Checking the Costs of War

Checking the Costs of War

*Sources of Accountability
in Post-9/11 US Foreign Policy*

EDITED BY SARAH E. KREPS
AND DOUGLAS L. KRINER

THE UNIVERSITY OF CHICAGO PRESS   CHICAGO AND LONDON

The University of Chicago Press, Chicago 60637
The University of Chicago Press, Ltd., London
© 2025 by The University of Chicago
"War Powers, the 'Deep State,' and Insurrection" by Rebecca Ingber © 2025 by Rebecca Ingber
All rights reserved. No part of this book may be used or reproduced in any manner whatsoever without written permission, except in the case of brief quotations in critical articles and reviews. For more information, contact the University of Chicago Press, 1427 E. 60th St., Chicago, IL 60637.
Published 2025
Printed in the USA

34 33 32 31 30 29 28 27 26 25   1 2 3 4 5

ISBN-13: 978-0-226-83414-6 (cloth)
ISBN-13: 978-0-226-83816-8 (paper)
ISBN-13: 978-0-226-83815-1 (e-book)
DOI: https://doi.org/10.7208/chicago/9780226838151.001.0001

Library of Congress Cataloging-in-Publication Data

Names: Kreps, Sarah E., editor. | Kriner, Douglas L., editor.
Title: Checking the costs of war : sources of accountability in post-9/11 US foreign policy / edited by Sarah E. Kreps and Douglas L Kriner.
Description: Chicago : The University of Chicago Press, 2025. | Includes bibliographical references and index.
Identifiers: LCCN 2024029671 | ISBN 9780226834146 (cloth) | ISBN 9780226838168 (paperback) | ISBN 9780226838151 (ebook)
Subjects: LCSH: Executive power—United States. | United States—Foreign policy—21st century.
Classification: LCC E895 .C446 2025 | DDC 352.23/50973—dc23/eng/20240723
LC record available at https://lccn.loc.gov/2024029671

♾ This paper meets the requirements of ANSI/NISO Z39.48-1992 (Permanence of Paper).

Contents

List of Illustrations   vii

CHAPTER 1. Unfettered Foreign Policy? Domestic Checks on Presidential Powers after 9/11   1
Sarah E. Kreps and Douglas L. Kriner

CHAPTER 2. Purely Partisan Warriors? Legislative Rhetoric in the Afghanistan and Iraq Wars   40
Sarah E. Kreps and Douglas L. Kriner

CHAPTER 3. Varieties of Bipartisanship: How Democrats and Republicans Align on Foreign and Domestic Policy   76
Jordan Tama

CHAPTER 4. Cassandra's Reward: The Electoral Benefits of Early Opposition to an Unpopular War   105
Benjamin O. Fordham

CHAPTER 5. Congressional Midterms, Presidential Reelection, and US Foreign Policy   135
Christopher Dictus and Philip B. K. Potter

CHAPTER 6. Modern Day Minutemen? Public Opinion and Reserve Component Mobilization   175
Jessica D. Blankshain and Lindsay P. Cohn

CHAPTER 7. Gender and the Political Costs of War: Partisan Cues, Gender Heuristics, and the Politics of Public Opposition to War   202
Aaron Childree, Katherine Krimmel, Max Palmer, and Douglas L. Kriner

CHAPTER 8. Nondominant Communal Groups and Casualty Sensitivity: Evidence from Israel, the United Kingdom, and the United States 231
Ronald R. Krebs and Robert Ralston

CHAPTER 9. "Hand-to-Hand Combat": Bureaucratic Politics and National Security 262
Andrew Rudalevige

CHAPTER 10. War Powers, the "Deep State," and Insurrection 299
Rebecca Ingber

CHAPTER 11. A Post-GWOT Syndrome? Institutional Response, Public Opinion, and the Future of US Foreign Policy 338
Sarah E. Kreps and Douglas L. Kriner

Acknowledgments 365

Index 367

Illustrations

Figures

Figure 1.1 Partisan Polarization in Congress over Time, 1945–2022 / 5
Figure 1.2 Partisan Polarization in Presidential Approval, 1953–2022 / 7
Figure 1.3 Changes in US Military Personnel over Time / 10
Figure 1.4 Drone Strikes in Afghanistan, Pakistan, Somalia, and Yemen, 2002–2020 / 12
Figure 2.1 Distribution of Hawkish Ideology by Party, 110th Congress / 48
Figure 2.2 Effects of Partisanship across Wars and Rhetoric Type / 56
Figure 2.3 Effects of Ideology on Rhetoric within Each Party Caucus: Iraq / 59
Figure 2.4 Effects of Ideology on Rhetoric within Each Party Caucus: Afghanistan / 59
Figure 2.5 Does District Partisanship Moderate the Effect of Member Partisanship on Rhetoric? / 62
Figure 3.1 Rates of Bipartisanship—CQ Key Votes / 85
Figure 3.2 Rates of Bipartisanship—Vote Smart Key Votes / 86
Figure 3.3 Rates of Bipartisanship—CQ Almanac Votes / 86
Figure 3.4 Variation of Bipartisanship and Polarization—CQ Key Votes / 88
Figure 3.5 Variation of Bipartisanship and Polarization—Vote Smart Key Votes / 88

Figure 3.6	Strong Polarization—CQ Key Votes / 89
Figure 3.7	Strong Polarization—CQ Almanac Votes / 89
Figure 3.8	Presidential Position Votes—CQ Key Votes / 90
Figure 3.9	Presidential Position Votes—Vote Smart Key Votes / 91
Figure 3.10	Presidential Position Votes—CQ Almanac Votes / 91
Figure 3.11	Presidential Position Foreign Policy Votes—CQ Key Votes / 93
Figure 3.12	Presidential Position Foreign Policy Votes—CQ Almanac Votes / 93
Figure 3A.1	Rates of Bipartisanship under Various Conditions—CQ Key Votes / 96
Figure 3A.2	Rates of Bipartisanship under Various Conditions—Vote Smart Key Votes / 97
Figure 3A.3	Rates of Bipartisanship under Various Conditions—Other CQ Almanac Votes / 97
Figure 6.1	Average Support for Military Action—Active Duty vs. Reserve Mobilization / 185
Figure 6.2	Average Support for Military Action by Reserve Mobilization Condition / 186
Figure 6.3	Direct Comparison of Voluntarism and Commonness Conditions / 188
Figure 6.4	Subjects' Beliefs about Historical Use of US Military Servicemembers / 190
Figure 6.5	Treatment Effects by Knowledge Level / 191
Figure 6.6	Perceptions of Servicemember Motivations by Experimental Condition / 193
Figure 6.7	Treatment Effects of Coercion vs. Volunteer Condition on Beliefs about Servicemember Motivations / 193
Figure 7.1	Salience of Wars in Iraq and Afghanistan over Time / 210
Figure 7.2	Coefficients on Gender by Party and Year: Iraq / 216
Figure 7.3	Coefficients on Gender by Party and Year: Afghanistan / 218
Figure 7.4	Marginal Effects of Gender on Afghanistan Withdrawal Assessments / 222
Figure 8.1	Predicted Probability of Tolerating Any Casualties: USA / 245
Figure 11.1	Isolationist Sentiment by Party, 1956–2020 / 351
Figure 11.2	Support for Cutting Defense Spending by Party, 1980–2020 / 355

Tables

Table 2.1 Effect of Member Partisanship on Wartime Rhetoric / 55
Table 2.2 Effect of Ideology within Each Party Caucus on Wartime Rhetoric / 58
Table 2.3 District Partisanship Moderates Effect of Member Partisanship / 61
Table 2.4 Partisanship and More Nuanced Afghanistan War Rhetoric / 63
Table 2.5 District Partisanship and Partisan Hedging / 64
Table 3.1 Typologies of Political Alignments / 79
Table 4.1 Democratic House Incumbent Vote Share in the 2002 Elections / 117
Table 4.2 Democratic House Incumbent Vote Share in the 2004 Elections / 119
Table 4.3 Expected Vote Share for Democratic Incumbents in 2004 / 120
Table 4.4 Democratic House Incumbent Vote Share in the 2006 Elections / 121
Table 4.5 Democratic House Incumbent Vote Share in Districts with High Military Casualties / 123
Table 4.6 Democratic House Incumbent Vote Share in Close Districts, 2002 Election / 124
Table 4.7 Republican House Incumbent Vote Share in 2004 and 2006 / 125
Table 5.1 Presidential and Congressional Elections 1946–2018 / 140
Table 5A.1 Presidential Domestic and Foreign Policy Achievements, Theoretical Expectations / 160
Table 6.1 Personnel Policies and Support for Military Action / 187
Table 6.2 Treatment Effects on Expected Costs and Benefits of Action / 195
Table 7.1 Believe US Made a Mistake Invading Iraq / 214
Table 7.2 Believe War in Afghanistan Was a Mistake, 2004–2015 / 218
Table 8.1 National Samples and Benchmarks / 237
Table 8.2 Casualty Sensitivity in Israel, the United Kingdom, and the United States / 241

CHAPTER ONE

Unfettered Foreign Policy?
Domestic Checks on Presidential Powers after 9/11

Sarah E. Kreps and Douglas L. Kriner

On September 11, 2001, more than 2,500 Americans died in the bloodiest attack on American soil since Pearl Harbor. The US economy was sent reeling from the shock, and millions of Americans became more anxious, fearful, and willing to support an aggressive response.[1] To prevent future attacks, Americans sacrificed a measure of privacy and civil liberties in the name of security. Twenty years later, more than a third of Americans say they are still more nervous when flying than they were pre-9/11. Two-thirds continue to believe that America changed forever.[2] And of course, within weeks of the attack the United States launched in Afghanistan what would become the longest war in American history, which was shortly followed by an even larger war in Iraq, as well as a myriad of other strikes and armed interventions across the globe.

Writing in 1787, James Madison presciently warned that "war is in fact the true nurse of executive aggrandizement."[3] History proved Madison right, as Polk, Lincoln, Wilson, and Roosevelt all expanded presidential power beyond prior constraints under the exigencies of war. Unsurprisingly, the response to 9/11 would prove no different. Following President Bush's address to a joint session of Congress in September 2001, in which he told Americans to prepare for a "lengthy campaign unlike any other we have ever seen," historian Michael Beschloss announced that "the imperial presidency is back."[4] While perhaps uncontroversial, the statement was ironic. Just nine months earlier, Beschloss had labeled Bush "the first post-imperial president," given the relative foreign and domestic tranquility under which he was elected. Beschloss was far from alone in his judgment. Arthur Schlesinger Jr. reissued his 1973 classic, *The Imperial Presidency*, with a new introduction anchored in the observation that the post-9/11 presidency had rendered obituaries of the imperial presidency from the 1990s far too premature.[5] In the tumultuous years that followed, scholarship plumbed the intellectual, legal, and historical origins of this resurgence of presidential imperialism,[6] while journalistic accounts warned of "the subversion of American democracy" under an ascendant executive.[7]

And yet, despite the continued resilience of Schlesinger's imperial presidency paradigm,[8] a new wave of scholarship straddling the 9/11 attacks pushed back against notions of virtually unchecked presidential preeminence in the military arena.[9] To be sure, even scholars asserting the continued relevance of domestic constraints acknowledged that the formal checks on presidential power in foreign policy are weak. For example, while the Constitution grants Congress considerable Article I powers to influence the course and conduct of military affairs, most importantly the power of the purse, legislators routinely fail to use these powers to push back against a wayward executive. Moreover, even in the rare instances when congressional critics endeavor to do so, collective action dilemmas and supermajoritarian requirements frequently thwart their efforts.

This does not mean that presidents enjoy an unfettered hand in conducting military affairs, but the nature of the domestic checks on the commander in chief are primarily political. Other institutional actors, and perhaps most importantly members of Congress, have the capacity to raise (or lower) the political costs presidents stand to incur by waging war. Central to these costs is public opinion. Presidents have strong incentives to cultivate public support. Public support is a reservoir of political capital that bolsters efforts to achieve key priorities on their programmatic agendas.[10] Ultimately, it is central to presidents' electoral fortunes, those of their copartisan successors, and of their party.[11] Opponents of presidential foreign policies know this and therefore focus considerable energy on the floor, in the hearing room, and through a myriad of actions in the public sphere seeking to sway public opinion against the president.[12] Presidents respond to changes in these costs—and to the anticipation of them—by adjusting and moderating their conduct of military affairs.[13]

However, precisely because these checks are informal, their strength and efficacy may critically depend on the nature of the political environment. Over the last two decades, the American polity has experienced significant changes that could have major ramifications for the capacity of other actors to check presidential actions in the foreign policy realm. Some of these changes are continuations and accelerations of trends that began before 9/11. Others are mostly new developments. Still others are products of presidents' own decisions on how to wage war in ways that might minimize domestic oversight.

In this chapter, we briefly review four main developments with the potential to weaken or fundamentally alter the operation of domestic constraints on presidential foreign policymaking. We then engage relevant literatures examining the influence of legislative, public opinion, and bureaucratic checks on the commander in chief and discuss how the chapters that follow address gaps in these literatures and tackle new questions about the continued viability of each check in a post-9/11 context.

Four Developments That Could Undermine the Efficacy of Domestic Checks

Polarization in Congress

Three days after the 9/11 attacks, Congress voted almost unanimously to authorize the use of force in Afghanistan and to grant the Bush Administration wide latitude to prosecute the global war on terror. However, that remarkable bipartisanship would prove short-lived. Over the years, partisan battle lines were reestablished over the execution of the war in Iraq. By the endgame of the war in Afghanistan, intense partisan politicking was on full display as many of the same Republicans who had supported President Trump's negotiated deal with the Taliban to withdraw US forces from Afghanistan savagely attacked President Biden for executing the agreement. Conversely, many Democrats who had criticized Trump held their fire under a copartisan president.

Of course, partisan polarization in Congress began long before 9/11. Figure 1.1 plots one of the most commonly used measures of elite-level polarization, the distance between the first dimension NOMINATE score, a widely used measure of ideological liberalism or conservatism, for the median member of each party from the 79th (1945–1946) through the 117th Congress (2021–2022). As shown in the top panel of figure 1.1, beginning in the 1970s, the median Republican steadily became considerably more conservative while the median Democrat became slightly more liberal over the intervening decades. This is consistent with arguments about asymmetric polarization, which hold that the increasingly rightward turn of congressional Republicans has disproportionately contributed to polarization.[14] The bottom panel of figure 1.1 plots the ideological gap between the median congressional Democrat and Republican. From 1945 through 1975, this gap grew only modestly. Since the 1970s, the pace of polarization has accelerated substantially.

Alongside this ideological polarization, the last three decades have witnessed a dramatic increase in partisan competition and animosity, or what Frances Lee has called "partisan teamsmanship." From 1933 through 1994, Democrats controlled the House of Representatives for all but four years. Since 1994, control of the House has oscillated between the parties multiple times. In this intensely contested era of narrow majorities, the House is seemingly always in play. This, in turn, has heightened incentives to stand by your party and to deny the other victories that might provide even a small, but decisive, edge at the next election.[15]

Despite the conventional wisdom asserting a "bipartisan consensus" through most of the Cold War era, partisanship played a key role in igniting and exacerbating most foreign policy battles since the end of World War II, from intense Republican criticism of Harry Truman's prosecution of the war in Korea to Democrat-led challenges of Ronald Reagan's policies in Central America, which culminated in the Iran-Contra hearings.[16] Partisan conflict over foreign affairs intensified in the 1990s with significant Republican pushback against Bill Clinton's humanitarian interventions on all fronts.[17] The 1996 Republican Party platform denounced Clinton's reckless interventions in Somalia and Haiti, while simultaneously chastising him for his *failure* to intervene in Rwanda and Burundi.[18] Yet throughout the pre-9/11 era, there were repeated, significant moments in which presidential foreign policies enjoyed both substantial bipartisan support and pushback. For example, while Democrats spearheaded legislative efforts to curtail and end the war in Vietnam, they were bolstered by support from key liberal Republicans, including John Sherman Cooper, Mark Hatfield, and Jacob Javits. Even in the intensely partisan late 1990s dominated by impeachment, Bill Clinton received a significant political boost from John McCain's support for the war in Kosovo (as well as trouble from his calls to escalate it) during a time when most Republicans opposed the war.

However, the ever-intensifying polarization and congressional partisanship since 9/11 raises important questions about the conditions under which legislative checks might still be effective in this transformed political environment. Will these developments render congressional pushback

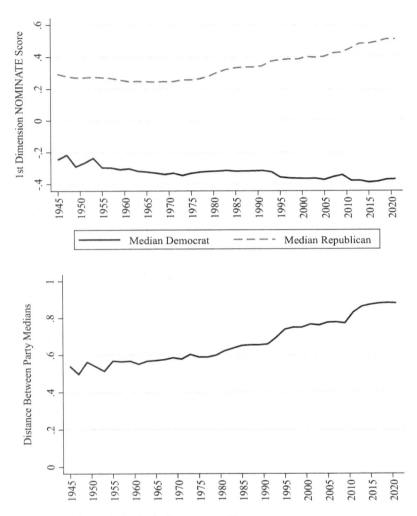

FIGURE 1.1 Partisan Polarization in Congress over Time, 1945–2022
Note: NOMINATE scores from https://voteview.com/.

exclusively a feature of divided government, with the majority party exploiting its agenda powers to the fullest to squelch dissent under unified government?[19] Will congressional criticism of presidential military policies be exclusively from the opposition party, rendering this pushback less influential and more easily dismissed as "cheap talk"?[20]

Partisan Tribalism among the Public

In the days after the 9/11 attacks, the American public came together against a common enemy, al-Qaeda. In the first Gallup poll fielded following the tragedy, President Bush had the support of 92 percent of Americans, the highest figure recorded in Gallup history and higher than President Truman's 87 percent rating after the end of World War II.[21] Yet this unprecedented national unity proved short-lived. Vice President Cheney's words that September 11 would take the country to "the dark side" proved prophetic.[22] Warrantless surveillance, an ill-fated war in Iraq, and dubious treatment of detainees had echoes of American behavior in wars past, when the onset of a crisis led to the internment of Japanese Americans in World War II, or the Alien and Sedition Acts from the Quasi-War with France in 1798. Unity gave way to acrimony as pockets of Americans questioned government overreach and judgment lapses. While many Americans initially rallied behind the Iraq War, significant partisan splits soon emerged, and from 2004 through the end of George W. Bush's presidency, the partisan approval gap for the war averaged 62 percent. As Gary Jacobson documents, Bush had become "a divider, not a uniter."[23]

This polarization in public opinion toward the Iraq War reflected a broader trend of increasing partisan tribalism in Americans' political assessments. Scholars continue to debate whether American public opinion is increasingly polarized ideologically or whether ideological polarization is primarily an elite-level phenomenon.[24] However, what few deny is that most Americans have become more tribal and partisan in their political assessments and behaviors over time. Increasingly, mass opinion is motivated by an antipathy for the other party.[25]

Consider the forces underlying presidential approval ratings. Decades of scholarship has tracked how presidential approval rises and falls in response to changes in the economy, wars, and other major international and domestic events.[26] However, as shown in figure 1.2, increasingly for most Americans one factor and only one factor predominates their assessment of the president's job performance: whether the president is of their party or hails from the opposition. The top panel of figure 1.2 plots the average approval rating for each president from Eisenhower through Biden, separated by party. Presidents have always enjoyed greater support from their copartisans than from the opposition party in the mass public. However, this gap has grown substantially over time. From Eisenhower through Carter, we see significant heterogeneity in the level of support presidents were able to secure from their copartisans in the mass public. However, be-

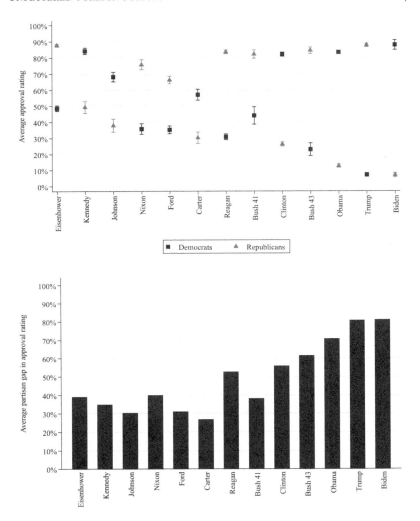

FIGURE 1.2. Partisan Polarization in Presidential Approval, 1953–2022

Note: Gallup presidential approval polling data, https://news.gallup.com/interactives/185273/presidential-job-approval-center.aspx; I-bars in top panel show 95 percent confidence intervals about each mean level of approval.

ginning with Reagan and continuing through present day, presidents have consistently secured overwhelming support from their fellow partisans. Perhaps the next most notable trend is the steady erosion of presidential approval among the opposition starting with Bill Clinton and continuing to the point where both Donald Trump and Joe Biden averaged less than

10 percent support among Democrats and Republicans, respectively. The bottom panel of figure 1.2 plots the gap in average approval across the two parties over time. From Eisenhower through Carter, the partisan gap ranged from 27 percent to 40 percent. Since Clinton, the gap has grown precipitously from 56 percent to in excess of 80 percent.

This development could have major implications for the strength of domestic checks on presidential conduct of military affairs and the conditions under which those checks may be effective. Will presidents have fewer incentives to be responsive to public opinion if a significant share of the electorate is already calcified in their assessments along party lines? Or will smaller shifts still be so politically decisive in an era of narrow electoral margins that the incentives to respond to even small changes in public opinion remain high? Similarly, changing public opinion is a key mechanism through which other institutional actors seek to influence a president's strategic calculus and bring political pressure to bear on an administration to change course. Will other actors' capacity to shift opinion be reduced in an era of intense tribalism? And how might these actors adjust their strategies accordingly in such a transformed environment?

The Increasingly Submerged Costs of War

On any metric, the costs of over two decades of war since 9/11 have been stark. Since 2001, overseas contingency operations appropriations have exceeded $2 trillion. The country has spent hundreds of billions more expanding and fortifying military bases, bolstering homeland security, and providing for veterans' health benefits and care. The Watson Institute's Costs of War Project estimates total post-9/11 war spending in excess of $8 trillion.[27] More than seven thousand US soldiers and eight thousand American contractors lost their lives in Iraq and Afghanistan, more than fifty thousand were wounded in action, and more than thirty thousand US service members have committed suicide since 9/11.[28]

An extensive literature in international relations scholarship argues that wartime public opinion formation is akin to a cost-benefit calculation.[29] Individuals weigh the costs of war against its perceived benefits, supporting the war when the latter exceeds the former and opposing it when the costs are greater. This represents a key potential domestic check on presidents' freedom of action. As a war's costs rise, public support may fade; this, in turn, may increase the political costs of staying the course. Moreover, presidents have strong incentives to anticipate any such erosion and to eschew policies that risk significant costs that could trigger a collapse in public support. However, this mechanism depends on the costs of war being transparent and readily available to citizens as well as to other political actors who might sound the alarm and raise war costs' public salience.[30]

Despite the massive costs of the post-9/11 "forever wars" in blood and treasure, a series of policy decisions, some beginning before 9/11 and others emerging since, have significantly reduced the visibility of many of these costs. First, the human costs of these wars have been borne by an ever-decreasing slice of the American public, insulating most Americans from direct exposure to the costs. As shown in the top panel of figure 1.3, the size of the US military has decreased dramatically since the end of the Cold War, even as the population has grown. As a result, less than half a percent of the population now serves.[31] Moreover, those who paid the greatest sacrifice—those killed and wounded in war—have come disproportionately from socioeconomically disadvantaged communities with less political visibility and clout. Indeed, these inequalities in the Iraq and Afghanistan Wars substantially exceeded those observed in all other major US wars of the past seventy years.[32]

Further insulating many Americans from the direct risks of fighting and dying in combat is a major shift in the way the United States recruits and supplies its military personnel needs. As American involvement in the Vietnam War ebbed, the government discontinued the draft in 1973 and shifted to an all-volunteer military. As shown in the bottom panel of figure 1.3, this represented a watershed change in policy and fundamentally changed the way that many Americans experienced the immediate costs of war. The United States conscripted more than ten million men into the Armed Forces during World War II. This draft authority lapsed in 1947 but was reinstated in 1948. Inductions peaked during the Korean War in 1951, when more than half a million men were drafted. Between 1948 and 1972, the United States averaged just under two hundred thousand draftees per year. Conscription—and the threat of it—exposed many if not most American families to the very real possibility that a family member would be forced to fight in a foreign war. As a result, scholarship employing a range of approaches from the historical to the experimental has shown that conscription significantly reduces public support for war.[33] The shift away from conscription has removed a significant source of public unease and therefore might weaken the nature of a popular check on sustained presidential military adventurism.

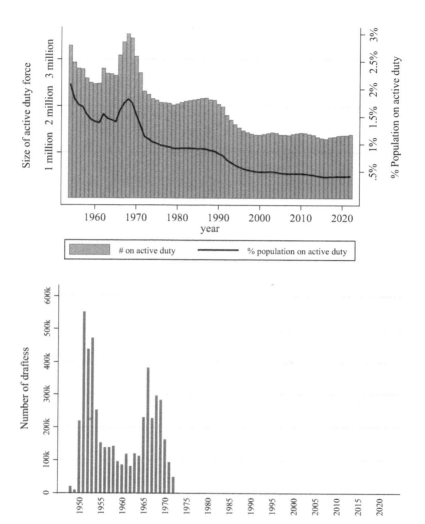

FIGURE 1.3. Changes in US Military Personnel over Time

Note: Data from Selective Service System Induction Statistics, https://www.sss.gov/history-and-records/induction-statistics/; active duty military strength data from DMDC, Office of the Secretary of Defense, https://dwp.dmdc.osd.mil/dwp/app/dod-data-reports/workforce-reports; US population data from United Nations—World Population Prospects, https://population.un.org/wpp/Download/Standard/CSV/.

This dramatic shift in how America recruits the forces to fight its wars was also accompanied by a revolution in how the United States pays for its wars. During the Vietnam War, President Johnson only reluctantly asked Congress for a tax increase to offset the conflict's escalating costs. While Johnson carried the day, support for the war steadily fell. This became another "lesson of Vietnam": taxation would inevitably erode support for war.[34] Policymakers learned this lesson well, so when the United States went to war after 9/11, first in Afghanistan and then in Iraq, it broke with all precedent from World Wars I and II, Korea, and Vietnam and funded those protracted conflicts exclusively through deficit spending.[35] By postponing the fiscal reckoning and keeping the costs of war largely hidden from public view, policymakers have proactively taken steps to undermine popular resistance, allowing them to wage ever more protracted and costly conflicts.[36]

Finally, the human cost of the post-9/11 wars has been staggering. However, over time technological and tactical innovations allowed policymakers to take steps to prosecute the war on terror in new ways that minimized the risk to US soldiers and therefore further removed the costs of war from the public consciousness. Perhaps the paradigmatic example of this is the dramatic increase in reliance on drone strikes as a key element of the counterterrorism campaign. The Bureau of Investigative Journalism (BIJ) estimates that since 2002 the United States has conducted more than fifteen thousand strikes—both in long-standing theaters of US military operations, such as Afghanistan, and in other areas where US forces are not publicly or only marginally engaged, such as Yemen. The top panel of figure 1.4 focuses on drone strikes in three theaters where neither Congress nor the United Nations has explicitly authorized the use of force: Pakistan, Somalia, and Yemen.[37] While the first US drone strike dates back to 2002 in Yemen, the program's scope expanded dramatically under President Obama, particularly during his final two years in office. As early as 2011, while reflecting on the drone strike that killed Anwar al-Awlaki, an American-born imam who had become an al-Qaeda leader in Yemen, Obama allegedly quipped to aides, "Turns out I'm really good at killing people. Didn't know that was gonna be a strong suit of mine."[38] The number of strikes then escalated further under the Trump Administration.

Moreover, as the United States sought to wind down its combat mission and circumscribe its footprint in Afghanistan, administrations from both parties increasingly turned to drones to continue to strike thousands

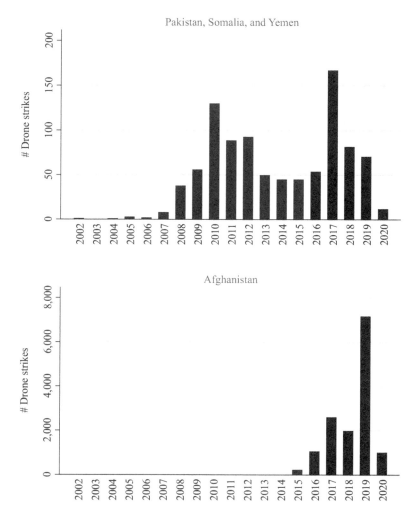

FIGURE 1.4. Drone Strikes in Afghanistan, Pakistan, Somalia, and Yemen, 2002–2020
Note: Data obtained from the Bureau of Investigative Journalism, https://www.thebureauinvestigates.com/stories/2017-01-01/drone-wars-the-full-data.

of targets in a way that almost eliminated the risk of American casualties and that minimized the political visibility of US military engagement. As shown in the bottom panel of figure 1.4, President Obama authorized hundreds of drone strikes in the final two years of his administration. The intensity of the drone war then grew dramatically under President Trump with the BIJ reporting more than seven thousand drone strikes in Afghanistan in 2019 alone.

This technological revolution has allowed presidents to project power almost anywhere on the globe and to strike with lethal precision with almost no direct risk to American life.[39] Moreover, while some drone strikes are highly publicized, most are shrouded in secrecy. The combination limits the political visibility of drone warfare in ways that could severely limit both congressional and public oversight, undermining any popular check on its exercise.

The Unitary Executive Theory, Reimagined

A fourth development with potentially major consequences for the nature of domestic checks on the presidential conduct of foreign affairs is internal to the executive branch itself: a new articulation of the unitary executive theory that would grant the president expanded, even unchecked powers in multiple spheres, coupled with a determination to put it into effect. Debates over the scope of executive power in the American constitutional system are as old as the republic. The Antifederalist author Cato denounced the "vague and inexplicit" language of Article II that could be construed as giving the president "great powers" that "would lead to oppression and ruin."[40] Perhaps one of the vaguest clauses is Article II, Section 1: "The executive Power shall be vested in a President of the United States of America." This ambiguous phrase has given rise to widely varying interpretations, including multiple variants of what is often called unitary executive theory.[41]

An earlier, weaker version of the unitary executive theory was articulated in the early Reagan Administration. At its core, this version argued that the president, as the unitary executive, had the power to provide direction to other executive branch actors and remove those who failed to comply; in short, its aim was to provide a constitutional foundation for resisting congressional efforts to influence the bureaucracy and to combat bureaucratic resistance to administration policies.[42] While even this more limited theory could produce bold claims—for example, that independent agencies were constitutionally suspect because they violated separation of powers and must be subject to presidential control—it pales in comparison to what Frederick Schwarz and Aziz Huq would call the theory's monarchical incarnation that emerged after 9/11.[43] Central to this argument is that the vesting clause grants presidents broad unenumerated powers, particularly in the field of foreign and military affairs. Perhaps the starkest expression of this view is encapsulated in an Office of Legal Counsel (OLC) memo written by John Yoo just two weeks after the 9/11 attacks.

The impetus for the OLC memo was Congress's refusal to grant Bush unfettered power to prosecute the war on terror anywhere in the world as he alone saw fit. Before passing the Authorization to Use Military Force (AUMF) in Response to the 9/11 Attacks, Congress struck a clause from the administration's initial draft. While the final resolution empowered the president "to use all necessary and appropriate force against those nations, organizations or persons he determines planned, authorized, harbored, committed, or aided in the planning or commission of the attacks against the United States that occurred on September 11, 2001," it refused to also grant him the power "to deter and preempt any future acts of terrorism or aggression against the United States."[44]

The Bush Administration then turned to OLC to provide it with the powers that Congress had explicitly denied it. Yoo obliged with a memo articulating the president's almost plenary inherent constitutional power to address the emergency militarily: "Neither statute (AUMF or the War Powers Resolution), however, can place any limits on the President's determinations as to any terrorist threat, the amount of military force to be used in response, or the method, timing, and nature of the response. *These decisions, under our Constitution, are for the President alone to make.*"[45] Almost twenty years later, Donald Trump would articulate a similar understanding of the president's constitutional powers in even plainer terms: "Article II allows me to do whatever I want."[46] Whereas Yoo focused on the propriety of legislative checks on the president's wartime authority, Trump's attorney general, William Barr, openly doubted whether there were even checks from advisers and other entities within the executive branch, stating, "Constitutionally, it is wrong to conceive of the President as simply the highest officer within the Executive branch hierarchy. He alone *is* the Executive branch."[47]

Many of the most extraordinary claims of unfettered presidential power articulated by OLC in the aftermath of 9/11 were reversed over time.[48] However, the theory continues to provide a legal framework for presidents eager to resist congressional interference in military affairs and to bring recalcitrant bureaucrats in the Department of Defense, the armed forces, and elsewhere to heel. For example, President Bush's first secretary of defense, Donald Rumsfeld, returned to Washington in 2001 determined to right what he saw as a serious imbalance in American civil-military relations.[49] Rumsfeld dismissed warnings and force requirement recommendations from military commanders and burst through bureaucratic barriers to plan and conduct the Iraq War according to his and the president's vision.[50]

The conventional wisdom emerging from Eisenhower's farewell address, warning about the power of the military industrial complex, has long held that while the massive federal bureaucracy was absolutely essential to the functioning of American foreign affairs, it could and did cause problems for presidents, and it pushed back at efforts to impose political control.[51] Presidential orders are rarely self-executing, and presidential-bureaucratic politics often amount to a game of persuasion in which the *primus inter pares* must persuade nominal subordinates that what the president wants is also in their own interests.[52] Modern incarnations of an expanded unitary executive theory do not eliminate the fundamental issues of the principal-agent relationship; however, these maximalist unitary executive claims do provide presidents with a legal rationale justifying extreme efforts to overcome bureaucratic resistance. If successful, this could weaken the nature of bureaucratic influences and checks on presidential conduct of foreign policy.

Reassessing Domestic Political Checks

In this volume, we reassess the continued strength of domestic political constraints on the use of force in a post-9/11 context. The subsequent chapters focus on the actors best positioned to push back against presidential overreach—Congress, the public, and the bureaucracy—and examine the conditions under which each can impose some check on the commander in chief. Each analysis also speaks to our overarching theme of whether changes in the political and institutional environment since 9/11 have weakened, strengthened, or conditionally influenced each domestic constraint. In so doing, the volume goes beyond the typical treatment of one branch or actor individually and instead engages a broader set of constraints that democratic leaders face when making decisions about how to use force abroad. The immediate focus is on the United States, given its special status as the direct target of the watershed event of 9/11 and leader of many of the consequential foreign policy actions in the years after. However, the volume also engages with cross-national evidence, and the lessons it distills about the nature of domestic checks on executive-led foreign policy have implications for other democracies. In the next sections, we briefly review the theoretical arguments describing how each actor can exercise a check on the commander in chief and how subsequent chapters enhance our understanding of these politics in the post-9/11 era.

Congress

Perhaps the most logical domestic constraint on presidential freedom of action in foreign affairs is Congress. After all, Article I grants the legislature a series of enumerated powers directly in the field of military affairs, including the power to declare war; grant letters of marque and reprisal (the eighteenth-century equivalent of limited war)[53]; raise, support, and regulate the armed forces; and, ultimately, the power of the purse. Weighing these considerable powers against the commander-in-chief clause and executive power of the president, the great legal scholar Edward Corwin famously called the Constitution an invitation for the two branches to struggle over control of the nation's foreign affairs.[54] The conventional wisdom has long held, however, that since World War II the struggle has been decidedly one-sided.[55]

Truman's decision to enter the Korean conflict without seeking congressional approval proved an inflection point in interbranch war powers,[56] marking the rise of an ascendant presidency. Some of Truman's successors have sought congressional authorization for their military ventures, while others have not. Even those who have done so, have assiduously maintained that while welcome, congressional support is legally unnecessary. While Congress tried to claw back some of its power after Watergate, the central instrument of that effort—the War Powers Resolution—has proven an ineffective tool. By refusing to acknowledge that US troops are in a zone of hostility, even when they are sustaining casualties, presidents avoid the triggering of the automatic withdrawal clock. And Congress has repeatedly shown itself unable to muster the requisite supermajorities to trigger it over a presidential veto.[57]

Similarly, the power of the purse repeatedly has proven an instrument too blunt to use successfully. For example, after regaining control of Congress in the 2006 midterms, running on a pledge to wind down the war in Iraq, the newly minted Democratic majorities included language in a Department of Defense Appropriations bill mandating a timetable for withdrawing US troops from Iraq. President Bush called their bluff and vetoed the bill. Rather than facing politically devastating charges of failing to support the troops in the field, Democrats caved and passed a clean bill without a timetable.

A new wave of scholarship, however, has questioned this conventional view of congressional weakness. While the formal legislative checks on presidential overreach in foreign affairs are weak, an exclusive focus on these failures overlooks the more informal yet still tangible ways in which members of Congress can raise the political costs of foreign policy actions for the president. Perhaps most importantly, Congress has a number of tools—from floor votes on initiatives to rein in a wayward military action,[58] to investigative oversight,[59] to floor speeches, interviews, and other engagement in the public sphere[60]—to challenge the president in the court of public opinion and raise the political costs of going it alone. Harry Truman committed hundreds of thousands of Americans to combat in Korea without a congressional declaration of war, and Congress never used its formal powers to end the fighting. Even in this case, commonly cited as a watershed moment in interbranch war politics heralding presidential ascendance, intense congressional criticism, driven primarily by opposition-party Republicans, dramatically weakened Truman politically.[61] Ultimately, Truman opted not to seek reelection in 1952, all but handing the presidency to the Republican Party for the first time in twenty years.

Building on the example of partisan contestation in the Korean War, most scholarship has focused on partisanship as a driver of congressional assertiveness and influence over presidential conduct of foreign policy. Research has shown that Congress is more likely in divided government to use the various levers at its disposal to erode the president's political capital, and presidents—anticipating this pushback—are more reticent to use force and reduce its scale and duration when deciding a military response is required.[62] But to what extent is partisanship the sole factor driving congressional opposition to presidential military policies? And how do these dynamics play out in an era of intense polarization?

Sarah Kreps and Douglas Kriner examine whether members of Congress are strictly partisan warriors versus the extent to which ideological leanings and electoral calculations help explain variation in congressional wartime criticism. Disentangling the relative influence of partisanship and ideology is empirically difficult. To gain leverage, Kreps and Kriner examine a rarely employed foreign policy—a military surge of troops—carried out first by a Republican (for the Iraq War) and then a Democrat (for the Afghanistan War). In the former case, partisanship and baseline ideological moorings (Democrats being more dovish than Republicans) align;

but in the latter they diverge, which helps separate the basis for position-taking on the use of force. Across both surges, Democrats were most likely to criticize presidential policies, regardless of whether a Republican or Democrat sat in the Oval Office. Intraparty ideological heterogeneity also explained variation in congressional rhetoric, as did electoral context and its interaction with partisanship. The results highlight the complex incentive structures underlying congressional engagement with military policy. Perhaps most importantly, they suggest that strong majorities of copartisans may not always insulate commanders in chief from costly congressional pushback, even in an age of intense partisan polarization when the incentives to maintain party loyalty are heightened.

Jordan Tama takes a different tack in his critique of recent scholarship emphasizing partisan divisions in Congress. He posits that despite the rising tide of partisan polarization engulfing the political landscape, many foreign policy questions continue to find support across the aisle. Examining legislative votes on important issues of foreign policy, he provides evidence of considerable bipartisanship and suggests that intraparty divisions may sometimes be more important than interparty differences in explaining domestic legislative divisions on foreign policy. The analysis demonstrates that reducing legislative influence to divided government—in which the opposition in the majority is associated with constraining executive behavior—offers an incomplete picture. In some cases, as in the aftermath of 9/11, bipartisanship even in periods of divided government can bolster the president's position and weaken the congressional check on potentially costly military policies. But in other contexts, Republican and Democratic legislators may actually work together to oppose or challenge presidential foreign policy decisions.

Tama shows that this "anti-presidential bipartisanship" is empirically far from rare. Indeed, a prominent, important, and recent example is the congressional response to the Biden Administration's chaotic withdrawal from Afghanistan. Republicans in Congress unsurprisingly jumped on the calamitous execution of the withdrawal. A minority report of the Senate Committee on Foreign Relations took the Biden Administration to task, alleging that "despite countless warnings that the Taliban had the ability to take the country swiftly, the Biden Administration failed to properly plan a coordinated evacuation of US citizens, Afghans, and allied partners."[63] But leading Democrats also sharply criticized the administration, lending the congressional pushback a decidedly bipartisan flavor, as Democratic Senators Bob Menendez (NJ), Edward Markey (MA), and Jeanne Shaheen (NH) joined the chorus of criticism about the withdrawal.[64] These insights suggest that the conventional focus on divided government is incomplete and highlight the need for a more nuanced theory of the conditions under which congressional checks might arise.

Public Opinion

One of the most important mechanisms through which Congress affects presidential calculations is its ability to influence public opinion. David Mayhew famously called Congress's most important investigations, many of which focused on foreign policy, "publicity probes" for a reason; by their very design they are crafted to attract attention and shine a light on perceived presidential missteps and misconduct.[65] Congressional position-taking more broadly—in the committee room, on the floor, or over the airwaves—can influence public support for war.[66] But Mayhew also famously wrote about the "electoral connection" and the relationship between legislators' policy positions and public opinion, specifically that members' goal is reelection and that they seek to avoid missteps that might interfere with that goal.

Elections are, of course, the ultimate expression of public opinion, where citizens can render their verdict and either return to or remove from office politicians who pursued a specific military course of action, supported it, or opposed it. While the electoral salience of foreign policy varies dramatically, with consistent regularity in the post-World War II era campaigns have seriously engaged questions of foreign affairs and voters have judged elected officials for their performance and policy prescriptions in military matters.[67] Even when foreign policy questions become electorally salient, which foreign policy messages and actions actually resonate with the public varies considerably across contexts.[68]

In 2002, the Bush Administration strategically pushed Congress to vote to authorize the use of force against Iraq in October before the midterm elections. The administration rightly calculated that with the scars of 9/11 still fresh in many voters' minds, moderate Democrats would feel increased political pressure to grant Bush the war authority, and more importantly the attendant political cover, he coveted. More broadly, that year the Republican Party bucked the trend of presidential party losses in midterms, riding the sustained rally around the flag effect and Bush's long coattails for a gain of eight seats in the House and two in the Senate. In 2004, President Bush won reelection despite having become bogged down in Iraq, if not to the extent that would become more manifestly obvious in subsequent years following the explosion of sectarian tensions that plunged the country into veritable civil war.[69] Moreover, the Democrats failed to offer a clear policy alternative,[70] and while public support for the war had softened, it had not yet cratered.[71]

Two years later, the midterm elections took on the flavor of a referendum on Iraq.[72] By then, the war had become unpopular and registered voters who opposed the war overwhelmingly favored Democrats in House races, which an ABC News poll suggested was the highest level of Democratic preference since 1984.[73] Antiwar fervor continued to motivate voters two years later, as Hillary Clinton's vote to authorize the Iraq War when she was a senator became a distinguishing feature in her battle with Barack Obama for the Democratic nomination. Clinton's vote for the war and Obama's opposition to it (while in the Illinois State Senate) proved a considerable advantage for the latter, who cited his opposition as an indicator of "the kind of judgment that will ensure that we are using our military power wisely."[74] Obama, of course, went on to solidly defeat John McCain, perhaps the only Republican as hawkish on Iraq as President Bush, in November 2008. McCain faced political headwinds on multiple fronts; however, survey evidence suggests that Iraq was a major liability. In the preelection 2008 American National Election Study, just under 80 percent of respondents judged the Iraq War not worth its costs. Of those, almost 70 percent said they planned to vote for Barack Obama.

The 2006 and 2008 elections clearly suggest that voters may retrospectively sanction presidents and their supporters in Congress for pursuing costly wars. But do voters subsequently reward those who presciently oppose military actions that later prove unpopular? Benjamin Fordham examines this question, and its critical implications for the nature of domestic political constraints on presidents when contemplating the use of force. As Fordham notes, preconflict opposition to war is important because it can invite greater scrutiny and expose flawed policies; moreover, because congressional pushback can shape public opinion and presidential anticipations of political costs, it can even influence the decision to intervene or not.

While assiduously maintaining that they do not need congressional approval, presidents routinely seek it for major military ventures precisely because of the valuable political cover it provides.[75] Supporting or opposing conflict, however, can also have electoral implications for legislators. Failing to support the president, particularly a popular one, can be politically costly; this logic is nicely captured in President Bush's demand for congressional action to authorize the use of force before the 2002 midterms, even though UN weapons inspectors were still in Iraq and military action was not imminent. The costs of opposition may be particularly acute if they are not offset by electoral benefits should a military venture later prove costly and unpopular.

Fordham examines the electoral consequences of voting against the Authorization for the Use of Military Force in Iraq and, correspondingly, speaking out against the intended war, focusing specifically on opposition Democrats. Fordham finds that speaking out against a war they do not think will succeed provides few electoral rewards. Rather, members of Congress appear to be rewarded for staying silent until the war begins to go badly, taking on the equivalent of a Monday morning quarterback role of second-guessing after the game. The lone exception is in constituencies that suffered high local casualty rates. Here, members who initially opposed the war did perform significantly better in 2024 than those who supported it; however, they did little better than those who refused to take a clear position. The finding is somewhat dispiriting from the perspective of checking unwise uses of force; Cassandras who prophetically warn of impending disaster are not rewarded when their predictions prove right, which could in turn mute such criticism ex ante. However, Fordham also finds that Democrats who later turned on the war and criticized it *post ex facto* appear to have reaped electoral benefits in subsequent elections. The knowledge that the opposition party will eventually look to capitalize on military failure should incentivize presidential caution when contemplating the use of force.

Christopher Dictus and Phillip Potter take a different tack on electoral incentives and constraints. In sharp contrast to some strands of diversionary logic speculating presidents might seek foreign policy victories to bolster their electoral fortunes, Dictus and Potter argue that presidents have strong incentives to focus on domestic policy as elections, both midterm and presidential, approach. Presidents who win reelection or pick up seats in Congress exploit this strengthened political position to prioritize their domestic agendas, rather than foreign policy. By contrast and perhaps paradoxically, it is presidents who narrowly win reelection or who suffer significant setbacks in the midterms who turn disproportionately to foreign policy as their capacity to advance their domestic agendas is weakened. The implications for democratic constraint are potentially stark. Presidents on the campaign trail tend to take their eye off the ball when it comes to foreign policy, and politically powerful presidents tend to shy away from foreign policy, instead concentrating their political capital on advancing their domestic agenda. This can lead directly to missed opportunities, lost diplomatic momentum, and crises. For example, Johnson's emphasis on domestic politics early in his term led directly to Democratic Party electoral successes but also contributed to neglect of a war effort in Vietnam that was increasingly going off the rails. Ironically, the presidents most incentivized to focus on foreign affairs may have the least to lose politically from foreign policy adventurism.

Even well in advance of Election Day, actual or anticipated shifts in public opinion and popular support—an ubiquitous measure of a president's political capital or lack thereof—can be consequential. But what drives public opinion, and under what conditions might it tangibly check presidential policy making? At least since Kant, theorists have speculated that because the public bears the burden in blood and treasure, democratic publics will be reluctant to support or will withdraw support from policies that they do not deem to be worth the sacrifice. This logic is a key mechanism underlying many theories of a democratic peace.[76] Unsurprisingly, decades of scholarship have therefore focused on the conditions under which this is true and how leaders adapt accordingly. Public support for war does often wane as casualties and other war costs mount.[77] However, this casualty sensitivity may be conditional, depending on the nature of the conflict itself,[78] perceptions of success,[79] or the reaction of political elites.[80]

Moreover, leaders who anticipate public backlash from costly military interventions have found ways to alleviate those constraints, whether by relying on drones, which do not impose risks on the military that uses them, or by paying for wars through debt rather than the more visible cost of taxes.[81] Others have shown that conscription institutions themselves reflect leaders' decisions about how to minimize the impact of war based on who within society experiences the costs.[82]

Jessica Blankshain and Lindsay Cohn pick up on the theme of how personnel policies affect public attitudes toward war. They observe that while previous research has investigated the effect of conscription on public support for war, with a focus on whether those likely to be affected by conscription are more likely to resist a conflict, we know little about whether reserve mobilization affects support for a proposed military intervention. This shift to the all-volunteer force in the waning days of the Vietnam War all but ensured that fighting and sustaining major wars in the future would require such mobilization. Does doing so erode public support for the use of force in the same way as conscription?

A number of scholars have considered whether some form of "skin in the game" affects the elasticity of support for war, speculating that when people have more to lose, whether in blood or treasure, their calculus changes, and they become more sensitive to the likely costs of a conflict.[83] Past research has focused on conscription, which directly exposes a wider swath of the public to combat risks and lowers support for war. But extensive and extended mobilizations of the National Guard and reserve, such as those that presidents relied on to prosecute the wars in both Iraq and Afghanistan,[84] also increase the number of Americans with skin in the game. Blankshain and Cohn, however, show that reserve mobilization does not affect support for proposed military action the same way as conscription, which points to ways that leaders manufacture support for war by reducing the apparent cost of conflict. What should have been a potentially powerful constraint—spreading the risk of direct costs to a wider swath of Americans—fails to generate much of a check, even when this mobilization is framed in different ways that emphasize its true costs.

To better understand when public opinion is more likely to serve as a constraint on presidential freedom of action in foreign affairs, public opinion scholars have also long sought to understand the individual-level determinants of public support for war. One of the most consistent empirical regularities is the gender gap.[85] While research has consistently shown that women are usually less supportive of war than men, the size of the gender gap varies widely across conflicts and contexts.[86] The gender gap may be even more politically important in contemporary politics because women have become an increasingly critical part of the Democrats' electoral coalition.[87]

Aaron Childree and colleagues examine the interaction of gender and partisan heuristics in shaping US public support for war in Vietnam, Iraq, and Afghanistan. They find that the magnitude and even existence of a gender gap in war support varies significantly across groups and over time. When partisan elites send clear signals to their fellow partisans in the mass public, partisanship drives wartime attitudes and gender plays little role. By contrast, when elites send mixed messages, the gender heuristic becomes more important in shaping attitudes. This dynamic again points to presidential incentives to tamp down elite criticism but from a different lens. Presidents that can rally elites from both sides of the aisle around their military policies may minimize another threat to broad public support—the gender gap. By contrast, when elites send mixed signals, women may be more likely to turn against the war, eroding the president's political position.

The final chapter in the public opinion section of the volume offers new insight into the relationships between race, ethnicity, and casualty sensitivity. In a cross-national study spanning the United States, the United Kingdom, and Israel, Robert Ralston and Ronald Krebs examine whether nondominant racial and ethnic groups are more or less sensitive to war casualties than dominant groups. Across cases, they find little ex ante evidence that racial and ethnic minorities were less supportive of the use of force in general. However, minorities were significantly more sensitive to casualties. This dynamic, as with the gender gap explored by Childree and colleagues, could pose a greater risk for Democratic presidents because an erosion in support among a key component of their electoral coalition could be particularly damaging.

The Bureaucracy

Long before contemporary laments about the "deep state" or the national security establishment "blob" that resists direction from political principals and threatens democratic accountability,[88] Norton Long noted in a 1952 *American Political Science Review* article that the bureaucracy "is often viewed as tainted with an ineradicable lust for power, it is alleged that, like fire, it needs constant control to prevent its erupting from beneficent servitude into dangerous and tyrannical mastery."[89] The bureaucracy is intended to be a neutral administrator, responsive to its political principals. At the same time, the bureaucracy is populated by civil servants who have their own political views and policy preferences, perhaps especially as the landscape has become more polarized.[90] Derided as the deep state by conspiracy theorists, members of the bureaucracy have been shown to play an independent role in administering policy, whether in providing continuity that reduces whiplash across presidential administrations or in more assertively checking the president. As Francis Fukuyama suggested in 2019, "American constitutional government depends on the existence of a professional, expert, nonpartisan civil service. Hard as it is to imagine in this moment of extreme partisan polarization, government cannot function without public servants whose primary loyalty is not to the political boss who appointed them but to the Constitution and to a higher sense of the public interest. Like all modern democracies, the U.S. needs a deep state, because it is crucial to fighting corruption and upholding the rule of law."[91]

Scholars of presidential unilateral power have increasingly examined the role of bureaucratic resistance in shaping what are often regarded as unilateral presidential directives. Many executive actions originate not from the White House, but from the departments and agencies themselves. Some presidential directives are changed significantly after repeated rounds of back and forth with bureaucratic actors, often blunting their intended effect. And in still other cases, bureaucratic resistance or delayed action can kill proposed administrative actions altogether.[92]

While international relations scholarship has long recognized the importance of bureaucratic politics in shaping foreign policy decisions,[93] more recent scholarship critiquing the imperial-presidency paradigm and emphasizing domestic constraints has paid comparatively little systematic attention to the role of the bureaucracy. This omission is glaring considering the ample evidence for the historical influence of bureaucratic pushback. In his 1960 classic *Presidential Power*, Richard Neustadt's first "case of command" focused on General Douglas MacArthur's resistance to Truman's more limited war policies in Korea and the steep costs Truman ultimately paid from his failure to persuade MacArthur to toe the line.[94] Bill Clinton faced considerable resistance from the foreign policy establishment on multiple fronts, from the intense pushback that scuttled his planned executive order to allow gay people to serve openly in the military (Don't Ask, Don't Tell was the messy compromise), to entrenched resistance to the administration's impulse to make protecting human rights a focal point of US post-Cold War foreign policy. The latter is perhaps best captured in Madeline Albright's exasperated lament to then chairman of the Joint Chiefs, Colin Powell, who opposed intervention in Bosnia, "What's the point of having this superb military that you're always talking about if we can't use it?"[95] Of course, ultimately, the United States *would* send troops to Bosnia, but only years later after thousands more lives were lost. Donald Trump came to power in 2016 promising an end to the "stupid wars" of his predecessors and the reorientation of US foreign policy away from its postwar commitments to liberal internationalism. While Trump denounced bureaucrats who resisted his initiatives as agents of an antidemocratic "deep state," he had little interest in creating new institutions or reorienting existing ones to better serve his iconoclastic policy prescriptions.[96] A more systematic incorporation of bureaucratic politics into contemporary debates over domestic constraint in foreign affairs is long overdue.

Andrew Rudalevige and Rebecca Ingber take up that challenge. Rudalevige argues that even the extraordinary claims of the post-9/11 variant of the unitary executive theory have failed to make it so; the president may be *primus inter pares*, but bureaucratic actors nominally under the president in the executive branch hierarchy have their own constituencies and independent bases of political power and authority. Similarly, while the massive growth of the administrative state has surely increased presidential power in absolute terms, this expansion alone is no guarantee that presidents can harness that power to effect desired innovations in policy. As the tortured history of presidential management of the two-decades-long war in Afghanistan makes clear, the same features of the bureaucracy that can at times bolster the executive's strength can also impose their own constraints on presidential freedom of action.

Ingber acknowledges that the bureaucracy can, at times, play a constraining role, as it did, at least in part, during the insurrection of January 6. However, in Ingber's assessment the bureaucracy expands and entrenches presidential power in foreign affairs more often than it constrains. The bureaucracy is empowered by Congress and is essential to congressional oversight; however, the very existence of a bureaucratic check mollifies Congress, making legislators more willing to countenance executive aggrandizement and to abdicate their own duty to check the growth of presidential power. Moreover, the norms and institutional incentives governing bureaucratic behavior encourage bureaucrats to advance and defend legal interpretations that maximize executive authority. In the realm of war powers, these dynamics have produced a ratchet effect over time and the increasing centralization of war powers within the executive branch.

* * *

With predictable regularity, critics will charge that, and the political punditry will debate whether, the current American president is imperial. However, the focus on specific presidents, or even specific moments within an individual presidency, obscures a more interesting and important question: what types of domestic constraints does a president face when making foreign policy, and how do those constraints vary across contexts and over time? These are the central questions that motivate the contributions to this volume. The analyses of legislative, public opinion, and bureaucratic checks on executive power offer insights into the domestic incentives and constraints influencing presidential behavior and the actions of elected officials more generally; the findings have major implications for the prospects for war and peace in a post-9/11 world, and now, more than twenty years out from 9/11, in a post-post-9/11 world.

While the analyses in subsequent chapters illuminate important aspects of each domestic check and how the four institutional changes discussed previously have influenced the efficacy of these constraints, we briefly reflect on two broader shifts in American politics that promise to shape the future of presidential power in foreign affairs for the foreseeable future. We return to these themes in the concluding chapter.

The first development is the reemergence of isolationist wings within both parties, but particularly within the Republican ranks. Candidate Trump's America First foreign policy promising a retrenchment in America's role on the world stage resonated, to the surprise of many, with a significant share of the Republican base disillusioned by fifteen years of inconclusive war.[97] While still a minority position, Trump's more inward-looking posture and his more conciliatory stance toward traditional adversaries including Russia and North Korea has taken hold over a significant share of the party. For example, in April 2024 House Speaker Mike Johnson (R-LA) was forced to resort to extraordinary tactics to pass legislation providing for desperately needed funds and military equipment to keep Ukraine afloat amid a renewed Russian offensive. Despite its supermajority on the Rules Committee, Republicans relied on Democratic votes to advance a complicated rule that allowed members to vote on four aid bills separately, including funds for Ukraine, Israel, and Taiwan, before combining them into a single package to send to the Senate.[98] The decision was politically parlous and violated the "Hastert Rule" as a majority of the Republican caucus ultimately voted against the Ukraine aid bill (101 yeas vs. 112 nays); Democrats by contrast unanimously backed the measure, ensuring its passage.[99] Republicans were considerably more united behind continued military aid to Israel. Yet here, too, a bloc of twenty-one Republican legislators voted no. Thirty-seven Democrats also bucked a president of their own party and voted against aid to Israel; however, given that each of these members voted for aid to Ukraine, this split better reflects a policy disagreement with the White House than isolationist sentiment writ large.[100]

The ultimate implications of this growing isolationist sentiment in Congress remain unclear. Given Trump's long shadow over almost the entire GOP caucus, there is little reason to believe that skeptics of interventionist policies would offer staunch resistance should Trump regain the White House and choose to pursue a more aggressive foreign policy stance. This dynamic could further complicate the political calculations of a Democratic president, however. As the following chapter shows, congressional pushback to President Obama's escalation of the war in Afghanistan arose primarily from doves within his own party. Given the Democratic Party's greater dovishness since the latter stages of the Vietnam War, Democratic presidents have always faced more difficult coalition management challenges when contemplating the use of force. When considering bold military action, many Democratic presidents have counted on support from more hawkish Republicans. If the resurgence of isolationism within the GOP continues, this may place further constraints on Democratic presidents' military policy calculations.

The second development is a significant shift in public opinion toward the use of force as an instrument of policy over the two decades since the 9/11 attacks. While elite and mass polarization, policy innovations, and the extraordinary assertions of presidential power backed by broad constitutional arguments may have weakened some checks on presidential freedom of action and changed the conditions under which they might operate, a broader undeniable shift in the underlying political environment has occurred. Contemporary and likely future presidents must now battle against war weariness and increasingly entrenched public skepticism of major wars. In December 2001, opinion polls routinely showed more than 90 percent of Americans supported the war in Afghanistan.[101] By Joe Biden's inauguration, 55 percent of Americans supported the new president's plan to withdraw all troops by September 11, 2021, versus just 23 percent who opposed it.[102] And that fall, while majorities criticized Biden's handling of the chaotic withdrawal, equally large, if not larger, majorities supported the decision to withdraw US forces and bring America's longest war to a close.[103]

In the 1970s and 1980s, it was common to speak of a Vietnam syndrome in which US foreign policy was hamstrung by the memory of the war in southeast Asia, the human carnage it produced, and the political toll it exacted on the presidential administrations that prosecuted it.[104] Recently, some analysts have declared the syndrome's return after years of costly and at best inconclusive, at worse self-defeating war in Iraq and Afghanistan.[105] The argument should not be pushed too far. Presidents have adapted strategically and tactically, projecting military power around the globe in ways that minimize the American footprint, largely evading domestic political notice and minimizing potential retribution. However, as old challenges have resurfaced and new threats arise, presidents must confront them amid a backdrop of growing public skepticism toward aggressively interventionist foreign policies.

Twenty years after 9/11, the United States finds itself in its first proxy war with Russia since the collapse of the Soviet Union; in a high stakes game with China as the United States tries to counter the ascendant power's ambitions in the Pacific; and increasingly mired in another conflict in the Middle East. In each case, presidents have consciously avoided any direct military involvement. Yet, the scale of the American responses is significant and the stakes high. Unsurprisingly, given the risk of a direct confrontation between nuclear superpowers, a majority of Americans have always opposed sending American forces to defend Ukraine from Russian aggression. However, since Russia's blitzkrieg invasion in February 2022, the United States has sent more than $100 billion in aid, making Ukraine the first European country to receive the greatest share of US foreign aid since Truman and the Marshall Plan.[106] This massive infusion of aid initially enjoyed strong support among a super-majority of Americans. However, this support has waned considerably over time from 70 percent supporting military aid versus just 13 percent opposing it in April 2022 to a bare majority, 53 percent supporting aid versus 40 percent opposing it two years later.[107]

The spring 2024 supplemental providing an additional $14 billion in military aid to Israel attracted far greater support in Congress than the more contentious battle to send more military aid to Ukraine. However, public support for the deepening American commitment is decidedly weaker on both sides of the partisan divide. Democratic divisions on Israel-Palestine have received the most media attention, and polling data confirms that the issue is highly divisive among Democratic identifiers. In a March 2024 Pew poll, 56 percent of Democrats said they would be less likely to support a presidential candidate who continues to support Israel with military aid versus 40 percent who said they would be more likely to support a pro-aid candidate. However, a significant share of Republicans shared this view with 34 percent saying they would be less likely to support a candidate who supports continued military aid to Israel. Independents were roughly evenly split on the issue, but a majority said they were less likely to prefer a candidate who favors continued aid to Israel.[108]

Thus far the Biden Administration has overcome congressional objections and secured continued funding for its policies, despite an erosion of popular support. As of summer 2024, the extent to which Ukraine and Israel will resonate with voters and influence their electoral calculus remains uncertain. Finally, this broad shift in public opinion is far from immutable, and a future focusing event and a resurgence of bipartisan elite consensus could well reverse contemporary public skepticism toward extended commitments of US troops abroad and bold interventionist military policies more broadly.

Yet, the overarching political environment has undeniably and inexorably changed in the two decades since the attacks on the Pentagon and World Trade Center. This fundamental reorientation shapes the incentives and calculations of presidents and legislators alike and all but ensures that the domestic politics of military force in the post-post-9/11 era are considerably more parlous for an imperial president than those that characterized the early years of the new millennium.

Notes

1. Leonie Huddy and Stanley Feldman, "Americans Respond Politically to 9/11: Understanding the Impact of the Terrorist Attacks and Their Aftermath," *American Psychologist* 66 (2011): 455–467.

2. Jennifer De Pinto, Anthony Salvanto, Fred Backus, and Kabir Khanna, "Twenty Years after 9/11, Most See a Country Forever Changed—CBS News Poll," *CBS News*, September 10, 2021, https://www.cbsnews.com/news/twenty-years-after-911-most-see-a-country-forever-changed-opinion-poll/.

3. James Madison, Helvidius Number 4, 1793, https://founders.archives.gov/documents/Madison/01-15-02-0070.

4. Quoted in Donald Wolfensberger, "The Return of the Imperial Presidency?," *Wilson Quarterly* 26, no. 2 (Spring 2002): 36–41.

5. Michael Beschloss, "The End of the Imperial Presidency," *New York Times*, December 18, 2000; Arthur Schlesinger Jr., *The Imperial Presidency* (Boston: Houghton Mifflin, 1973), ix.

6. Andrew Rudalevige, *The New Imperial Presidency: Renewing Presidential Power after Watergate* (Ann Arbor: University of Michigan Press, 2005).

7. Charlie Savage, *Takeover: The Return of the Imperial Presidency and the Subversion of American Democracy* (Boston: Little, Brown & Company, 2007).

8. See, for example, Paul Peterson, *The President, the Congress, and the Making of Foreign Policy* (Norman: The University of Oklahoma Press, 1994); Barbara Hinckley, *Less than Meets the Eye: Foreign Policy Making and the Myth of the Assertive Congress* (Chicago: University of Chicago Press, 1994); Louis Fisher, *Congressional Abdication on War and Spending* (College Station: Texas A&M University Press, 2000); James Meernik, "President Decision Making and the Political Use of Military Force," *International Studies Quarterly* 38 (1994): 121–138; James Meernik, "Congress, the President, and the Commitment of the US Military," *Legislative Studies Quarterly* 20 (1995): 377–392.

9. For scholarship advocating for a continued role for congressional and other

domestic checks on the commander in chief, see David Clark, "Agreeing to Disagree: Domestic Institutional Congruence and US Dispute Behavior," *Political Research Quarterly* 53 (2000): 375–400; William Howell and Jon Pevehouse, *While Dangers Gather: Congressional Checks on Presidential War Powers* (Princeton, NJ: Princeton University Press, 2007); Ralph Carter and James Scott, *Choosing to Lead: Understanding Congressional Foreign Policy Entrepreneurs* (Durham, NC: Duke University Press, 2009); Douglas Kriner, *After the Rubicon: Congress, Presidents, and the Politics of Waging War* (Chicago: University of Chicago Press, 2010); Douglas Kriner and Eric Schickler, *Investigating the President: Congressional Checks on Presidential Power* (Princeton, NJ: Princeton University Press, 2016).

10. Brandice Canes-Wrone and Scott de Marchi, "Presidential Approval and Legislative Success," *Journal of Politics* 64 (2002): 491–509.

11. Paul Gronke, Jeffrey Koch, and Matthew Wilson, "Follow the Leader? Presidential Approval, Presidential Support, and Representatives' Electoral Fortunes," *Journal of Politics* 65 (2003): 785–808; Alan Abramowitz, "Forecasting the 2008 Presidential Election with the Time-for-Change Model," *PS: Political Science & Politics* 41 (2008): 691–695.

12. David Mayhew, *America's Congress: Actions in the Public Sphere, James Madison through Newt Gingrich* (New Haven, CT: Yale University Press, 2000).

13. Howell and Pevehouse, *While Dangers Gather*; Kriner, *After the Rubicon*.

14. Jacob Hacker and Paul Pierson, *Off Center: The Republican Revolution and the Erosion of American Democracy* (New Haven, CT: Yale University Press, 2005); Sean Theriault, *The Gingrich Senators: The Roots of Partisan Warfare in Congress* (New York: Oxford University Press, 2013).

15. Frances Lee, *Beyond Ideology: Politics, Principles, and Partisanship in the US Senate* (Chicago: University of Chicago Press, 2009); Frances Lee, *Insecure Majorities: Congress and the Perpetual Campaign* (Chicago: University of Chicago Press, 2016).

16. Robert David Johnson, *Congress and the Cold War* (New York: Cambridge University Press, 1995); Kriner, *After the Rubicon*.

17. Kenneth Schultz, "Tying Hands and Washing Hands: The U.S. Congress and Multilateral Humanitarian Intervention," in *Locating the Proper Authorities: The Interaction of Domestic and International Institutions*, ed. Daniel Drezner, 105–142 (Ann Arbor: University of Michigan Press, 2003); Sarah Kreps, *Coalitions of Convenience: United States Military Interventions after the Cold War* (New York: Oxford University Press, 2011).

18. "Republican Party Platform of 1996," August 12, 1996. Republican Party Platforms, *The American Presidency Project*, ed. Gerhard Peters and John T. Woolley, accessed March 21, 2024, https://www.presidency.ucsb.edu/node/273441.

19. On negative agenda power, see Sean Gailmard and Jeffery Jenkins, "Negative Agenda Control in the Senate and House: Fingerprints of Majority Party Power," *Journal of Politics* 69 (2007): 689–700; Jeffery Jenkins and Nathan

Monroe, "Buying Negative Agenda Control in the US House," *American Journal of Political Science* 56 (2012): 897–912.

20. Matthew Baum and Tim Groeling, "Shot by the Messenger: Partisan Cues and Public Opinion Regarding National Security and War," *Political Behavior* 31 (2009): 157–186.

21. David Moore, "Bush Job Approval Highest in Gallup History: Widespread Public Support for War on Terrorism," *Gallup.com*, September 24, 2001, https://news.gallup.com/poll/4924/bush-job-approval-highest-gallup-history.aspx.

22. Joseph Margulies, *What Changed When Everything Changed: 9/11 and the Making of National Identity* (New Haven, CT: Yale University Press, 2013, 6).

23. Gary Jacobson, *A Divider, Not a Uniter: George W. Bush and the American People* (New York: Longman, 2011).

24. Alan Abramowitz and Kyle Saunders, "Is Polarization a Myth?" *Journal of Politics* 70 (2008): 542–555; Joseph Bafumi and Robert Shapiro, "A New Partisan Voter," *Journal of Politics* 71 (2009):1–24. Morris Fiorina, Sam Abrams, and Jeremy Pope, *Culture War: The Myth of a Polarized America* (New York: Pearson Longman, 2005).

25. Alan Abramowitz and Steven Webster, "Negative Partisanship: Why Americans Dislike Parties But Behave Like Rabid Partisans," *Political Psychology* 39 (2018): 119–135; Liliana Mason, *Uncivil Agreement: How Politics Became Our Identity* (Chicago: University of Chicago Press, 2018); Nathan Kalmoe and Liliana Mason, *Radical American Partisanship: Mapping Violent Hostility, Its Causes, and the Consequences for Democracy* (Chicago: University of Chicago Press, 2022).

26. For an overview, see Paul Gronke and Brian Newman, "FDR to Clinton, Mueller to?: A Field Essay on Presidential Approval," *Political Research Quarterly* 56 (2003): 501–512.

27. Neta C. Crawford, "The U.S. Budgetary Costs of the Post-9/11 Wars," *20 Years of War: A Costs of War Research Series*, 2021, https://watson.brown.edu/costsofwar/files/cow/imce/papers/2021/Costs%20of%20War_U.S.%20Budgetary%20Costs%20of%20Post-9%2011%20Wars_9.1.21.pdf.

28. US Department of Defense, "Casualty Status as of 10 a.m. EDT April 9, 2024," https://www.defense.gov/casualty.pdf; "U.S. & Allied Killed," Costs of War, updated July 2021, https://watson.brown.edu/costsofwar/costs/human/military/killed.

29. Alvin Richman, "When Should We Be Prepared to Fight?" *Public Perspective* 6 (1995): 44–47; Eric Larson, *Casualties and Consensus: The Historical Role of Casualties in Domestic Support for U.S. Military Operations* (Santa Monica, CA: Rand, 1996); Louis Klarevas, "The 'Essential Domino' of Military Operations: American Public Opinion and the Use of Force," *International Studies Perspectives* 3 (2002): 417–437.

30. Douglas Kriner and Francis Shen, "Responding to War on Capitol Hill: Battlefield Casualties, Congressional Response, and Public Support for the War in Iraq," *American Journal of Political Science* 58 (2014): 157–174.

31. US Department of Defense, "Population Representation in the Military Services: Fiscal Year 2019 Summary Report," accessed March 21, 2024, https://prhome.defense.gov/Portals/52/Documents/POPREP/2019%20summary_1.pdf?ver=k_GmX9ohPA04VovH5lnWXg%3d%3d.

32. Douglas Kriner and Francis Shen, *The Casualty Gap: The Causes and Consequences of American Wartime Inequalities* (New York: Oxford University Press, 2010); Douglas Kriner and Francis Shen, "Invisible Inequality: The Two Americas of Military Sacrifice," *University of Memphis Law Review* 46 (2014): 545–636.

33. Daniel Bergan, "The Draft Lottery and Attitudes toward the Vietnam War," *Public Opinion Quarterly* 73 (2009): 379–384; Robert Erikson and Laura Stoker, "Caught in the Draft: The Effects of Vietnam Draft Lottery Status on Political Attitudes," *American Political Science Review* 105 (2011): 221–237; Michael Horowitz and Matthew Levendusky, "Drafting Support for War: Conscription and Mass Support for Warfare," *Journal of Politics* 73 (2011): 1–11; Joseph Vasquez, "Shouldering the Soldiering: Democracy, Conscription, and Military Casualties," *Journal of Conflict Resolution* 49 (2005): 849–873; Douglas Kriner and Francis Shen, "Conscription, Inequality, and Partisan Support for War," *Journal of Conflict Resolution* 60 (2016): 1419–1445.

34. Bartholomew Sparrow, "Limited Wars and the Attenuation of the State: Soldiers, Money, and Political Communication in World War II, Korea, and Vietnam," in *Shaped by War and Trade: International Influences on American Political Development*, ed. Ira Katznelson and Martin Shefter (Princeton, NJ: Princeton University Press, 2002), 267–300.

35. Rosella Cappella Zelinsky, *How States Pay for Wars* (Ithaca, NY: Cornell University Press, 2016).

36. Sarah Kreps, *Taxing Wars: The American Way of War Finance and the Decline of Democracy* (New York: Oxford University Press, 2018).

37. Of course, the language of the 2001 AUMF is broad as it authorized the president "to use all necessary and appropriate force against those nations, organizations, or persons he determines planned, authorized, committed, or aided the terrorist attacks that occurred on September 11, 2001, or harbored such organizations or persons, in order to prevent any future acts of international terrorism against the United States by such nations, organizations or persons." This opens the door for arguments that AUMF authorized strikes in Pakistan, which harbored al-Qaeda leaders including Osama bin Laden, and in Yemen and Somalia, where the Obama administration argued that groups such al-Qaeda in the Arabian Peninsula, despite the fact that these groups did not form until after 9/11. Shoon Kathleen Murray, "Stretching the 2001 AUMF: A History of Two Presidencies," *Presidential Studies Quarterly* 45 (2015): 175–198.

38. Mark Halperin and John Heilemann, *Double Down: Game Change 2012* (New York: Penguin, 2013, 52).

39. John Kaag and Sarah Kreps, *Drone Warfare* (New York: John Wiley & Sons, 2014).

40. See Cato IV (November 8, 1787) and Cato V (November 22, 1787), accessed March 21, 2024, https://teachingamericanhistory.org/document/cato-iv/; https://teachingamericanhistory.org/document/cato-v/.

41. Among others, see Steven Calabresi and Christopher Yoo, *The Unitary Executive* (New Haven, CT: Yale University Press, 2008); Stephen Skowronek, John Dearborn, and Desmond King, *Phantoms of a Beleaguered Republic: The Deep State and the Unitary Executive* (New York: Oxford University Press, 2021).

42. Mark Tushnet, "A Political Perspective on the Theory of the Unitary Executive," *University of Pennsylvania Journal of Constitutional Law* 12 (2009): 313–329.

43. Frederick Schwarz Jr. and Aziz Huq, *Unchecked and Unbalanced: Presidential Power in a Time of Terror* (New York: New Press, 2008); Jack Goldsmith, *The Terror Presidency: Law and Judgment Inside the Bush Administration* (New York: W.W. Norton & Company, 2007); Robert Sloane, "The Scope of Executive Power in the Twenty-First Century: An Introduction," *Boston University Law Review* 88 (2008): 341–351.

44. Richard Grimmett, "Authorization for Use of Military Force in Response to the 9/11 Attacks (P.L. 107-40): Legislative History," CRS Report RS22357, January 16, 2007.

45. John Yoo, "The President's Constitutional Authority to Conduct Military Operations against Terrorists and Nations Supporting Them," September 25, 2001, http://fas.org/irp/agency/doj/olc092501.html#. Emphasis added.

46. John Haltiwanger, "Trump Claimed Article 2 of the Constitution Gives Him the Right to Do 'Whatever I Want as President,' But That's Not True," *Business Insider*, July 23, 2019.

47. Memorandum from Bill Barr to Deputy Attorney General Rod Rosenstein and Assistant Attorney General Steve Engel, re: Mueller's "Obstruction" Theory, at 9 (June 8, 2018). Emphasis in the original.

48. Jack Goldsmith, "Executive Branch Crisis Lawyering and the Best View," *Georgetown Journal of Legal Ethics* 31 (2018): 261–276.

49. Thomas Owens Mackubin, "Rumsfeld, the Generals, and the State of U.S. Civil-Military Relations," *Naval War College Review* 59 (2006): 68–80.

50. Stephen Dyson, "'Stuff Happens': Donald Rumsfeld and the Iraq War," *Foreign Policy Analysis* 5 (2009): 327–347; Donald Drechsler, "Reconstructing the Interagency Process After Iraq," *Journal of Strategic Studies* 1 (2007): 3–30.

51. Graham Allison, *Essence of Decision: Explaining the Cuban Missile Crisis* (Boston: Little Brown, 1971); I.M. Destler, *Presidents, Bureaucrats and Foreign Policy* (Princeton, NJ: Princeton University Press, 1972); Robert Art, "Bureaucratic Politics and American Foreign Policy: A Critique," *Policy Sciences* 4 (1973): 467–490; Amy Zeggart, *Flawed by Design: The Evolution of the CIA, JCS, and NSC* (Palo Alto, CA: Stanford University Press, 1999).

52. Richard Neustadt, *Presidential Power* (New York: New American Library, 1960).

53. William Young, "A Check on Faint-Hearted Presidents: Letters of Marque and Reprisal," *Washington and Lee Law Review* 66 (2009): 896–940.

54. Edward Corwin, *President, Office and Powers* (New York: New York University Press, 1948).

55. Schlesinger Jr., *Imperial Presidency*; James Lindsay, "Congress, Foreign Policy, and the New Institutionalism," *International Studies Quarterly* 38 (1994): 281–304; Hinckley, *Less Than Meets the Eye*.

56. Gordon Silverstein, *Imbalance of Powers: Constitutional Interpretation and the Making of American Foreign Policy* (New York: Oxford University Press, 1997); Stephen Griffin, *Long Wars and the Constitution* (Cambridge, MA: Harvard University Press, 2013).

57. Louis Fisher and David Gray Adler, "The War Powers Resolution: Time to Say Goodbye," *Political Science Quarterly* 113 (1998): 1–20; Michael Glennon, "Too Far Apart: Repeal the War Powers Resolution," *University of Miami Law Review* 50 (1995): 17. For a more sanguine view of the War Powers Resolution and its practical effects on policy, see David Auerswald and Peter Cowhey, "Ballotbox Diplomacy: The War Powers Resolution and the Use of Force," *International Studies Quarterly* 41 (1997): 505–528.

58. Kriner, *After the Rubicon*.

59. Kriner and Schickler, *Investigating the President*.

60. Mayhew, *America's Congress*; Howell and Pevehouse, *While Dangers Gather*.

61. David McCullough, *Truman* (New York: Simon and Schuster, 2003).

62. David Clark, "Agreeing to Disagree: Domestic Institutional Congruence and U.S. Dispute Behavior," *Political Research Quarterly* 53 (2000): 375–401; Howell and Pevehouse, *While Dangers Gather*; Kriner, *After the Rubicon*; Roseanne McManus, *Statements of Resolve: Achieving Coercive Credibility in International Conflict* (New York: Cambridge University Press, 2017).

63. Senate Committee on Foreign Relations, Minority Report, "Left Behind: A Brief Assessment of the Biden Administration's Strategic Failures during the Afghanistan Evacuation," February 2022, https://www.foreign.senate.gov/imo/media/doc/Risch%20Afghanistan%20Report%202022.pdf.

64. Barbara Sprunt, "There's a Bipartisan Backlash to How Biden Handled the Withdrawal from Afghanistan," *NPR*, August 17, 2021, https://www.npr.org/2021/08/16/1028081817/congressional-reaction-to-bidens-afghanistan-withdrawal-has-been-scathing.

65. David Mayhew, *Divided We Govern: Party Control, Lawmaking, and Investigations, 1946–1990* (New Haven, CT: Yale University Press, 1991).

66. John Zaller and Dennis Chiu, "Government's Little Helper: U.S. Press Coverage of Foreign Policy Crises, 1945–1991," *Political Communication* 13 (1996): 385–405; Matthew Baum and Tim Groeling, "Crossing the Water's Edge: Elite Rhetoric, Media Coverage, and the Rally-Round-the-Flag Phenomenon," *Journal of Politics* 70 (2008): 1065–1085.

67. John Aldrich, John Sullivan, and Eugene Borgida, "Foreign Affairs and Issue Voting: Do Presidential Candidates 'Waltz Before a Blind Audience?'" *American Political Science Review* 83 (1989): 123–141; Peter Trumbore and David Dulio, "Running on Foreign Policy: Examining the Role of Foreign Policy Issues in the 2000, 2002, and 2004 Congressional Campaigns," *Foreign Policy Analysis* 9 (2013): 267–286.

68. Miroslav Nincic and Barbara Hinckley, "Foreign Policy and the Evaluation of Presidential Candidates," *The Journal of Conflict Resolution* 35, no. 2 (June 1991): 333–355.

69. Though even in 2004, Bush did lose vote share in states and counties that had suffered high casualties. David Karol and Edward Miguel, "The Electoral Cost of War: Iraq Casualties and the 2004 US Presidential Election," *Journal of Politics* 69 (2007): 633–648.

70. Adam Berinsky, "Assuming the Costs of War: Events, Elites, and American Public Support for Military Conflict," *Journal of Politics* 69 (2007): 975–997.

71. Jacobson, *Divider, Not a Uniter*.

72. Douglas Kriner and Francis Shen, "Iraq Casualties and the 2006 Senate Elections," *Legislative Studies Quarterly* 32 (2007): 507–530; Christian Grose and Bruce Oppenheimer, "The Iraq War, Partisanship, and Candidate Attributes: Variation in Partisan Swing in the 2006 U.S. House Elections," *Legislative Studies Quarterly* 32 (2007): 531–557; Scott Gartner and Gary Segura, "All Politics are Still Local: The Iraq War and the 2006 Midterm Elections," *PS: Political Science & Politics* 41 (2008): 95–100.

73. Gary Langer, "Midterm Election: Referendum on War," *ABC News*, October 23, 2006, https://abcnews.go.com/Politics/story?id=2600146&page=1.

74. Roger Simon, "Obama Beats Hillary over Head with Iraq," *Politico*, January 31, 2008, https://www.politico.com/story/2008/01/obama-beats-hillary-over-head-with-iraq-008248.

75. Douglas Kriner, "Obama's Authorization Paradox: Syria and Congress's Continued Relevance in Military Affairs," *Presidential Studies Quarterly* 44 (2014): 309–327.

76. Philip Potter and Matthew Baum, "Democratic Peace, Domestic Audience Costs, and Political Communication," *Political Communication* 27 (2010): 453–470.

77. John Mueller, *War, Presidents, and Public Opinion* (New York: John Wiley and Sons Inc., 1973); Scott Gartner and Gary Segura, "War, Casualties, and Public Opinion," *Journal of Conflict Resolution* 42 (1998): 278–320.

78. Bruce Jentleson, "The Pretty-Prudent Public: Post-Vietnam American Opinion on the Use of Force," *International Studies Quarterly* 36 (1992): 49–73.

79. Christopher Gelpi, Peter Feaver, and Jason Reifler, *Paying the Human Costs of War: American Public Opinion and Casualties in Military Conflicts* (Princeton: Princeton University Press, 2009).

80. John Zaller, *The Nature and Origins of Mass Opinion* (New York: Cambridge University Press, 1992); Adam Berinsky, *In Time of War: Understanding*

American Public Opinion from World War II to Iraq (Chicago: University of Chicago Press, 2009).

81. Kaag and Kreps, *Drone Warfare*.

82. Joanne Gowa, *Ballots and Bullets: The Elusive Democratic Peace* (Princeton, NJ: Princeton University Press, 2000); Horowitz and Levendusky, "Drafting Support."

83. Vasquez, "Shouldering the Soldiering"; Horowitz and Levendusky, "Drafting Support"; Kriner and Shen, "Conscription."

84. The US has even mobilized the reserve to combat COVID-19. Jules Hurst, "No Way to Get to the War: Mobilization Problems and the Army Reserve," *Modern War Institute*, October 30, 2020, https://mwi.usma.edu/no-way-to-get-to-the-war-mobilization-problems-and-the-army-reserve/.

85. Pamela Conover and Virginia Sapiro, "Gender, Feminist Consciousness, and War," *American Journal of Political Science* 37 (1993): 1079–1099; Lisa Brandes, "Public Opinion, International Security Policy, and Gender: The United States and Great Britain since 1945" (PhD diss., Yale University, 1994); Miroslav Nincic and Donna Nincic, "Race, Gender, and War," *Journal of Peace Research* 39 (2002): 547–568.

86. Richard Eichenberg, "Gender Differences in Public Attitudes Toward the Use of Force by the United States," *International Security* 28 (2003): 110–141; Richard Eichenberg, "Gender Differences in American Public Opinion on the Use of Military Force, 1982–2013," *International Studies Quarterly* 60 (2016): 138–148; Deborah Brooks and Benjamin Valentino, "A War of One's Own: Understanding the Gender Gap in Support for War," *Public Opinion Quarterly* 75 (2011): 270–286.

87. Karen Kaufmann, John Petrocik, and Daron Shaw, *Unconventional Wisdom: Facts and Myths about American Voters* (New York: Oxford University Press, 2008).

88. Stephen Walt, "The Donald Versus 'The Blob,'" in *Chaos in the Liberal Order: The Trump Presidency and International Politics in the Twenty-First Century*, ed. Robert Jervis, Francis Gavin, Joshua Rovner, and Diane Labrosse (New York: Columbia University Press, 2018).

89. Norton Long, "Bureaucracy and Constitutionalism," *American Political Science Review* 46 (1952): 808.

90. Daniel Drezner, *The Ideas Industry* (New York: Oxford University Press, 2017).

91. Francis Fukuyama, "American Democracy Depends on the 'Deep State,'" *Wall Street Journal*, December 20, 2019.

92. Andrew Rudalevige, "Executive Orders and Presidential Unilateralism," *Presidential Studies Quarterly* 42 (2012): 138–160; Josh Kennedy, "'Do This! Do that! and Nothing Will Happen': Executive Orders and Bureaucratic Responsiveness," *American Politics Research* 43 (2015): 59–82; Andrew Rudalevige, *By Executive Order: Bureaucratic Management and the Limits of Presidential Power* (Princeton, NJ: Princeton University Press, 2021).

93. Allison, *Essence of Decision*.

94. Richard Neustadt, *Presidential Power: The Politics of Leadership* (New York: John Wiley & Sons, 1960).

95. Andrew Bacevich, "Policing Utopia: The Military Imperatives of Globalization," *The National Interest* 56 (1999): 7.

96. Daniel Drezner, "Present at the Destruction: The Trump Administration and the Foreign Policy Bureaucracy," *Journal of Politics* 81 (2019): 723–730.

97. Douglas Kriner and Francis Shen, "Battlefield Casualties and Ballot-Box Defeat: Did the Bush-Obama Wars Cost Clinton the White House?" *PS: Political Science and Politics* 53, no. 2 (2020): 248–252.

98. Mychael Schnell, "Democrats Hel Advance Ukraine, Israel, Aid in Rare Rules Move," Roll Call, April 19, 2024, https://thehill.com/homenews/house/4604231-democrats-ukraine-israel-aid-rare-rules-move/.

99. Roll call 151, H.R. 8035, Ukraine Security Supplemental Appropriations Act, April 20, 2024, https://clerk.house.gov/Votes/2024151.

100. Roll call 152, H.R. 8034, Israel Security Supplemental Appropriations Act, April 20, 2024, https://clerk.house.gov/Votes/2024152.

101. Among others, see Newsweek, "Defining Victory/Reforming Islam, Question 6 [USPSRNEW.01NW22.Q05]," Princeton Survey Research Associates, Cornell University (Ithaca, NY: Roper Center for Public Opinion Research, 2001); Fox News, "Fox News Poll: December 2001, Question 13 [USODFOX.121401.R15]," Opinion Dynamics, Cornell University (Ithaca, NY: Roper Center for Public Opinion Research, 2001); CBS News, "CBS News/New York Times Poll: Civil Liberties/Afghanistan/Terrorism, Question 66 [USCBSNYT.121101.R57]," CBS News, Cornell University (Ithaca, NY: Roper Center for Public Opinion Research, 2001).

102. Ipsos, "Ipsos Understanding Society: Wave 2 April 2021, Question 6 [31118528.00005]," Ipsos, Cornell University (Ithaca, NY: Roper Center for Public Opinion Research, 2021).

103. For example, see Washington Post/ABC News, "ABC News/Washington Post Poll, Question 4 [31118604.00003]," Abt Associates, Cornell University (Ithaca, NY: Roper Center for Public Opinion Research, 2021).

104. Geoff Simons, *The Vietnam Syndrome: Impact on US Foreign Policy* (New York: St. Martin's Press, 1997).

105. Marvin Kalb, "It's Called the Vietnam Syndrome, and It's Back," *Brookings*, January 22, 2013, https://www.brookings.edu/blog/up-front/2013/01/22/its-called-the-vietnam-syndrome-and-its-back/.

106. Jonathan Masters and Will Merrow, "How Much U.S. Aid is Going to Ukraine?" Council on Foreign Relations, May 9, 2024, https://www.cfr.org/article/how-much-us-aid-going-ukraine.

107. ABC News, ABC News/Ipsos Poll: 2022 Wave 43, Question 11, 31119491.00010, Ipsos, (Cornell University, Ithaca, NY: Roper Center for Public Opinion

Research, 2022), Survey question, DOI: 10.25940/ROPER-31119491; Quinnipiac University Polling Institute, Quinnipiac University National Poll, Quinnipiac University Polling Institute, (Cornell University, Ithaca, NY: Roper Center for Public Opinion Research, 2024), Dataset, DOI: 10.25940/ROPER-31121000.

108. "Americans Split on Continuing Military Aid to Israel," Pew, March 1, 2024, https://www.ipsos.com/en-us/americans-split-continuing-military-aid-israel.

CHAPTER TWO

Purely Partisan Warriors?
Legislative Rhetoric in the Afghanistan and Iraq Wars

Sarah E. Kreps and Douglas L. Kriner

In *Federalist* no. 47, Madison described the accumulation of powers in one branch of government as "the very definition of tyranny."[1] Yet between 1788 and the middle of the twentieth century, American presidents pushed the bounds of their authority, seeking to conduct the nation's foreign policy with limited congressional influence. Truman's decision to go to war in Korea without seeking legislative sanction accelerated the consolidation of executive power. By the early 1970s, historian Arthur Schlesinger Jr. opined that in questions of war and peace the American president had become "the most absolute monarch (with the possible exception of Mao Tse-tung of China) among the great powers of the world."[2] While Congress endeavored to battle back against presidential imperialism after Watergate, the conventional wisdom has held that the practical consequences of its resurgence amounted to much "less than meets the eye."[3]

The view of an imperial presidency has not gone unscathed. To be sure, as Benjamin Fordham shows in his chapter, members of Congress have few electoral incentives to oppose the use of force ex ante and try to head-off a potentially costly military misadventure. Even when presidential wars fail to go according to plan, Congress rarely succeeds in using the power of the purse or the War Powers Resolution to legally compel a wayward commander in chief to change course. Yet, by pushing back against other presidential priorities,[4] holding investigative hearings,[5] and battling the president in the public sphere,[6] members of Congress are frequently able to raise the costs of ignoring congressional preferences, even when they cannot legislatively mandate a change in policy. If Christopher Dictus and Phillip Potter's chapter is any guide, these tools should be all the more important in circumstances in which the tendency for foreign policy ambition is more likely, which is when executives emerge from an election weakened by the results.

In this chapter, we engage ongoing debates about the circumstances under which Congress exercises its checks on foreign policy. Most scholarship asserting Congress's continued relevance privileges partisanship as the predominant driver of members' willingness to use the tools at their disposal to push back against presidents and check the commander in chief. (For an important critique, see Jordan Tama's chapter and his assessment of "anti-presidential bipartisanship," in which members of Congress set aside partisan loyalties and challenge the executive in a unified, bipartisan manner). Political competition, according to these arguments, is channeled more through political parties than between branches, creating a separation of parties rather than a separation of powers. As Daryl Levinson and Richard Pildes put it, "the practical distinction between party-divided and party-unified government thus rivals, and often dominates, the constitutional distinction between the branches in predicting and explaining interbranch political dynamics. Recognizing that these dynamics will shift from competitive when government is divided to cooperative when it is unified calls into question basic assumptions of separation of powers."[7]

If a separation-of-parties system operates, then unified government will defang Madisonian checks and balances. Solid copartisan majorities insulate presidents from politically costly pushback. Only when presidents confront a strong opposition party should they anticipate considerable institutional resistance to their policy proposals. Accordingly, scholars point to the partisan composition of Congress as a strong predictor of the frequency with which presidents use force abroad,[8] the probability with which they respond to foreign crises,[9] and the scope and duration of American military actions.[10]

As discussed in the introductory chapter, there are strong theoretical reasons to believe that these partisan dynamics should have grown even stronger in the post-9/11 era given the continued acceleration of both partisan ideological polarization and pure teamsmanship in an era of an evenly divided electorate with partisan control up for grabs at each election.[11] If legislators ever had other incentives—ideological, electoral, institutional, or otherwise—to push back against wayward presidential military policies, these developments risk subsuming them completely to partisan forces.

A number of popular accounts of contemporary foreign policy accord with the separation-of-parties perspective. For example, in 2013, at the height of President Obama's counterterrorism strikes, peace activist Medea Benjamin accused Democratic legislators of playing politics on the use of force. She observed that if President Bush had been expanding counterterrorism operations, Democrats "would have been yelling and screaming about it." Instead, she argued, "Democrats are too concerned with party politics and they fall in line with President Obama."[12] Under President Trump, Peter Beinart warned that "Democrats are hypocrites for condemning Trump over Syria," noting that they criticized Trump's Syria withdrawal and abandonment of the Kurds "but want the U.S. to pull out of Afghanistan under similar conditions."[13]

The almost-exclusive focus on partisanship gives short shrift to other factors that might guide legislative position-taking on the use of force. If ideology also shapes members' positions, such that hawks favor more aggressive postures and doves prefer diplomatic overtures, then congressional checks will not disappear under unified government.[14] Far from becoming enamored with force when a copartisan sits in the White House, Democratic doves, for example, may maintain ideological consistency and continue to challenge proposals for military force.[15] Indeed, when President Biden authorized strikes in Syria without congressional approval, Chris Murphy (D-CT) said that "Congress should hold this administration to the same standard it did prior administrations, and require clear legal justifications for military action, especially inside theaters like Syria, where Congress has not explicitly authorized any American military action."[16] Electoral pressures may also animate legislators. John Aldrich, John Sullivan, and Eugene Borgida show that the public does discern differences among candidates on foreign policy and that these differences affect vote choice,[17] although again, Fordham's chapter in this volume shows that these incentives do not operate preemptively to check a proposed use of force but rather align once the operation has gone badly. If ideological and electoral factors also influence congressional positions on the use of force, then the separation of powers may remain intact under unified government, challenging arguments grounded in partisanship.

Isolating the effect of partisanship from motives of ideology and electoral incentives presents methodological challenges because these factors are often collinear.[18] Traditionally used dependent variables, such as roll call votes, are increasingly controlled by party leaders, limiting opportunities to assess important heterogeneity across members in positions and in engagement.[19] Moreover, the volume of data necessary to analyze other forms of legislative behavior, including speechmaking, has been prohibitively large.[20] We therefore apply advances in machine learning to study congressional rhetoric in the context of a rarely employed foreign policy—a military surge first in Iraq during the 110th Congress and then in Afghanistan during the 111th Congress—undertaken by presidents of both parties. Surges across presidents of two different parties provide a paired comparison for understanding the basis for legislative position-taking on two of the most consequential foreign policy decisions of the post-9/11 era. Although President Bush initiated both wars, President Obama quickly owned the Afghanistan War when he chose not to end it after coming to power but actually increased troop levels;[21] the Afghanistan War colloquially came to be known as "Obama's War." Comparing the response of congressional Democrats and Republicans across these two cases can help tease out the relative importance of ideological leanings versus raw partisanship in shaping legislative position-taking on the use of force.

Despite partisanship defining the contemporary political landscape, we challenge the separation-of-parties thesis with evidence that it does not exclusively define political competition on the use of force. While congressional rhetoric on the Iraq War largely fell along partisan lines, legislative positions on the Afghanistan surge during the Obama administration did not. Democrats challenged the Obama surge despite partisan ties to its architect. Conversely, Republicans largely refrained from issuing antiwar statements despite the potential for partisan gain, even if many tempered their prowar rhetoric by largely refraining from publicly supporting the administration itself. Members' ideological leanings drove significant intrapartisan variation in position-taking. Finally, electoral pressures consistently moderated the influence of partisanship on members' wartime position-taking.

Our analysis offers new insights into the conditions under which congressional checks on executive power are most likely. Most importantly, our findings offer an important corrective to scholarship warning about the primacy of partisan forces in driving congressional engagement on the use of force.[22] By demonstrating the importance of ideological and constituency pressures, we challenge arguments suggesting that unified government and the strength of partisan loyalty effectively neutralize legislative checks on wartime executive behavior.[23] Unified government does not guarantee all presidents a complacent Congress. Rather, because partisanship and ideology both influence member engagement with military matters, Democratic presidents face greater pushback in unified government than do Republicans. Understanding when members are likely to speak out in the public sphere and either support or challenge the president and his policies offers important insights into the political costs of military action, the president's freedom of action, and the likelihood of force.

Why Rhetoric Matters

Debates on the separation of powers often lament the legislature's lackluster influence when it comes to checking executive power on the use of force.[24] Weighing in on whether Congress effectively exercises its constitutional responsibility to raise militaries, provide funding, and authorize wars, thereby standing in the way of a unilateral executive, Louis Fisher argues that "on matters of war, we have what the framers thought they had put behind them: a monarchy. Checks and balances? Try to find them."[25] More recently, Jack Goldsmith observes "a steady 230-year rise in presidential power over foreign (and domestic relations) that responds to massive changes in the US role in a much more dangerous and complex world."[26]

Arguments about the imperial presidency often hinge on observations about whether Congress authorized the use of force and the frequency with which presidents initiated force without congressional approval. Such evidence refers to the "hard powers" of Congress to check executive power. Congress also, however, has enormous "soft powers" that refer to its powers of persuasion and its capacity to bring political pressure to bear on the White House: these include the ability to set the agenda, determine rules of proceedings, launch high profile investigations, and, perhaps most importantly, engage in speech and debate.[27]

Political rhetoric, whether through morning business floor speeches, grandstanding, explaining votes, or high-profile filibusters, is more than cheap talk; it is a "mechanism of persuasion."[28] Congressional speeches are an important way members of Congress communicate with each other and, perhaps even more importantly, with their constituents in order to elicit accord.[29] As President Obama observed at the end of his presidency, "it matters to have Congress with you, in terms of your ability to sustain what you set out to do."[30] Scholars have shown "the voice of Congress (or lack thereof)"[31] affects constraints on executive decision-making via several mechanisms. One is through an agenda-setting process within Congress. Expressing reservations in the context of legislative debate can in turn perform an agenda-setting function, producing political momentum for more assertive and constraining functions, such as appropriations and investigations that hamper a policy's sustainability.[32]

The influence of legislative position-taking may also operate via signaling to a domestic political audience. Responding to the puzzle of why members give speeches even when the chamber is almost empty, James Snyder and Michael Ting argue that such speeches allow members to claim credit for taking a clear position on a particular issue.[33] Congressional rhetoric is covered on television programs (whether through specialized coverage such as C-Span or highlights on news programs), in print, on social media, and in the press releases legislators send to constituents explaining achievements in Washington.[34] The media also plays a critically important role in amplifying institutional challenges to the commander in chief and his policies.[35] A significant literature employing both observational[36] and experimental[37] evidence shows that the public positions taken by members of Congress can shape public opinion. Perhaps most importantly, congressional criticism can significantly erode public support for war and impose political costs on the White House for staying the course.

Lastly, legislative position-taking has the potential to strengthen or undermine international adversaries. International politics is always a two-level game, with the executive branch needing to maintain support from domestic constituencies while striking bargains with international actors.[38] Those international actors always cue off the signals of the foreign domestic audience, where domestic division can strengthen the bargaining position of the international actor.[39] Russia's online interference strategy identifies and then insinuates itself into domestic debates about race, foreign policy, and immigration, divisions they can glean from the internet and from the quite visible partisan debates in Congress.[40] In the context of foreign interventions, groups such as the Taliban could draw strength upon hearing vociferous domestic opposition in the United States, an indication that the domestic political situation is fragile, suggesting that the Taliban try to collapse support altogether through a few well-placed attacks, or simply wait out the occupation.

Legislative scholars have long debated the relative influence of various factors in driving congressional behavior. From this research, we generate analytical expectations about how both partisanship and ideology might influence members' wartime positions as well as how electoral context could moderate position-taking behavior.

Partisan Loyalty

By many accounts, legislative decisions to voice support for or opposition to executive policies are partisan in nature. Partisan loyalty, in which members are more likely to line up with the president on the use of force when they share party ties and to oppose it when they do not, is a strong force for several reasons. First, presidents tend to have informational advantages, especially at the outset of conflict.[41] In the absence of full information about the wisdom of a particular intervention, members of Congress look to the White House. The president's partisan allies in Congress are more likely to cue off the judgments of their copartisans in the White House and both trust and support administration initiatives.[42] By contrast, for opposition partisans, administration cues are less trustworthy and therefore less influential.

Second, partisan loyalty can help members secure power within the institution, perhaps most importantly powerful committee assignments.[43] Membership on influential committees confers power through gatekeeping, preferential access to information, and the power to set the legislative agenda. For example, membership on the appropriations committee is clearly associated with an institutional advantage in terms of funding decisions.[44] Prestigious committee assignments, however, depend on whether individuals have demonstrated loyalty to the party leader, the president, and his key initiatives such as military force.

Finally, and most importantly, partisan electoral incentives may encourage the president's copartisans to rally around their leader in the White House. Legislators are poised to reap electoral benefits when their party is viewed as logging policy successes. Party loyalty makes the collective goals of passing legislation or approving foreign policy initiatives more likely, which then has the potential for positive externalities for the individual members who are associated with those partisan successes.[45] In the context of military force, the dynamic might consist of benefiting from the president's "rally around the flag" increase in approval, in which members of Congress hope to ride these coattails to electoral advantage.[46]

The corollary of partisan loyalty is negative partisanship in which antipathy toward the other party drives legislative behavior.[47] Opposing the other party's initiative irrespective of its policy merits becomes the coin of the realm, a vehicle for eroding support for the administration, damaging that party's brand, and weakening all those running under its banner at the next election.[48] Frances Lee finds that even on low-stakes issues in which there is general ideological agreement between conservatives and liberals, Republicans and Democrats will nonetheless fight with each other, in part because the presidency is polarized and presidential leadership has spillover effects in the legislative chambers.[49] If so, then partisans would derive benefit from having denied the president of the opposing party a foreign policy victory by challenging a policy, even if they would have supported it if proposed by a president of the same party.[50]

Taken together, the arguments above point to partisanship as an important determinant of legislative position-taking on foreign policy. Whether a legislator supports or opposes the use of force is a function of whether he or she shares the party of the president.

> H1: Members of Congress from the partisan opposition will give more antiwar speeches and fewer prowar speeches than the president's copartisans, all else equal.

Ideological Loyalty

A second theoretical driver of legislative position-taking is ideological loyalty.[51] Although electoral benefits may accrue to partisan loyalists, legislators may also benefit by acting as policy loyalists who vote consistently with their ideological brand and are rewarded for rising above the partisan fray and acting on principle. Legislators, according to this view, take positions on the basis of policy views that correspond with their ideological moorings.[52]

Indeed, scholars have found that voters punish policy inconsistency—particularly if a legislator opposes a policy under an opponent but supports it under a copartisan—as the behavior of a "partisan hack."[53] These concerns may be particularly acute in foreign policy as members want to avoid charges of playing politics with questions of national security. Joanne Gowa, for example, finds no relationship between partisanship—whether that of the president or partisan composition of Congress—and decisions to use force.[54] Instead, support or opposition is anchored in a

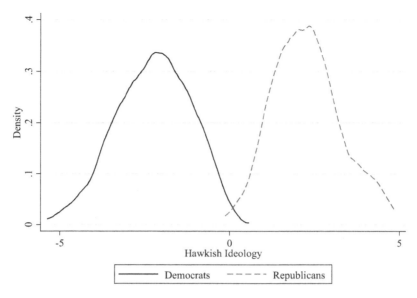

FIGURE 2.1. Distribution of Hawkish Ideology by Party, 110th Congress
Source: Foreign policy ideology scores described in Gyung-Ho Jeong, "Measuring Foreign Policy Positions of Members of the U.S. Congress," *Political Science Research and Methods* 6, no. 1 (2018): 181–196.

legislator's ideology, such that defense hawks favor a muscular foreign policy, support for higher defense spending, and the use of force more than doves, irrespective of who is in the White House, and doves express opposition.

During the early Cold War, hawks and doves populated both parties. Senator Henry "Scoop" Jackson, for example, a Democrat from Washington state, was a hawk who took militarily assertive positions regardless of who occupied the White House.[55] Post-Vietnam, party and hawk–dove ideology have increasingly converged because Republicans have become more consistent in their prowar positions and Democrats more antiwar, with increasingly few exceptions.[56] Senator Joe Lieberman, for example, a defense hawk, "ended up in a foreign-policy centrist no-man's land," in which he abandoned the Democratic Party, ran as an independent, and ultimately retired.[57] As shown in figure 2.1, foreign policy ideology scores constructed by Gyung-Ho Jeong and Paul J. Quirk suggest that by the 110th Congress congressional Democrats and Republicans were so highly polarized on questions of foreign policy; that almost every Democrat was more dovish than the most dovish Republican.[58] If ideology also drives congressional wartime position-taking—and in some cases is even the dominant factor—then we would expect the following:

> H2: Democrats will be more likely to take antiwar positions than Republicans, regardless of the party of the president; conversely, Republicans will take more prowar positions than Democrats.
>
> H3: Members' ideology will explain intrapartisan variation in public position-taking; ideological hawks will give fewer antiwar and more prowar speeches than doves.

While Democratic legislators may be more dovish than Republicans, presidents of both parties frequently use military force,[59] which presents potential tensions. Assuming that a Democratic president proposes the use of force, the dilemma for Democrats in Congress is that a supportive position would be a gesture of partisan unity but come at the expense of ideological purity. For Republicans, the dilemma is the opposite. The use of force under a Republican president presents no such dilemmas. Democrats can oppose for both partisan and ideological reasons, and Republican legislators can support for both reasons.

Legislators need not choose between partisan and ideological loyalty, however. Members' overall positions toward war may reflect their basic ideological orientation, while their support for or criticism of the administration's conduct of it may better reflect partisan motives. For example, Republicans could continue to support the war in Afghanistan and embrace the surge in 2009, which would be consistent with their ideological worldview, but criticize President Obama's management of and competence on the war. Democrats, conversely, might criticize the protracted conflict, brandishing their dovish credentials, but praise their copartisan's policies and administration of the war effort. In cross-pressured moments when ideological and partisan preferences conflict, we expect a degree of hedging in which members find ways to embrace aspects consistent with both their ideology and partisanship. These cross-pressures are particularly salient when a Democrat is in the White House because Democrats have ideological priors causing them to oppose most wars but back a copartisan president, and vice versa for Republicans. Under these circumstances we expect the following:

> H4: Under a Democratic president, congressional Democrats will be more likely to give speeches that are critical of the war but supportive of the administration's conduct of it than Republicans; conversely, Republicans will be more likely to criticize the administration and its policies but support the war itself.

Electoral Context

Finally, given the long-standing emphasis in congressional scholarship on the electoral connection,[60] electoral context could significantly moderate the influence of partisanship on members' wartime position-taking.[61] Reelection-minded legislators have strong incentives not to stray too far from their constituents, the logic being that constituents are more likely to reelect individuals who represent their views through policy positions.[62]

With increasing polarization, incumbency rates have risen considerably.[63] However, even in recent Congresses, a sizable contingent of legislators has represented a state or district that leans toward the opposite party, that is, Democrats who represent a red state or district and Republicans who represent a blue state or district.[64] For these members, electoral pressures may blunt partisan incentives and narrow partisan gaps in wartime rhetoric, leading to the following predictions:

> H5: Representing a constituency that leans toward the other party (i.e., a Democrat from a red district or a Republican from a blue district) will weaken the effect of member partisanship on the volume of anti- and prowar rhetoric.
>
> H6: Representing a constituency that leans toward the other party will also encourage "hedging"; that is, making cross-pressured members take positions similar to those advanced by members of the other party.

A Tale of Two Wars

The discussion above points to several potential determinants of legislative position-taking on war. Legislators may be partisan warriors rallying behind a copartisan president or battling an opposition party executive in the court of public opinion for electoral and political gain. They might act as policy loyalists and pursue a consistent prowar or antiwar position irrespective of who is in the White House, a copartisan or otherwise. Finally, electoral context might play a crucial role in moderating the influence of partisan forces on wartime position-taking.

In some cases, the outcomes these dynamics produce might be observationally equivalent. If we looked only at the initiation of the Iraq War, for example, we would likely see a disproportionate number of Democrats opposing the war and Republicans supporting it. Unfortunately, however, studying just the Iraq War aligns both partisan and ideological incentives, since it was a Republican-initiated war and Democrats are more likely to be associated with adversarial attitudes toward assertive defense postures. Opposition to the Iraq War then would be consistent with an ideology that corresponds with Democrats tending toward dovishness and Republicans toward hawkishness but also Democrats opposing a Republican war and Republicans supporting their copartisan's initiative.

To tease out differences across these factors—partisanship, ideology, and constituent preferences—requires identifying a policy that is similar in nature but continues across changes in these key parameters. We therefore study a key aspect of military operations in Afghanistan and Iraq. The Afghanistan War began in 2001 as a response to the 9/11 terrorist attacks. The Iraq War began in 2003 as an effort to overthrow Saddam Hussein. In the middle of both wars, policy makers initiated strategic reviews to identify why the United States was not winning and how to transition to an approach that might improve the likelihood of success. In both cases, the American military proposed a surge of 30,000 troops that the president endorsed. Analytically, the timing of each surge is fortuitous. The first took place in 2007 during the Iraq War under a Republican president, George Bush, and the second in 2009 during the Afghanistan War under a Democratic president, Barack Obama.

One criticism of comparing these two wars is that they were different in partisan political terms. The Iraq War was clearly a Republican project. Bush's responsibility for the Iraq War made the outcome and progress of the war more of a benchmark for assessing his presidency. In contrast, the Afghanistan War was at best a bipartisan project. If these premises are correct, then comparing the partisan basis of legislative support for each surge would be inappropriate since Democrats would more clearly have incentives to criticize the Iraq surge than Republicans the Afghanistan surge.

While it is true that President Bush started both wars, research on executive culpability—the degree to which voters hold leaders accountable for a war's outcome—suggests that voters quickly associated President Obama with the Afghanistan War when he did not withdraw from the war but rather held a review and ordered a surge of troops.[65] For most of the Bush administration, Afghanistan was a low salience, almost forgotten war. Under Obama's escalation, the costs of the war and its salience rose dramatically. For example, just over five hundred Americans died in Afghanistan during the entire Bush presidency. By contrast, the US suffered more than eight hundred casualties during President Obama's first two years in office alone. Bob Woodward referred to the Afghanistan surge as one of *Obama's Wars*, laying responsibility at Obama's feet for the escalatory action that came to entrench the United States' enduring commitment to the war.[66] While no two historical cases are exactly parallel, the strong similarities in these two surges across a Republican and Democratic president offer a fruitful way to tease out the effect of partisanship from ideology and from constituent loyalty on legislative position-taking.

Empirical Strategy

To explain legislative position-taking on these two troop surges, we study the 110th Congress (2007–2009), which corresponds to the Iraq War surge, and the 111th Congress (2009–2011), corresponding to the Afghanistan War surge. Nuances within speech allow us to evaluate not just support for and opposition to the surge but whether and how legislators rhetorically hedge, for example, whether Democrats criticize the Afghanistan War while defending the president's approach, or Republican hawks criticize Obama's approach to the war while not abandoning their general stance in favor of the conflict.

As the basis of our position-taking analysis, we used the *Congressional Record*, the official record of proceedings from the United States Congress, which includes the nearly 180 days per year that Congress is in session. We then wrote a program that took the aggregated *Record* and split it into speeches—from the beginning of one individual's intervention until an interruption—each with its own metadata. The program then iterated over each of these speeches (there are 6,215,134 in the dataset), and for each one it attempted to match its speaker with a member of Congress in the United States Legislators dataset.[67]

We then developed an algorithm to search the *Record* for proceedings about the Iraq or Afghanistan Wars, resulting in a total of 10,253 speeches in the Congressional Record being included for Iraq and 3,543 speeches for Afghanistan. For the Iraq War, we adopted a simple coding scheme classifying speeches as either prowar, antiwar, or irrelevant. For Iraq, most members' partisan and ideological incentives reinforced each other. Democratic doves had multiple incentives to criticize President Bush's Iraq War surge, while hawkish Republicans had multiple incentives to back the president and his policies.[68] For the war in Afghanistan, we developed a more nuanced coding system. As in Iraq, speeches were first classified as relevant or irrelevant. Then, we coded relevant speeches along two dimensions: whether they were prowar or antiwar, and (if they took a clear position), whether they were explicitly supportive or critical of the administration and its conduct of the war/surge.[69] The approach allowed us to examine whether members with conflicting partisan and ideological incentives moderated their rhetoric by taking positions that diverged in terms of support for the war and the administration.

For the Iraq War, coding involved an iterative process of hand-coding and machine learning (ML). In the first stage, a team of coders initially coded a training set of five hundred speeches and classified them as relevant to the surge/war or irrelevant. Speeches that raise concerns about the sustainability, cost, strategy, or consequences of the war were coded as relevant. We then used this training set to inform a naive-bayesian classifier to predict the relevance of the remaining speeches in our data set. We then compared the results from this model to a new set of hand-coded speeches not included in the training set to examine the inter-coder reliability between the ML and human approaches. Additional details are available in the online appendix.[70]

For Iraq, our team of coders then created a second training set sampled at random from the subset of relevant speeches, and they coded each speech as either prowar or antiwar. This training set was then used to generate a new ML model to predict the tone of speeches. The model performed well, and its errors were predictable. The main source of error was the model coding speeches as antiwar that humans coded as prowar. In almost 90 percent of these cases, the model incorrectly coded Republican speeches as antiwar. Almost all of the other errors (e.g., the model coding a speech as prowar that a human coded as antiwar) were speeches by Democrats. We hand-coded all speeches that the model coded as "contratype"—that is all speeches by Republicans that the model coded as antiwar (n=1,286) and all speeches by Democrats initially coded by the model as prowar (n=148).

The more nuanced, two-dimensional coding scheme for Afghanistan War speeches, however, proved more difficult to predict with a high degree of reliability using a ML model.[71] Moreover, the model errors were not as predictable for Afghanistan. In addition, the number of relevant speeches for the Afghanistan War/surge in the 111th Congress was far smaller, leading us to rely exclusively on human coders to code relevant speeches along the two substantive dimensions. Leveraging the nuance of rhetoric, and the possibility that legislators might try to hedge their ideological and partisan bets by being for a war and against the president's conduct, we coded both prowar or antiwar sentiment and pro-president versus anti-president sentiment.

Having assembled the number of relevant substantive war speeches of each type given by each member for both wars, which serve as the dependent variables in the analyses that follow, we accounted for the key independent variables associated with our hypotheses. To account for partisanship, we included a dummy variable identifying members of the opposition party in the model of antiwar speeches and a corresponding indicator variable for presidential copartisans in the model of prowar speeches. In subsequent models of intrapartisan variation in rhetoric, to account for ideology we used the measure of legislator foreign policy ideological hawkishness/dovishness devised by Jeong.[72]

In addition, we include a range of individual-level controls. We control for several institutional factors, including each member's chamber seniority, whether a member is part of each party's leadership structure, and membership on foreign policy committees, which could give members clout with which to confront the executive and defend legislative authority to check presidential power.[73] We also control for veteran status, which could give members credibility for challenging executive foreign policy decisions. More than two-thirds of the 110th Congress previously served in the 107th when both the House and Senate voted to authorize the use of military force against Iraq. To examine the extent to which subsequent variation in rhetoric concerning the surge can be explained by members' initial stance toward the war, our models include a pair of dummy variables identifying members who voted for and against the Iraq AUMF in 2002. Finally, the models include demographic controls for each member's race and gender as well as an indicator for senators.

Results

To investigate the influence of partisanship on members' wartime rhetoric, table 2.1 presents a series of negative binomial event count models.[74] The first two models examine the factors driving congressional criticism of the Iraq War and surge in the 110th Congress; models three and four examine congressional criticism of the war in Afghanistan in the 111th Congress. In these models, criticism of the war is broadly defined as opposition to either the war or the Obama administration's conduct of it, as op-

TABLE 2.1 **Effect of Member Partisanship on Wartime Rhetoric**

	Iraq		Afghanistan	
	Antiwar	Prowar	Antiwar	Prowar
Opposition party	3.27***	−3.41***	−2.12***	0.50***
	(0.14)	(0.20)	(0.38)	(0.18)
Leader	0.90***	1.11***	−0.97	1.85***
	(0.30)	(0.34)	(0.91)	(0.37)
Foreign policy committee memberships	0.30***	0.47***	0.59**	0.98***
	(0.11)	(0.12)	(0.28)	(0.15)
Seniority in chamber	0.02*	0.02	0.08***	0.05***
	(0.01)	(0.01)	(0.03)	(0.01)
Military veteran	0.25	0.04	0.60	0.44**
	(0.17)	(0.17)	(0.44)	(0.20)
Female	0.08	−0.28	0.34	−0.24
	(0.16)	(0.22)	(0.43)	(0.26)
Latino	−0.74***	0.30	−2.28**	−0.20
	(0.26)	(0.41)	(0.91)	(0.41)
African American	0.01	−0.59	−0.62	−0.13
	(0.21)	(0.63)	(0.57)	(0.37)
Senator	0.57***	0.78***	−1.23***	0.36*
	(0.18)	(0.21)	(0.42)	(0.21)
Ln (alpha)	0.32***	0.28***	2.12***	0.76***
	(0.08)	(0.10)	(0.13)	(0.13)
Constant	−1.02***	1.01***	−0.47	−1.47***
	(0.15)	(0.13)	(0.29)	(0.18)
Observations	548	548	550	550

Note: All models are negative binomial regressions. Standard errors in parentheses. All significance tests are two-tailed.
* p<0.10, ** p<0.05, *** p<0.01

erationalized above. Subsequent models examine more nuanced rhetoric that takes diverging positions on the war and the Obama administration's conduct of it. Figure 2.2 shows the effect of partisanship on each category across both wars while holding all other factors constant at their median values.

The results for Iraq War rhetoric are broadly consistent with H1 and the primacy of partisanship. The median opposition party Democrat was predicted to give about a dozen floor speeches critical of the war, all else equal.[75] By contrast, the median Republican gave fewer than one. Prowar speeches were disproportionately concentrated among President Bush's partisan allies in Congress. Our model predicts that the median Republican gave approximately three prowar speeches, whereas the median Democrat gave virtually zero. This is strong prima facie evidence for the power of partisanship in shaping wartime rhetoric.[76] However, in the case

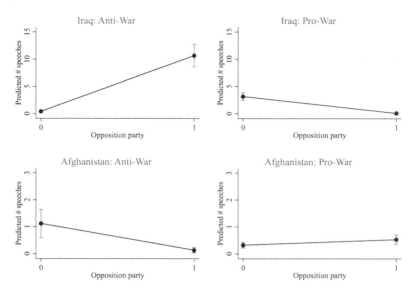

FIGURE 2.2. Effects of Partisanship across Wars and Rhetoric Type
Note: I-bars indicate 95 percent confidence intervals.

of Iraq partisan and ideological incentives reinforced each other, making it all but impossible to tease out the relative importance of each.

During the Afghanistan surge, on the other hand, opposition party Republicans were actually less critical, on average, than were President Obama's Democratic allies in Congress.[77] After eight years of inconclusive conflict, openly prowar speeches were relatively rare. However, far from trumpeting the surge policies of a copartisan president, congressional Democrats actually gave fewer floor speeches supporting the war in Afghanistan in the 111th Congress, all else being equal, than did opposition party Republicans. These patterns are sharply inconsistent with H1 and past research emphasizing the primacy of partisan motivations. Instead, they are more consistent with H2 and explanations emphasizing the importance of ideology and policy preferences.

Several of our institutional and demographic controls were also significant predictors of a member's volume of anti- and prowar rhetoric. Members with greater institutional standing—party leaders, members of the foreign policy committees, and members of more senior committees—were more likely to take positions on both wars, both positive and negative.[78] Military veterans were both more likely to speak out in favor of and against the war in Afghanistan (the latter coefficient narrowly misses conventional thresholds of statistical significance), though there is little evidence that veteran status influenced congressional rhetoric concerning Iraq. While we find no evidence of a gender gap in congressional wartime position-taking, Latino members were less critical of both wars than other members. Finally, perhaps reflecting the greater opportunities each senator has to command the floor, we find that senators gave more speeches both for and against the Iraq War surge than did House members. Senators also gave more speeches supporting the Afghanistan surge; however, senators gave significantly fewer speeches criticizing the Afghanistan surge, all else being equal.[79]

Ideology and Intrapartisan Variation in Rhetoric

To more fully examine the influence of ideology on wartime position-taking, table 2.2 re-estimates the models in table 2.1 for each partisan caucus and examines the influence of members' foreign policy ideology on intraparty variation in wartime rhetoric. Figure 2.3 illustrates the effects for Iraq War rhetoric and figure 2.4 illustrates the effects on position-taking regarding the war in Afghanistan.

Strongly consistent with H3, in each case member ideology had significant effects on Iraq War rhetoric. Our model predicts that the most dovish Democrat gave about twenty antiwar speeches during the 110th Congress. By contrast, the most moderate Democrat was predicted to have given fewer than ten, all else being equal. Similarly, among Republicans criticism of the war was sharply concentrated within the moderate wing of the caucus. As ideological hawkishness increases, the predicted number of antiwar speeches quickly approaches zero. Increasing hawkishness significantly increased prowar rhetoric among Republican members; among congressional Democrats, the effects were also positive, though substantively smaller. Ideology was a less consistent predictor of intrapartisan variation in Afghanistan War rhetoric; however, more dovish Democrats gave significantly more antiwar speeches than more hawkish Democrats.

Taken together, the data strongly suggest that many Democrats' ideological preferences led them to criticize large-scale military interventions like Iraq and Afghanistan, regardless of who sits in the Oval Office, and vice versa for Republicans.

TABLE 2.2 **Effect of Ideology within Each Party Caucus on Wartime Rhetoric**

	Iraq				Afghanistan			
	Democrats		Republicans		Democrats		Republicans	
	Anti	Pro	Anti	Pro	Anti	Pro	Anti	Pro
Hawkish	-0.26***	0.58**	-1.26***	0.60***	-0.39**	0.05	-0.46	-0.01
ideology	(0.08)	(0.27)	(0.17)	(0.07)	(0.17)	(0.13)	(0.34)	(0.12)
Leader	0.99***	1.88**	1.44**	0.99***	-1.32	2.30***	-15.80	1.71***
	(0.36)	(0.92)	(0.56)	(0.31)	(0.96)	(0.51)	(2,609.18)	(0.50)
Foreign policy	0.18	0.80*	0.32	0.47***	0.31	1.13***	0.58	0.68***
committees	(0.11)	(0.44)	(0.21)	(0.11)	(0.29)	(0.19)	(0.73)	(0.20)
Seniority in	-0.00	0.06*	-0.01	0.05***	0.08***	0.05***	0.17*	0.07***
chamber	(0.01)	(0.03)	(0.02)	(0.01)	(0.03)	(0.02)	(0.10)	(0.02)
Military	-0.27	-1.45*	0.56*	0.34**	-1.04**	0.18	1.47*	0.86***
veteran	(0.18)	(0.77)	(0.29)	(0.15)	(0.46)	(0.29)	(0.79)	(0.26)
Female	-0.20	-2.37**	-0.15	0.07	0.22	-0.12	2.13	-0.76
	(0.17)	(1.15)	(0.46)	(0.23)	(0.45)	(0.31)	(1.54)	(0.52)
Latino	-0.71***	0.60	-17.04	1.25**	-2.34***	-1.63**	-16.62	1.62**
	(0.25)	(0.91)	(2,698.00)	(0.52)	(0.86)	(0.66)	(2,311.26)	(0.80)
African	-0.15	0.34	—	—	-0.79	-0.12	—	—
American	(0.19)	(0.86)			(0.51)	(0.38)		
Senator	0.82***	0.51	0.26	0.63***	-0.33	0.43	-4.08**	-0.20
	(0.21)	(0.77)	(0.37)	(0.18)	(0.48)	(0.28)	(1.85)	(0.33)
Ln (alpha)	0.08	1.51***	0.26	-0.19	1.79***	0.55***	2.56***	0.60***
	(0.08)	(0.43)	(0.29)	(0.12)	(0.15)	(0.20)	(0.43)	(0.19)
Constant	1.93***	-1.76***	1.26***	-0.84***	-1.18***	-1.45***	-2.83***	-1.05**
	(0.18)	(0.60)	(0.43)	(0.25)	(0.45)	(0.33)	(1.38)	(0.41)
Observations	292	292	256	256	319	319	223	223

Note: All models are negative binomial regressions. Standard errors in parentheses. All significance tests are two-tailed.
* $p<0.10$, ** $p<0.05$, *** $p<0.01$

The Moderating Role of Electoral Context

Regarding Afghanistan, the parties' different ideological leanings on military questions was a better predictor of wartime rhetoric than partisan orientation relative to the incumbent president, and ideology also explains significant intrapartisan variation in members' rhetoric. However, the influence of partisanship may also vary across individual electoral contexts. Specifically, H5 posits that electorally vulnerable members will weaken the effect of partisanship on wartime rhetoric.

Measuring electoral vulnerability on congressional races is far from straightforward. Perhaps the most direct measure would be to use a member's electoral margin in his or her last race. However, given the stark vari-

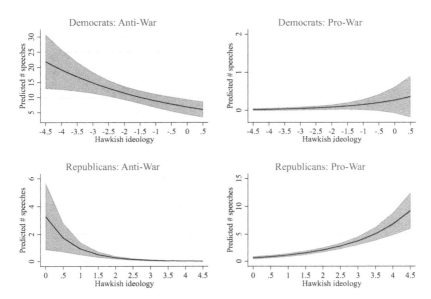

FIGURE 2.3. Effects of Ideology on Rhetoric within Each Party Caucus: Iraq
Note: Shaded bands indicate 95 percent confidence intervals.

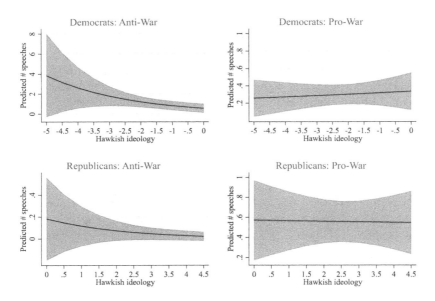

FIGURE 2.4. Effects of Ideology on Rhetoric within Each Party Caucus: Afghanistan
Note: Shaded bands indicate 95 percent confidence intervals.

ance in challenger quality from election cycle to cycle, and even whether there is a serious challenger at all, this may afford a crude measure at best. For example, in 2008 Rep. John Spratt (D-SC) coasted to reelection for the thirteenth time in South Carolina's fifth congressional district, winning by almost 25 percent. Just two years later, he lost his bid for reelection to Mick Mulvaney by more than 6 percent. Perhaps a better indicator of the electoral pressures Spratt faced was that the Republican presidential candidate carried his district in 2008.

Accordingly, we construct two measures of electoral vulnerability. The analyses in the chapter employ an indicator variable identifying members who represent a constituency that leans toward the opposition party as determined by its vote in the last presidential election (i.e., Democrats from red states/districts or Republicans from blue states/districts). Additional analyses yielding substantively similar results and reported in the online appendix employ an indicator variable identifying members from swing constituencies that were decided by 10 percent or less in the last presidential election race.

The models in table 2.3 replicate the earlier analyses from table 2.1 but with two additional variables: a dummy variable indicating Democratic members from red states/districts and Republican members from blue states/districts, and the interaction of this variable with the dummy variable identifying members not from the president's party. Figure 2.5 illustrates the effects.

For three of the four types of speeches, the results offer at least some evidence that electoral context significantly moderates the influence of partisanship on members' wartime rhetoric (H5). Hailing from a red state or district significantly reduced the number of antiwar speeches the median Democrat is predicted to give by almost 30 percent. Similarly, whereas the median Republican from a red state or district was predicted to give zero antiwar speeches, our model predicts that the median Republican from a blue state or district responded to that pressure by giving at least a couple of speeches critical of the war, all else being equal. Representing a red state or district had no significant influence on prowar speechmaking by Democrats. However, representing a blue state or district significantly reduced the number of speeches supporting the Iraq War by the median Republican.

Consistent with H2, Democrats from blue states/districts gave more speeches critical of the war in Afghanistan, even under a Democratic president, than did Republicans. However, Democrats from red states/

TABLE 2.3 **District Partisanship Moderates Effect of Member Partisanship**

	Iraq		Afghanistan	
	Antiwar	Prowar	Antiwar	Prowar
Opposition party	3.55***	−3.43***	−1.94***	0.36*
	(0.16)	(0.23)	(0.41)	(0.20)
Opposition party X District leans other party	−1.78***	0.58	0.35	0.43
	(0.41)	(0.52)	(1.00)	(0.42)
District leans other party	1.48***	−0.64*	−2.25***	−0.27
	(0.37)	(0.35)	(0.53)	(0.30)
Leader	1.26***	1.26***	−1.46*	1.90***
	(0.30)	(0.33)	(0.88)	(0.37)
Foreign policy committee memberships	0.36***	0.57***	0.40	1.03***
	(0.10)	(0.12)	(0.28)	(0.14)
Seniority in chamber	0.03***	0.04***	0.09***	0.06***
	(0.01)	(0.01)	(0.03)	(0.01)
Military veteran	0.26	0.01	0.47	0.44**
	(0.17)	(0.17)	(0.44)	(0.20)
Female	−0.02	−0.29	0.42	−0.27
	(0.16)	(0.22)	(0.43)	(0.26)
Latino	−0.58**	0.32	−2.48***	−0.32
	(0.26)	(0.42)	(0.88)	(0.42)
African American	−0.16	−0.74	−0.70	−0.30
	(0.21)	(0.64)	(0.56)	(0.37)
Ln (alpha)	0.31***	0.31***	2.05***	0.76***
	(0.08)	(0.10)	(0.13)	(0.13)
Constant	−1.18***	1.00***	−0.43	−1.36***
	(0.16)	(0.13)	(0.30)	(0.19)
Observations	548	548	550	550

Note: All models are negative binomial regressions. Standard errors in parentheses. All significance tests are two-tailed.
* $p<0.10$, ** $p<0.05$, *** $p<0.01$

districts were much more circumspect in their public criticism of the war and, indeed, were indistinguishable from Republicans.

Partisan Hedging with More Nuanced Rhetoric

Within the context of the war in Afghanistan, the role of partisan incentives appears relatively muted when examining the volume of members' war rhetoric examined in general terms. Rather, Republicans gave more prowar speeches and fewer antiwar speeches than did Democrats, even with President Obama in the White House. Ideological hawks in both parties were more reticent to criticize the war publicly than were more

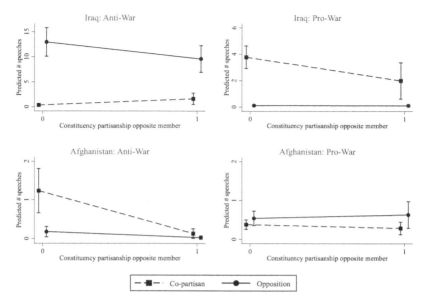

FIGURE 2.5. Does District Partisanship Moderate the Effect of Member Partisanship on Rhetoric?

Note: I-bars indicate 95 percent confidence intervals.

dovish members.[80] However, H4 expected that members torn by competing partisan and ideological incentives might respond by engaging in more nuanced wartime position-taking. In the context of Afghanistan, Democrats should be more likely to criticize the war but rally behind President Obama and his conduct of it. By contrast, Republicans should be more likely to support the war effort writ large but criticize the Obama Administration's conduct of wartime operations.

To test these dueling predictions of H4, we use the more nuanced coding scheme for Afghanistan war speeches. Table 2.4 presents counts of each type of speech that took a position for or against both the war and the administration. The first column presents the counts of each of the four speech types for all members, the second presents the tallies for Democratic members, and the third presents the relevant tallies for Republican members.

Most speeches that explicitly took positions on both the war and the administration offered consistent assessments: they either supported both

TABLE 2.4 **Partisanship and More Nuanced Afghanistan War Rhetoric**

	All	Democrats	Republicans
Antiwar/Anti-admin.	249	214	35
Antiwar/Pro-admin.	41	38	3
Ratio	*6:1*	*6:1*	*12:1*
Prowar/Pro-admin.	248	132	116
Prowar/Anti-admin.	53	12	41
Ratio	*5:1*	*11:1*	*3:1*

Note: Non-italicized cells present the number of speeches in each category of rhetoric. Ratios rounded to whole numbers.

the war and the administration's conduct of it or opposed both. However, as shown in column one, a substantial minority of speeches involved more nuanced positions in which members took contrasting positions on the war effort as a whole and the administration's conduct of it. Strongly consistent with H4, Democrats were significantly more likely to hedge their antiwar criticism by simultaneously expressing their support for a copartisan president and his war policies. As shown previously in figure 2.2, contra simple partisan narratives, Democrats gave significantly more antiwar speeches during the 111th Congress than did Republicans. However, many Democrats tempered this criticism by also expressing their support for the administration. Among Democrats, the ratio of antiwar/anti-administration speeches to antiwar/pro-administration speeches was 6:1. To be sure, this means that most Democratic war rhetoric was critical and potentially quite costly to President Obama. However, hedging was much more prominent among Democrats than among Republicans. When Republicans spoke out against the war, few felt the need to defend the new administration; among Republicans, this same ratio was 12:1.

Instead, many Republicans, consistent with their overall greater hawkishness on foreign policy, were openly supportive of the war in Afghanistan. However, a significant number of their prowar speeches also hedged by coupling general support for the war with criticism of the Obama Administration. Among Republicans, the ratio of prowar/pro-administration speeches to prowar/anti-administration speeches was 3:1. By contrast, prowar/anti-administration speeches were exceedingly rare among Democrats, and among the president's copartisans this ratio was 11:1.

In sum, we find strong support for H4 in that ideology and partisanship routinely interacted and encouraged many members to take more

TABLE 2.5 **District Partisanship and Partisan Hedging**

	Aligned with constituency partisanship		Not aligned with constituency partisanship	
	Democrat	Republican	Democrat	Republican
Antiwar/Pro-admin.	0.137	0.017	0.032	0.000
Prowar/Anti-admin.	0.042	0.227	0.016	0.020

Note: Average number of speeches of each type for each partisan/electoral context group. Bolded means are significantly different from one another, p<0.10, two-tailed test.

nuanced positions on the Afghanistan War—positions that likely hurt or were of limited benefit to the Obama Administration. War support from the opposition party can be politically advantageous, but any political benefits are likely tempered if not eliminated completely when it is coupled with open criticism of the administration and its policies. Similarly, copartisan criticism of the war that is nonetheless supportive of the administration is doubtless preferable to rhetoric that is critical on both dimensions. However, antiwar copartisan cues are costly signals that risk a politically damaging erosion of public support for the war, even if tempered by support for the administration.

The analysis concludes by examining whether electoral pressures also moderated partisans' willingness to hedge by taking more nuanced positions that rendered split judgments on the war and the administration's conduct of it. Table 2.5 compares the mean number of antiwar/pro-administration speeches and prowar/anti-administration speeches across partisan groups and electoral contexts.

Among partisans who align with their district's partisan orientation (about 80 percent of members), we see the significant partisan splits also shown in the summary statistics from table 2.4. Democrats were much more likely to give speeches critical of the war but supportive of the Obama Administration's handling of it than were Republicans, and vice versa for speeches supportive of the war but critical of the administration.[81] However, among cross-pressured members—Democrats from red constituencies and Republicans from blue constituencies—the gap between these members and members of the other party disappear. In this context and strongly consistent with H6, electoral pressures almost completely negate the estimated effect of member partisanship.

Conclusion

Scholars long spoke of a bipartisan consensus that sustained American foreign policy through the Cold War. In important senses, this is accurate. In others, it is overstated; under constant fire first for allegedly "losing" China and then for his inability to swiftly win the war in Korea, President Truman likely would have found such platitudes baffling. Over the past twenty years, scholarship has challenged such assertions and demonstrated empirically that partisan forces significantly shaped the course and conduct of American military policy throughout the postwar era.[82] During the Cold War and after it, before Vietnam and after the last troops came home, presidents have consistently enjoyed a freer hand when bolstered by strong copartisan majorities in Congress. By contrast, when the opposition holds sway on Capitol Hill, critics of administration policies enjoy multiple levers to cause political headaches for the administration should its policies fail to proceed according to plan. Presidents regularly both anticipate and respond to these costs by adjusting their policy choices accordingly. That such strong partisan dynamics arose even in the mid-twentieth century, an era of relatively low polarization, is somewhat surprising. As the parties have polarized rapidly in the intervening decades, the theoretical logic suggests this dynamic should have strengthened further still.

However, our analysis of congressional pushback to the wars in Iraq and Afghanistan suggest that this almost exclusive focus on partisanship is misleading and obscures the importance of other incentives that also lead some legislators to push back against presidential policies. Although partisan polarization has reached record heights in the two decades since 9/11, we find that it has not defined interbranch contestation on the use of force. Our core findings help allay concerns of activists and scholars that unified government invariably insulates presidents from institutional pushback in ways that would green-light the use of force without meaningful legislative debate. Congress is unlikely to give the executive a pass on the use of force for long in almost any political context. Republican presidents presiding over unified government are in the strongest position with their copartisans in charge of the floor and the committee gavels. However, even in these circumstances, minority Democrats have both partisan and ideological incentives to exploit windows of opportunity to attack the administration and its wartime policies should windows of opportunity arise. Indeed, in the summer and fall of 2003, after President George W. Bush declared "mission accomplished," the Democratic minority in Congress amassed considerable pushback against the war.

Democrats presiding over unified government also cannot count on iron-clad support from their copartisans on Capitol Hill. During the Afghanistan surge, Democrats, at least in the rank and file, did not abandon their dovish preferences to side with their copartisan in the White House but took more antiwar and fewer prowar positions than Republicans. An important exception were members of the Democratic leadership, who gave more prowar statements than their peers. This is significant and speaks to the power of the imperative to support a copartisan standard-bearer in the White House. However, while the separation-of-parties logic applied to leaders, public defections and criticism among many rank and file Democrats was both newsworthy and costly.

Ideological hawkishness may lead some Republicans to back the use of force, providing a Democratic administration with valuable political cover, but competing partisan and ideological forces may also lead many to hedge and qualify their public positions. Under President Obama Republicans gave more pro-Afghanistan War speeches than Democrats writ large, but many also tempered this public support with criticism of the administration's conduct of the war. Analogously, some Democrats softened their opposition to the war by backing the Obama Administration's handling of it. Electoral forces also moderated the influence of partisanship, narrowing and sometimes eliminating the gaps between presidential copartisans and members of the opposition.

While both Presidents Bush and Obama faced considerable political pushback from Congress in unified and divided government alike, one might still ask whether this pushback had anything more than symbolic value. After all, Democratic efforts to mandate a timetable for withdrawal from Iraq as part of the 2007 appropriations battle failed. And President Obama proceeded with not one but two troop surges in 2009, nearly tripling the number of troops in Afghanistan. A full examination of the effects of congressional opposition is beyond the scope of this chapter. However, we note that there is considerable evidence that pushback in both cases was politically costly. While significant debate remains about the ultimate efficacy of the 2007 surge, internal violence and US casualties both fell sharply over the last two years of the Bush presidency.[83] Congressional criticism offered a potent counter-narrative to the Bush administration's efforts to proclaim success in Iraq in 2007–2008, and public support for the war remained flat and low. Opposition to the war buoyed the Obama campaign first in the primaries and then in the general election, and the political climate eased his decision to bring the war to an end in 2011.

In 2009, President Obama ordered two major troop surges in Afghanistan, and the second surge in the fall provoked considerable opposition from within his own party. Clearly, this congressional pushback did not deter Obama from ordering the surge. However, it did affect his strategic calculus.[84] In a national address announcing the surge, President Obama declared, "I have determined that it is in our vital national interest to send an additional 30,000 U.S. troops to Afghanistan." But in the very next sentence, he made important concessions to critics, including many skeptics within his own party, "After 18 months, our troops will begin to come home."[85] This second announcement won over key skeptics, with House Speaker Nancy Pelosi declaring the president has "articulated a way out of this war," even as Obama's timetable sparked sharp criticism from congressional hawks such as his defeated rival John McCain.[86] Obama's policy then is best understood as a political compromise between hawkish and dovish forces within his own administration (with Vice President Biden leading the charge against the surge) as well as contrasting pressures from Congress, including considerable opposition to the surge from key members of his own party.[87] These pressures may not preclude or end the use of force, but they do significantly factor in to a president's decision calculus.

Finally, because the episodes of force we examined are among the most important military decisions of the post-Vietnam era, they do raise questions of scope conditions. For example, in the 1990s Republicans aggressively opposed Clinton's foreign interventions both on the floor and in the public sphere,[88] and they also voted against President Obama's engagement in Libya.[89] The type of military force deployed or the strategic objectives pursued may therefore condition the degree to which partisanship, ideology, and electoral pressures manifest themselves. As Fordham observes in his chapter, legislative position taking once a war begins can be shaped by a combination of public perceptions of the war and reelection timing. Thus, although an important first step in the analysis of legislative behavior on foreign policy, we suggest that these machine-learning tools be used to examine congressional position-taking on a wider range of foreign policy issues to identify how the influence of partisanship, ideology, and electoral pressures vary across issues and contexts.

Notes

1. James Madison, "Federalist Papers No. 47," February 1, 1788, The Avalon Project, Yale Law School, last accessed April 21, 2024, https://avalon.law.yale.edu/18th_century/fed47.asp.

2. Arthur Schlesinger Jr., *The Imperial Presidency* (Boston: Houghton Mifflin, 1973), ix.

3. Barbara Hinckley, *Less than Meets the Eye: Foreign Policymaking and the Myth of the Assertive Congress* (Chicago: University of Chicago Press, 1994).

4. Richard Neustadt, *Presidential Power* (New York: New American Library, 1960).

5. Douglas Kriner and Eric Schickler, *Investigating the President: Congressional Checks on Presidential Power* (Princeton, NJ: Princeton University Press, 2016).

6. David Mayhew, *America's Congress: Actions in the Public Sphere, James Madison through New Gingrich* (New Haven, CT: Yale University Press, 2000); William Howell and Jon Pevehouse, *While Dangers Gather: Congressional Checks on Presidential War Powers* (Princeton, NJ: Princeton University Press, 2007); Eric Posner and Adrian Vermeule, *The Executive Unbound: After the Madisonian Republic* (New York: Oxford University Press, 2010); Douglas Kriner, *After the Rubicon: Congress, Presidents, and the Politics of Waging War* (Chicago: University of Chicago Press, 2010); Josh Chafetz, *Congress's Constitution: Legislative Authority and the Separation of Powers* (New Haven, CT: Yale University Press, 2017).

7. Daryl Levinson and Richard Pildes, "Separation of Parties, Not Powers," *Harvard Law Review* 119, no. 8 (2006): 2311.

8. David Clark, "Agreeing to Disagree: Domestic Institutional Congruence and US Dispute Behavior," *Political Research Quarterly* 53, no. 2 (2000): 375–400; Howell and Pevehouse, *While Dangers Gather*; Jong Hee Park, "Structural Change in US Presidents' Use of Force," *American Journal of Political Science* 54 (2010): 766–782.

9. Howell and Pevehouse, *While Dangers Gather*.

10. Kevin Wang, "Presidential Responses to Foreign Policy Crises: Rational Choice and Domestic Politics," *Journal of Conflict Resolution* 40, no. 1 (1996): 68–97; Clark, "Agreeing to Disagree"; Kriner, *After the Rubicon*.

11. Frances Lee, *Insecure Majorities: Congress and the Perpetual Campaign* (Chicago: University of Chicago Press, 2016).

12. Paul Harris, "Democrats' Silence on Drones Leaves Right in Unlikely Alliance with Activists," *The Guardian*, March 8, 2013.

13. Peter Beinart, "Democrats Are Hypocrites for Condemning Trump Over Syria," *The Atlantic*, October 18, 2019.

14. For this analysis, we exclude airstrikes and humanitarian intervention, which we consider qualitatively different in terms of the resources at stake and

the motivation from larger-scale interventions to overthrow governments, install democratic institutions, or hold territory.

15. Martin Hollis and Steve Smith, "Roles and Reasons in Foreign Policy Decision Making," *British Journal of Political Science* 16, no. 3 (1986): 269–286; Sarah Kreps, Elizabeth Saunders, and Kenneth Schultz, "The Ratification Premium: Hawks, Doves, and Arms Control," *World Politics* 70, no. 4 (2018): 479–514; Kenneth Schultz, "The Politics of Risking Peace: Do Hawks or Doves Deliver the Olive Branch?" *International Organization* 59, no. 1 (2005): 1–38.

16. Jonah Shepp, "What were the Legal (and Strategic) Grounds for Biden's Syria Airstrikes?" *New York Magazine*, February 27, 2021, https://nymag.com/intelligencer/2021/02/the-legal-and-strategic-grounds-for-bidens-syria-strikes.html.

17. John Aldrich, John Sullivan, and Eugene Borgida, "Foreign Affairs and Issue Voting: Do Presidential Candidates 'Waltz Before a Blind Audience?'" *American Political Science Review* 83, no. 1 (1989): 123–141. See also Christian Grose and Bruce Oppenheimer, "The Iraq War, Partisanship, and Candidate Attributes: Variation in Partisan Swing in the 2006 U.S. House Elections," *Legislative Studies Quarterly* 32, no. 4 (2007): 531–557; Scott Sigmund Gartner and Gary Segura, "All Politics are Still Local: The Iraq War and the 2006 Midterm Elections," *PS: Political Science & Politics* 41, no. 1 (2008): 95–100.

18. Barber and Pope (2019) similarly note the collinearity between party and ideology but tease out partisan and policy ideology at the constituency rather than legislative level. Michael Barber and Jeremy C. Pope, "Does Party Trump Ideology? Disentangling Party and Ideology in America," *American Political Science Review* 113, no.1 (2019): 38–54.

19. Kathryn Pearson, *Party Discipline in the U.S. House of Representatives* (Ann Arbor: University of Michigan Press, 2015).

20. Dan Hopkins and Gary King, "A Method of Automated Nonparametric Content Analysis for Social Science," *American Political Science Review* 54, no. 1 (2010): 229–247.

21. Sarah Croco, "The Decider's Dilemma: Leader Culpability, War Outcomes, and Domestic Punishment," *American Political Science Review* 105, no. 3 (2011): 457–477.

22. Howell and Pevehouse, *While Dangers Gather*.

23. Levinson and Pildes, "Separation of Parties."

24. Hinckley, *Less than Meets the Eye*.

25. Louis Fisher, "A Dose of Law and Realism for Presidential Studies," *Presidential Studies Quarterly* 32, no. 4 (2002): 676–677.

26. Jack Goldsmith, "The Contributions of the Obama Administration to the Practice and Theory of International Law," *Harvard International Law Journal* 57 (2016): 470.

27. Chafetz, *Congress's Constitution*.

28. Ronald Krebs and Patrick Thaddeus Jackson, "Twisting Tongues and Twisting Arms: The Power of Political Rhetoric," *European Journal of International Relations* 13, no. 1 (2017): 35; Mariah Zeisberg, *War Powers: The Politics of Constitutional Authority* (Princeton, NJ: Princeton University Press, 2013).

29. John Kingdon, *Congressmen's Voting Decisions* (Ann Arbor: University of Michigan Press, 1989), 212; Justin Grimmer, "Appropriators Not Position Takers: The Distorting Effects of Electoral Incentives on Congressional Representation," *American Journal of Political Science* 57, no. 3 (2013): 624–642.

30. Jeffrey Goldberg, "The Obama Doctrine," *The Atlantic* 317, no. 3 (2016): 70–90, https://www.theatlantic.com/magazine/archive/2016/04/the-obama-doctrine/471525/.

31. Howell and Pevehouse, *While Dangers Gather*, 105.

32. Cheryl Schonhardt-Bailey, "The Congressional Debate on Partial-Birth Abortion: Constitutional Gravitas and Moral Passion," *British Journal of Political Science* 38, no. 3 (2008): 383–410.

33. James Snyder and Michael Ting, "Why Roll Calls? A Model of Position-Taking in Legislative Voting and Elections," *Journal of Law, Economics, and Organization* 21, no. 1 (2005): 154.

34. David Broockman and Daniel Butler, "The Causal Effects of Elite Position-Taking on Voter Attitudes: Field Experiments with Elite Communication," *American Journal of Political Science* 61, no. 1 (2017): 208–221; Justin Grimmer, "A Bayesian Hierarchical Topic Model for Political Texts: Measuring Expressed Agendas in Senate Press Releases," *Political Analysis* 18, no. 1 (2010): 1–35.

35. W. Lance Bennett, "Toward a Theory of Press-State Relations in the US," *Journal of Communication* 40, no. 2 (1990): 103–127; Jonathan Mermin, *Debating War and Peace: Media Coverage of US Intervention in the Post-Vietnam Period* (Princeton, NJ: Princeton University Press, 1999).

36. John Zaller and Dennis Chiu, "Government's Little Helper: U.S. Press Coverage of Foreign Policy Crises, 1945–1991," *Political Communication* 13, no. 4 (1996): 385–405; Adam Berinsky, *In Time of War: Understanding American Public Opinion from World War II to Iraq* (Chicago: University of Chicago Press, 2009); Timothy Groeling and Matthew Baum, "Crossing the Water's Edge: Elite Rhetoric, Media Coverage, and the Rally-Round-the-Flag Phenomenon," *Journal of Politics* 70, no. 4 (2008): 1065–1085.

37. Matthew Baum and Timothy Groeling, *War Stories: The Causes and Consequences of Public Views of War* (Princeton, NJ: Princeton University Press, 2010); Howell and Pevehouse, *While Dangers Gather*.

38. Robert Putnam, "Diplomacy and Domestic Politics: The Logic of Two-Level Games," *International Organization* 42, no. 3 (1988): 427–460.

39. Dennis Foster, "An 'Invitation to Struggle'? The Use of Force against 'Legislatively Vulnerable' American Presidents," *International Studies Quarterly* 50, no. 2 (2006): 421–444.

40. Conor Friedersdorf, "Trump and Russia Both Seek to Exacerbate the Same Political Divisions," *The Atlantic*, January 23, 2018.

41. Baum and Groeling, *War Stories*.

42. William Howell and Jon Pevehouse, "Presidents, Congress, and the Use of Force," *International Organization* 59, no. 1 (2005): 215–216.

43. Wayne Leighton and Edward López, "Committee Assignments and the Cost of Party Loyalty," *Political Research Quarterly* 55, no. 2 (2002): 59–90; Nicole Asmussen and Adam Ramey, "When Loyalty Is Tested: Do Party Leaders Use Committee Assignments as Rewards?" *Congress and the Presidency* 45, no. 1 (2018): 41–65.

44. D. Roderick Kiewiet and Mathew McCubbins, *The Logic of Delegation: Congressional Parties and the Appropriations Process* (Chicago: University of Chicago Press, 1991), 83; Bryan Marshall, Brandon Prins, and David Rohde, "Fighting Fire with Water: Partisan Procedural Strategies and the Senate Appropriations Committee," *Congress and the Presidency* 26, no. 2 (1999): 113–132.

45. René Lindstädt and Ryan J. Vander Wielen, "Dynamic Elite Partisanship: Party Loyalty and Agenda Setting in the US House," *British Journal of Political Science* 44, no. 4 (2014): 741–772.

46. Howell and Pevehouse, "Presidents," 216.

47. Alan Abramowitz and Steven Webster, "The Rise of Negative Partisanship and the Nationalization of US Elections in the 21st Century," *Electoral Studies* 41 (2016): 12–22; Lee, *Insecure Majorities*.

48. Gary Jacobson, *The Politics of Congressional Elections* (New York: Pearson Longman, 2004).

49. Frances Lee, *Beyond Ideology: Politics, Principles, and Partisanship in the US Senate* (Chicago: University of Chicago Press, 2009).

50. Howell and Pevehouse, *While Dangers Gather*; Kreps, Saunders, and Schultz, "Ratification Premium," 486.

51. Wars may shift legislators' ideologies, temporarily bringing them into closer alignment with the president; see William Howell, Saul Jackman, and Jon Rogowski, *The Wartime President: Executive Influence and the Nationalizing Politics of Threat* (Chicago: University of Chicago Press, 2013). However, more than five years after 9/11 and following the 2006 midterms, there are strong reasons to expect ideology to drive wartime position-taking.

52. Richard Fenno Jr., "US House Members in Their Constituencies: An Exploration," *American Political Science Review* 71, no. 3 (1977): 883–917.

53. Jamie Carson, Gregory Koger, Matthew Lebo, and Everett Young, "The Electoral Costs of Party Loyalty in Congress," *American Journal of Political Science* 54, no. 3 (2010): 603.

54. Joanne Gowa, "Politics at the Water's Edge: Parties, Voters, and the Use of Force Abroad," *International Organization* 52, no. 2 (1998): 320.

55. Robert Kaufman, *Henry M. Jackson: A Life in Politics* (Seattle, WA: University of Washington Press, 2000), 138.

56. Michael Cohen, "When Democrats Became Doves," *Foreign Policy*, December 2, 2011, https://foreignpolicy.com/2011/12/02/when-democrats-became-doves/; I. M. Destler, Leslie Gelb, and Anthony Lake, *Our Own Worst Enemy* (New York: Simon and Schuster, 1984); Benjamin Fordham, "The Evolution of Republican and Democratic Positions on Cold War Military Spending: A Historical Puzzle," *Social Science History* 31, no. 4 (2007): 603–636.

57. Gyung-Ho Jeong and Paul J. Quirk, "Division at the Water's Edge: The Polarization of Foreign Policy," *American Politics Research* 41, no. 1 (2019): 68.

58. For a parallel figure for the 111th Congress, see the online appendix. We acknowledge that roll-call based scores that purport to measure ideology from roll-call voting behavior—at least as distinct from party—can be problematic. However, in the statistical analyses that follow, we look for evidence that ideology drives intraparty variation in congressional rhetoric. We do not include partisanship and the roll-call based ideology measures in the same model to try to parse out the relative influence of partisanship and ideology.

59. Benjamin Fordham, "Partisanship, Macroeconomic Policy, and US Uses of Force 1949–1994," *Journal of Conflict Resolution* 42, no. 4 (1998): 418–439.

60. David Mayhew, *Congress: The Electoral Connection* (New Haven, CT: Yale University Press, 1974).

61. Electoral factors could also moderate the influence of ideology. We explore this dynamic in more detail in the online appendix. While the effects are not consistent across all types of rhetoric and both wars, in multiple cases we find that electoral forces (e.g., representing a constituency that leaned toward the other party) encouraged moderate members to adjust their rhetoric in ways that would be more appealing to the baseline partisan orientation of their constituencies. However, given our main focus of elucidating the more nuanced relationship between partisanship and legislative wartime position-taking, we address here the way electoral factors moderate the influence of partisanship on rhetoric.

62. James Stimson, Michael Mackuen, and Robert Erikson, "Dynamic Representation," *American Political Science Review* 89, no. 3 (1995): 543–565.

63. Alan Abramowitz, Brad Alexander, and Matthew Gunning, "Incumbency, Redistricting, and the Decline of Competition in US House Elections," *Journal of Politics* 68, no. 1 (2006): 75–88.

64. Following common practice, we use the two-party presidential election vote as a proxy for state/district partisanship; see, for example, Stephen Ansolabehere, James Snyder, and Charles Stewart III, "Candidate Positioning in US House Elections," *American Journal of Political Science* 45, no. 1 (2001): 136–159.

65. Croco, "Decider's Dilemma," 474.

66. Bob Woodward, *Obama's Wars* (New York: Simon and Schuster, 2010). Democratic Congressman Peter DeFazio made this point clearly in a June 16, 2009, floor speech *before* Obama's troop surge: "With a new White House strategy, a new commanding general, and 21,000 additional troops, I believe this is now President

Obama's war" (*Congressional Record*, vol 115, pt. 11, 15309. June 16, 2009). Even the president's partisan allies recognized that Obama's dramatic escalation had now appropriated the war.

67. From the United States project, https://github.com/unitedstates/congress-legislators.

68. Hand-coding of a subset of speeches revealed almost no clear examples of speeches that were either prowar but anti-administration or antiwar but pro-administration.

69. All relevant speeches were either prowar or antiwar; however, not all relevant speeches took an explicit position either pro- or anti-administration.

70. Online appendix available on Harvard Dataverse: https://doi.org/10.7910/DVN/OEOIM3.

71. For Afghanistan, the model and human coders agreed more than 80 percent of the time for a Cohen's kappa of 0.65.

72. To construct these measures, Jeong employs a Bayesian item response theory model using all foreign policy votes. Gyung-Ho Jeong, "Measuring Foreign Policy Positions of Members of the U.S. Congress," *Political Science Research and Methods* 6, no. 1 (2018): 181–196; Jeong and Quirk, "Division at the Water's Edge."

73. Douglas Kriner and Francis Shen, "Responding to War on Capitol Hill: Battlefield Casualties, Congressional Response, and Public Support for the War in Iraq," *American Journal of Political Science* 58, no. 1 (2014): 163.

74. For additional details on the distribution of pro- and antiwar speeches across members as well as robustness checks given the prevalence of zeros in several speech categories, see the online appendix. Additional analyses presented in the appendix modeling the probability of simply taking an anti- or prowar position (instead of the number of each type of speech) yield substantively similar results. Finally, some members gave both pro- and antiwar speeches. Additional analyses examining the factors that led members to take split positions are also presented in the online appendix.

75. To simplify comparisons, all first differences calculated by setting both Iraq AUMF vote indicators to 0.

76. Results for partisanship are substantively similar even after controlling for whether a member voted for or against the authorization to use military force against Iraq if they were in the chamber in 2002 (see Online Appendix SI table 8). In each model specification the partisan coefficient is of the same sign and roughly the same magnitude as those reported in table 2.1. Members who voted for the AUMF against Iraq were significantly less likely to criticize the surge, and members who voted against the AUMF gave significantly fewer prowar speeches than those who voted for it.

77. As discussed previously, members gave many fewer speeches during the Afghanistan surge than during the Iraq surge, and even fewer speeches that were openly critical of the surge/war. As a robustness check, we also reestimated our

analyses using a zero-inflated model to account for the large number of members who did not give any speeches critical of the war (see the online appendix). Republicans were significantly more likely to not give any floor speeches critical of the war than were Democrats. Among members who did give at least one antiwar speech, there is almost no partisan difference in frequency (e.g., the average Democrat who gave at least one antiwar speech gave 4.42 such speeches vs. 4.43 for the average Republican who gave at least one antiwar speech).

78. The only exception is that members of the leadership were, if anything, slightly less likely to criticize the war in Afghanistan than other members, though the coefficient is not statistically significant.

79. None of our hypotheses predict interchamber differences in the relationships between partisanship, ideology, and electoral context and congressional wartime rhetoric. However, as a robustness check, we estimated separate models for House members and Senators respectively (see Online Appendix SI table 9). The results are substantively similar across chambers. Most importantly, while opposition partisans were significantly more likely to speak out against the Iraq War surge in the 100th Congress, they were significantly less likely to do so against the Afghanistan War surge in the 111th Congress. This result, which is strongly consistent with H2, holds for members of both chambers.

80. Interacting the hawkish ideology measure and party dummy in model four of table 2.1 yields a substantively small and statistically insignificant coefficient.

81. The first difference in means (0.137 vs. 0.017) is statistically significant, $p<0.10$, two-tailed test. The second difference in means (0.227 vs. 0.042) is statistically significant, $p<0.01$, two-tailed test.

82. Howell and Pevehouse, *While Dangers Gather*; Kriner, *After the Rubicon*.

83. See, for example, David Hastings Dunn and Andrew Futter, "Short-Term Tactical Gains and Long-Term Strategic Problems: The Paradox of the US Troop Surge in Iraq," *Defence Studies* 10 (2010): 195–214.

84. See Kevin Marsh, "Obama's Surge: A Bureaucratic Politics Analysis of the Decision to Order a Troop Surge in the Afghanistan War," *Foreign Policy Analysis* 10, no. 3 (2014): 265–288.

85. Jesse Lee, "The New Way Forward—the President's Address," December 1, 2009, https://obamawhitehouse.archives.gov/blog/2009/12/01/new-way-forward-presidents-address.

86. Kelly McHugh, "A Tale of Two Surges: Comparing the Politics of the 2007 Iraq Surge and the 2009 Afghanistan Surge," *Sage Open* 5, no. 4 (2015): 1–16. For McCain's criticism, see "*Meet the Press* Transcript for December 6, 2009," NBC News, December 6, 2009, https://www.nbcnews.com/id/wbna34280265.

87. Douglas Kriner, "Congress, Public Opinion, and the Political Costs of Waging War," in *Congress Reconsidered*, 11th ed., ed. L. Dodd and B. Oppenheimer (Washington, DC: CQ Press, 2017, 421–450).

88. Kenneth Schultz, "Tying Hands and Washing Hands: The U.S. Congress and

Multilateral Humanitarian Intervention," in *Locating the Proper Authorities: The Interaction of Domestic and International Institutions*, ed. Daniel Drezner, 105–142 (Ann Arbor: University of Michigan Press, 2003). However, both the Clinton and Obama Administrations tried to justify at least some of these missions on nonhumanitarian grounds.

89. Authorizing the Limited Use of the United States Forces in Support of the NATO Mission in Libya, H.J. Res 68, 112th Cong. (2011), https://clerk.house.gov/Votes/2011493.

CHAPTER THREE

Varieties of Bipartisanship

How Democrats and Republicans Align on Foreign and Domestic Policy

Jordan Tama

How do Democratic and Republican elected officials align on foreign and domestic policy, and how do these alignments influence congressional checks on the president? For many followers of American politics, the answers to these questions might seem obvious and straightforward—namely that, regardless of the issue, the two parties have separated themselves into opposing camps, weakening the ability of Democratic and Republican members of Congress to band together to constrain the president.[1] Studies of US foreign policy have also highlighted rising polarization, showing that Democrats and Republicans have diverged on international issues since the 1960s.[2] Foreign policy scholars have further shown that polarization diminishes congressional checks on the president—for instance, by weakening congressional oversight of the executive branch[3] and giving the president greater incentive to act unilaterally.[4] Even when members of Congress criticize presidential actions, presidents may be able to effectively dismiss the criticism as partisan sniping if it only comes from the opposition party, as Sarah Kreps and Douglas Kriner observe in their introduction to this volume.

Yet other research suggests that bipartisanship remains alive. Some of this work shows that bipartisan cosponsorship of legislation is still common and that the enactment of legislation on major issues continues to involve bipartisan cooperation.[5] On foreign policy, some scholars have found that congressional bipartisanship has not declined when accounting for the increased use of procedural votes on Capitol Hill,[6] that the foreign policy identities of the two parties are not very distinct,[7] and that the worldviews of Democratic and Republican foreign policy elites continue to overlap to a considerable degree.[8] Other studies demonstrate that Congress exercises more influence on foreign policy than is commonly appreciated, calling into question claims that polarization has resulted in an imperial presidency.[9]

In this chapter, I add to these more nuanced understandings of political dynamics on foreign policy and show that Congress remains surprisingly capable of constraining the president on international issues in a bipartisan manner. First, I show that bipartisanship continues to occur regularly in Washington and more often than one might think based on media headlines featuring polarization. Second, I highlight how bipartisanship regularly takes different forms, including bipartisan congressional support for the president, which I call *pro-presidential bipartisanship*; bipartisan congressional opposition to the president, which I label *anti-presidential bipartisanship*; and competing bipartisan coalitions generated by intra-party division, or *cross-partisanship*. Importantly, each of these types of bipartisanship has different implications for the extent of congressional constraint on the president, with congressional constraint being weakest in instances of pro-presidential bipartisanship and strongest in cases of anti-presidential bipartisanship. Third, I examine how patterns of bipartisanship and polarization vary across foreign and domestic policy. I find that anti-presidential bipartisanship occurs far more often on international issues, indicating that Congress checks the president in a bipartisan manner more often when it turns its attention overseas than when it focuses on matters at home.

My multifaceted conception of bipartisanship departs from standard understandings of the term. Analyses of Congress often treat bipartisanship and polarization as binary concepts. In one standard approach, a congressional vote is considered to be bipartisan if a majority of Democrats and a majority of Republicans vote the same way, and it is considered to be polarized if a majority of Democrats vote against a majority of Republicans. A limitation with this approach is that it does not distinguish between stronger or weaker degrees of bipartisanship or polarization. While some studies employ more fine-grained measures of bipartisanship and polarization, there have been relatively few efforts to conceptualize bipartisanship or polarization in ways that do not treat them as binary categories. One of the contributions of this chapter is to distinguish conceptually between stronger and weaker levels of bipartisanship and polarization. This facilitates a more fine-grained understanding of political alignments while foregrounding the importance of intraparty divisions in cases where neither bipartisanship nor polarization is strong.

I also bring the president more directly into the picture by distinguishing between cases in which lawmakers in the two parties support the president's positions and cases in which lawmakers in the two parties oppose the president's positions. The standard image of bipartisanship involves the two parties in Congress lining up with the president. In foreign policy, this image is captured by the truism that politics should "stop at the water's edge."[10] This image also underlies "two presidencies" research that examines whether the president receives stronger support from Congress on international than on domestic issues.[11] But Democratic and Republican lawmakers sometimes work together to challenge, rather than back, presidential policies, generating a combination of bipartisan agreement within Congress and interbranch conflict—a combination that is particularly well-suited to constrain presidential behavior.

I outline three typologies designed to capture different dimensions of and nuances in political alignments (see table 3.1). The first typology reflects the standard conceptions of congressional bipartisanship and polarization, defining *bipartisanship* as the situation in which majorities of Democrats and Republicans vote together, and defining *polarization* as the situation in which majorities of Democrats and Republicans vote against each other. While this typology lacks nuance, it is highly intuitive and quite useful for analyzing trends across issues or over time.

The second typology takes into account differences in the strength of congressional bipartisanship or polarization. It divides congressional votes into three categories: *strong bipartisanship*, in which at least 90 percent of Democrats line up on the same side as at least 90 percent of Republicans; *strong polarization*, in which 90 percent or more of lawmakers in each party take opposing positions; and *cross-partisanship*, in which more than 10 percent of the lawmakers in a party vote against their party's dominant position.[12] Use of this typology can be particularly informative because strong polarization is likely to generate much larger governance pathologies than more moderate levels of polarization, while the cross-partisanship category highlights the type of intraparty division that can have an outsized impact on legislative outcomes when congressional majorities are small.[13] Given that cross-partisanship occurs often, this also points to important limits in the extent to which congressional constraint

TABLE 3.1 **Typologies of Political Alignments**

Typology 1	
Bipartisanship	Majorities of two parties vote together
Polarization	Majorities of two parties vote against each other

Typology 2	
Strong bipartisanship	At least 90 percent of members of both parties vote together
Strong polarization	At least 90 percent of members of both parties vote against each other
Cross-partisanship	More than 10 percent of members of a party vote against party's dominant position

Typology 3	
Pro-presidential bipartisanship	Majorities of two parties vote with president
Anti-presidential bipartisanship	Majorities of two parties vote against president
Polarization	Majorities of two parties vote against each other

on the president is determined by unified or divided party control of government, as Sarah Kreps and Douglas Kriner discuss in their chapter on the politics of US troop surges in Iraq and Afghanistan.

The third typology incorporates both congressional and presidential positions on legislation. Focusing on instances when the president supports or opposes a piece of legislation, it distinguishes between *pro-presidential bipartisanship*, in which majorities of both parties support the president's position; *anti-presidential bipartisanship*, in which majorities of both parties oppose the president's position; and *polarization*, in which a majority of Democratic lawmakers line up against a majority of Republican lawmakers. This typology centers attention on the extent to which Congress follows or challenges the president, which is central to understanding the strength of congressional checks on the president.

In what follows, I use three sets of data on congressional votes since the end of the Cold War to examine how the prevalence of these varieties of bipartisanship and polarization differ across foreign and domestic policy. Across all three data sets, I find that levels of bipartisanship, cross-partisanship, and anti-presidential bipartisanship have been higher on foreign policy than on domestic matters. In one of the most striking findings, rates of anti-presidential bipartisanship are roughly three times higher in foreign policy than in domestic policy in two of the data sets and twelve times higher in foreign policy in the third data set. Moreover, rates of antipresidential bipartisanship in foreign policy have not significantly changed since the September 11, 2001, terrorist attacks. In another indication of the frequent willingness of members of the president's party to defect from the president's position on foreign policy, I find that more than 10 percent of the president's copartisans vote against the president in about half of foreign policy votes. In addition, the data show that strong polarization is much less common on international than on domestic issues. Each of these patterns has also been maintained since the 9/11 attacks. Collectively, these findings suggest that Congress has remained more capable of constraining the president on foreign policy over the past two decades than much of the foreign policy literature would suggest.

Contributors to Political Alignments

Before examining the data, in this section I discuss why the prevalence of different political alignments might vary across foreign and domestic policy even during a time of high overall polarization. One possible source of higher rates of bipartisanship on international issues is the way in which major national security threats can bring Democrats and Republicans together through a shared sense of danger or the phenomenon of rallying around the flag.[14] For instance, after the September 11, 2001, terrorist attacks, the House and Senate approved in unanimous or nearly unanimous votes an authorization to use military force against the perpetrators of the attack and legislation that expanded the government's counterterrorism powers.[15] But major crises such as 9/11 represent an anomaly and cannot explain why patterns of bipartisanship and polarization would differ across foreign and domestic policy during more normal times. Moreover, recent research has found that crises and security threats no longer reliably generate bipartisan unity, calling into question the continued significance of this dynamic.[16]

Other aspects of domestic politics, including the ideological landscape, interest group advocacy, and the electoral incentives of lawmakers and the president can also contribute to variation in political alignments across policy areas.[17] While ideological polarization is generally high among both the public and elites in the United States,[18] public and elite views are much more polarized on some issues than others. Overall, the attitudes of liberals and conservatives are farther apart on domestic than on foreign policy matters.[19] On most major domestic issues, from health care to taxes, liberals and conservatives have strikingly different views. But such ideological polarization does not characterize foreign policy across the board. To be sure, some foreign policy debates are polarized ideologically. For instance, conservatives tend to be more pro-military and less supportive of multilateral institutions than liberals.[20] However, other foreign policy debates do not map onto distinct liberal and conservative positions. For example, many liberals and conservatives support the maintenance of international alliances and the imposition of sanctions on countries engaged in objectionable behavior,[21] while debates over international trade or the use of military force for humanitarian purposes often feature ideological splits within the parties.[22] These different ideological contexts can foster bipartisan agreement or cross-partisanship among elected officials.

The interest group landscape can also facilitate different varieties of polarization and bipartisanship. Many advocacy groups, from the National Rifle Association to Planned Parenthood, have a strong partisan orientation, enjoying close ties to one of the two parties and much weaker ties to the other party. Such groups tend to contribute to polarization on the issues that they care about.[23] But other advocacy groups, such as many defense contractors and ethnic constituencies, maintain strong links to both parties, which can allow them to be a force for bipartisanship on those matters where they choose to get engaged. On the whole, campaign contribution data show that, compared to advocacy groups focused on domestic issues, foreign policy interest groups give a greater share of their donations to centrist politicians or to politicians in both parties.[24] Such donations tend to foster bipartisan cooperation in Washington. At the same time, there exists a relatively large number of foreign policy issues that feature relatively little interest group advocacy.[25] On such issues, lawmakers typically have more leeway to adopt different positions, facilitating cross-partisanship.

A final factor—the differing electoral incentives of lawmakers and the president—helps to explain why lawmakers in both parties sometimes line up together in opposition to the president on foreign policy. Although presidents sometimes act in parochial ways,[26] they generally have an incentive to advance the overall security and welfare of the country because voters hold them accountable for the nation's safety and well-being.[27] By contrast, voters hold members of Congress accountable for their positions on issues, but rarely hold them accountable for policy outcomes.[28] This pattern gives lawmakers a greater incentive than the president to favor positions that are popular with important constituencies, even if those positions might not be in the best interest of the country. At the same time, the weaker accountability of lawmakers than of the president for policy outcomes can give members of Congress more political freedom than the president to adopt positions based on their own principled views, particularly on issues that are not highly salient.[29] Since the contrast between the incentives facing lawmakers and the president is starkest on foreign policy given the president's much greater electoral accountability for protecting national security, international issues can be more conducive than domestic matters to anti-presidential bipartisanship.

Examining empirically whether and how each of these factors—the existence of crises, the ideological landscape, interest group advocacy, and differing congressional and presidential incentives—influences political alignments on foreign and domestic policy is beyond the scope of this chapter but is examined in more depth in other research.[30] My purpose in outlining these potential contributors to political alignments is simply to offer plausible explanations for why alignment patterns might differ across these policy areas. In the next section, I investigate whether patterns of bipartisanship and polarization do actually vary across international and domestic issues.

Data on Important Congressional Votes

To investigate patterns of bipartisanship and polarization on foreign and domestic policy, I created three data sets of important congressional votes.[31] Many congressional votes are trivial, dealing with matters of little public consequence.[32] Yet voting patterns on these trivial issues might differ systematically from voting patterns on more important ones. Since congressional behavior matters primarily to the extent that it affects the ability of the government to address important issues, it makes sense to isolate votes on important issues and investigate how Democrats and Republicans align on them.

Given that there are multiple ways to identify important congressional votes, I created three data sets that incorporate different sets of important votes. The similarities in empirical patterns across the three data sets enhance the validity of my findings.

The first data set includes all votes identified as "key votes" by Congressional Quarterly (CQ) from 1991 to 2020.[33] These are the House and

Senate votes considered by CQ to have been the most important votes in a given year. CQ typically gives this label to a select group of about ten to fifteen votes from each chamber each year. I chose to include the years 1991 to 2020 in the data set because polarization in American politics was generally high during this period, making it a period when one might expect bipartisanship to be rare. Moreover, this period follows the end of the Cold War, which should make it a hard test for my argument that bipartisanship is more common on foreign than on domestic policy given that the end of the Cold War is commonly associated with a decline in bipartisan cooperation on international issues.[34] The data set includes a total of 834 votes. Twenty-five percent of these votes concerned foreign policy and 75 percent involved domestic policy.[35]

A second data set allows me to home in on the most recent part of this thirty-year time period, when overall polarization in American politics reached new heights. The relatively small number of CQ key votes per year makes it difficult to identify clear patterns for small subsets of years, particularly when comparing patterns in different policy areas. I therefore turn to a second source, Vote Smart, which identifies a larger set of congressional key votes for each year.[36] I coded all Vote Smart key votes from 2013 to 2020, a period spanning the second term of Barack Obama's presidency and Donald Trump's presidential term. Examining these years in-depth enables consideration of the extent to which different types of bipartisanship existed on international and domestic issues when many measures of polarization in American politics attained record levels.[37] This data set includes a total of 1,444 roll call votes. Twenty-two percent of the votes involved foreign policy and 78 percent concerned domestic issues.

While these key vote data sources are very valuable, they share an important limitation. CQ and Vote Smart only give the key vote label to roll call votes. This is problematic when it comes to analyzing patterns of polarization and bipartisanship because roll call votes differ systematically from voice votes and unanimous consent votes in the extent of bipartisan support for legislation. When legislation enjoys strong bipartisan support, House or Senate leaders often bring it to the floor for a voice vote or unanimous consent vote rather than a roll call vote.[38] By contrast, congressional leaders typically use roll call votes for legislation that enjoys weaker support on Capitol Hill. Excluding voice votes and unanimous consent votes from an analysis of voting patterns can therefore lead to a large underestimation of the actual average level of bipartisan backing for legislation.

I therefore created a third data set that includes important roll call votes as well as important voice votes and unanimous consent votes. Until 2017, the annual publication Congressional Quarterly Almanac (or CQ Almanac) included articles that summarized congressional activity in a given policy area, such as defense or agriculture, during that year. Each article typically lists important votes in that area in the text box "Box Score." Notably, these box scores included voice votes and unanimous consent votes as well as roll call votes. My third data set includes the votes mentioned in one of these box scores.[39] Whereas these votes typically were not as important as the CQ key votes, they were still important enough for CQ Almanac editors to have considered them worthy of being highlighted in the publication. Since it would have been very time-consuming to code every vote highlighted in CQ Almanac from 1991 to 2020, my research assistants and I coded these votes for every third year, starting with 1992.[40] This data set includes a total of 2,080 votes. Twenty percent of the votes concern foreign policy and 80 percent involve domestic matters. Sixty-five percent of the votes were roll call votes, while 35 percent were voice votes or unanimous consent votes.

In what follows, I use tabulations from these three data sets to compare foreign and domestic policy voting patterns. I find that the same types of differences exist between foreign and domestic policy voting across these data sets. The empirical patterns provide strong support for my expectation that foreign policy debates are more conducive to bipartisanship, including different types of bipartisanship, than domestic policy debates. In two of the most striking differences, strong polarization has been much more common on domestic than on foreign policy, whereas anti-presidential bipartisanship has been far more common on international than on domestic issues. I further find that rates of pro-presidential bipartisanship and anti-presidential bipartisanship are similar in the pre-9/11 and post-9/11 eras, suggesting that the 9/11 attacks did not generate a lasting change in the willingness of congressional Democrats and Republicans to join together to support or challenge the president.

The Frequency of Bipartisanship

In this section, I compare foreign and domestic policy voting patterns in these data using a simple measure of the rate of bipartisan voting. This measure is based on a dichotomous indicator of whether a majority of

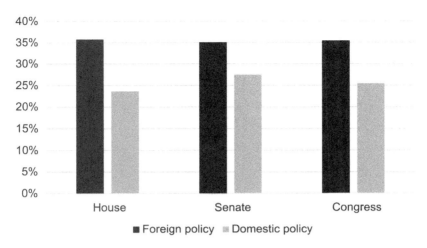

FIGURE 3.1. Rates of Bipartisanship—CQ Key Votes

Democrats voted the same way as a majority of Republicans on a given piece of legislation. Using this dichotomous indicator, I define the rate of bipartisanship as the share of a set of votes on which majorities of the two parties voted together.

Across all three data sets, the rate of bipartisanship was stronger on foreign than on domestic policy. Among CQ key votes from 1991 to 2020, a majority of Democrats voted with a majority of Republicans in 35 percent of foreign policy votes and 25 percent of domestic policy votes (see figure 3.1).[41] Sizable gaps also separate the two policy areas among the Vote Smart key votes from 2013 to 2020, though the bipartisanship scores for these recent years are lower overall, as one would expect. Among the Vote Smart key votes, majorities of Democrats and Republicans voted together 31 percent of the time on foreign policy and 18 percent of the time on domestic policy (see figure 3.2).

A gap of similar magnitude separates the rate of bipartisanship in foreign and domestic policy votes when examining the CQ Almanac roll call and non-roll call votes from every third year, but the frequency of bipartisanship is higher across-the-board in these votes than in the CQ and Vote Smart key votes. In tabulating these votes, I treat voice votes and unanimous consent votes as votes in which majorities of Democrats and Republicans voted together, since these voting procedures are typically used when a measure has strong bipartisan backing.[42] Using this

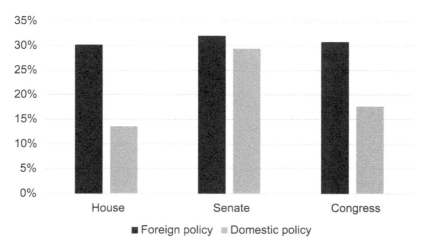

FIGURE 3.2. Rates of Bipartisanship—Vote Smart Key Votes

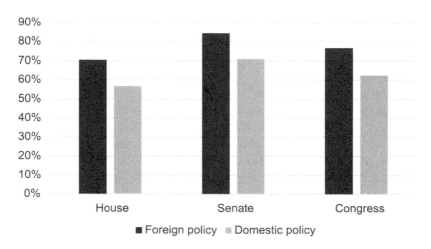

FIGURE 3.3. Rates of Bipartisanship—CQ Almanac Votes

approach reveals that majorities of Democrats and Republicans voted together 77 percent of the time on foreign policy and 63 percent of the time on domestic policy in this set of votes (see figure 3.3). The greater frequency of bipartisanship in these votes than in the data sets of key votes likely reflects both the inclusion of voice votes and unanimous consent votes in the tabulations as well as the somewhat lower public salience of many of these votes compared to the key votes, as polarization tends to be lower on less salient issues.[43]

These patterns hold when looking only at House votes or only at Senate votes. Among House votes, the rates of bipartisanship are higher on foreign than on domestic policy in each of the three data sets. Among Senate votes, bipartisanship levels are also higher on international than on domestic issues in each of the data sets, but this gap is not statistically significant for the Vote Smart key votes.

The rate of bipartisanship remains higher on foreign than on domestic policy in each of the three data sets when breaking down the data in a variety of other ways, including when excluding procedural and amendment votes, immigration votes, or spending votes from the tabulations. Levels of bipartisanship are also higher on international than on domestic issues in each of the data sets under different configurations of unified or divided party control of the House, Senate, and presidency (see figures 3A.1–3A.3 in the printed appendix). Collectively, these patterns support my argument that foreign policy debates are generally more conducive to bipartisanship than domestic policy ones.

The two data sets that span the entire 1991–2020 period further indicate that rates of bipartisanship in foreign policy did not change dramatically between the pre- and post-9/11 eras. In the CQ key votes data set, majorities of Democrats and Republicans voted together on foreign policy 34 percent of the time before 9/11 and 36 percent of the time after 9/11. In the data set including CQ Almanac roll call, voice, and unanimous consent votes, majorities of Democrats and Republicans voted together on foreign policy 70 percent of the time before 9/11 and 62 percent of the time after 9/11.

Variations of Bipartisanship and Polarization

The data sets tell a similar story with respect to the prevalence of strong polarization and cross-partisanship on foreign and domestic policy. For each of the data sets, strong polarization, in which at least 90 percent of Democrats vote on the opposite side as at least 90 percent of Republicans, is much more common on domestic than on international issues. Among the CQ key votes, 14 percent of the foreign policy votes and 29 percent of the domestic policy votes were strongly polarized (see figure 3.4). Among the Vote Smart key votes, 36 percent of the foreign policy votes and 55 percent of the foreign policy votes were strongly polarized (see

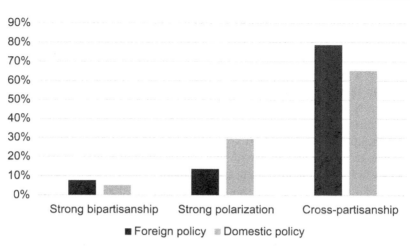

FIGURE 3.4. Variation of Bipartisanship and Polarization — CQ Key Votes

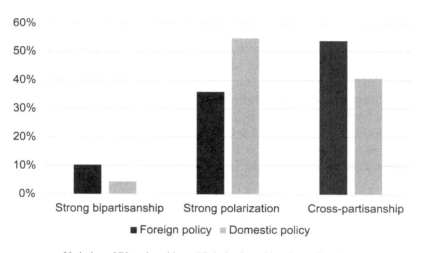

FIGURE 3.5. Variation of Bipartisanship and Polarization — Vote Smart Key Votes

figure 3.5). Among the set of CQ Almanac votes that includes both roll call and non-roll call votes, 13 percent of foreign policy votes and 26 percent of domestic policy votes were strongly polarized. Moreover, rates of strong polarization were considerably lower on foreign policy than on domestic policy both before and after 9/11, suggesting that Democrats and Republicans in Congress have remained more capable of cooperating on international than on domestic issues in recent years (see figures 3.6 and 3.7). However, as figures 3.6 and 3.7 also show, strong polarization has become more common on foreign policy since 9/11 than it was before 9/11, indicating that the broader trend of increased polarization in American politics has affected Congress on international as well as domestic issues.

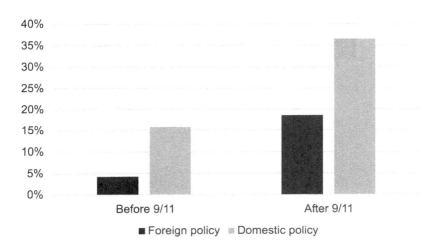

FIGURE 3.6. Strong Polarization—CQ Key Votes

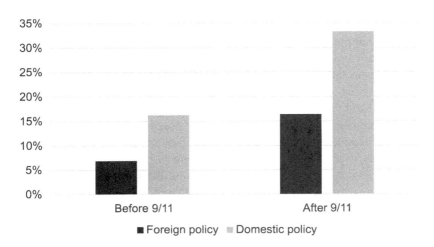

FIGURE 3.7. Strong Polarization—CQ Almanac Votes

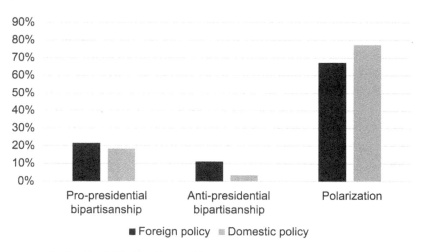

FIGURE 3.8. Presidential Position Votes—CQ Key Votes

If this trend continues, it will bode poorly for the ability of Congress to serve as an effective check on the president as time goes on.

The data also show that cross-partisanship, in which more than 10 percent of the members of a party vote against their party's dominant position, is more common on foreign than on domestic policy. Among the CQ key votes, 79 percent of foreign policy votes and 65 percent of domestic policy votes featured cross-partisanship (see figure 3.4). Among the Vote Smart key votes, 54 percent of foreign policy votes and 41 percent on domestic policy votes involved cross-partisanship (see figure 3.5).[44] These findings support my expectation that foreign policy debates are characterized not only by more frequent agreement between Democrats and Republicans but also by more frequent division within the parties.

Restricting the analysis to presidential position votes—votes on which the president took a clear position—illuminates the prevalence of pro-presidential bipartisanship, in which majorities of both parties vote in line with the president's position, and anti-presidential bipartisanship, in which majorities of both parties vote against the president's position. While there does not exist a statistically significant difference between foreign and domestic policy in rates of pro-presidential bipartisanship in any of the data sets, anti-presidential bipartisanship is much more common on foreign than on domestic policy in all three data sets. Among the CQ key votes, 11 percent of foreign policy votes and 4 percent of domestic policy votes featured anti-presidential bipartisanship (see figure 3.8). Among the

Vote Smart key votes, 12 percent of foreign policy votes and 1 percent of domestic policy votes were marked by anti-presidential bipartisanship (see figure 3.9). Among the set of CQ Almanac votes that includes voice votes and unanimous consent votes, 21 percent of foreign policy votes and 7 percent of domestic policy votes involved anti-presidential bipartisanship (see figure 3.10).

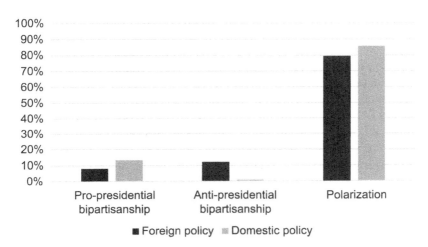

FIGURE 3.9. Presidential Position Votes—Vote Smart Key Votes

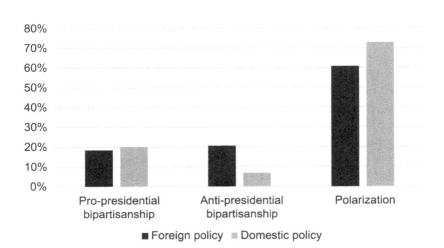

FIGURE 3.10. Presidential Position Votes—CQ Almanac Votes

Although these rates of anti-presidential bipartisanship may seem low across the board, it is striking that they are roughly three times higher in two of the data sets and twelve times higher in the third data set on international than on domestic issues. It is also remarkable that, during a time of high overall polarization, majorities of Democrats and Republicans would band together to vote against the president on foreign policy even as often as one out of ten or one out of five times. These rates of anti-presidential bipartisanship are all the more notable given the extent to which the president is widely considered to be the dominant foreign policy actor. Whereas the two-presidencies model suggests that presidents get their way in Congress more often on foreign than on domestic policy,[45] these data suggest that lawmakers actually challenge presidents more often on international than on domestic matters. They also suggest that any claims of presidential dominance of contemporary foreign policy should be qualified to recognize those instances when Congress pushes foreign policy in a direction that the president opposes.

Moreover, the presidential position votes reveal that it is common for a substantial number of members of the president's own party to defect from the president on foreign policy votes. More than 10 percent of the president's party voted in opposition to the president's position in 48 percent of the CQ presidential position key votes involving foreign policy and in 53 percent of the Vote Smart key votes involving foreign policy. These data indicate that the president often cannot fully rely on congressional copartisans for insulation from legislative challenges on international issues.

The data further indicate that rates of pro-presidential bipartisanship and anti-presidential bipartisanship in foreign policy were similar in the decade prior to 9/11 and the two decades after 9/11, suggesting that 9/11 did not bring a significant lasting change in the degree of congressional constraint on the presidency, at least when it comes to foreign policy legislation. Among presidential position votes in the CQ key vote data set, pro-presidential bipartisanship characterized 24 percent of foreign policy votes before 9/11 and 20 percent of foreign policy votes after 9/11, while anti-presidential bipartisanship marked 8 percent of foreign policy votes before 9/11 and 13 percent of foreign policy votes after 9/11 (see figure 3.11). For the CQ Almanac data set that includes roll call and non-roll call votes, the rate of pro-presidential bipartisan voting on foreign policy inched up from 22 percent to 23 percent between the two periods, while the rate of anti-presidential bipartisanship on foreign policy dipped from 16 percent to 11 percent (see figure 3.12). Taken together, these data point to a lim-

VARIETIES OF BIPARTISANSHIP

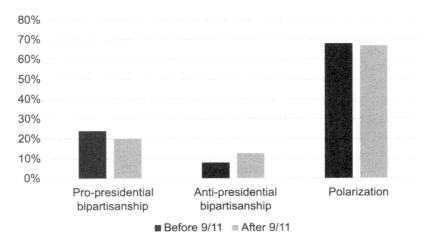

FIGURE 3.11. Presidential Position Foreign Policy Votes—CQ Key Votes

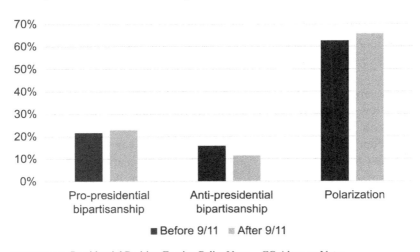

FIGURE 3.12. Presidential Position Foreign Policy Votes—CQ Almanac Votes

ited overall change in the willingness of Democrats and Republicans to cooperate in support of or in opposition to the president.

Conclusion

The data presented in this chapter show that Democratic and Republican elected officials line up differently on foreign than on domestic policy and that Congress can still serve as a check on the president when it turns its attention overseas. Across three data sets of congressional votes, bipartisanship, cross-partisanship, and anti-presidential bipartisanship are all more common on international issues than on domestic matters. Conversely, strong polarization is much more common on domestic than on foreign policy. Strikingly, these patterns hold for the full period since the end of the Cold War, including both the pre-9/11 and post-9/11 years, as well as for the Obama and Trump presidencies, when overall polarization in American politics reached new heights. Considered collectively, these patterns suggest that the politics of foreign policy differ from the politics of domestic policy in some important ways. The findings also indicate that members of Congress in the two parties have remained capable of cooperating to constrain the president on foreign policy in recent decades, despite the shock of 9/11 and other factors highlighted in this volume that have facilitated the exercise of strong presidential power.

Developments during the first two years of Joe Biden's presidency point to the continued relevance of distinctions among types of bipartisanship and polarization, the persistence of differences between foreign and domestic policy, and the ongoing ability of Congress to support and constrain the president in a bipartisan manner on international matters. On several highly salient domestic issues, Democrats and Republicans were nearly entirely polarized along partisan lines. For instance, hardly any members of Congress crossed party lines in key votes on a major pandemic relief and economic stimulus package; Ketanji Brown Jackson's confirmation as a Supreme Court justice; and legislation funding extensive green energy investments, setting a ceiling on the cost of prescription drugs, boosting the capacity of the Internal Revenue Service, and increasing some corporate taxes.[46] Some other domestic issues, including legislation funding major infrastructure investments and providing protections for same-sex and interracial marriages, were marked by cross-partisanship, with substantial numbers of Republican lawmakers joining with most or all Democrats.[47]

On foreign policy issues, strong polarization was rare during Biden's first two years in office, but pro-presidential partisanship, anti-presidential bipartisanship, and cross-partisanship marked a variety of important issues. Democratic and Republican members of Congress lined up nearly entirely on opposite sides on the question of whether to support Biden's efforts to pursue a new nuclear agreement with Iran.[48] But when Russia invaded Ukraine, strong majorities of lawmakers in both parties banded together to support Biden's approach to the conflict and to European security more broadly by providing large amounts of military aid to Ukraine and approving the admission of Sweden and Finland into NATO.[49] On another issue of great power relations, China policy was marked by strong bipartisanship in Congress as well as substantial tensions between Congress and the president. When Speaker of the House Nancy Pelosi traveled to Taiwan in the summer of 2022, her trip was criticized by the Biden administration but defended by both Democratic and Republican lawmakers.[50] Similarly, the Biden administration urged Congress not to approve legislation elevating the diplomatic status of Taiwan and designating Taiwan a major non-NATO ally, but majorities of Democrats and Republicans on the Senate Foreign Relations Committee voted to advance the legislation nevertheless.[51] On a war powers issue, meanwhile, substantial numbers of Republican lawmakers crossed the aisle to vote with nearly all the Democrats to repeal an authorization for the use of military force dating back to 2002.[52]

None of this is to suggest that polarization is not increasing on foreign policy or that partisanship does not shape foreign policy behavior. Indeed, recent work finds that polarization in congressional voting on both foreign and domestic policy continued to rise under Obama and Trump,[53] while a spate of other research shows that members of Congress are often influenced by partisan concerns when making foreign policy decisions.[54] Moreover, the data presented here indicate that strong or moderate polarization characterizes a large share of congressional foreign policy votes. But the heavy emphasis on polarization and partisanship in analyses of the contemporary politics of US foreign policy has resulted in too little appreciation of the continued prevalence of intraparty divisions and different forms of bipartisanship on international issues.

The persistence of anti-presidential bipartisanship on foreign policy is also notable in that it points to the continued importance of Congress on foreign policy, underscoring that Congress still matters when it comes to world affairs. Moreover, it shows that lawmakers remain capable of constraining the president on international issues not only through tools such as hearings, investigations, and public criticism—which have been the focus of some of the most important research on congressional influence[55]—but also through their formal legislative powers. The ability of Democrats and Republicans to work together on some important international issues, either in support of or in opposition to the president, suggests too that the United States remains capable of acting in a bipartisan manner in support of the liberal international order.[56] In short, from a normative standpoint, the glass is both half-empty and half-full.

Further research could seek to integrate the three typologies that I have outlined into a single, multidimensional model of political affiliation.[57] In this chapter, I chose to keep the three typologies distinct from each other so that each typology would focus on a single variable of interest—in the first typology, whether majorities of the two parties vote together; in the second typology, whether the strength of bipartisanship or polarization passes the 90 percent threshold; and in the third typology, whether Democrats and Republicans in Congress are lining up in support of, or in opposition to, the president. Combining these typologies might enable a more parsimonious understanding of political alignments, further advancing knowledge of the capacity of Congress to act effectively and rein in the president in foreign affairs.

Appendix

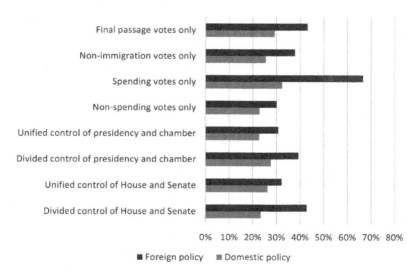

FIGURE 3A.1. Rates of Bipartisanship under Various Conditions—CQ Key Votes

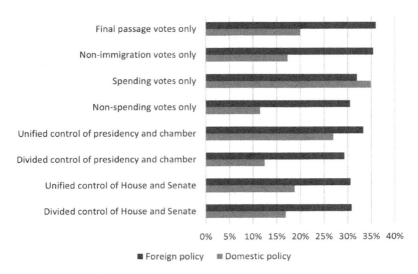

FIGURE 3A.2. Rates of Bipartisanship under Various Conditions—Vote Smart Key Votes

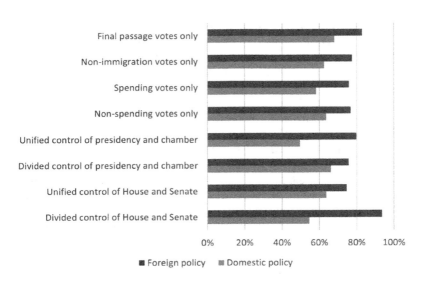

FIGURE 3A.3. Rates of Bipartisanship under Various Conditions—CQ Almanac Votes

Notes

1. On the rise of polarization in American politics, see Sean M. Theriault, *Party Polarization in Congress* (Cambridge: Cambridge University Press, 2008); Nolan McCarty, Keith T. Poole, and Howard Rosenthal, *Polarized America: The Dance of Ideology and Unequal Riches*, 2nd ed. (Cambridge, MA: MIT Press, 2016); Lilliana Mason, *Uncivil Agreement: How Politics Became Our Identity* (Chicago: University of Chicago Press, 2018); Shanto Iyengar et al., "The Origins and Consequences of Affective Polarization in the United States," *Annual Review of Political Science* 22 (2019): 129–146.

2. James M. McCormick and Eugene R. Wittkopf, "Bipartisanship, Partisanship, and Ideology in Congressional-Executive Foreign Policy Relations, 1947–1988," *Journal of Politics* 52, no. 4 (1990): 1077–1100; Jeffrey S. Peake, "Presidential Agenda Setting in Foreign Policy," *Political Research Quarterly* 54, no. 1 (2001): 69–86; Brandon C. Prins and Bryan W. Marshall, "Congressional Support of the President: A Comparison of Foreign, Defense, and Domestic Policy Decision Making during and after the Cold War," *Presidential Studies Quarterly* 31, no. 4 (2001): 660–678; C. James DeLaet and James M. Scott, "Treaty-Making and Partisan Politics: Arms Control and the U.S. Senate, 1960–2001," *Foreign Policy Analysis* 2, no. 2 (2006): 177–200; Charles A. Kupchan and Peter L. Trubowitz, "Dead Center: The Demise of Liberal Internationalism in the United States," *International Security* 32, no. 2 (2007): 7–44; Jack Snyder, Robert Y. Shapiro, and Yaeli Bloch-Elkon, "Free Hand Abroad, Divide and Rule at Home," *World Politics* 61, no. 1 (2009): 155–187; Peter Hays Gries, *The Politics of American Foreign Policy: How Ideology Divides Liberals and Conservatives over Foreign Affairs* (Stanford, CA: Stanford University Press, 2014); Gyung-Ho Jeong and Paul J. Quirk, "Division at the Water's Edge: The Polarization of Foreign Policy," *American Politics Research* 47, no. 1 (2019): 58–87; Gordon M. Friedrichs and Jordan Tama, "Polarization and US Foreign Policy: Key Debates and New Findings," *International Politics* 59, no. 5 (2022): 767–785.

3. Linda L. Fowler, *Watchdogs on the Hill: The Decline of Congressional Oversight of U.S. Foreign Relations* (Princeton, NJ: Princeton University Press, 2015); James M. Goldgeier and Elizabeth N. Saunders, "The Unconstrained Presidency: Checks and Balances Eroded Long Before Trump," *Foreign Affairs* 97, no. 5 (2018): 144–156.

4. William G. Howell, *Power without Persuasion: The Politics of Direct Presidential Action* (Princeton, NJ: Princeton University Press, 2003). For additional work on negative effects of polarization on the conduct of US foreign policy, see Jeffrey S. Peake, Glen S. Krutz, and Tyler Hughes, "President Obama, the Senate and the Polarized Politics of Treaty-Making," *Social Science Quarterly* 93, no. 5 (2012): 1295–1315; Kenneth A. Schultz, "Perils of Polarization for U.S. Foreign Policy," *Washington Quarterly* 40, no. 4 (2017): 7–28; Daniel W. Drezner, "This Time Is Different: Why U.S. Foreign Policy Will Never Recover," *Foreign Affairs* 98,

no. 3 (2019): 10–17; Peter Trubowitz and Peter Harris, "The End of the American Century? Slow Erosion of the Domestic Sources of Usable Power," *International Affairs* 95, no. 3 (2019): 619–639; Rachel Myrick, "The Reputational Consequences of Polarization for American Foreign Policy: Evidence from the U.S.–U.K. Bilateral Relationship," *International Politics* 59, no. 5 (2022): 1004–1027.

5. Laurel Harbridge, *Is Bipartisanship Dead? Policy Agreement and Agenda-Setting in the House of Representatives* (New York: Cambridge University Press, 2015); James M. Curry and Frances E. Lee, *The Limits of Party: Congress and Lawmaking in a Polarized Era* (Chicago: University of Chicago Press, 2020), 10–11.

6. Stephen Chaudoin, Helen V. Milner, and Dustin Tingley, "The Center Still Holds: Liberal Internationalism Survives," *International Security* 35, no. 1 (2010): 75–94.

7. Joshua D. Kertzer, Deborah Jordan Brooks, and Stephen G. Brooks, "Do Partisan Types Stop at the Water's Edge?" *Journal of Politics* 83, no. 4 (2021): 1764–1782.

8. Dina Smeltz et al., *United in Goals, Divided on Means: Opinion Leaders Survey Results and Partisan Breakdowns from the 2014 Chicago Survey of American Opinion on US Foreign Policy* (Chicago: Chicago Council on Global Affairs, 2015).

9. Lisa L. Martin, *Democratic Commitments: Legislatures and International Cooperation* (Princeton, NJ: Princeton University Press, 2000); William G. Howell and Jon C. Pevehouse, *While Dangers Gather: Congressional Checks on Presidential War Powers* (Princeton, NJ: Princeton University Press, 2007); Douglas L. Kriner, *After the Rubicon: Congress, Presidents, and the Politics of Waging War* (Chicago: University of Chicago Press, 2010); David P. Auerswald, "Arms Control," in *Congress and the Politics of National Security*, ed. David P. Auerswald and Colton C. Campbell, 189–212 (New York: Cambridge University Press, 2012); James M. Scott and Ralph G. Carter, "The Not-So-Silent Partner: Patterns of Legislative-Executive Interaction in the War on Terror, 2001–2009," *International Studies Perspectives* 15, no. 2 (2014): 186–208; David P. Auerswald and Colton C. Campbell, eds., *Congress and Civil-Military Relations* (Washington, DC: Georgetown University Press, 2015); Helen V. Milner and Dustin Tingley, *Sailing the Water's Edge: The Domestic Politics of American Foreign Policy* (Princeton, NJ: Princeton University Press, 2015); Douglas Kriner and Eric Schickler, "The Resilience of Separation of Powers? Congress and the Russia Investigation," *Presidential Studies Quarterly* 48, no. 3 (2018): 436–455; Jeffrey S. Lantis, *Foreign Policy Advocacy and Entrepreneurship: How a New Generation in Congress Is Shaping US Engagement with the World* (Ann Arbor: University of Michigan Press, 2019); Jordan Tama, "Forcing the President's Hand: How the US Congress Shapes Foreign Policy through Sanctions Legislation," *Foreign Policy Analysis* 16, no. 3 (2020): 397–416; Shannon Carcelli, "Congressional Polarization and Limitation Riders in Foreign Aid Appropriations," *International Politics* 59, no. 5 (2022): 898–924.

10. Ellen C. Collier, *Bipartisanship and the Making of Foreign Policy: A Historical Survey*, 2nd ed. (Lexington, KY: Xlibris, 2011); Fowler, *Watchdogs on the Hill*, 173.

11. Aaron Wildavsky, "The Two Presidencies," *Trans-action* 4, no. 2 (1966): 7–14; Richard Fleisher et al., "The Demise of the Two Presidencies," *American Politics Quarterly* 28, no. 1 (2000): 3–25; Brandice Canes-Wrone, William G. Howell, and David E. Lewis, "Toward a Broader Understanding of Presidential Power: A Reevaluation of the Two Presidencies Thesis," *Journal of Politics* 70, no. 1 (2008): 1–16.

12. Joseph Cooper and Garry Young, "Partisanship, Bipartisanship, and Crosspartisanship in Congress since the New Deal," in *Congress Reconsidered*, ed. Lawrence C. Dodd and Bruce I. Oppenheimer, 246–273 (Washington, DC: CQ Press, 1997); Martha L. Gibson, *Conflict Amid Consensus in American Trade Policy* (Washington, DC: Georgetown University Press, 2000).

13. Frances E. Lee, *Insecure Majorities: Congress and the Perpetual Campaign* (Chicago: University of Chicago Press, 2016).

14. John E. Mueller, *War, Presidents, and Public Opinion* (New York: Wiley, 1973); John R. Oneal and Anna Lillian Bryan, "The Rally 'Round the Flag Effect in U.S. Foreign Policy Crises, 1950–1985," *Political Behavior* 17, no. 4 (1995): 379–401; Joanne Gowa, "Politics at the Water's Edge: Parties, Voters, and the Use of Force Abroad," *International Organization* 52, no. 2 (1998): 307–324; Marc J. Hetherington and Michael Nelson, "Anatomy of a Rally Effect: George W. Bush and the War on Terrorism," *PS: Political Science & Politics* 36, no. 1 (2003): 37–42.

15. Adrian Vermeule, "Emergency Lawmaking after 9/11 and 7/7," *University of Chicago Law Review* 75 (2008): 1155–1190; Shoon Kathleen Murray, "Stretching the 2001 AUMF: A History of Two Presidencies," *Presidential Studies Quarterly* 45, no. 1 (2015): 175–198.

16. Rachel Myrick, "Do External Threats Unite or Divide? Security Crises, Rivalries, and Polarization in American Foreign Policy," *International Organization* 75, no. 4 (2021): 921–958.

17. Jordan Tama, *Bipartisanship and US Foreign Policy: Cooperation in a Polarized Age* (Oxford: Oxford University Press, 2024).

18. Pew Research Center, *Political Polarization in the American Public*, June 12, 2014; Abramowitz, *The Great Alignment: Race, Party Transformation, and the Rise of Donald Trump (New Haven, CT: Yale University Press, 2018)*.

19. Delia Baldassarri and Andrew Gelman, "Partisans without Constraint: Political Polarization and Trends in American Public Opinion," *American Journal of Sociology* 114, no. 2 (2008): 408–446; Hans Noel, *Political Ideologies and Political Parties in America* (New York: Cambridge University Press, 2013).

20. Brian C. Rathbun, *Trust in International Cooperation: International Security Institutions, Domestic Politics and American Multilateralism* (Cambridge, NY: Cambridge University Press, 2012); Georg Wenzelburger and Florian Böller, "Bomb or Build? How Party Ideologies Affect the Balance of Foreign Aid and Defence

Spending," *British Journal of Politics and International Relations* 22, no. 1 (2019): 3–23; Tim Haesebrouck and Patrick Mello, "Patterns of Political Ideology and Security Policy," *Foreign Policy Analysis* 16, no. 4 (2020): 565–586; Tapio Raunio and Wolfgang Wagner, "The Party Politics of Foreign and Security Policy," *Foreign Policy Analysis* 16, no. 4 (2020): 515–531; Wolfgang Wagner, *The Democratic Politics of Military Interventions: Political Parties, Contestation, and Decisions to Use Force Abroad* (Oxford: Oxford University Press, 2020); William Bendix and Gyung-Ho Jeong, "Beyond Party: Ideological Convictions and Foreign Policy Conflicts in the US Congress," *International Politics* 59, no. 5 (2022): 827–850; Michael Flynn and Benjamin O. Fordham, "Everything Old Is New Again: The Persistence of Republican Opposition to Multilateralism in American Foreign Policy," *Studies in American Political Development* 37, no. 1 (2022): 1-18, https://doi.org/10.1017/S0898588X22000165; Gries, *The Politics of American Foreign Policy*.

21. Dina Smeltz et al., *The Foreign Policy Establishment or Donald Trump: Which Better Reflects American Opinion?* (Chicago: Chicago Council on Global Affairs, 2017); Tama, "Forcing the President's Hand."

22. Brian Rathbun, "Wedges and Widgets: Liberalism, Libertarianism, and the Trade Attitudes of the American Mass Public and Elites," *Foreign Policy Analysis* 12, no. 1 (2016): 85–108; Patrick Homan and Jeffrey S. Lantis, *The Battle for U.S. Foreign Policy: Congress, Parties, and Factions in the 21st Century* (Cham: Palgrave Macmillan, 2020); Sarah Maxey, "The Power of Humanitarian Narratives: A Domestic Coalition Theory of Justifications for Military Action," *Political Research Quarterly* 73, no. 3 (2020): 680–695; Gordon Friedrichs, "Polarized We Trade? Intra-Party Polarization and U.S. Trade Policy," *International Politics* 59, no. 5 (2022): 956–980.

23. Frank R. Baumgartner et al., *Lobbying and Policy Change: Who Wins, Who Loses, and Why* (Chicago: University of Chicago, 2009); Matt Grossman, "Who Gets What Now? Interest Groups under Obama," *The Forum* 7, no. 1 (2009), https://doi.org/10.2202/1540-8884.1298; Kathleen Bawm et al., "A Theory of Political Parties: Groups, Policy Demands and Nominations in American Politics," *Perspectives on Politics* 10, no. 3 (2012): 571–597; Michael T. Heaney, "Bridging the Gap between Political Parties and Interest Groups," in *Interest Group Politics*, ed. Allan J. Cigler and Burdett A. Loomis, 194–218 (Washington, DC: CQ Press, 2012); Mark J. Rozell, Clyde Wilcox, and Michael M. Franz, *Interest Groups in American Campaigns: The New Face of Electioneering*, 3rd ed. (New York: Oxford University Press, 2012); David Karol, "Party Activists, Interest Groups, and Polarization in American Politics," in *American Gridlock: The Sources, Character, and Impact of Political Polarization*, ed. James A. Thurber and Antoine Yoshinaka, 68–85 (New York: Cambridge University Press, 2015).

24. Adam Bonica, "Ideology and Interests in the Political Marketplace," *American Journal of Political Science* 57, no. 2 (2013): 294–311; Emilie M. Hafner-Burton, Thad Kousser, and David G. Victor, "Lobbying at the Water's Edge: Corporations

and Congressional Foreign Policy Lobbying" (ILAR working paper, San Diego, CA, 2015).

25. Wildavsky, "The Two Presidencies"; Karol, "Party Activists, Interest Groups, and Polarization in American Politics."

26. B. Dan Wood, *The Myth of Presidential Representation* (New York: Cambridge University Press, 2009); Douglas L. Kriner and Andrew Reeves, "Presidential Particularism and Divide-the-Dollar Politics," *American Political Science Review* 109, no. 1 (2015): 155–171.

27. Stephen D. Krasner, *Defending the National Interest: Raw Materials Investments and U.S. Foreign Policy* (Princeton, NJ: Princeton University Press, 1978); James Meernik and Elizabeth Oldmixon, "The President, the Senate, and the Costs of Internationalism," *Foreign Policy Analysis* 4, no. 2 (2008): 187–206; William G. Howell, Saul P. Jackman, and Jon C. Rogowski, *The Wartime President* (Chicago: University of Chicago Press, 2013).

28. David R. Mayhew, *Congress: The Electoral Connection* (New Haven, CT: Yale University Press, 1974); Roger H. Davidson et al., *Congress and Its Members*, 16th ed. (Thousand Oaks, CA: CQ Press, 2018).

29. Richard F. Fenno Jr., *Congressmen in Committees* (Boston: Little, Brown and Company, 1973); James M. Lindsay, *Congress and the Politics of U.S. Foreign Policy* (Baltimore: Johns Hopkins University Press, 1994); James M. McCormick and Neil J. Mitchell, "Commitments, Transnational Interests, and Congress: Who Joins the Congressional Human Rights Caucus?" *Political Research Quarterly* 60, no. 4 (2007): 579–592; Ralph G. Carter and James M. Scott, *Choosing to Lead: Understanding Congressional Foreign Policy Entrepreneurs* (Durham, NC: Duke University Press, 2009); Ellen A. Cutrone and Benjamin O. Fordham, "Commerce and Imagination: The Sources of Concern about International Human Rights in the U.S. Congress," *International Studies Quarterly* 54, no. 3 (2010): 633–655; Sarah B. Snyder, *From Selma to Moscow: How Human Rights Activists Transformed U.S. Foreign Policy* (New York: Columbia University Press, 2018); Lantis, *Foreign Policy Advocacy and Entrepreneurship*.

30. Tama, *Bipartisanship and US Foreign Policy*.

31. I thank Harrison Brooks, James Bryan, Gabriel Exposito, and Balazs Martonffy for their excellent work on the data sets.

32. David R. Mayhew, *Divided We Govern: Party Control, Lawmaking, and Investigations, 1946–2002*, 2nd ed. (New Haven, CT: Yale University Press, 2005), 202–203.

33. CQ lists these key votes in a section of its annual publication, CQ Almanac. See, for instance, CQ Roll Call, *CQ Almanac 2019: 116th Congress*, 1st Session (Washington, DC: CQ Press, 2021).

34. Prins and Marshall, "Congressional Support of the President"; DeLaet and Scott, "Treaty-Making and Partisan Politics"; Kupchan and Trubowitz, "Dead Center"; Snyder, Shapiro, and Bloch-Elkon, "Free Hand Abroad, Divide and Rule at Home"; Jeong and Quirk, "Division at the Water's Edge."

35. I classified a vote as a foreign policy vote if the Congressional Research Service categorized the legislation in one of the following policy areas: armed forces and national security, international affairs, foreign trade and international finance, or immigration. Since many of the immigration votes concerned domestic as well as international issues, I exclude immigration from the foreign policy category in some alternative specifications presented in the printed appendix to this chapter.

36. Vote Smart key votes are available at https://justfacts.votesmart.org/bills (last accessed November 17, 2022).

37. Nolan McCarty, *Polarization: What Everyone Needs to Know* (New York: Oxford University Press, 2019); Ezra Klein, *Why We're Polarized* (New York: Simon & Schuster, 2020); Abramowitz, *The Great Alignment*.

38. Mayhew, *Divided We Govern*, 222; Harbridge, *Is Bipartisanship Dead?*, 75.

39. If an article lacks a box score, the data set includes the votes mentioned in the body of the article.

40. Coding votes from every third year, rather than every other year or every fourth year, greatly reduces the possibility that selection bias could be introduced by the overrepresentation or underrepresentation of presidential or congressional election years in the data set. Unfortunately, CQ Almanac stopped publishing these types of articles after 2017. I therefore replaced what would have been the 2019 data with votes highlighted by CQ Almanac in 2017, to ensure that the years included in the data set were temporally balanced across the thirty-year period. The result is that the data set includes votes from 1992, 1995, 1998, 2001, 2004, 2007, 2010, 2013, 2016, and 2017.

41. All differences highlighted in the chapter are statistically significant at the 5 percent level unless otherwise noted.

42. Harbridge, *Is Bipartisanship Dead?*, 75.

43. Baumgartner et al., *Lobbying and Policy Change*. Indeed, salience is one of the criteria used by CQ and Vote Smart to identify key votes. One of the CQ criteria for identifying a key vote is that it represents a matter of major controversy, while one of the Vote Smart criteria for identifying a key vote is that it received media attention.

44. I do not present cross-partisanship data for the other CQ Almanac votes since it is difficult to determine whether a voice vote involved cross-partisanship.

45. Wildavsky, "The Two Presidencies"; Fleisher et al., "The Demise of the Two Presidencies"; Canes-Wrone, Howell, and Lewis, "Toward a Broader Understanding of Presidential Power."

46. Senate Vote 110 and House Vote 72 on American Rescue Plan Act of 2021, H.R. 1319, 117th Cong. (2021); Senate Vote 134 on the Confirmation of Ketanji Brown Jackson as an Associate Justice of the Supreme Court of the United States, 117th Cong. (2022); Senate Vote 325 and House Vote 420 on Inflation Reduction Act of 2022, H.R. 5376, 117th Cong. (2022).

47. Senate Vote 314 and House Vote 369 on Infrastructure Investment and Jobs Act, H.R. 3684, 117th Cong. (2021) ; House Vote 373 and Senate Vote 356 on Respect for Marriage Act, H.R. 8404, 117th Cong. (2022).

48. Haris Alic, "49 Senate Republicans Pledge to Reject Any New Iran Deal Negotiated by Biden," *Washington Times*, March 14, 2022.

49. Catie Edmondson and Emily Cochrane, "House Passes $40 Billion More in Ukraine Aid, with Few Questions Asked," *New York Times*, May 10, 2022; Karoun Demirjian, "Senate Votes to Approve NATO Membership for Sweden and Finland," *New York Times*, August 3, 2022.

50. Jacob Knutson, "McConnell, 25 Senate Republicans Say They Support Pelosi's Taiwan Trip," *Axios*, August 2, 2022.

51. Andrew Desiderio, "U.S.-Taiwan Bill Sails through Senate Panel Despite White House Misgivings," Politico, September 14, 2022.

52. House Vote 172 on To Repeal the Authorization for Use of Military Force against Iraq Resolution of 2002, H.R. 256, 117th Cong. (2021).

53. James Bryan and Jordan Tama, "The Prevalence of Bipartisanship in U.S. Foreign Policy: An Analysis of Important Congressional Votes," *International Politics* 59, no. 5 (2022): 874–898.

54. Peter Trubowitz, *Politics and Strategy: Partisan Ambition and American Statecraft* (Princeton, NJ: Princeton University Press, 2011); Gustavo A. Flores-Macías and Sarah E. Kreps, "Political Parties at War: A Study of American War Finance, 1789–2010," *American Political Science Review* 107, no. 4 (2013): 833–848; Timothy Hildebrandt et al., "The Domestic Politics of Humanitarian Intervention: Public Opinion, Partisanship, and Ideology," *Foreign Policy Analysis* 9, no. 3 (2013): 243–266; Douglas L. Kriner and Francis X. Shen, "Conscription, Inequality, and Partisan Support for War," *Journal of Conflict Resolution* 60, no. 8 (2016): 1419–1445; Howell and Pevehouse, *While Dangers Gather*.

55. Howell and Pevehouse, *While Dangers Gather*; Kriner, *After the Rubicon*; Fowler, *Watchdogs on the Hill*; Kriner and Schickler, "The Resilience of Separation of Powers?"

56. Stephen Chaudoin, Helen V. Milner, and Dustin Tingley, "Down But Not Out: A Liberal International American Foreign Policy," in *Chaos in the Liberal Order: The Trump Presidency and International Politics in the Twenty-First Century*, ed. Robert Jervis, Francis J. Gavin, Joshua Rovner and Diane N. Labrosse (New York: Columbia University Press, 2018), 61–97; G. John Ikenberry, *A World Safe for Democracy: Liberal Internationalism and the Crises of Global Order* (New Haven, CT: Yale University Press, 2020).

57. I thank one of the anonymous peer reviewers of the chapter for this suggestion.

CHAPTER FOUR

Cassandra's Reward

The Electoral Benefits of Early Opposition to an Unpopular War

Benjamin O. Fordham

As Sarah Kreps and Douglas Kriner point out in the opening chapter of this volume, members of Congress provide the most important political check on the president's ability to wage war. They have a variety of tools for increasing the political cost to the president for using military force. Whether members of Congress are actually willing to use these tools depends in part on how they think the public will respond at the polls. Will their constituents reward them if they agree with their criticisms, or punish them if they do not? These political concerns are not members' only motive but they are a systematic and important one. The expected political rewards for criticizing the president's policy are crucial not only for determining what members of Congress will do but also for shaping whether the president contemplates such a military action in the first place.

The main means through which Congress can restrain the president is its criticism of wars that the public has come to see as excessively costly or misguided. We need not observe frequent Congressional criticism of presidential uses of military force for this mechanism to work. The expectation that such a war will be the target of costly political attacks from the opposition party should be enough to make the president cautious. Indeed, previous research has shown that divided government and the strength of legislative opposition restrain presidents in the international arena.[1] This institutional constraint is the basis for claims that democracies have wartime advantages, because it contributes to meaningful debate that can check executive decision making. Such debate should expose foolhardy plans for military action and push the executive toward those that are wise and winnable.[2]

Unfortunately, the caution this mechanism has induced has not been enough to avoid costly and unpopular military adventures in Korea, Vietnam, Iraq, Afghanistan, and elsewhere since 1945. In crucial instances, such as the decisions to advance to the Yalu River in 1950, to commit larger combat forces to Vietnam in 1965, or to invade Iraq in 2003, the executive branch has brushed aside important questions about whether these actions were necessary and about how costly they might become. Shared but faulty assumptions or advisers' desire to support the president and maintain internal unity, among other things, have hampered deliberations within the executive branch. Ideally, public debate involving their congressional opponents should force the president and his advisers to answer the hard questions before taking military action. If legislators can expect sufficiently large electoral rewards for opposing an unsuccessful use of force, then even some members of the president's party might choose this course. It could create an instance of the anti-presidential bipartisanship that Jordan Tama discusses in his contribution to this volume. It would increase presidential caution even beyond the level we would expect because of fear of the consequences of an unsuccessful operation after the fact.

While such an outcome would be nice, this chapter offers evidence that members of Congress can generally expect little electoral reward for opposing a costly military operation before it is launched. In the pages that follow, I will revisit the debate that preceded the March 2003 US invasion of Iraq and the elections that followed. The rewards for early opposition to a war that later becomes unpopular should actually be realized in this case. The war was politically salient enough to make a difference in elections. There was also ample time for debate before the war began. Both the House and Senate debated and passed a resolution authorizing the use of force five months before the invasion, and the Bush administration's intentions were apparent well before that. There were good reasons to question both the premises of the war and its prospects for success. Even Army Chief of Staff Eric Shinseki raised questions about whether the force assembled for the invasion was sufficient to occupy the country after the war, a position that would usher him into early retirement.[3] Finally, many of the prewar concerns about the invasion were ultimately borne out—including Shinseki's doubts about the adequacy of the occupation force—and it was widely unpopular by 2005. If there are ever electoral benefits for opposing military action before the war began, they should be apparent in this case.

Unfortunately, the evidence offers little support for the existence of these electoral incentives. For members of the opposition party, speaking out against a war that they believe will be unsuccessful provides few electoral rewards. Indeed, there appear to be perverse incentives to keep silent until disaster actually ensues. Members of Congress who turned against the war only after it became unpopular did as well or better at the polls as members who spoke out before the invasion. In the longer term, the electoral benefits of opposing the war accrued to the opposition party as a whole rather than to individual members who spoke out against it, giving them little incentive to take the risk of moving early. Knowing that the opposition party will capitalize on a military failure should still lead presidents to be careful in using military force. The track record of disasters like those in Iraq, Afghanistan, and Vietnam suggests that executive caution is not always enough. Moreover, political incentives that reduce serious debate deprive the United States of other theoretical advantages that a democracy should enjoy in international conflict.

Why Preconflict Opposition Matters

The opposition party's freedom to dissent from government policy in a democracy has important implications for crisis bargaining and military conflict. These extend beyond the president's anticipation of congressional criticism over a costly and unpopular war. Opposition can also directly rein in costly military adventures after they begin.[4] United States military casualties directly affect presidential reelection.[5] They can also damage the electoral fortunes of the president's party in Congress and motivate further congressional opposition, especially from members whose districts are home to those killed or wounded.[6]

These mechanisms all concern congressional opposition after a war has become unpopular, but congressional action after the executive has issued a military threat yet before a conflict begins is also theoretically important. Presidents often use force without informing Congress in advance, allowing little or no time for debate, but this is not always the case. There was substantial time for public debate before the most serious

American military adventures since World War II, including the interventions in Vietnam in 1964–1965, Kuwait in 1991, Afghanistan in 2001, and Iraq in 2003. In cases like these, the positions that members of the opposition party take make a difference. If they do not dissent, wider public debate is unlikely. Research on the media finds that coverage of the debate is indexed to the conflict among public officials, especially members of Congress.[7] Democratic opposition should help expose flawed policies that might have gone unchallenged in an autocracy, making military success more likely or at least reducing the chance of a resounding failure.[8]

The opposition party also plays a theoretically important role in signaling resolve during a crisis, affecting the probability of avoiding war. Kenneth Schultz's account of international crisis bargaining suggests that opposition support for the executive's threats sends a powerful signal to international adversaries that the government is not bluffing. This added credibility makes a peaceful crisis outcome more likely.[9]

Electoral incentives are sure to influence opposition party legislators' decisions to support or oppose a prospective military action. Schultz's account of these incentives in *Democracies and Coercive Diplomacy* is especially careful and explicit. He contends that electoral incentives suggest support for military actions that the opposition expects the public to view favorably, those in which "the costs of war are anticipated to be low relative to the stakes of the dispute." On the other hand, "when military and political conditions are such that the resort to force would be politically undesirable . . . domestic opposition parties have incentives to publicly oppose the use of force."[10] The logic behind these incentives is straightforward: it pays to be right. "It makes sense to assume that voters reward opposition parties that either support successful policies or oppose unsuccessful policies, and they punish parties that oppose successful policies."[11]

Schultz is not alone in his understanding of the electoral incentives for opposing an unwise military commitment. In their work on the politics of military conflict, Jack Levy and William Mabe criticize many of Schultz's other assumptions, but they share his views on this point. "If the opposition expects that war will be unsuccessful and unpopular, it will go on record opposing war in order to exploit the resulting political discontent and improve its future electoral prospects."[12] Other scholars considering the role of the political opposition in a democracy have suggested similar mechanisms.[13]

This account of electoral incentives is certainly plausible, and Schultz provides empirical support in *Democracy and Coercive Diplomacy* for hypotheses about international conflict that follow from it using data on 1,800 crises involving 170 states from 1816 through 1984.[14] Nevertheless, existing research raises some uncomfortable questions about whether electoral incentives have actually operated this way in the United States since 1945, where the president has rarely had trouble getting support from the opposition party for prospective military action. Many observers note that Congress rarely refuses executive demands for support when it contemplates military action, usually providing it without much debate.[15] Even scholars who argue that Congress is more influential than its silence suggests still acknowledge that it is usually reactive and deferential when it comes to prospective uses of force.[16] This pattern may be partly due to presidents' selection of military efforts that are highly likely to succeed, but Congress has also acquiesced in cases where there was ample reason to worry about the outcome before the operation was launched, as there was before the wars in Vietnam and Iraq.

Whether the electoral incentives for opposition work as assumed in the United States matters, even if the assumptions are correct for other democracies. The absence of political rewards for early opposition to wars that become unpopular would undermine genuine public deliberation, making support appear more widespread than it actually is. The lack of these incentives for real preconflict debate would also mean that the behavior of the opposition party would send no reliable signal to international adversaries, depriving the United States of a bargaining advantage that other democracies enjoy. In both ways, it would put the country at greater risk for costly and unsuccessful military operations. The track record of major American military interventions since World War II, and the debates leading up to them, does not rule out this unfortunate possibility. The United States has become involved in several unsuccessful and unpopular military adventures, often with overwhelming public and congressional support at the outset.

There is evidence that members of Congress who oppose declarations of war are disproportionately likely to retire or be punished at the polls afterward, at least in the case of successful wars.[17] By contrast, the claim that members of the opposition party who speak out against unsuccessful military adventures at the outset get a corresponding reward at the polls has received less scrutiny. Examining the electoral consequences of the Vietnam War, Scott Gartner, Gary Segura, and Bethany Barratt found that voters punished incumbents for local casualties but that these incumbents could shield themselves from this effect by opposing the war.[18]

However, because the 1964 Gulf of Tonkin Resolution passed 416–0 in the House and 88–2 in the Senate, it is clear that the incumbents who gained this advantage nearly all did so in spite of supporting the war at the outset. Research on congressional elections during the Iraq War generally finds a similar pattern: members of the incumbent party may be punished for local casualties, especially if they supported the war, but members of the opposition party get no corresponding reward even if they initially opposed the conflict.[19]

The paucity of empirical support for the conjecture that members of the opposition party will be rewarded for opposing an unsuccessful military operation make sense when one considers the practical problems of taking this position in the postwar United States. For one thing, while some military operations have failed, the overwhelming military power of the United States has meant that these failures have rarely happened quickly. The US military has faced few opponents who could promptly defeat it since 1945. Opponents of the war must thus survive politically for some time before receiving any electoral reward for anticipating the eventual failure. Another problem is that reaping any political benefit from a national failure is fraught. Outspoken opponents of the war may be branded as unpatriotic, blamed for undermining public support, and perhaps even charged with contributing to the military defeat. From an electoral standpoint, remaining silent until the war actually becomes unpopular might be a safer course. The absence of an electoral reward for opposing an unsuccessful military action in its early stages does not mean there will be no such opposition, but it does remove a strong incentive for it.

Research Design

While previous research has found little evidence of an electoral reward for anticipating a war's unpopularity, this outcome has not been the primary focus of that research. It remains possible that a more thorough search might turn up evidence of the expected reward, at least under favorable circumstances. For reasons I noted at the outset, the Iraq War is a case where these electoral rewards ought to be realized. It was highly salient. There was ample opportunity to speak out before the invasion. There was plenty of information raising doubts about the reasons for the war and its likely course. Most importantly, the war really did become unpopular. While electoral rewards for opposing the war should be apparent in this case, assessing them raises several important research design issues.

Electoral Rewards for Opposition to the Iraq War

The Iraq War was a significant issue in at least three elections: 2002, 2004, and 2006. I will focus on the fortunes of incumbent House Democrats in these three elections.[20] These are not the only elections in which opposition to the war before it began was potentially relevant, but they have some important research design advantages. I have identical expectations about Senate Democrats running for reelection, but there are too few of these contests in each election cycle to permit a meaningful quantitative analysis. The war certainly affected Republican electoral prospects, but the theoretically important expectations about electoral rewards concern the opposition party. Similarly, candidates challenging incumbents might have benefited from opposition to the war before it was launched but they occupied a different political position than did incumbents holding office during the prewar debates of late 2002 and early 2003. Their positions do not bear as directly on the theoretical stakes as those of incumbents.

The dependent variable in the analysis that follows is the incumbent's share of all non-spoiled ballots, including those cast for third-party candidates and those where the voter did not select a candidate in the congressional race. The central theoretical issue here is whether voters reward or punish incumbents for their position on the war. They might do so by voting for the candidate of the other major party, but they might instead support a third-party candidate or decline to indicate a preference in the congressional race even though they voted in other races on the ballot. These alternative choices are important because a substantial number of incumbents ran unopposed, or at least faced no major party opponent. Moreover, opposition to the war was especially strong among those on the left and right ideological fringes of American politics. These voters might have preferred to express their approval or disapproval of the incumbent's position through some means other than supporting the other major party candidate, who might be quite ideologically distant from them. An analysis restricted to the incumbent's share of the two-party vote, which is included in the online appendix, does not change the results reported here in any substantively important way.[21]

I will examine the three elections separately because the implications of opposing the war were different in each one. An electoral reward was unlikely in 2002 because the war had not yet begun and the prospect of it was generally popular with the public. It is possible that opponents of military action paid a political price that fall. If the punishment for taking a position against the war was sufficiently large, it could cancel out any reward in later elections when the conflict became unpopular. Electoral benefits for early opposition to the war are increasingly likely in 2004 and 2006, as the war became steadily less popular. There is ample evidence that the war contributed to the Democratic electoral success in 2006, when Democrats gained control for the House for the first time since 1994.[22] The question here is whether Democrats who had opposed the war before it began reaped a disproportionate share these electoral rewards.

The fact that the war affected at least two elections after it began raises the question of whether Democrats who had initially supported the war, or who had remained silent, could reap a political reward by turning against the war after it became unpopular. Douglas Kriner and Francis Shen found that House members from districts that suffered high casualties became increasingly critical of the war.[23] The ability of members to change their positions in order to protect themselves from punishment at the polls is theoretically important because it would further reduce the electoral incentive to oppose the war before it began. Why should members risk punishment for opposing a potentially popular military action when they could simply change positions on the matter if and when things go wrong? Such a shift would not be difficult to explain to voters. After all, members of Congress are genuinely unlikely to have any influence over military strategy or full information about conditions on the ground in advance of the conflict, considerations that could readily excuse their change of mind.

Testing a Negative Proposition

Another important research design issue arises from the fact that the conjecture tested here is a negative one. I suspect that opposition members of Congress received little or no electoral reward for opposing a war that later became unpopular. This exercise is interesting because there is a substantial and important body of theory that assumes the existence of these electoral rewards. An equally plausible but less candid way of framing this chapter would be as a test of those affirmative claims about electoral incentives. The research design issue is that conventional hypothesis testing assumes the null to be true, then evaluates whether the evidence provides grounds for rejecting it. Given the high bar for rejecting the null, persuasive evidence requires that the scales be rebalanced in favor of the claim that there are some electoral rewards for early opposition to a war that goes badly. I will do this re-balancing in several ways.

First, to account for imperfections in indicators of House members' positions on the war, I will examine several of them. The indicator of prewar opposition most widely used is the vote on final passage of the resolution authorizing the use of force in Iraq, approved in the House by a vote of 297–133 on October 10, 2002. While this highly visible vote is a good indicator of members' positions on the war, it lacks nuance. In fact, many members sought to qualify their stance on the war resolution in ways that could be electorally relevant. I will consider two additional indicators that better capture these efforts to shade their position.

A second indicator uses the other three votes taken during the debate on the authorization resolution. Each of these were on measures intended to qualify the resolution's support for the use of force to some extent. The first, offered by Dennis Kucinich (D-OH), was a motion to recommit the measure to committee with instructions to provide more information on several issues, including the likely cost of a war. It was rejected 101–325. The second was a substitute amendment offered by Barbara Lee (D-CA) that would have urged the administration to seek a peaceful resolution to the dispute with Iraq. It was rejected 72–355. The third, which garnered the most support, was a substitute by John Spratt (D-SC) that would have required another vote of support from Congress if the administration was unable to secure a resolution from the United Nations Security Council authorizing the use of force. It failed 155–270. The proportion of the four votes on which they opposed the war offers a more nuanced indicator of member's positions.

A third indicator uses floor speeches on the war. Counts of the number of prowar and antiwar speeches each member gave provide another indicator of the intensity of their position on the war.[24] These are useful because members had more control over the number and content of their speeches than they did over the measures that came up for a roll call vote. Of course, the House floor is not the only venue where members could take a public position, but it was an especially important one. Members who spoke out on the war in the media were likely to have done so on the floor as well. To measure positions on the war, I coded all the floor speeches that mentioned "Iraq" between September 1, 2002, and the beginning of the war on March 19, 2003, according to whether they broadly supported or opposed military action. The coding rules were intended to mirror those developed by Douglas Kriner and Francis Shen to examine speeches given after the war began.[25] Because the war was clearly on the horizon during this debate, the coding process was not difficult. Some members refrained from taking an explicit position on the anticipated use of military force but even most of these offered considerations that weighed for or against it. The speeches that took no position at all were mainly those concerning procedures for conducting the debate.

In addition to considering more than one indicator of members' prewar positions, I will also examine circumstances where electoral rewards were especially likely. Previous research suggests that local casualties had a strong and negative impact on local views of both the wars in Iraq and in Vietnam. Even if other issues overshadowed the war in the rest of the country, it might still matter in these areas. I will evaluate whether high-casualty districts gave greater rewards to members of Congress who had opposed the war from the beginning. I will also consider whether electoral rewards were more apparent in electorally close districts, and whether the few Republicans who opposed the war before it began were able to escape the electoral punishment meted out to their party after the war became unpopular.

The Endogeneity of Election Results and Prewar Position-Taking

The very notion of an electoral incentive assumes that politicians can anticipate the public's response to positions they take on salient issues like the Iraq War. Election results and position-taking might be endogenous for reasons less cynical than a self-conscious effort to pander to voter preferences. The endogeneity might also arise from a process in which districts with many activists concerned about the issue persuade their representative of the merits of their position, then support that representative at the polls, and perhaps in other electorally useful ways.

Regardless of the precise process, endogeneity biases estimates of the effect of members' positions on election results. For electoral punishments, estimates should be biased downward. Members will tend not to take positions that antagonize their voters, or they may only do so when they have reason to believe electoral punishment will be slight. By the same logic, estimates of electoral rewards will be biased upward. Members' strategic pursuit of electoral advantage will make these rewards appear widespread, especially when members have reason to think the rewards could be large. These biases can be reduced by including variables indicating characteristics of the district correlated with the strategic behavior, but they cannot be entirely eliminated because members have more information about the likely responses of their constituents than these variables contain. While important, this source of bias is not as serious a problem in this analysis as it might appear. Because the conjecture tested here is that these rewards are small or non-existent, the upward bias in estimates of them makes the test more difficult. Like the steps discussed in the preceding subsection, it helps rebalance the analysis in favor of finding some electoral benefits.

Which members should have expected the greatest electoral rewards from early opposition to the war? The most obvious group are those whose constituents were likely to turn against the war. With the benefit of hindsight, we know that Democrats in the general public were more likely to follow this course. The Iraq War was an intensely polarizing event. Democratic approval of the war was between 50 and 60 percent at the time it began but fell to less than 20 percent by the end of the Bush Administration, a drop of roughly forty percentage points. On the other hand, Republican support began at around 90 percent at the start of the war and fell off to around 75 percent by the end of the Bush Administration, a drop of only about fifteen points.[26] Growing partisan polarization was nothing new in 2002. Professional politicians should have anticipated this pattern, even if they may have been surprised by its extent. If so, members from more Democratic districts should tend to oppose the war before it began. The models of the electoral effect of opposition to the war will include the most recent presidential vote in each district to help control for the effect of strategic position-taking.[27]

Members' expectations about the competitiveness of their districts could also influence their willingness to take a risky position. While there were ample reasons to think the war might be a mistake before it began, no one could be sure precisely how it would go. Its initial popularity made speaking out against it a risky choice, just as the potential for substantial American casualties made full-throated support dicey. Members who held relatively safe seats should have been more likely to take a strong position on the war. Given baseline partisan mistrust of the Bush Administration among Democrats, this position was more likely to be negative than positive among these members. To capture electoral safety or precarity, the models in the next section will include variables indicating the proportion of the vote the member received in the last election and whether they were running unopposed in the election being analyzed.

Empirical Analysis

To assess whether voters rewarded House members for their prewar positions, I will analyze election results from 2002, 2004, and 2006. Previous research indicates that the Iraq War substantially affected the congressional elections in 2006.[28] There is evidence that they also affected presidential election results in 2004, though obviously not enough to unseat the incumbent.[29] While the course of the war certainly appears to have affected election outcomes, the question of whether prewar position-taking had any effect is somewhat different.

I begin with the 2002 election, which took place less than a month after Congress passed the resolution authorizing the use of force. At the time, most of the public approved of the impending invasion of Iraq. Gallup polls from the fall of 2002 consistently found greater than 50 percent support in the general public. The poll closest to the election (November 8–10) found 59 percent in favor, 35 percent opposed and 6 percent with no opinion.[30] If voters punished House members for taking antiwar positions, it should have happened in this election. As I noted earlier, if the electoral backlash is large enough, it could eliminate the incentive for prewar opposition even for members who believed the war would later become unpopular. At the same time, strategic behavior by members should limit the extent to which we actually observe electoral punishment.

Table 4.1 presents the results of four OLS regression models of incumbent Democrats' share of the vote in November 2002 House races, each using a different indicator of the member's stance on the war. They also include three controls for the partisan character of the district and the competitiveness of the race: district partisanship as captured by the 2000 presidential vote, the member's share of the vote in the 2000 election, and a dummy indicating whether the member had no major party opposition. These should reduce bias arising from the endogeneity of position-taking and election results, though they will not entirely eliminate it. Estimates of electoral punishment, expected in this election, will be biased downward. Those of electoral rewards in subsequent elections will be biased upward.

The results underscore the importance of strategic position-taking on the war by Democrats. Contrary to the expectation of electoral punishment in 2002, Democrats who opposed the war did better at the polls than those who did not. This result holds using two of the three indicators of prewar positions. Members who gave three antiwar speeches, a number that placed them among the most vocal critics of the war, received a vote share roughly 4.3 percentage points higher than Democrats who gave no antiwar speeches at all. Prowar speeches had no apparent effect. Those who voted against the war authorization resolution received roughly 3.8 percentage points more support at the polls than those who voted for

TABLE 4.1 **Democratic House Incumbent Vote Share in the 2002 Elections**

	Model 1	Model 2	Model 3	Model 4
Vote against final passage of war authorization resolution		0.04* (0.01)		
Proportion of votes against war in 2002 authorization debate			0.04 (0.02)	
Antiwar speeches prior to the 2002 election (log)				0.03* (0.01)
Prowar speeches prior to the 2002 election (log)				−0.01 (0.02)
Democratic share of 2000 presidential vote in district	0.07 (0.05)	0.02 (0.06)	0.03 (0.06)	0.02 (0.06)
Incumbent vote share in 2000 election	0.50* (0.06)	0.49* (0.05)	0.49* (0.05)	0.50* (0.05)
No Republican opponent	0.17* (0.02)	0.17* (0.02)	0.17* (0.02)	0.17* (0.02)
Constant	0.27* (0.04)	0.28* (0.04)	0.28* (0.04)	0.28* (0.04)
Observations	188	187	188	188
R-squared	0.61	0.63	0.62	0.63
Adjusted R-squared	0.61	0.62	0.61	0.62

Note: The dependent variable is the proportion of the total vote the incumbent received. Standard errors in parentheses.
* $p<0.05$

it. Given the general popularity of the war at the time, the most sensible way to interpret the results is that Democrats who opposed the war came from districts where voters did not share the majority view. These Democratic incumbents probably knew their constituents would support their antiwar position.

The bottom line is that Democrats who opposed the war during the fall 2002 debate over it escaped electoral punishment that year. Perhaps mainly due to strategic position-taking, this potential barrier to receiving electoral rewards once the war became unpopular does not appear to have been a problem. It is worth emphasizing that the electoral rewards antiwar representatives appear to have reaped in 2002 are not the ones that are most theoretically important. These should come from anticipating the subsequent unpopularity of the war. At the time of the 2002 election, the invasion of Iraq had not yet happened and remained prospectively popular.

If there are rewards for correctly anticipating the disastrous course of the war, they should begin to appear during the 2004 election. After more than a year of searching, no weapons of mass destruction had been found. It was clear well before the election that the United States faced a growing insurgency in Iraq. After the killing of four armed contractors in the city of Fallujah in March 2004, the US military proved unable to regain control of the city. It would not finally do so until mounting a major military operation in November. The Abu Ghraib torture scandal broke in April 2004, making a mockery of the humanitarian justifications for the war. Even though George W. Bush was reelected as president, the public as a whole was about evenly divided on the war, and the trends were clearly unfavorable.[31] Among Democrats, the decline was especially steep. Around 50 percent of them had supported the war in March 2003, but less than 20 percent did so by mid-2004.[32] Members from heavily Democratic districts—those most likely to have opposed the war before it began—should have reaped an electoral benefit. The central question here is whether they did, and whether these benefits exceeded those given to members who spoke out against the war only after it became unpopular.

Table 4.2 presents the results of six models of Democratic incumbent vote shares in the 2004 election. They provide no evidence that Democrats were rewarded for taking an antiwar position in the prewar period. Neither the authorization votes nor speeches concerning the war in the period between September 1, 2002 and the start of the conflict on March 19, 2003 appear to have affected the results of the 2004 election. In spite of the incentive for members to strategically select themselves into the groups most likely to be rewarded for an antiwar position, and the fact that those who opposed the war had been rewarded in 2002, no comparable rewards accrued to these representatives in 2004.

Model 4 provides evidence that voters did punish members who had supported the war before it began. Members who gave three prowar speeches received 4.7 percent less at the polls than members who gave no prowar speeches. Unfortunately, because there was no reward for vocal opposition to the war, this is an incentive to remain silent, not to oppose the war. The results in model 6 are even worse from the standpoint of incentivizing prewar opposition, suggesting that prewar speeches both for and against the war had negative effects in the 2004 election. Because their prewar speeches influenced the 2002 result, which is included in the model here, they had an additional positive indirect effect of just over one percentage point through this independent variable. This was roughly the amount needed to offset the negative coefficient on prewar speeches in model 6 if members also gave three or more speeches against the war

TABLE 4.2 **Democratic House Incumbent Vote Share in the 2004 Elections**

	Model 1	Model 2	Model 3	Model 4	Model 5	Model 6
Vote against final passage of war authorization resolution		0.01 (0.01)				
Proportion of votes against war in 2002 authorization debate			0.003 (0.02)			
Antiwar speeches before war (log)				−0.01 (0.01)		−0.03* (0.01)
Prowar speeches before war (log)				−0.03* (0.01)		−0.04* (0.01)
Antiwar speeches after war began (log)					0.01 (0.01)	0.02* (0.01)
Democratic share of 2000 presidential vote in district	0.32* (0.04)	0.32* (0.05)	0.32* (0.05)	0.31* (0.05)	0.31* (0.05)	0.32* (0.05)
Incumbent vote share in 2002 election	0.25* (0.04)	0.27* (0.05)	0.27* (0.05)	0.26* (0.04)	0.25* (0.04)	0.26* (0.04)
No Republican Opponent	0.19* (0.02)	0.19* (0.02)	0.19* (0.02)	0.19* (0.02)	0.19* (0.02)	0.18* (0.02)
Constant	0.31* (0.03)	0.29* (0.04)	0.29* (0.04)	0.33* (0.04)	0.30* (0.03)	0.31* (0.04)
Observations	190	172	173	190	190	190
R-squared	0.67	0.67	0.67	0.68	0.68	0.69
Adjusted R-squared	0.66	0.66	0.66	0.67	0.67	0.68

Note: The dependent variable is the proportion of the total vote the incumbent received. Standard errors in parentheses.
* $p<0.05$

after it began. Members who had opposed the war before it began were not really punished in 2004, but they were not rewarded either.

The biggest electoral winners were members who had stayed silent before the war but spoke out against it after it became unpopular. Members who gave three antiwar speeches after the invasion could expect a 2.2 percentage point boost at the polls in 2004. This effect is only evident in model 6, which controls for prewar position-taking. Not surprisingly, most members who had opposed the war before it began also opposed it after it became unpopular. They did not enjoy the benefit accorded members who turned against it later. If they had, then the coefficient on antiwar speeches after the war began would have been significant in model 5 as well as model 6. Voters apparently preferred Monday morning quarterbacks even if those who played on Sunday had won the game.

To clarify these effects, table 4.3 shows the expected vote share for otherwise identical Democrats based on the positions they took before the war and after it began. By far the most electorally advantageous course of action was to take no position on the war before it began, then turn against it as it became unpopular before the 2004 election. Democrats who opposed the war before it began did slightly better than those who had supported the war but only by a small and statistically insignificant margin. They could expect to receive nearly four percentage points less at the polls in 2004 than a member who did not turn against it until after the fighting began, though. This electorally optimal course of action had the considerable advantage of sparing the member the need to anticipate the course of the war in advance.

In view of these incentives, it is not surprising that a substantial number of Democrats who had been silent, or had supported the war before it began, turned against it during the 108th Congress. In all, forty Democratic House members who had given no antiwar speeches before the invasion gave at least one afterward. Of these converts, twenty-seven had given at least one prowar speech before hostilities started. The point here is not to question the sincerity of these changes of mind but to point out that their position was the one that made the most electoral sense. Voters should arguably have discounted newly emergent opposition to the war and rewarded those who had taken this position when it was less obviously advantageous. This is not what happened, though.

TABLE 4.3 **Expected Vote Share for Democratic Incumbents in 2004**

		Position after war began:	
		Three antiwar speeches	No antiwar speeches
Prewar position:	Three antiwar speeches	**67.2%** (65.6, 68.8)	**64.9%** (62.1, 67.8)
	No prewar speeches	**71.0%** (68.6, 73.3)	**68.7%** (66.7, 70.8)
	Three prowar speeches	**65.7%** (62.5, 68.8)	**63.5%** (60.2, 66.7)

Note: Upper and lower bounds of the 95-percent confidence interval are in parentheses. Predicted vote shares are based on model 6 in table 4.2. They assume the member had a Republican opponent, received the mean vote share for a Democrat in 2002, and were from a district where the Democratic presidential candidate received the mean vote share for a Democratic district in 2000.

Electoral rewards for opposition to the war were arguably even more likely in 2006 than in 2004. The war was broadly unpopular by this time. Every Gallup Poll on the issue taken in 2006 showed a majority of respondents felt the war had been a mistake.[33] Mounting US casualties contributed to this trend.[34] There is ample evidence that the war played a role in the Democratic electoral success that year, helping Democrats gain control of the House for the first time since 1994.[35] How much of this electoral reward did Democrats who had opposed the war before it began enjoy?

Table 4.4 presents the results of six models of Democratic incumbent vote shares in the 2006 election. They are identical to the models of the 2004 election in table 4.2. In this case, none of the variables indicating positions on the war is related to election outcomes, including speeches given during the 109th Congress that preceded the 2006 election. How should we interpret this result in light of the general consensus that the unpopularity of the war contributed to Democratic success that year? The most likely answer

TABLE 4.4 **Democratic House Incumbent Vote Share in the 2006 Elections**

	Model 1	Model 2	Model 3	Model 4	Model 5	Model 6
Vote against final passage of war authorization resolution		0.003 (0.01)				
Proportion of votes against war in 2002 authorization debate			−0.01 (0.02)			
Antiwar speeches before war (log)				0.003 (0.01)		0.005 (0.01)
Prowar speeches before war (log)				0.01 (0.02)		0.01 (0.02)
Antiwar speeches in 109th Congress (log)					−0.001 (0.005)	−0.002 (0.006)
Democratic share of 2004 presidential vote in district	0.17* (0.05)	0.15* (0.06)	0.17* (0.06)	0.18* (0.06)	0.17* (0.05)	0.18* (0.06)
Incumbent vote share in 2004 election	0.32* (0.06)	0.39* (0.06)	0.39* (0.06)	0.37* (0.06)	0.32* (0.06)	0.37* (0.06)
No Republican Opponent	0.16* (0.01)	0.13* (0.01)	0.13* (0.01)	0.14* (0.01)	0.16* (0.01)	0.14* (0.01)
Constant	0.37* (0.03)	0.33* (0.04)	0.33* (0.04)	0.33* (0.04)	0.37* (0.03)	0.33* (0.04)
Observations	191	155	156	172	191	172
R-squared	0.62	0.62	0.62	0.64	0.62	0.64
Adjusted R-squared	0.62	0.61	0.61	0.63	0.62	0.62

Note: The dependent variable is the proportion of the total vote the incumbent received. Standard errors in parentheses.
* $p<0.05$

is that the electoral advantage accrued to the party as a whole, not just to its most antiwar members. The Democratic Party was broadly antiwar by the 2006 election. Taking an antiwar position did not make a Democratic incumbent stand out to voters. During the 109th Congress, 64 percent of House Democrats gave at least one antiwar speech. By comparison, the party's position had been far less clear before the war began. Although the leadership had promised every member who wanted to address the House on the war resolution time to do so in the fall of 2002, only 32 percent of Democrats took the opportunity to speak against the war. Another 25 percent spoke in favor of it. A 43 percent plurality said nothing on the floor.

If opposition to the war advantaged the Democrats as a group in 2006, as appears to be the case, it would offer yet another electoral reason for individual Democratic legislators to avoid taking a position before the war began even if they thought it would probably go badly. Why take the individual risk when the eventual reward would accrue to the entire party? Even if there is some other explanation for the electoral irrelevance of antiwar speeches by individual House members, these results provide no support for the expectation that prewar opposition would provide an electoral payoff.

Were There Narrower Electoral Rewards?

The analysis presented thus far suggests that, in general, early Democratic opponents of the war received little electoral reward. However, it is possible that some narrower subsets of these members still benefited. First, members whose districts were especially strongly affected by the war might have been rewarded for opposing it before it began. There is ample evidence that casualties have an impact on both public opinion and electoral outcomes. Voters in districts where casualties were concentrated might have behaved differently. The models in table 4.5 seek to answer this question by estimating the effect of early positions on the war in districts where the population within a fifty-mile radius had suffered casualties at least one standard deviation above the mean for all congressional districts.

There is some evidence that these districts were more attentive to prewar positions, though most of it suggests the punishment of hawks rather than rewarding of doves. Prewar opposition has no statistically significant effect on vote share in either 2004 or 2006, though it comes close in the models using the proportion of votes against the war in the 2002 debate.

TABLE 4.5 **Democratic House Incumbent Vote Share in Districts with High Military Casualties**

	2004 Election				2006 Election			
Vote against final passage of war authorization resolution	0.02 (0.02)				0.001 (0.02)			
Proportion of votes against war in 2002 authorization debate		0.04 (0.02)				0.02 (0.04)		
Antiwar speeches before war (log)			−0.02 (0.01)	−0.01 (0.02)			0.03 (0.02)	0.04 (0.02)
Prowar speeches before war (log)			−0.05* (0.02)	−0.05* (0.02)			0.02 (0.02)	0.02 (0.02)
Antiwar speeches after war began (log)				−0.01 (0.01)				−0.002 (0.01)
Democratic share of preceding presidential vote in district	0.17* (0.07)	0.18* (0.07)	0.16* (0.07)	0.14 (0.08)	0.24* (0.10)	0.23* (0.10)	0.18 (0.09)	0.18 (0.09)
Incumbent vote share in last election	0.67* (0.07)	0.66* (0.07)	0.65* (0.07)	0.65* (0.07)	0.52* (0.12)	0.49* (0.13)	0.51* (0.10)	0.51* (0.10)
No Republican opponent	0.09* (0.02)	0.08* (0.02)	0.09* (0.02)	0.09* (0.02)	0.09* (0.02)	0.09* (0.02)	0.09* (0.02)	0.09* (0.02)
Constant	0.11 (0.06)	0.10 (0.05)	0.18* (0.06)	0.20* (0.06)	0.19* (0.08)	0.21* (0.08)	0.21* (0.07)	0.21* (0.07)
Observations	51	51	56	56	37	37	41	41
R-squared	0.83	0.83	0.80	0.80	0.75	0.75	0.79	0.79
Adjusted R-squared	0.81	0.82	0.78	0.78	0.72	0.72	0.76	0.75

Note: The dependent variable is the proportion of the total vote the incumbent received. Standard errors in parentheses.
* p<0.05

War supporters were punished in these districts, however, especially in 2004. Voters in high-casualty districts also gave no discernible reward to members who turned against the war only after it became unpopular. They appear to have discounted these statements and focused on prewar positions.

Voting patterns in these high-casualty districts in 2004 come closest to the assumptions that Schultz and other theorists make about the public response to war. Even here, however, several important caveats apply. Remaining silent before the war was still the best course of action. Early

TABLE 4.6 **Democratic House Incumbent Vote Share in Close Districts, 2002 Election**

	Model 1	Model 2	Model 3	Model 4
Vote against final passage of war authorization resolution		0.06* (0.03)		
Proportion of votes against war in 2002 authorization debate			0.10* (0.04)	
Antiwar speeches prior to the 2002 election (log)				0.09* (0.03)
Prowar speeches prior to the 2002 election (log)				0.02 (0.04)
Democratic share of 2000 presidential vote in district	0.07 (0.14)	−0.04 (0.14)	−0.09 (0.15)	−0.05 (0.14)
Incumbent vote share in 2000 election	0.27 (0.36)	0.03 (0.36)	0.04 (0.36)	0.09 (0.35)
No Republican opponent	0.20* (0.04)	0.22* (0.04)	0.22* (0.04)	0.19* (0.04)
Constant	0.39 (0.22)	0.54* (0.22)	0.55* (0.22)	0.50* (0.22)
Observations	52	52	52	52
R-squared	0.35	0.41	0.41	0.46
Adjusted R-squared	0.30	0.36	0.36	0.40

Note: The dependent variable is the proportion of the total vote the incumbent received. Close districts are those where the incumbent had received less than 60 percent of the vote in 2000. Standard errors in parentheses.
* $p<0.05$

supporters of the war were punished but those who spoke out against it received no comparable reward. Moreover, even this pattern was short-lived, applying in 2004 but not 2006.

Another possibility is that Democrats in electorally close districts were rewarded for early opposition. These members had more room for electoral improvement than did their copartisans who routinely won by large margins. Electoral benefits might thus be easier to discern. To test this possibility, I replicated the analysis of the 2002, 2004, and 2006 elections in tables 4.1, 4.2, and 4.4 using a sample restricted to districts where the incumbent had won with less than 60 percent of the vote. Prewar opposition had statistically significant effects only in the 2002 election. Table 4.6 presents the results. Results for the other two elections can be found in the online appendix.

The electoral rewards Democratic incumbents received in close districts in 2002 were larger than those evident among all Democrats. Those who voted against the war resolution did 6.3 percentage points better than those who did not. Those who consistently voted against the war during

TABLE 4.7. **Republican House Incumbent Vote Share in 2004 and 2006**

	2004 Election			2006 Election		
Vote against final passage of war authorization resolution	0.05 (0.03)			−0.04 (0.03)		
Proportion of votes against war in 2002 authorization debate		0.11 (0.06)			−0.07 (0.06)	
Antiwar speeches before war (log)			0.04 (0.02)	0.01 (0.03)		−0.01 (0.02)	−0.03 (0.03)
Prowar speeches before war (log)			−0.003 (0.01)	−0.004 (0.01)		0.001 (0.01)	0.001 (0.01)
Antiwar speeches after war began (log)				0.02 (0.02)			0.02 (0.02)
Democratic share of preceding presidential vote in district	−0.21* (0.06)	−0.20* (0.07)	−0.20* (0.06)	−0.19* (0.06)	−0.43* (0.08)	−0.48* (0.07)	−0.48* (0.07)
Incumbent vote share in last election	0.25* (0.04)	0.25* (0.04)	0.24* (0.04)	0.24* (0.04)	0.26* (0.05)	0.22* (0.04)	0.22* (0.04)
No Democratic opponent	0.22* (0.01)	0.22* (0.01)	0.24* (0.01)	0.24* (0.01)	0.21* (0.02)	0.21* (0.02)	0.22* (0.04)
Constant	0.55* (0.04)	0.55* (0.04)	0.56* (0.04)	0.55* (0.04)	0.59* (0.06)	0.64* (0.05)	0.63* (0.05)
Observations	175	175	208	208	153	182	182
R-squared	0.72	0.72	0.74	0.74	0.63	0.62	0.62
Adjusted R-squared	0.72	0.72	0.73	0.73	0.62	0.61	0.61

Note: The dependent variable is the proportion of the total vote the incumbent received. Standard errors in parentheses.
* p≤0.05

the fall debate could expect to receive 9.7 percentage points more than members who voted consistently for it. Those who gave three antiwar speeches gained a towering 11.8 percentage point advantage, a decisive margin in a close district. These results strongly suggest that Democrats in close districts judged their voters' reactions correctly in deciding whether to oppose the impending war, in spite of its national popularity. However, these members were no more likely to receive an electoral benefit in the 2004 or 2006 elections than were Democratic incumbents in general.

A third possibility is that even though Democrats who opposed the war received few electoral benefits, perhaps Republicans who did were able to escape the punishment that voters visited on their party after the war became unpopular. While this possibility does not bear directly on the incentives facing the opposition party, it is still substantively important because it would give members of the president's party who thought the war was a mistake an incentive to cross party lines and join the opposition while there was still time to stop it. Table 4.7 applies the analysis of the 2004 and 2006 elections to Republicans.

Few House Republicans opposed the war in 2002, so the tests in table 4.7 rest on the activity of a small number of people. Only 6 of 221 House Republicans voted against the war resolution. Only 7 gave at least one antiwar floor speech during the debate. The results in table 4.7 indicate that this small group may have received some benefit during the 2004 election but none in 2006, when the greatest electoral punishment of their party occurred. In the first three models of incumbent vote shares in the 2004 election, the coefficients on antiwar votes and speeches narrowly miss the conventional threshold for statistical significance, but the signs are positive. This is not true for the 2006 election. These results jibe with the fate of the six Republicans who voted against the war resolution. Of the four who ran for reelection in 2004, all were successful. (Connie Morella [R-MD] had been defeated in 2002, and Amory Houghton [R-NY] decided not to seek another term in 2004.) Things went poorly for this group in 2006, however. Both John Hostetler (R-IN) and Jim Leach (R-IA) were defeated. Only Jimmy Duncan (R-TN) and Ron Paul (R-TX) served beyond the 2006 election, retiring from Congress in 2018 and 2012 respectively.

Discussion

The evidence presented here casts doubt on the electoral incentives widely thought to influence opposition party decisions to oppose a prospective military action. It would be wrong to assume that patterns evident during the Iraq War generalize to all prospective wars or beyond the United States. However, conditions for observing the electoral rewards thought to follow from opposing a military action that later becomes unpopular were especially favorable in this case. Wars with less time for prewar deliberation or less information about the potential problems with the rationale for military action and the plans for carrying it out make the prospect of political rewards for early opposition even dimmer. Despite the favorable circumstances, data from the 2002, 2004, and 2006 elections offer little evidence of an electoral incentive for early opposition to war. Those who opposed the Iraq War before it began did well at the polls in 2002 but were overshadowed by more recent position-taking in 2004. In districts that had suffered unusually high casualties, they fared better in the 2004 election than members who had supported the war, but those who had taken no position did just as well.

This paucity of evidence is not due to the endogeneity of congressional position-taking and election results. Members generally avoid taking positions likely to antagonize their supporters, either because of deliberate electoral strategy or through less cynical processes of representation. This endogeneity certainly biases estimates of the electoral effects of members' positions, but the bias runs against the argument that there is little electoral reward for taking an early antiwar position. Members' tendency to seek out electoral advantages should make these rewards appear larger than they actually are, just as they would make electoral punishments appear smaller.

Why did voters not reward members for taking positions against the war before it began? The evidence suggests two main reasons. First, positions on the Iraq War mattered to voters, but recent positions appear to have mattered more. The antiwar positions that some Democratic representatives took in the fall of 2002 made a difference in the November election that year. In a mark of the importance of strategic position-taking and other endogenous processes, even though the prospect of war was popular nationally, the Democrats who opposed it were rewarded, not punished, at the polls. By contrast, in the next two election cycles when the war really was unpopular, these representatives received no further electoral benefit. Instead, in 2004, voters rewarded antiwar positions taken in the more recent past instead, even if they were taken by members who had previously supported the war.

This recency bias is important in the US context. For one thing, because of the overwhelming military power of the United States, immediate military failures are likely to be uncommon. Major American military reversals since World War II have more often come in the form of a persistent and costly failure to achieve military and political goals, as in Vietnam, Iraq, and Afghanistan. Because time must pass before such a failure is evident, positions taken before the conflict began may be effectively forgotten by the time the war becomes unpopular. This myopia devalues those earlier positions, even though they reveal more about the wisdom and principles of the representatives who took this stand. After all, early opponents of the war were taking a risk rather than simply adopting a position that was already popular.

Voters' focus on recent events also gives members of Congress an incentive to avoid speaking out on a prospective military action. Doing so is undeniably risky, regardless of the position one takes. Prewar statements are hostages to fortune. A future political opponent could exploit them if things do not go as the member predicts. If the member can simply adopt the position later and reap most of the political benefits of doing so, then even some who privately have doubts about the wisdom of the proposed operation may choose to follow this course. Of course, those with intense ideological objections or constituencies that are already antiwar will still speak out, but their views are easier to discount than those of more moderate or conflicted members. This is especially likely because the reticence of their colleagues makes the views of war opponents appear more extreme and anomalous than they really are.

Districts that had suffered unusually high casualties appear to constitute a limited exception to voters' tendency to focus on recent statements. This raises the possibility that things might have worked differently during historical periods when the United States expected to suffer more casualties than it has in recent interventions. If members of Congress thought casualties could be heavy, especially in their district, then they would have more motive to speak out against an intervention they thought would fail. Current developments in military technology, such as the increasing use of drones and improved battlefield medicine, make a return to these circumstances unlikely.

The second reason for the absence of electoral rewards for early opposition to the Iraq War is the tendency to accord rewards or punishments to the party as a whole rather than to individual members. Previous research has turned up substantial evidence that Democratic gains in the 2006 election were due in part to the unpopularity of the war. However, because nearly the entire party opposed the war by that time, the members who had done so when things were far less unanimous received no additional benefit.

This creates yet another incentive for members to avoid taking an early position.

Conclusion

What is the broader significance of the limited electoral incentives for opposing a prospective military operation? Above all, a circumscribed debate in Congress could affect the way the war is discussed in the media and in the public more broadly. There are reasons to think it could make a difference for the quality of deliberation about war and peace.

The absence of electoral incentives does not mean no members of Congress will criticize the move toward war. Some will still do so out of ideological conviction or because they represent an antiwar constituency. These two considerations go together as more liberal constituencies elect more liberal members of Congress. Of the 211 Democrats present for the debate prior to the 2002 election, 53 gave at least two speeches against the war before the November election. Not surprisingly, these members were more liberal than most Democrats, with an average first-dimension DW-NOMINATE score of -0.45 compared to the party median of -0.37. In their districts, the Democratic presidential nominee won an average of 65 percent of the vote in the 2000 election, compared to 59 percent for all districts with a Democratic representative. The absence of electoral incentives almost certainly had a greater effect on the behavior of members of the party who lacked an ideological conviction about the war. The lack of electoral incentives does not rule out debate, but it does circumscribe it.

Congressional debate matters for broader public discussion of a proposed military operation. As William Howell and Jon Pevehouse put it, "more than anyone else, members of Congress determine whether the president's case for military action is given a free pass or widely contested in the national media."[36] A substantial body of research has found that media coverage of war and peace is closely tied to the views of government officials, including members of Congress.[37] Howell and Pevehouse found that this was also the case during the fall 2002 debate over the Iraq War.[38] When there was debate in Congress, the media paid attention to the controversy. When the debate ceased as members went home to campaign for reelection in late October, coverage of the issue greatly declined.

The fact that opponents of the war were generally more liberal than most Democrats also made it easier to dismiss their critique of the war as extreme, even though many of the key arguments they made were widely shared by experts and even many officials within the executive branch. The claim that Iraq possessed substantial stocks of weapons of mass destruction, that it might share these weapons with terrorists, and that the regime had contacts with al Qaeda were all disputed within the intelligence community.[39] The Department of Defense, which dominated prewar planning, resisted serious consideration of the postwar occupation of Iraq.[40] If more moderate Democrats had joined in criticizing the war on these points, they might have been taken more seriously. Moreover, a broader set of critics in Congress might have been able to provide political cover for administration officials who wanted to raise concerns about the proposed military operation. As the case of General Shinseki shows, they were not able to do so in 2002–2003. The limited character of the congressional debate may be at the root of the widely shared impression that the "marketplace of ideas" failed to function in run up to the Iraq War, allowing specious arguments to carry the day.[41]

Are the limits of congressional debate in cases like the Iraq War enough to deprive the United States of the advantages democracies are generally thought to have in making decisions about war and peace? The knowledge that members of the opposition party will turn against an unpopular war, even if their prewar opposition is limited, ought to be enough to induce caution in a president contemplating military action. We should still observe few such outcomes. Certainly, costly failures like those in Vietnam, Afghanistan, and Iraq ought to be well off the equilibrium path, and even smaller debacles like those in Lebanon during the early 1980s or Somalia in the early 1990s ought to be rare. Unfortunately, as these examples suggest, they are not rare enough. There are at least two reasons that a lack of vigorous prewar debate may be partly responsible for these outcomes.

First, a circumscribed public debate makes it harder for critics of the prospective war to present their position, let alone get it taken seriously. In the cases of Iraq and Vietnam, there was substantial skepticism about the prospects for military success even within the executive branch.[42] With little real public debate, it proved remarkably easy for hawks in the Johnson and Bush Administrations to sweep these doubts aside. Indeed, coupled with the pervasive assumption of American military superiority, the absence of public debate appears to have made it difficult for those with doubts about the war even to express their opinions privately. Doing so would associate them with a position that found support only on the ideological fringes. Instead, officials in the Johnson and Bush Administrations ended up believing their own dubious justifications for war, or at least pretending to do so.

Second, the perfunctory character of public debate and the reticence of the more ideologically centrist parts of the political opposition deprives the United States of the signaling advantages that Schultz theorized. The limited opposition did not really demonstrate a widely shared conviction that the war would go well, or that the nation as a whole was determined to see it through. Instead, American military adversaries could expect that the opposition party would turn against the war if it became sufficiently costly, regardless of the positions its members had taken before the war began. As Saddam Hussein's fate illustrates, surviving to this point in the face of American military attack is no sure thing. However, the military opponents of the United States are certainly aware that it is a potentially effective strategy. There is no clear reason that determined rhetoric from the executive branch, even with support from the opposition party, should persuade them that US resolve will persist through time or overcome significant costs.

Finally, the evidence reviewed here comes from one major intervention, the war in Iraq. As Sarah Kreps and Douglas Kriner noted in the introduction this volume, the high level of polarization in contemporary American politics, already quite high in the early 2000s, might diminish the constraints on the president. There are reasons to suspect that polarization might diminish the electoral rewards for early opposition to a prospective use of force. Lower polarization might allow early opponents of the war to win over supporters of the president's party once the costs of the war became clear, something that did not happen to a very great extent in this case. A change of heart by these voters would increase the chance that early opponents who lived in divided districts would be rewarded at the polls. Under lower polarization, voters might also distinguish among individual members of each party rather than attribute support or opposition to the war to the party as a whole, as they appeared to do in 2006. This would also make rewards for early opponents more likely. Intraparty differences over the Iraq War really were smaller than they were during the Vietnam War, for instance. It was thus more difficult to infer a member's position on the Vietnam War from his or her party affiliation than it was during the Iraq War. An analysis of congressional position-taking on Vietnam might reveal patterns somewhat different from those found here.

Notes

1. David H. Clark, "Agreeing to Disagree: Domestic Institutional Congruence and U.S. Dispute Behavior," *Political Research Quarterly* 53, no. 2 (2000): 375–401;

William Howell and Jon Pevehouse, *While Dangers Gather* (Princeton, NJ: Princeton University, 2007).

2. Dan Reiter and Allan Stam, *Democracies at War* (Princeton, NJ: Princeton University Press, 2002).

3. Robert Draper, *To Start a War: How the Bush Administration Took American into Iraq* (New York: Penguin Books, 2020), 328–330.

4. Douglas L. Kriner, *After the Rubicon* (Chicago: University of Chicago Press, 2010).

5. For example, see David Karol and Edward Miguel, "The Electoral Cost of War: Iraq Casualties and the 2004 U.S. Presidential Election," *Journal of Politics* 69, no. 3 (2007): 633–648.

6. For example, see Scott Sigmund Gartner, Gary M. Segura, and Bethany A. Barratt, "War Casualties, Policy Positions, and the Fate of Legislators," *Political Research Quarterly* 57, no. 3 (2004): 467–477; Douglas Kriner and Francis Shen, "Responding to War on Capitol Hill: Battlefield Casualties, Congressional Response, and Public Support for the War in Iraq," *American Journal of Political Science* 58, no. 1 (2014): 157–174.

7. Howell and Pevehouse, *While Dangers Gather*, 155–191; Jonathan Mermin, *Debating War and Peace* (Princeton, NJ: Princeton University Press, 1999).

8. Reiter and Stam, *Democracies at War*, 23; Kenneth N. Waltz, *Foreign Policy and Democratic Politics* (Boston, MA: Little, Brown, and Company, 1967).

9. Kenneth A. Schultz, "Domestic Opposition and Signaling in International Crises," *American Political Science Review* 92, no. 4 (1998): 829–844; Kenneth A. Schultz, *Democracy and Coercive Diplomacy* (New York: Cambridge University Press, 2001).

10. Schultz, *Democracy and Coercive Diplomacy*, 8–9.

11. Schultz, *Democracy and Coercive Diplomacy*, 89.

12. Jack Levy and William F. Mabe Jr., "Politically Motivated Opposition to War," *International Studies Review* 6, no. 4 (2004): 79.

13. For example, see Philip Arena, "Success Breeds Success? War Outcomes, Domestic Opposition, and Elections," *Conflict Management and Peace Science* 25, no. 2 (2008): 136–151; Philip Arena, "Crisis Bargaining, Domestic Opposition, and Tragic Wars," *Journal of Theoretical Politics* 27, no. 1 (2015): 108–131; Kristopher W. Ramsay, "Politics at the Water's Edge: Crisis Bargaining and Electoral Competition," *Journal of Conflict Resolution* 48, no. 4 (2004): 459–486; Patrick Shea, Terence K. Teo, and Jack S. Levy, "Opposition Politics and International Crises: A Formal Model," *International Studies Quarterly* 58, no. 4 (2014): 741–751; Laron K. Williams, "Hawks, Doves, and Opportunistic Opposition Parties," *Journal of Peace Research* 51, no. 1 (2014): 111–125.

14. Schultz, *Democracy and Coercive Diplomacy*, 12.

15. For example, see Barbara Hinkley, *Less than Meets the Eye* (Chicago: University of Chicago Press, 1994), 82.

16. For example, see Howell and Pevehouse, *While Dangers Gather*, 19–21; Kriner, *After the Rubicon*, 10–11.

17. James L. Regens, Ronald Keith Gaddie, and Brad Lockerbie, "The Electoral Consequences of Voting to Declare War," *Journal of Conflict Resolution* 39, no. 1 (1995): 168–182.

18. Gartner, Segura, and Barratt, "War Casualties, Policy Positions, and the Fate of Legislators."

19. Scott Sigmund Gartner and Gary M. Segura, "All Politics Are Still Local: The Iraq War and the 2006 Midterm Elections," *PS: Political Science and Politics* 41, no. 1 (2008): 95–100; Christian R. Grose and Bruce I. Oppenheimer, "The Iraq War, Partisanship, and Candidate Attributes: Variation in Partisan Swing in the 2006 U.S. House Elections," *Legislative Studies Quarterly* 32, no. 4 (2007): 531–557; Kriner and Shen, "Responding to War on Capitol Hill."

20. House election data are from MIT Election Data and Science Lab, "U.S. House, 1976–2018," 2021, https://electionlab.mit.edu/data. These are results reported by the Clerk of the House of Representatives.

21. The appendix for this chapter can be found online on the Harvard Dataverse: https://doi.org/10.7910/DVN/OEOIM3.

22. Grose and Oppenheimer, "The Iraq War, Partisanship, and Candidate Attributes."

23. Kriner and Shen, "Responding to War on Capitol Hill."

24. I will use separate variables for pro-war and anti-war speeches because combining them into a single indicator assumes that they have symmetric effects. The empirical evidence in the next section suggests that this is not the case.

25. Kriner and Shen, "Responding to War on Capitol Hill."

26. Gary C. Jacobson, "Perception, Memory, and Partisan Polarization on the Iraq War," *Political Science Quarterly* 125, no. 1 (2010): 32.

27. Data on presidential election results by congressional district in 2000 and 2004 are from Congressional Quarterly, *CQ's Politics in America 2002 for the 107th Congress* (Washington, DC: Congressional Quarterly, Inc., 2001); Congressional Quarterly, *CQ's Politics in America 2004 for the 108th Congress* (Washington, DC: Congressional Quarterly, Inc., 2003); and Congressional Quarterly, *CQ's Politics in America 2006 for the 109th Congress* (Washington, DC: Congressional Quarterly, Inc., 2005).

28. Gartner and Segura, "All Politics Are Still Local"; Grose and Oppenheimer, "The Iraq War, Partisanship, and Candidate Attributes."

29. Karol and Miguel, "The Electoral Cost of War."

30. Gallup Poll, "Iraq," 2021, https://news.gallup.com/poll/1633/iraq.aspx. The specific question was, "Would you favor or oppose invading Iraq with U.S. ground troops in an attempt to remove Saddam Hussein from power?"

31. Gallup Poll, "Iraq.".

32. Jacobson, "Perception, Memory, and Partisan Polarization on the Iraq War."

33. Gallup Poll, "Iraq." The exact wording of the question was, "In view of the developments since we first sent our troops to Iraq, do you think the United States made a mistake in sending troops to Iraq, or not?"

34. Gartner and Segura, "All Politics Are Still Local"; Kriner and Shen, "Responding to War on Capitol Hill."

35. Grose and Oppenheimer, "The Iraq War, Partisanship, and Candidate Attributes."

36. Howell and Pevehouse, *While Dangers Gather*, 163.

37. For example, see Mermin, *Debating War and Peace*.

38. Howell and Pevehouse, *While Dangers Gather*, 155-191.

39. Draper, *To Start a War*, 133-156; 201-219; 267-269.

40. For example, see Draper, *To Start a War*, 233.

41. For example, see Chaim Kaufman, "Threat Inflation and the Failure of the Marketplace of Ideas," *International Security* 29, no. 1 (2004): 5-48; Jane Kellett Kramer, "Militarized Patriotism: Why the U.S. Marketplace of Ideas Failed Before the Iraq War," *Security Studies* 16, no. 3 (2007): 489-524.

42. On Vietnam, see Daniel Ellsberg, ed., "The Quagmire Myth and the Stalemate Machine," in *Papers on the War* (New York: Simon & Schuster, 1972), 42-135; also, Kai Bird, *The Color of Truth* (New York: Touchstone, 2000). On Iraq, see Draper, *To Start a War*; Kaufman, "Threat Inflation and the Failure of the Marketplace of Ideas"; and James Fallows, *Blind into Baghdad* (New York: Vintage, 2009).

CHAPTER FIVE

Congressional Midterms, Presidential Reelection, and US Foreign Policy

Christopher Dictus and Philip B. K. Potter

The events of 9/11 changed how presidents approached foreign policy. Expanded presidential powers, congressional polarization, and decades on a war footing conspired to further erode the already weakened constraints on presidential authority. This evolution has occurred in the context of more durable electoral institutions that ultimately determine who holds power and what limitations are placed on them. It is, therefore, essential to understand how mounting presidential foreign policy powers intersect with the incentives and constraints imposed by the electoral cycle.

The electoral cycle shapes foreign policy by altering presidential power, expertise, and incentives. The result is systematic pressure on foreign policy from both the last election's outcome and the shadow of the next. Most work on this relationship focuses on the election of new presidents.[1] However, this chapter explores the additional impact of presidential reelection campaigns and congressional midterm elections. We establish that presidents on the campaign trail focus on policies that provide the greatest electoral reward. Because the American public prioritizes domestic concerns over foreign policy, that means maximizing achievements at home while minimizing international initiatives and obligations. In other words, in the immediate lead-up to both midterm and second-term elections, presidents have a systematic incentive to neglect foreign policy in favor of domestic achievements.

This contradicts the longstanding concern that presidents may resort to diversionary foreign policy to spark a rally in popularity ahead of voting.

Instead, we find that presidents are far more likely to avoid foreign policy altogether when on the campaign trail for themselves or their congressional colleagues. While less flashy than the idea of "wagging the dog" with the use of force abroad, neglect can have a pernicious effect on US foreign policy, particularly in delicate matters of state that benefit from consistency and the careful maintenance of diplomatic relationships.

The outcomes of these elections also shape US foreign policy in predictable ways. Both midterms and presidential reelections are referenda on the sitting president's policies. The results, therefore, influence presidential power. These contests not only change the partisan composition of Congress, potentially leading to divided government, but also provide a clear indication of presidential strength. Significant domestic initiatives require political capital; those who emerge victorious obtain that capital. In contrast, those who lose seats in Congress or scrape by in their reelection bid will find themselves politically constrained and must look disproportionately abroad for policy achievements.

In short, the electoral cycle shapes presidential agendas by altering presidential power and incentives, the party in control of the White House and Congress, and the balance of power between the parties. This chapter will detail these forces and their relationship with foreign and domestic policy.

Midterm Elections

Even though the president is not personally up for election, midterm elections are a broad-based referendum on how well the president's policies are playing with voters. The results of midterms indicate the president's political power and popularity, and can directly limit or enhance the prospects for presidential priorities by changing the partisan composition of Congress. This is a longstanding, durable, and commonly understood relationship. For example, a *TIME Magazine* article on January 26, 1970, discussed the midterm elections that year, saying they "will serve as the first broad referendum on the Nixon Administration's policies."[2] Similarly, a 1998 CNN article noted, "It was the great 'impeachment election' that never was. Americans shunned the opportunity to turn Tuesday's midterm elections into a referendum on President Bill Clinton's behavior, dashing Republican hopes of gaining seats in the House and Senate."[3]

Because presidents stand to gain or lose so much due to these elections, particularly if there is a change in House or Senate control, they position their policies to maximize favorable results. We argue that this leads them to prioritize domestic over foreign policy in the months leading up to voting. Given voters' comparative indifference to foreign affairs, dedicating time and attention to such matters promises comparatively little in terms of electoral reward.[4] In contrast, retrospective voting and established voter attentiveness to pocketbook issues lead presidents who are closing in on a moment of electoral oversight to burnish their domestic record. Put succinctly, presidents are incentivized to neglect foreign policy in favor of issues at home in the lead-up to elections.

After the election, presidents face a new set of incentives and constraints. If the midterms prove favorable, the president is empowered. Since the political return to (and constraints on) domestic policies are higher than that of foreign policy, empowered presidents will disproportionately use this capital to pursue their domestic priorities. If, on the other hand, the midterms prove to be a political setback, the president will be constrained domestically and forced into the comparatively unconstrained realm of foreign affairs.[5]

These forces lead to three expectations:

1. In the lead-up to midterm elections, presidents will seek to emphasize domestic issues rather than foreign policy.
2. After a favorable midterm result, newly emboldened presidents will favor their domestic policy agenda.
3. After a poor midterm result, the weakened administration will seek refuge in foreign policy.

Presidential Reelection

Of course, for a sitting president, a reelection bid is even more significant than the midterms. Few elected to the highest office in the United States have passed on an attempt to keep it.[6] However, despite the heightened personal stakes, the relationship between reelection campaigns and policy agendas is similar to that governing midterm elections.

Campaigning for reelection demands considerable presidential time and attention. With the window for direct accountability fast approaching, presidents pursue policies that appeal most to voters, pushing them toward any domestic achievements that might be available. For example, David Lindsey and William Hobbs find that presidents spend considerably less time on foreign priorities before presidential elections.[7] As James Carville more colloquially noted in 1992, "it's the economy, stupid."

As Carville implied, domestic policy brings home the electoral bacon. Presidents who can trumpet their successes at home will do so to show their ability to address the concerns of everyday Americans. Presidents forced to rely on foreign policy successes in a reelection bid do so at their peril. Indeed, George H. W. Bush's failure to address the deficit and other economic concerns led to his defeat by Bill Clinton, regardless of his impressive foreign policy record. Despite overseeing and successfully handling the collapse of the Berlin War; Mikhail Gorbachev's fall from power; the crumbling of the Soviet Union; and Iraq's invasion of Kuwait, Bush was unable to convince the American public that he deserved a second term in office. Indeed, his approval rating fell from 89 percent in March 1991 to 29 percent in August 1992 due almost entirely to the flagging economy.[8]

If a president succeeds in a reelection bid, the margin of victory prominently signals the administration's strength or weakness, shaping policy *after* the election. Presidents who win reelection in a landslide are empowered to pursue significant domestic policy reforms. For example, Lyndon Johnson won in 1964 with a 61–39 margin. He leveraged this strength to finalize his Great Society programs: creating Medicare and Medicaid and passing the Voting Rights and Elementary and Secondary School Acts. Notably, he deferred action in Vietnam as much as he could.[9]

Therefore, presidential incentives and constraints around reelection are similar to those governing midterm elections but more exaggerated. This leads to three additional expectations:

1. In the lead-up to reelection, presidents will seek to emphasize domestic issues rather than foreign policy.
2. Presidents who win reelection by a large margin or with new strength in Congress will disproportionately pursue their domestic policy agenda.
3. A president emerging from reelection weakened by the results will turn to foreign policy.

Elections since 1945

To assess the validity of these expectations, we explore presidential domestic and foreign policy behavior around midterm and reelection campaigns since 1945 (table 5.1). These presidents served after the passage of the 22nd Amendment and faced broadly similar circumstances after World War II.

Table 5.1 bears out one of the enduring trends of midterm elections: the president's party tends to lose seats. David Crockett finds, for example, that between 1830 and 1998 the president's party lost an average of 32.2 seats in the House and 1.64 seats in the Senate in midterm elections.[10] Only Kennedy (1962), Nixon (1970), Clinton (1998), Bush (2002), and Trump (2018) gained seats in either the House or the Senate. Only Bush (2002) saw his party gain in the House and the Senate.

While they rarely achieve their preferred outcome, presidents must do what they can to at least mitigate their losses. The opportunity to improve their prospects in Congress and demonstrate public support for presidential initiatives gives presidents every incentive to campaign actively. They tend to do so on the merits of their domestic record.

Richard Nixon and the 1970 Midterms

Richard Nixon's approach to the 1970 midterm illustrates the pressures that midterm election campaigns place on presidents. Early on, Nixon "took centralized control of the campaign" by personally recruiting prominent Senate candidates, including George H. W. Bush in Texas and Richard Roudebush in Indiana, managing the distribution of funds to Republican candidates, and imposing a common theme on the campaigns. This engagement in the midterms came even though he had publicly indicated an inclination "not to do any active campaigning in 1970."[11]

Despite these interventions, Nixon still dedicated too much time to foreign policy in the early parts of the electoral cycle and suffered the consequences. He wrote, "When the campaign began to heat up around the middle of September, I was deeply involved in preparations for my second European trip, which lasted from September 27 to October 5. When I left, it seemed as if we actually had a chance to pull off an upset victory and pick up some seats. When I returned, I discovered that we were in serious trouble in almost every major race."[12]

When Nixon recognized his mistake, he began to take a much more active role in the midterms and consciously submerged his foreign policy engagements in voters' minds. Nixon wrote that after returning from his foreign trip, "I decided to reverse my earlier decision and announced that

TABLE 5.1. Presidential and Congressional Elections 1946–2018

Year	Election	President	Party	Winner	Pop. Vote %	Senate	Senate Result	House	House Result
1946	midterm	Truman	Democrat			R+12	R gain	R+55	R gain
1948	reelection	Truman	Democrat	Truman	49.6/45.1/2.4	D+9	D gain	D+75	D gain
1950	midterm	Truman	Democrat			R+5	D hold	R+28	D hold
1952	election		Republican	Eisenhower	55.2/44.3	R+2	R gain	R+22	R gain
1954	midterm	Eisenhower	Republican			D+2	D gain	D+19	D gain
1956	reelection	Eisenhower	Republican	Eisenhower	57.4/42.0	no change	D hold	D+2	D hold
1958	midterm	Eisenhower	Republican			D+15	D hold	D+49	D hold
1960	election		Democrat	Kennedy	49.72/49.55	R+1	D hold	D+10	D hold
1962	midterm	Kennedy	Democrat			D+4	D hold	R+1	D hold
1964	reelection	Johnson	Democrat	Johnson	61.1/38.5	D+2	D hold	D+37	D hold
1966	midterm	Johnson	Democrat			R+3	D hold	R+47	D hold
1968	election		Republican	Nixon	43.4/42.7/13.5	R+5	D hold	R+5	D hold
1970	midterm	Nixon	Republican			R+1	D hold	D+12	D hold
1972	reelection	Nixon	Republican	Nixon	60.7/37.5	D+2	D hold	R+12	D hold
1974	midterm	Ford	Republican			D+4	D hold	D+49	D hold
1976	reelection	Ford	Republican	Carter	50.1/48.0	R+1	D hold	D+1	D hold
1978	midterm	Carter	Democrat			R+3	D hold	R+15	D hold
1980	reelection	Carter	Democrat	Reagan	50.7/41.0/6.6	R+12	R gain	R+34	D hold

Year	Type	President	Party	Candidate	Vote %	Pres approval	House	Senate	Outcome
1982	midterm	Reagan	Republican			D+1	R hold	D+26	D hold
1984	reelection	Reagan	Republican	Reagan	58.8/40.6	D+2	R hold	R+16	D hold
1986	midterm	Reagan	Republican			D+9	D gain	D+5	D hold
1988	election	Bush	Republican	Bush	53.4/45.6	D+1	D hold	D+2	D hold
1990	midterm	Bush	Republican			D+1	D hold	D+7	D hold
1992	reelection	Bush	Republican	Clinton	43.0/37.4/18.9	no change	D hold	R+9	D hold
1994	midterm	Clinton	Democrat			R+8	R gain	R+54	R gain
1996	reelection	Clinton	Democrat	Clinton	49.2/40.7/8.4	R+2	R hold	D+2	R hold
1998	midterm	Clinton	Democrat			no change	R hold	D+5	R hold
2000	election	Bush	Republican	Bush	47.9/48.4	D+4	D gain	D+1	R hold
2002	midterm	Bush	Republican			R+2	R gain	R+8	R hold
2004	reelection	Bush	Republican	Bush	50.7/48.3	R+4	R hold	R+3	R hold
2006	midterm	Bush	Republican			D+6	D gain	D+31	D gain
2008	election	Obama	Democrat	Obama	52.9/45.7	D+8	D hold	D+21	D hold
2010	midterm	Obama	Democrat			R+6	D hold	R+63	R gain
2012	reelection	Obama	Democrat	Obama	51.1/47.2	D+2	D hold	D+8	R hold
2014	midterm	Obama	Democrat			R+9	R gain	R+13	R hold
2016	election	Trump	Republican	Trump	46.1/48.2	D+2	R hold	D+6	R hold
2018	midterm	Trump	Republican			R+2	R hold	D+41	D gain

I would campaign personally for our candidates in a number of key races. During the three weeks before the election I devoted seven full days to campaigning for candidates in twenty-two states."[13] Nixon recognized the impossibility of focusing on foreign affairs if he wished to make substantial gains, and he attributed the "trouble" in the major races to his time abroad.

After returning home and hitting the campaign trail, Nixon's prioritization of domestic politics is also evident in what he emphasized to his audiences. In his memoirs, he discusses the importance of the book *The Real Majority* to his thinking about the campaign. The book, by Kennedy's Census Bureau Director Richard Scammon and former Johnson speechwriter Ben Wattenberg, argued that the "Social Issue" would decide the elections in 1970 and 1972. In this view, the average American voter in the election was a forty-seven-year-old housewife, married to a machinist, and living on Dayton's outskirts. Scammon and Wattenberg wrote:

> To know that the lady in Dayton is afraid to walk the streets alone at night ... to know that she has a mixed view about blacks and civil rights because before moving to the suburbs she lived in a neighborhood that became all black, to know that her brother-in-law is a policeman, to know that she does not have the money to move if her new neighborhood deteriorates, to know that she is deeply distressed that her son is going to a community junior college where LSD was found on campus—to know all this is the beginning of contemporary wisdom.[14]

After reading the book, Nixon felt that the "Republican counterstrategy was clear: we should preempt the Social Issue in order to get the Democrats on the defensive. We should aim our strategy primarily at disaffected Democrats, at blue-collar workers, and at working-class white ethnics. We should set out to capture the vote of the forty-seven-year-old Dayton housewife."[15] Of course, nothing in the fictionalized description of the forty-seven-year-old housewife is about foreign affairs. To Nixon, she cared about the rule of law, civil rights, race, economics, and crime—all domestic issues.

Nixon took this strategy out on the campaign trail, and his stump speeches uniformly prioritized domestic issues. Vietnam was the only substantive foreign policy issue mentioned and Nixon minimized it to the extent possible, which was a challenge given the increasingly difficult circumstances that the conflict presented. Nixon was busy during the 1970 midterm campaign, visiting Pennsylvania, Wisconsin, Vermont, New Jersey, Ohio, North Dakota, Missouri, Tennessee, North Carolina, Indiana, Maryland, Florida, Texas, Illinois, Minnesota, Nebraska, California, Arizona, New Mexico, Nevada, and Utah. The speech in support of the Republican ticket in Vermont is representative of Nixon's focus during the midterms:

> I have come to Vermont to support a great United States Senator, Win Prouty, a great Governor, Deane Davis, and the entire Republican ticket. While here, I also want to reassure the people of Vermont and of New England about a matter that has become a cause of great concern to many: the question of *fuel supply*. I have talked with Senator Prouty and Governor Davis about this. I have investigated the situation. I want to say that despite all the discussion, and despite all the alarms, there is now *no fuel crisis*. And we are taking all necessary steps to ensure that Vermont and New England have *adequate supplies of fuel* this winter.... Senator Prouty has been one of the great leaders in the Senate *in education, in health, in transportation, in getting a better break for the elderly*. He understands what it takes to achieve our goal in the world of a full generation of peace ... With Winston Prouty in the Senate and Bob Stafford in the House, the people of Vermont can be sure that the voice of Vermont will be heard—and heeded. Let me say a word, too, about Governor Davis. Two years ago, Governor Davis inherited a *fiscal mess* from his predecessor—and he had the courage and the determination to do what was needed to clean it up. He knows what it takes to make State government work. He knows how to *fight crime*. Under his leadership, Vermont is setting an example for the Nation in *fighting pollution*. If we are to get power back to the States and back to the people—where it belongs—we need more Governors like Deane Davis... [emphasis added][16]

This speech reflects Nixon's emphasis on domestic issues: the fuel supply, education, health, transportation, care for the elderly, fiscal responsibility, fighting crime, and reducing pollution. Insofar as there is any reference to foreign affairs, it is to achieving a "full generation of peace." However, in the American mind, peace is usually framed as an opportunity to look inward and focus on domestic priorities.[17] Put simply, Nixon sought to maximize his gains during the midterm election, and he did so by focusing on the domestic issues most likely to be salient to voters.

How well did Nixon's approach pay off? The results were mixed. Republicans gained one seat in the Senate, but the Democrats added twelve seats to their House majority.[18] Mason argues that Nixon failed in his 1970 strategy: the midterms did not change the partisan balance of Congress, many of Nixon's hand-picked candidates were unsuccessful, and voters did not change their ideas about the Republican Party.[19]

Nixon, however, disagreed and argued that there were signs of success: "In fact, this was an excellent showing because in past election years in which unemployment was on the rise, the average loss of seats by the party controlling the White House was forty-six. In that respect, we had defied overwhelming historical trends. It was also particularly gratifying to me that some extreme liberals were among those senators retired by the voters."[20] The 1970 midterm cycle conforms with key elements of our argument: presidents navigating congressional midterms have strong incentives to emphasize domestic policy at the expense of foreign policy.

Presidents have a similar vested interest in emphasizing domestic policy during their bids for reelection. Facing an electorate that cares about their everyday problems, presidents seeking reelection do better by focusing (to the greatest extent possible) on national rather than international concerns. Furthermore, while the results of midterm elections reflect indirectly on presidents, the results of their reelection campaigns are unambiguous. To illustrate how this works in practice, we explore Lyndon Johnson's successful campaign to win the presidency in his own right in 1964 and George H. W. Bush's loss in 1992.

Lyndon Johnson and the Sweep of 1964

Lyndon Johnson assumed the presidency under tragic circumstances but was well-positioned to work toward a significant domestic agenda. Before becoming vice president, he had been a two-term senator, serving as majority leader from 1955 to 1961, minority leader from 1953 to 1955, and majority whip from 1951 to 1953. Before joining the Senate, he served in the House from 1937 to 1949. Johnson was intimately familiar with the mechanics of the United States Congress. He used that experience to pass several significant pieces of legislation on the road to his landslide victory in 1964.

To ensure victory in 1964, Johnson concentrated his efforts on the domestic policy achievements he knew would resonate with the American electorate. In 1964 alone, Johnson helped to usher through some of the most significant domestic legislation of the twentieth century. In January, the Twenty-Fourth Amendment abolished poll taxes. On May 22, during a speech at the University of Michigan, Johnson announced his Great Society and, later that summer, passed the Civil Rights Act, which outlawed discrimination on the basis of race, color, sex, religion, or national origin. After accepting the presidential nomination in August, Johnson initiated the War on Poverty by signing the Economic Opportunity Act and creating the Office of Economic Opportunity.[21]

While Johnson fervently believed in the legislation he signed, he designed his domestic initiatives to increase his electoral appeal leading up to the election. Johnson biographer Robert Dallek notes, "An attack on poverty had much appeal to LBJ. Not only was it his kind of program, it also gave him a platform for 1964." Dallek goes on to say, "Despite all the good news on his popularity, Johnson believed that if he were going to win in November, he needed, first, to enact the liberal agenda—the tax cut, war on poverty, and civil rights—and, second, to demonstrate that he was a President who could rise above politics to serve the national interest."[22]

The GOP's decision to nominate Sen. Barry Goldwater enabled Johnson to run to the center in hopes of winning a mandate for his domestic programs. In his memoirs, Johnson wrote,

> I knew that the Republican party's swing to the right gave me a rare opportunity to further the cause of *social reform*. Having inherited the entire political center, if only for the time being, I decided to seek a new mandate from the people ... I asked [the voters] for a mandate to *expand [social security] with Medicare*. Goldwater called for a return to a sink-or-swim policy toward the poor; I called for an expanded government program to *eradicate poverty*. Goldwater called for a strengthening of states' rights; I called for more *federal protection for civil rights*. Goldwater favored what amounted to an unregulated economy; I favored *imaginative fiscal and monetary policies* that would eliminate the old cycles of boom and bust.[23] [emphasis added]

Johnson doubled down on this program during his speech accepting the Democratic nomination for president, saying,

> Most Americans want *medical care* for older citizens. And so do I. Most Americans want *fair and stable prices and decent incomes* for our farmers. And so do I. Most Americans want a *decent home* in a decent neighborhood for all. And so do I. Most Americans want an *education* for every child to the limit of his ability. And so do I. Most Americans want a *job* for every man who wants to work.

And so do I. Most Americans want victory in our *war against poverty*. And so do I. Most Americans want continually expanding and *growing prosperity*. And so do I. These are your goals. These are our goals. These are the goals and will be the achievements of the Democratic Party.[24] [emphasis added]

Johnson's Great Society was the centerpiece of his election strategy, presenting a domestic agenda he knew would resonate with the American electorate. Voters responded to Johnson's emphasis on domestic policy with an overwhelming mandate endorsing the president's platform.

Johnson based his focus on domestic policy on the belief that the people wanted a frugal government that could still meet its needs. He noted in a memo that "government can be both progressive and compassionate on the one hand and prudent on the other."[25] He worked to ensure that the government would not be seen as a "reckless spender" and trumpeted how his cost-saving measures allowed the administration to "improve the Nation's well-being, promote better education, and develop our natural resources; the war on poverty; urban mass transportation; Housing Act Of 1964; major education bills; Land and Water Conservation Fund Act."[26] Notably, he does not mention Vietnam or any other foreign policy issue.

While Johnson vigorously pursued his domestic agenda in 1964, he actively avoided the challenges presented by Vietnam in the lead-up to the election. Most prominently, he actively delayed any declaration from Congress sanctioning additional advisers until after the election. Dallek writes that the "strongest inhibitions Johnson saw on pushing a resolution were the 1964 election and pending bills in Congress."[27]

Johnson's emphasis on domestic policy (and corresponding minimization of foreign affairs) paid off. He obtained one of the most resounding victories ever enjoyed by a sitting president, winning forty-four states with a 486–52 margin in the electoral college and a popular vote margin of 43,129,484 to 27,178,188. Johnson's dominance at the top of the ticket drove significant Democratic gains in Congress. Democrats picked up two seats in the Senate for a 68–32 advantage and added thirty-seven seats in the House for a 295–140 margin. In his memoirs, Johnson wrote, "The people responded to that program with an enthusiasm that made its mark on American history. Not only did the voters give the Democratic ticket the most extensive plurality in history, but they also sent to the Congress the largest Democratic majority since 1936."[28]

Johnson said that his favorite assessment of the election came from one of his Democratic challengers: Robert Kennedy. In 1967, in a speech to the New York State Democrats, Sen. Kennedy said, "In 1964 [President Johnson] won the greatest popular victory in modern times.... He has led us to build schools and clinics and homes and hospitals, to clean the water and to clear the air, to rebuild the city and to recapture the beauty of the countryside, to educate children and to heal the sick and comfort the oppressed on a scale unmatched in our history."[29] Coming from someone with whom he had a notoriously frosty relationship, the words meant a great deal. More importantly, for our purposes, Kennedy highlights how domestic politics enabled Johnson's victory and then fueled his domestic priorities postelection.

Not all presidents, however, follow Johnson's lead, usually to their detriment. To illustrate, we consider George H. W. Bush—a president who failed to emphasize domestic politics in a reelection bid and paid the price.

George H. W. Bush and the Neglect of Domestic Policy

George H. W. Bush epitomizes the foreign policy president. Before ascending to the highest office, the elder Bush served as ambassador to the United Nations under Richard Nixon, ambassador to the People's Republic of China and director of the Central Intelligence Agency under Gerald Ford, and vice president under Ronald Reagan. Substantively, this experience in foreign affairs served Bush well. As president, he faced the collapse of the Soviet Union, Iraq's invasion of Kuwait, and the Tiananmen Square protests in China. It did not, however, always benefit him politically.

Bush was acutely aware that this inclination toward foreign policy was a potential liability, writing, "It is said of me that I much prefer to work on international affairs.... Well, I am fully engrossed in this international crisis [in the Gulf], and I must say I enjoy working all the parts of it and I get into much more detail than I do on the domestic scene."[30] And, "They say I don't concentrate on domestic affairs, and I expect that charge is true; but how can you when you hold the life and death of a lot of young troops in your hand?"[31]

While indisputably successful in international affairs, Bush was concerned that his opponents would attack him on his handling of the economy and comparatively thin domestic agenda. Moreover, Bush faced an uphill battle in his 1992 reelection bid due to the state of the economy. Bush biographer Jon Meacham discusses an early campaign meeting:

"On the first weekend in August, Bush convened a political meeting at Camp David. The subject: the dreaded 1992 presidential campaign. There were about thirty people there, and the session opened with a dispiriting presentation from Bob Teeter, whose polling suggested that *domestic and economic concerns* were more important than global ones. . . . While Bush's foreign policy was viewed positively by 72 percent of voters, only 21 percent approved of his handling of the home front"[32] (emphasis added).

Bush foresaw the economy's effect on his reelection chances. His diary entries from the months before the election consistently return to the hope that the economy would recover in time to deliver a victory. But hope is not a strategy, and Bush lacked tangible domestic policy successes to hang his hat on. He had signed significant legislation on the environment, education, and disabilities, but these accomplishments happened early in his term and were long forgotten.

With no meaningful domestic successes to boast about, Bush had no choice but to campaign on foreign policy. He revealed the weakness of his position by touting his international accomplishments in his nomination acceptance speech:

> Just pause for a moment to reflect on what we've done. *Germany* is united, and a slab of the Berlin Wall sits right outside this Astrodome. *Arabs and Israelis* now sit face to face and talk peace, and every hostage held in *Lebanon* is free. The conflict in *El Salvador* is over, and free elections brought democracy to *Nicaragua*. Black and white *South Africans* cheered each other at the Olympics. The *Soviet Union* can only be found in history books. The captive nations of *Eastern Europe* and the *Baltics* are captive no more. And today on the rural streets of *Poland*, merchants sell cans of air labeled "the last breath of communism."[33] (emphasis added)

If Bush had been able to outline his domestic policy successes or a prospering economy, he would have done so.

President Bush again failed to present a meaningful domestic record at a rally in St. Louis. Instead, he attacked Clinton's record as governor of Arkansas:

> Here's a man who wants to be President of the United States, and here is the Arkansas record. They're good people there. Barbara and I lived next door to them. They're entitled to something better: 50th in the quality of environmental initiatives; 50th in the percentage of adults with a college degree; 50th in

per capita spending on criminal justice; 49th in per capita spending on police protection; 48th in percentage of adults with a high school diploma; 48th in spending on corrections; 46th on teachers' salary; 45th in the overall well-being of children. And he said in the last debate, "I want to do for America what I've done for Arkansas." No way! No way![34]

Bush's failure to speak to the everyday problems of the American electorate came to a head in his performance at a presidential debate at the University of Richmond on October 15, 1992. In one famous exchange, an audience member asked the candidates how the national debt had personally affected their lives. President Bush floundered, responding, "Well, I think the national debt affects everybody. Obviously, it has a lot to do with interest rates. I'm sure it has [affected me personally]. . . . If the question—maybe I get it wrong. Are you suggesting that if somebody has means that the national debt doesn't affect them?" After the audience member clarified their question, speaking about laid-off employees unable to afford their mortgages or car payments, Bush replied, "I mean, you've got to care. Everybody cares if people aren't doing well. But I don't think it's fair to say you haven't had cancer, therefore, you don't know what it's like. I don't think it's fair to say, whatever it is, if you haven't been hit by it personally."[35]

In contrast, Governor Clinton responded,

> I've been Governor of a small state for 12 years. I'll tell you how it's affected me. Every year, Congress and the President sign laws that make us do more things; it gives us less money to do it with. I see people in my state, middle class people, their taxes have gone up from Washington and their services have gone down, while the wealthy have gotten tax cuts. . . . When people lose their jobs there's a good chance I'll know them by their names. When a factory closes, I know the people who ran it. When the businesses go bankrupt, I know them. And I've been out here for 13 months, meeting in meetings just like this ever since October with people like you all over America, people that have lost their jobs, lost their livelihood, lost their health insurance.[36]

Bush's opponents could easily paint him as out of touch or insensitive to people's problems on the home front. Without a longstanding record of domestic policy programs, Bush could not point to concrete ways he had addressed the things the American electorate cared about most.

Despite broad admiration for his handling of foreign affairs, Bush could not convince voters that he was the best qualified to handle the nation's domestic problems. "The political tragedy of George Bush came in the last eighteen months or so of his presidency," Meacham wrote, "when he seemed a caretaker at a time when voters were in the market for a dreamer."[37] The voters did not ignore Bush's emphasis on foreign policy but did not reward it either. Despite his noteworthy achievements abroad, Bush failed to deliver domestic solutions and was consequently unable to win reelection.

The Impact of Elections

The results of elections, not just the campaigns that precede them, alter policy priorities. We posit that more favorable election outcomes empower presidents to pursue domestic priorities. In contrast, weaker showings force presidents into the less constrained domain of foreign policy.

The appendix to this chapter, printed in this volume, provides a table of all analyzed elections that identifies key domestic and foreign policy initiatives and the extent to which evidence conforms with expectations. We distilled these lists from the UVA Miller Center's Key Events for each president since 1945, which allows us to assess the nature and type of accomplishments each president had after each election.[38] Looking at the examples of what presidents achieved provides more concrete evidence of how political capital was gained and spent.

Some elections provide ambiguous results about whether the electorate is endorsing a president's policies. For example, President Clinton won his 1996 reelection easily (49% to 40%). Still, the Democrats only gained two seats in the House, while Republicans picked up two seats in the Senate and retained control of both chambers. While Clinton was able to win reelection himself, the Democrats' poor congressional performance muted any perceived endorsement of the president's policies. We, therefore, have mixed expectations about what kinds of policies Clinton should pursue. After his reelection, Clinton largely acted in foreign policy (a sign of relative political weakness). However, this may have been more due to the Lewinsky scandal than the election results.

First-Term Midterms

To refresh, we anticipate that presidents turn disproportionately to their foreign policy agendas after a setback in the congressional midterm elections.

That story is born out in four out of twelve instances: Truman after the 1946 election, Eisenhower after 1954, Bush 41 after 1990, and Clinton after 1994.

After the 1946 midterm, Truman worked to implement the Marshall Plan, recognize Israel, conduct the Berlin airlift, and institute the Truman Doctrine. From 1954 until his reelection campaign in 1956, Eisenhower also had a strong foreign policy focus. During this time, he signed a mutual defense pact with Taiwan, levied nuclear threats against China, and approved U2 reconnaissance flights over the Soviet Union. As noted, George H. W. Bush had a strong predisposition toward foreign policy, as was evident in his agenda after the 1990 midterm. Most significantly, he sent troops to Saudi Arabia and focused on the Gulf War after Saddam Hussein's invasion of Kuwait. Finally, following a major setback in the 1994 midterms, Clinton extended loans to Mexico, recognized Vietnam, conducted NATO strikes against Serbia, attempted a rapprochement with Russia, worked toward the Dayton Peace Accords, sent troops to Bosnia, launched missile strikes against Iraq, and implemented a nuclear test ban. These four cases support the notion that presidents have little choice but to focus on foreign policy if midterm elections confront them with a setback.

After the 1978 midterm election, Carter's agenda also leaned toward foreign policy: granting full diplomatic status to the People's Republic of China; signing the SALT II agreement; implementing PD-59; and announcing the Carter Doctrine, which established human rights as a central tenet of American foreign policy. However, Carter pursued a significant domestic agenda in parallel: implementing the Phase II energy plan, establishing the Department of Education, and commenting on the state of public opinion with the malaise speech.

There is one instance in which the midterm election produced mixed results, but the president was nonetheless able to pursue a vigorous domestic agenda: Nixon in 1970. While we already discussed Nixon's actions in the lead-up to the 1970 midterm, it is worth noting that he focused more on domestic policy after the election—signing the Occupational Safety and Health Act (OSHA), Emergency Employment Act, and Economic Stabilization Act, among others.

Kennedy faced similarly mixed results in 1962, with the Democrats picking up seats in the Senate but the Republicans gaining in the House. Kennedy did not govern long after the 1962 midterms, but his agenda trended toward foreign policy. He gave an address at American University outlining American priorities concerning the Soviet Union and went on to sign a nuclear test ban treaty.

In three cases, presidents diverged somewhat from an anticipated emphasis on foreign policy (Ford in 1974, Reagan in 1982, and Obama in 2010). After the 1974 election, despite Democratic gains in both the Senate and the House, Ford pursued an agenda that largely focused on addressing the economic problems in the United States. Domestic efforts included the Whip Inflation Now (WIN) campaign, the "reluctant" signing of the Tax Reduction Act of 1975, the Energy Policy Conservation Act, and the Federal Election Commission Act. By contrast, his most significant foreign policy accomplishments were withdrawing from Vietnam, visiting Japan, conducting airstrikes on Cambodia, and evacuating Americans from Lebanon.

In 1982, Reagan similarly focused on domestic affairs after Democrats picked up seats in both the Senate and the House. Reagan emphasized the economy: increasing the gas tax, pursuing the SDI, reforming social security, appointing Paul Volcker to a second term as head of the US Federal Reserve, implementing tax cuts, and making a deficit-reduction push. Reagan did, however, preside over the invasion of Grenada and the withdrawal from Lebanon.

Lastly, after the 2010 elections delivered six more Republicans to the Senate and sixty-three to the House, President Obama also focused more on domestic policy, counter to our expectations. On the home front, Obama instituted a federal pay freeze, extended tax cuts, repealed Don't Ask, Don't Tell, signed the Budget Control Act, presented the American Jobs Act, and instituted the STOCK Act. Notably, however, nearly all these actions were accomplished by executive order rather than through Congress. By contrast, his significant foreign policy achievements were New START, the killing of Osama bin Laden, and the end of the Iraq War.

Though we anticipated a domestic focus after the 2002 midterm, President George W. Bush spent more political capital on foreign policy. The election was one of the rare instances in which the president's party gained seats in both the House and the Senate. With such defiance of historical precedent, our theory anticipates that Bush would have utilized his political capital to pursue more difficult but electorally rewarding domestic actions. Bush, however, concentrated on justifying the invasion of Iraq and its eventual execution. His domestic actions included tax cuts (later reversed to fund the war), a late-term abortion ban, and an overhaul of Medicare.

Second-Term Midterms

The dynamics of agendas after the second term are heavily influenced by presidential term limits and the resulting lame duck period.[39] Four cases in which the president emphasized foreign policy adhere to our expectations (Truman after the 1950 midterm, Eisenhower after 1958, Reagan after 1986, and Obama after 2014). In two instances, however, the president's agenda trended toward foreign policy where we would expect a domestic focus (Clinton in 1998 and GW Bush after 2006).

The 1950 midterms saw Republicans gain five seats in the Senate and twenty-eight seats in the House. While Democrats retained control of both chambers, we would expect Truman to be more constrained and focused on foreign policy, as indeed he was. Truman was consumed with the Korean War, particularly after the Chinese intervened. During this time, Truman relieved Douglas MacArthur of command, tested a hydrogen bomb, and signed a large-scale foreign aid program. In contrast, his domestic actions after the 1950 elections centered on wage and price controls and handling a steel strike. Similarly, Democratic gains of fifteen seats in the Senate and forty-nine in the House in the 1958 midterm diminished Eisenhower's position. Eisenhower did pursue some domestic action, including Hawaii's statehood, the Landrum Griffin Act, the use of Taft-Hartley against steel and dockworkers, and addressing civil rights. However, Eisenhower's involvement in international affairs was more consequential. He hosted Soviet premier Khrushchev at Camp David, started preparing the CIA for the Bay of Pigs invasion, severed relations with Cuba, and addressed the fallout after Gary Powers was shot down over the Soviet Union.

In the 1986 midterm, Democrats gained nine seats and control of the Senate while adding five seats to their House majority. Reagan also reacted to this deterioration in his political position with the predicted shift toward his foreign policy agenda, selling arms to Iran to fund Nicaraguan Contras, visiting the Soviet Union, and signing a nuclear treaty. Reagan limited his major domestic actions to the Water Quality Control Act (which he failed to veto) and prohibitions against abortion assistance.

In 2014, Republicans gained nine seats and control of the Senate while adding thirteen seats to their House majority. As expected, these legislative headwinds pushed President Obama toward international affairs. He pursued and signed the Joint Comprehensive Plan of Action (JCPOA) and the Paris Climate Accords. On the home front, Obama passed the Clean Power Plan and the Veteran Suicide Act, while making failed attempts at immigration reform and free community college.

It is clear, however, that the outcomes of midterm elections are among several drivers of presidential agendas. In two cases (Clinton after 1998 and Bush after 2006), presidents pursued foreign policy objectives despite solid showings in the midterm. Clinton authorized strikes against Iraq and NATO attacks against Serbia, signed a trade deal with China, hosted a peace summit with Israel and Palestine, and held talks with new Russian president Vladimir Putin. However, this exception proves the rule, because the ongoing Lewinsky investigation sapped Clinton's political power coming out of the election. Conversely, after the 2006 elections, President Bush reoriented toward domestic policies despite Democratic gains in both the Senate and House (Democrats gained six seats in the Senate and thirty-one in the House). While Bush continued to deal with the Iraq War, including the surge of troops, he also was confronted with a mounting financial crisis. Bush made significant strides in domestic policy, including the passage of an antiterrorism bill, a fuel efficiency bill, a stimulus package, and the takeover of Fannie Mae and Freddie Mac.

Second-Term Presidents

The outcome of a reelection bid is the ultimate signal from the American electorate of its support for the president's policies. Reelections can affirm broad public support. Of course, this is the end of the line for some presidents. However, a president can win without obtaining a ringing endorsement of their policies and emerge weakened but still in power.

Of the eight presidents to win reelection since 1946, six prioritized domestic politics after victory on the strength of their mandates. Two, however, (Regan in 1984 and Clinton in 1996) primarily pursued foreign policy after securing a second term with a substantial margin.

The 1948, 1956, 1964, 1972, 2004, and 2012 elections relatively neatly adhere to the logic that electorally empowered presidents will expend that capital on domestic priorities. In 1948, President Truman secured an unexpected second presidential term by a narrow margin. However, his political prospects were bolstered by the congressional election results, with Democrats adding nine seats in the Senate and seventy-five in the House, gaining control of both chambers. Despite confronting the emerging threat of the Cold War with the formation of NATO and the start of the war in Korea, Truman pursued an ambitious slate of domestic priorities. He instituted the Fair Deal program, which instituted sweeping social reforms. While Congress did not act on all the items on Truman's twenty-one-point plan, a number were instituted, including a national health insurance plan; aid to education; voting rights; tax cuts; expanded social security; additional public housing; an increase in the minimum wage; a public works project; and the creation of the Department of Welfare. Thus, Truman used the political capital from the election to enact his domestic priorities over the objections of conservatives in Congress.

In 1956, despite a middling result in the congressional races, Eisenhower won reelection with a resounding 57.4 to 42.0 margin over Adlai Stevenson. The balance of the Senate did not change, while Democrats added two seats in the House and retained control of both chambers. Eisenhower obtained significant domestic policy advancements on the strength of his personal mandate despite facing an opposition Congress. Perhaps most significantly, Eisenhower oversaw the passage of the Civil Rights Act of 1957 and sent troops to Little Rock, Arkansas, to enforce its provisions. Eisenhower also passed the National Defense Education Act to bolster American science and math teaching and funding. On the foreign policy side, President Eisenhower instituted, and Congress approved, the Eisenhower Doctrine, allowing countries to request aid if threatened by another state.[40] Eisenhower also bolstered the strength of the Sixth Fleet in the Mediterranean and deployed and withdrew US Marines from Lebanon. However, on balance, his domestic achievements required a greater expenditure of political capital, which Eisenhower could only muster because of his strong showing in the 1956 election.

The 1964 election that brought Lyndon Johnson his first presidential term on his own merits is also consistent with the expectation that a strong reelection outcome will empower a president to focus on domestic political priorities. Johnson convincingly defeated Barry Goldwater 61.1 to 38.5. Democrats also increased their margins of control in the House and Senate. Even though Johnson's term came to be defined by the Vietnam War, he fought against that shift at every turn. His policy priorities were domestic. Johnson worked to pass the Voting Rights Act and the Elementary and Secondary Education Act. His efforts also led to the creation of Medicare and Medicaid. Despite the shadow of Vietnam, after his election in 1964, Johnson worked to make good on his domestic promises through his Great Society programs.

President Nixon's reelection in 1972 is another prominent example of a president who focused on domestic politics after winning a convincing mandate. While Nixon's second term would later be defined by the Watergate scandal, with cover-ups and diversions taking center stage, the president did work to institute a series of domestic reforms after the election. Nixon used the strong signal of support from the election to address the stagflation crisis that would hinder the Ford and Carter administrations. Before resigning, Nixon took executive action on the economy by instituting Phase Three and Four price controls, setting a sixty-day price freeze, increasing the minimum wage, and bolstering social security. Before Watergate unraveled the administration, Nixon used the political tailwinds gained from his reelection to prioritize domestic policy.

George W. Bush's reelection in 2004 over Senator John Kerry brought forth a similar dynamic. Bush used the political capital from his victory to pass domestic priorities, despite spending much of the term tending to the deteriorating situation presented by the Iraq War. Almost immediately after his election, Bush signed legislation overhauling the national security apparatus. The Intelligence Reform and Terrorism Prevention Act was signed in December and provided for the creation of the Director of National Intelligence.

The legislation addressed what many saw as intelligence inadequacies that created a permissible environment for the 9/11 attacks. In addition to the IRTPA, Bush also worked to ensure the passage of the Energy Policy Act of 2005, providing tax exemptions and loan guarantees for many types of energy production. Bush also oversaw the appointment and confirmation of Chief Justice John Roberts and Associate Justice Samuel Alito to the Supreme Court. Thus, while the Iraq War (including the siege of Fallujah, the surge in Iraq, and the trial of Saddam Hussein) consumed a great deal of time and attention within the Bush White House, the president used the political capital from his election victory to institute a series of domestic reforms.

The last case that clearly illustrates how presidents apply electorally obtained political capital to domestic priorities comes from President Obama's defeat of Mitt Romney in 2012. Obama won with a slimmer margin (51.1 to 47.2) but a nonetheless meaningful one in the more polarized politics of the period. Democrats also gained two seats in the Senate and eight in the House. While Democrats held the Senate until 2014, Republicans retained control of the House after their sweep in the 2010 midterms. Even before his second inauguration, President Obama used the signal of support from the American public to focus on domestic politics. In January 2013, Obama signed the American Taxpayer Relief Act, which extended tax breaks for many Americans but increased the tax rate for the upper-income bracket. After his reelection, President Obama oversaw the Violence Against Women Reauthorization Act, providing increased funding and services for women suffering from abuse. He also instituted the Bipartisan Student Loan Certainty Act, outlining how the government distributes student loans. The Federal Agriculture Reform and Risk Management Act boosted awareness and spending on agriculture and nutrition programs. Obama also extensively used executive orders to achieve domestic policy goals, signing orders on immigration reform, climate actions, and a minimum wage bump for federal contractors. President Obama dealt with the growing crises in Syria and Ukraine after the 2012 election. Still, he used the incentives he gained in his victory over Romney to take extensive action on domestic policy priorities.

Finally, we turn to the two cases that contradict our expectations, the 1984 and 1996 elections. Despite strong showings by Reagan and Clinton in their bids for reelection, both prioritized foreign policy at the start of their second terms. In 1984, Reagan won in a 58.8 to 40.6 landslide over former vice president Walter Mondale. More importantly, he won the electoral votes from every state except Minnesota (Mondale's home) and Washington, DC. However, the capstone of Reagan's second term was several in-person meetings with Soviet general secretary Mikhail Gorbachev. These meetings changed the tenor of the Cold War by lowering the perceived threat level and finding areas for cooperation. Reagan's domestic achievements were more muted: signing a deficit-reduction bill, moving Associate Justice William Rehnquist to chief, and appointing Antonin Scalia to the bench. Reagan also worked to revise the tax code during this time. Thus, while Reagan did not neglect domestic policy, his signature achievements and the preponderance of his efforts in his second term were on the foreign policy side of the ledger.

President Clinton's achievements during his second term also centered more on foreign than on domestic policy. But, again, Clinton faced a series of scandals early in his second term that sapped his political strength. The Lewinsky scandal started to build momentum, and the FBI was also investigating allegations that the Clinton campaign accepted contributions from foreign nations. Amid these scandals, Clinton turned to foreign policy, where he was less constrained. Clinton met with Russia's President Yeltsin in Helsinki to negotiate nuclear arms reductions (START III). Other significant Clinton foreign policy actions include stabilizing the financial crisis in Southeast Asia; a six-day, twelve-country tour of Africa; the Good Friday Peace Accords between Catholic and Protestant leaders in Northern Ireland; and addressing the embassy bombings in Kenya and Tanzania. Clinton also oversaw the Wye River Memorandum, an agreement between Israel and Palestine to resume negotiations over the West

Bank and Gaza Strip. Thus, because of the scandals facing his administration, Clinton turned to the relatively unconstrained realm of foreign policy despite his substantial electoral victory in 1996.

When considering how presidents react to reelection campaigns, the empirical evidence provides broad support for our expectations. In six out of eight cases in which a president won reelection, they used their newfound political capital to achieve domestic policy reforms. Only Presidents Reagan and Clinton decided to focus instead on foreign policy. In the case of Clinton, the scandals weighing on the administration drove the decision by sapping any congressional will to work with the president on domestic policy. The overall record suggests that presidents will use a reelection victory to focus on priorities that reap more electoral rewards for them and their party.

Conclusion

Electoral cycles systematically influence presidential engagement with foreign policy. We demonstrate that presidents often neglect foreign policy in the lead-up to midterms and reelection. Existing scholarship on the foreign policy implications of campaigns has primarily considered whether electoral incentives might cause leaders to spur a "rally" to boost their prospects. Our findings indicate no strong evidence that presidents engage in this behavior. The potential pathology is effectively the opposite—presidents are far more inclined to systematically neglect foreign policy in favor of domestic policy on the campaign trail. This effect manifests as diminished presidential involvement in diplomacy and reduced use of force abroad. The results of the elections, meanwhile, either empower or constrain executive actions. Strong presidents spend their political capital on domestic achievements (thus minimizing their attention to international affairs). In contrast, weak presidents, constrained on the home front, turn to foreign policy to leave their mark.

What do these electorally driven incentives and constraints mean for post-9/11 foreign policy? While the underlying institutional and electoral features remain unchanged, events since 9/11 have reinforced and hardened the dynamics we discuss. Two points are particularly salient for this discussion: (1) congressional polarization has narrowed the window for bipartisan cooperation, and (2) congressional constraints on presidential foreign policy powers have continued to erode.

Congressional polarization heightens the distinctions between strong and weak presidents. The deepening partisan divide between the parties in Congress since 9/11 has reduced the space for bipartisan cooperation. For example, while President Nixon could feasibly reach across the aisle for pollution legislation, equivalent bipartisan action on climate change is minimal at the present political moment. Weak presidents have little hope of enacting any significant domestic policy, particularly if the opposing party holds Congress. They are therefore constrained to act through executive action and in the foreign policy arena, where they are less constrained. Second, strong presidents know that their chance to pass landmark legislation on the home front is fleeting. This translates to a hyperfocus on domestic initiatives in the brief political moments when they become possible, leading to even greater neglect of foreign policy. If the hope for bipartisan cooperation is essentially zero, strong presidents must move quickly and purposefully before the next election potentially diminishes their political strength.

Second, politics no longer stops at the "water's edge"—to the extent it ever did. Because presidents, especially weak ones, cannot count on congressional support for international initiatives (much less domestic ones), they use the powers of the unitary executive to go it alone. President Obama's push for the Paris Climate Accords and for the JCPOA after the 2014 midterms highlights this. In that election, Republicans gained control of the Senate and added to their majority in the House. President Obama, weakened by these results, turned to foreign policy for substantive achievements. Neither the Paris Climate Accords nor the JCPOA required congressional ratification and both relied on the powers of the executive office (as shown by the Trump Administration's subsequent decision to withdraw from both). In other words, because President Obama's prospects for domestic reforms were essentially nil, he utilized the powers of the executive to make concrete foreign policy strides.

The post-9/11 period has therefore fortified the effects of midterms and reelection campaigns on executive branch concern with foreign policy. While presidents will continue to minimize foreign policy on the campaign trail, we expect elections' empowering and constraining effects to become more pronounced.

Appendix

TABLE 5A.1. **Presidential Domestic and Foreign Policy Achievements, Theoretical Expectations**

Election Year	Anticipated Emphasis	Theory Fit	Domestic Evidence	Foreign Policy Evidence
1946	Foreign Policy	Strong	-EO 9835: Federal Employee Loyalty Program; EO 9981: desegregates armed forces -Congress overrides Taft-Hartley veto -first president to address NAACP -National Security Act of 1947 -Requests legislation on housing, civil rights, and price controls	-Truman Doctrine -Marshall Plan -Recognizes Israel -Berlin airlift
1948	Domestic Policy	Strong	-Fair Deal program, Housing Act, minimum wage raise -Revenue Act of 1950, 1950 Social Security Amendments	-Forms NATO -Plans to develop H-bomb -Sends troops to Korea
1950	Foreign Policy	Strong	-Congress overrides Internal Security Act veto -Declares state of emergency over Communism; wage and price controls -Blocks steel strike; seizes control of steel industry, later declared unconstitutional -Congress overrides McCarren-Walter immigration bill veto	-Mutual Security Act -China counterattacks in Korea -Truman relieves MacArthur -Tests H-bomb
1952	None	N/A	-Wiley-Dander Seaway Act; Submerged Lands Act -Lifts price controls -Creates Department of Health, Education, and Welfare -"Chance for Peace" speech -Rosenberg execution -Proposes Social Security coverage increase -Refugee Relief Act -Requests changes in Taft-Hartley -Warren appointment	-US refuses to sign Geneva Accords -Signs SEATO -Mutual defense agreement with Japan -Korean armistice -Mossadegh overthrown in Iran with CIA backing -"Atoms for Peace" speech -Guatemalan coup

Year	Category	Rating	Domestic	Foreign
1954	Foreign Policy	Strong	-Announces plan to launch artificial satellites -ICC bans segregated transportation -Federal Highway Act -Social Security Act of 1956 -Brennan appointment	-US-Taiwan mutual defense pact -Makes atomic threats against China -Geneva conference proposes "open skies" -Releases U235 for peaceful purposes
1956	Mixed	Strong	-Civil Rights Act of 1957; meets with civil rights leaders -Sends troops to Little Rock; requests aid for education -Signs stimulus for housing construction to combat recession -Recommends civilian agency for space exploration -Alaska statehood -National Defense Education Act -Hawaii statehood	-Approves U2 flights -Eisenhower Doctrine -Doubles strength of 6th fleet in Mediterranean -Sends Marines to Lebanon -Withdraws Marines from Lebanon
1958	Foreign Policy	Strong	-Refuses to end steel strike; Taft-Hartley used against dockworkers, steelworkers -Landrum-Griffin Act -Civil Rights Act of 1960	-Proposes nuclear test ban -Khrushchev visits Camp David -Severs relations with Cuba; CIA trains for Bay of Pigs -Soviets shoot down Gary Powers; Paris Summit ends
1960	No expectation	N/A	-EO 10924; creates Peace Corps -Pledges support to space program -Reduces import duties	-Bay of Pigs; Cuban Missile Crisis -Meets Khrushchev in Berlin -Geneva Conference ends without agreement
1962	Mixed	Strong		-Ends trade with Cuba -American University address on USSR; test ban -Signs nuclear test ban

continues

TABLE 5A.1. (*continued*)

Election Year	Anticipated Emphasis	Theory Fit	Domestic Evidence	Foreign Policy Evidence
1964	Domestic Policy	Strong	-Voting Rights Act -Elementary and Secondary Education Act -Creates Medicare and Medicaid -Urges Congress for civil rights action -Marshall appointment	-Begins bombings in Vietnam; increases troops in Vietnam -Sends troops to Dominican Republic
1966	Foreign Policy	Mixed		-Tet Offensive -Begins Paris peace talks -Visits Brussels
1968	No expectation	N/A	-Selective Service Reform bill; ends draft deferments -Postal Reorganization Act establishes independent US Postal Service -Consolidates federal aid; proposes welfare reform -Aims to end segregation -Requests wage and price restraints -Creates the EPA -Approves plan to form Interagency Committee on Intelligence	-Resumes surveillance over North Korea -Warns Viet Cong; proposes Vietnam withdrawal -Cuts overseas government personnel -Nixon Doctrine; encourages Latin American self-sufficiency -Meets Israeli PM Golda Meir -Five Point Peace Plan for Vietnam
1970	No expectation	N/A	-Signs more than sixty bills, including the Occupational Health and Safety Act, Clean Air Act, Wage Price Controls bill, Emergency Employment Act -Extends Economic Stabilization Act -Declares Keynesian economic outlook -Delays cross-Florida canal -Declares Phase 1 and 2 price freezes -Vetoes national day care -Opposes busing -Passes legislation devaluing the dollar -Start of Watergate; attempts to halt investigation; denies involvement -Endorses revenue bill -Enhances EPA's regulatory power -Increases Social Security taxes and boosts disabled benefits	-Visits China -Authorizes additional bombing in Vietnam -Visits USSR

		Domestic Policy		Foreign Policy
1972	Strong	-Clears entire administration -Declares Phase 3 and 4 price controls; declares sixty-day price freeze -Takes responsibility for Watergate -Watergate coverup; refuses to turn over subpoenaed tapes -Agnew resigns; Ford appointed as VP -Addresses energy crisis -Discloses personal finances -Increases Social Security benefits; increases minimum wage -US v. Nixon over tapes -Resigns		-Signs Paris Peace Accords
1974	Weak	-Announces Whip Inflation Now campaign -FOIA passes over veto; Privacy Act of 1974 -Creates Rockefeller commission to review CIA abuses -Proposes tax cut; "reluctantly" signs Tax Reduction Act; requests tax reductions -Gives address on US energy policy -Refuses federal aid to NYC, then requests loans for NYC -Kissinger out as Nat. Sec. Adviser; Colby out as DCI; Schlesinger out as SecDef -Signs Energy Policy Conservation Act -Reorganizes intelligence community -Builds oil reserves; plans to stockpile oil -Requests Congress accept timetable for regulatory reform -Accepts Congressional revisions of FEC, Federal Election Campaign Act -Viking I lands on Mars -56th veto (funding for electric automobile engine; overridden) -Proposes Puerto Rican statehood		-Visits Japan -Withdraws from Vietnam -Orders airstrikes on Cambodia -European trip; signs Helsinki Accords -Limits nuclear underground testing -Evacuates Americans from Lebanon -Declares peace in Lebanon

continues

TABLE 5A.1. (*continued*)

Election Year	Anticipated Emphasis	Theory Fit	Domestic Evidence	Foreign Policy Evidence
1976	No expectation	N/A	-Pardons draft evaders -Signs Emergency Natural Gas Act; proposes cabinet-level Dept. of Energy -Proposes program on energy conservation; "moral equivalent of war" -Opposes B1 production -Invokes Taft-Hartley to end coal strike -Signs National Energy Act; Humphrey-Hawkins full employment bill	-Secretary Vance to Middle East to reconvene Geneva -Supports Soviet dissident Andrei Sakharov -Emphasizes human rights -Meets Israeli PM Begin, Polish FS Gierek, Shah of Iran -Multi-nation tour -Camp David Accords
1978	Foreign Policy	Moderate	-Announces Phase 2 energy plan -Approves MX missile development -Delivers Malaise speech -Five cabinet members resign -Establishes Department of Education -Announces anti-inflation program -Boycotts Moscow Summer Olympics	-Grants full diplomatic status to PRC -Signs SALT II -Iran hostage crisis and failed rescue -Asks Senate to table SALT II; Soviet grain embargo -Carter Doctrine -Signs PD-59, strategy for fighting limited nuclear war
1980	No expectation	N/A	-Tax Equity and Fiscal Responsibility Act -Proposes increase in defense spending -Budget plan includes funding cuts for 200 programs -O'Connor appointment -Signs tax cuts -Dismisses air traffic controllers after strike -Military buildup (including B1 bombers and MX missiles) -Establishes President's Private Sector Survey on Cost Control	-Lifts Soviet grain embargo -No IRBMs in Europe -Sanctions Poland following imposition of martial law -Addresses Parliament on Falklands conflict -Visits West Berlin

1982	Foreign Policy	Weak	-Signs gas tax, Social Security reform
-Nominates Volcker for 2nd term
-Final tax cuts go into effect; urges deficit reduction
-MX missile compromise with Congress; urges development of SDI	-Bombing of Lebanon barracks; withdrawal from Lebanon
-Invades Grenada
-Signs scientific and cultural exchange with China
1984	No expectation	N/A	-Farm credit crisis; eases rules on loan-guarantee program
-Signs Gramm-Rudman deficit-reduction bill
-Rehnquist to Chief Justice; Scalia appointment
-Signs tax code revision	-Announces trade embargo against Nicaragua
-West Germany cemetery ceremony
-Sanctions South Africa over martial law declaration
-Holds summit with Gorbachev in Geneva and Iceland
1986	Foreign Policy	Strong	-Congress overrides Water Quality Control Act veto
-Prohibits abortion assistance	-Iran-Contra affair
-Signs INF treaty with Russia; visits Soviet Union
1988	No expectation	N/A	-Announces bailout plan for savings and loans banks
-Bans semi-automatic rifles
-Signs Financial Institutions Reform, Recovery, and Enforcement Act of 1989
-Signs Fair Labor Standards Amendments of 1989
-Signs anti-drug law; Americans with Disabilities Act; Budget Enforcement Act
-Proposes new taxes
-Vetoes Civil Rights Act of 1990	-Offers assistance to Poland
-Condemns Tiananmen Square
-Fall of the Berlin Wall
-Meets with Gorbachev
-Invades Panama
-US-Soviet arms reduction agreement

continues

TABLE 5A.1. (*continued*)

Election Year	Anticipated Emphasis	Theory Fit	Domestic Evidence	Foreign Policy Evidence
1990	Foreign Policy	Strong	-Signs Clean Air Act of 1990 -Signs Immigration Act of 1990 -Thomas appointment -Signs Civil Rights Act of 1991 -Signs supplemental appropriations act providing aid to inner cities -Signs Unemployment Compensation Amendments of 1992	-US troops to Saudi Arabia; Somalia -Signs CFE treaty; START I; nuclear arms reduction agreements -Gulf War starts -Removes sanctions on South Africa -Meets Yeltsin -Announces aid plan to Soviet Union; nuclear agreement -Attends Earth Summit
1992	No expectation	N/A	-Announces HRC will handle healthcare; unveils healthcare plan -Signs Family Medical Leave Act; proposes welfare reform -Appoints Gore to head National Performance Review -Implements Don't Ask, Don't Tell -Ginsburg appointment -Omnibus Budget Reconciliation Act -Signs NAFTA -Violent Crime Control and Law Enforcement Act (1994 crime bill); Brady Act	-Orders Navy to attack Baghdad -Ambush in Mogadishu; withdraws troops from Somalia -Attends NATO summit -Lifts Vietnam trade embargo -Renews China's Most Favored Nation trade status -Meets with leaders of Israel and Jordan for talks -Haiti's military government cedes power -Sends troops to Middle East to deter Kuwait invasion

Year	Category	Strength	Actions
1994	Foreign Policy	Strong	-Senate approves GATT -Signs Congressional Accountability Act -Government shutdown after confrontation with Speaker Gingrich -Signs line item veto measure -Vetoes partial birth abortion restrictions -Signs Health Insurance Portability and Accountability Act -Signs The Personal Responsibility and Work Opportunity Reconciliation Act	-Signs START I; supports UN measure on nuclear test ban -Authorizes emergency loans to Mexico -Recognizes Vietnam -NATO strikes against Serbia -Improves relations with Russia -Urges peace efforts in Northern Ireland -Troops remain in Bosnia; Dayton Peace Accords -Orders missile strikes against Iraq
1996	Mixed	N/A	-Senate ratifies chemical weapons ban -Signs legislation to balance budget by 2002	-Agrees to negotiate with Russia on START III -Contributes funds to stabilize Indonesia -Visits six countries in Africa; embassy bombings in Africa -Good Friday Accords; Wye River memorandum
1998	Domestic Policy	Weak	-Faces impeachment; later acquitted -Senate votes down Comprehensive Test Ban Treaty -Announces longest economic expansion in American history	-Retaliatory strikes against Iraq -NATO attacks Serbia -Trade relations with China normalize after joining WTO -Summit meeting with Putin -Hosts Israeli peace summit

continues

TABLE 5A.1. (*continued*)

Election Year	Anticipated Emphasis	Theory Fit	Domestic Evidence	Foreign Policy Evidence
2000	No expectation	N/A	-Reinstates ban on aid to international groups performing or counseling abortion -Creates Office of Faith Based and Community Initiatives -Signs $1.35 trillion tax cut -Halts stem cell research -Creates Department of Homeland Security after 9/11 attacks -Signs No Child Left Behind Act -Calls for new laws focusing on corporate abuses	-Attack Iraqi radar sites -Withdraws from Kyoto Protocol; signs SORT in Moscow -Officially pledges military support to Taiwan -Begins Operation Enduring Freedom in Afghanistan -Withdraws from 1972 ABM treaty -Calls on Arafat to end attacks on Israel -Powell travels for talks with Israel-Palestine -Continues trade embargo against Cuba -Congress authorizes force against Iraq; UNSC on Iraq
2002	Domestic Policy	Weak	-Plans $674 billion tax cuts, reduced to $350 billion cut to fund war -Forbids law enforcement from considering race during patrol -Bans late-term abortions -Overhauls Medicare -Calls for constitutional amendment banning same-sex marriage	-CIA announces North Korea has nuclear missiles -Declares war on Iraq -Meets with Israel-Palestine to develop peace plan

Year	Policy Area	Strength	Actions
2004	Domestic Policy	Strong	-Powell out, Rice in at State Department -Creates ODNI; appoints John Negroponte as DNI -Signs Energy Policy Act of 2005 -Roberts appointment; Alito appointment -Same-sex marriage amendment (fails, but Bush supported) -Vetoes bill to lift constraints on stem cell research -Approves border fence
	Foreign Policy		-US forces launch assault to retake Fallujah -Takes diplomatic trip to Europe -Tries Saddam Hussein for war crimes -Works with South Korea on North Korean diplomacy -Vietnamese premier visits to discuss human rights -Admits forces will remain in Iraq
2006		Weak	-Signs Antiterrorism Bill; fuel efficiency bill -Proposes stimulus package to ease housing crisis and oil prices -Congress overrides Farm Bill veto -Treasury takes over Fannie Mae, Freddie Mac -Signs $700 billion bailout plan for bank assets; signs GM, Chrysler bailout
			-Saddam Hussein hanged in Baghdad -US attacks AQ in Somalia; announces troop surge in Iraq -Vetoes congressional bill limiting war spending -Hosts Middle East Peace Conference -Senate ends ban on trading nuclear fuels to India

continues

TABLE 5A.1. (*continued*)

Election Year	Anticipated Emphasis	Theory Fit	Domestic Evidence	Foreign Policy Evidence
2008	No expectation	N/A	-EO to close Guantanamo Bay -Signs Lilly Ledbetter Fair Pay Act; American Recovery and Reinvestment Act -Caps executive pay for companies receiving bailouts; announces Volcker rule -Overturns stem cell research restrictions -Sotomayor appointment; Kagan appointment -Lifts HIV travel ban -Signs Matthew Shepard and James Byrd Jr. Hate Crimes Prevention Act -Guarantees loans for nuclear reactor construction -Grants $900 million to schools accepting new reforms -Signs Affordable Care Act -Approves oil/gas drilling in Gulf of Mexico and off Virginia's coast -Proposes additional NASA funding -Dodd-Frank Wall Street Reform and Consumer Protection Act -Reforms veteran education; institutes post-9/11 GI Bill -Signs Rosa's Law on diction of federal statutes -Institutes Twenty-First Century Communications and Video Accessibility Act	-Awarded Nobel Peace Prize -Pledges aid to Haiti -Signs START

Year	Area	Strength	Actions
2010	Foreign Policy	Weak	-Signs New START -Authorizes raid that kills Osama bin Laden -Announces end of Iraq war -Sanctions Iran over "deceptive practices" -Federal employee pay freeze -Issues nine pardons -Signs Tax Relief, Unemployment Insurance Reauthorization, and Job Creation Act -Repeals Don't Ask, Don't Tell policy; announces support of same sex marriage -Budget Control Act; American Jobs Act; Healthy, Hunger-Free Kids Act -Signs Stop Trading on Congressional Knowledge Act
2012	Domestic Policy	Strong	-American Taxpayer Relief Act; Bipartisan Student Loan Certainty Act -Outlines proposal for comprehensive immigration reform -Signs Violence Against Women Reauthorization Act -EO 13653: climate change preparation; announces Climate Action Plan -Government shuts down after Congress fails to agree on funding legislation -EO 13672: protects LGBT employees -Signs Federal Agriculture Reform and Risk Management Act -EO 13658: increases minimum wage for workers on federal contracts
2014	Foreign Policy	Strong	-Draws red line in Syria over chemical weapons -Sanctions Russia over Crimea -Signs Child Care and Development Block Grant -Clay Hunt Suicide Prevention for American Veterans Act -Announces plan to use executive orders on immigration reform -Proposes free community college; introduces Clean Power Plan -Attends and helps institute Paris Climate Accords -Announces JCPOA (Iran deal) -Visits Cuba

Notes

1. Miroslav Nincic, "Elections and US Foreign Policy," in *The Domestic Sources of American Foreign Policy: Insights and Evidence*, ed. Eugene Wittkopf and James McCormick (Lanham, MD: Rowman and Littlefield, 2004); John Aldrich et al., "Foreign Policy and the Electoral Connection," *Annual Review of Political Science* 9 (2006): 477–502; Philip Potter, "Does Experience Matter? American Presidential Experience, Age, and International Conflict," *Journal of Conflict Resolution* 51 (2007): 351–378.

2. "Nation: Politics: They're Off Running for 1970," *TIME Magazine*, January 26, 1970. https://content.time.com/time/subscriber/article/0,33009,878703,00.html.

3. "Election '98 Lewinsky Factor Never Materialized," CNN, November 4, 1998, http://www.cnn.com/ALLPOLITICS/stories/1998/11/04/impeachment/.

4. Michael Delli Carpini and Scott Keeter, *What Americans Know about Politics and Why It Matters* (New Haven, CT: Yale University Press, 1996); Ole Holsti, *Public Opinion and American Foreign Policy*, rev. ed. (Ann Arbor: University of Michigan Press, 2004).

5. Aaron Wildavsky, "The Two Presidencies," *Trans-Action/Society* 4 (1966): 7–14; Brandice Canes-Wrone, William Howell, and David Lewis, "Toward a Broader Understanding of Presidential Power: A Reevaluation of the Two Presidencies Thesis," *Journal of Politics* 70 (2008): 1–16; Paul Peterson, *The President, the Congress, and the Making of Foreign Policy* (Norman: University of Oklahoma Press, 1994).

6. Only six presidents have deliberately decided against running for a second term: James K. Polk, James Buchanan, Rutherford B. Hayes, Calvin Coolidge, Harry Truman, and Lyndon Johnson. The latter three all took over the office of president after their predecessor died, so they served longer than the four years constitutionally allocated to a single term. Coolidge served from 1923–1929; Truman from 1945–1953; and Johnson from 1963–1969. There are other instances in which the incumbent president failed to secure party nomination for their reelection bid. Examples include John Tyler, Millard Filmore, Franklin Pierce, Andrew Johnson, and Chester A. Arthur.

7. David Lindsey and William Hobbs, "Presidential Effort and International Outcomes: Evidence for an Executive Bottleneck," *Journal of Politics* 77 (2015): 1089–1102.

8. Data on approval rating taken from UC Santa Barbara's American Presidency Project, last accessed April 23, 2024, https://www.presidency.ucsb.edu/statistics/data/presidential-job-approval.

9. There are exceptions, but even they tend to prove the rule. Bill Clinton, despite winning reelection in 1996 by a healthy 49–41 margin, was not able to marshal support for his domestic agenda. This, however, was largely because he was embroiled in an impeachment inquiry. As a consequence of being tied up in Congress, Clinton was forced to pursue his aspirations in foreign policy, where he had

a freer hand to act. After the 1996 election, Clinton pursued nuclear negotiations, attempted to stabilize Southeast Asia, made trips to Africa, and helped to negotiate the Good Friday Accords.

10. David Crockett, *The Opposition Presidency: Leadership and the Constraints of History* (College Station: Texas A&M University Press, 2002), 229.

11. Richard Nixon, *The Memoirs of Richard Nixon* (New York: Grossett and Dunlap, 1978), 545.

12. Nixon, *The Memoirs of Richard Nixon*, 545.

13. Nixon, *The Memoirs of Richard Nixon*, 545.

14. Richard M. Scammon and Ben J. Wattenberg, *The Real Majority: An Extraordinary Examination of the American Electorate.* New York: Coward-McCann, 1970.

15. Nixon, *The Memoirs of Richard Nixon*, 544.

16. Richard Nixon, "Statement in Support of Republican Candidates in Vermont." October 17, 1970. American Presidency Project, UC Santa Barbara, last accessed May 19, 2024, https://www.presidency.ucsb.edu/node/241136.

17. See, for example, Gray, who notes that there is "an American tendency to make many foreign security commitments during periods of conflict but to turn inward after the conflict is over." Colin Gray, *War, Peace, and Victory: Strategy and Statecraft for the Next Century* (New York: Simon and Schuster, 1991), 48.

18. It is important to note that the Republicans technically gained two seats in the regularly scheduled election but lost a seat in a special election.

19. Robert Mason. *Richard Nixon and the Quest for a New Majority.* Chapel Hill, NC: University of North Carolina Press, 2005.

20. Nixon, *The Memoirs of Richard Nixon*, 548.

21. See Table 5A.1 in the appendix for a full list of significant actions by president.

22. Robert Dallek, *Flawed Giant: Lyndon Johnson and His Times, 1961–1973* (New York: Oxford University Press, 1998), 61.

23. Lyndon B. Johnson, *Vantage Point: Perspectives on the Presidency, 1963–1969* (New York: Holt, Rinehart, and Winston, 1971), 103.

24. Lyndon B. Johnson. "Remarks Before the National Convention upon Accepting the Nomination." August 27, 1964. American Presidency Project, UC Santa Barbara, last accessed May 19, 2024, https://www.presidency.ucsb.edu/node/241812.

25. Lyndon B. Johnson, "Memorandum Outlining Some of the Major Issues of the Campaign," October 11, 1964, American Presidency Project, UC Santa Barbara, last accessed April 23, 2024, https://www.presidency.ucsb.edu/documents/memorandum-outlining-some-the-major-issues-the-campaign.

26. Johnson, "Memorandum."

27. Dallek, *Flawed Giant*, 104.

28. Lyndon Johnson, *Vantage Point: Perspectives on the Presidency, 1963–1969* (New York: Holt, Rinehart, and Winston, 1971), 104–105.

29. Johnson, *Vantage Point*, 110–111.

30. Jon Meacham, *Destiny and Power: The American Odyssey of George Herbert Walker Bush* (New York: Random House, 2016), 442.

31. Meacham, *Destiny and Power*, 454.

32. Meacham, *Destiny and Power*, 480.

33. George H. W. Bush, "Remarks Accepting the Presidential Nomination at the Republican National Convention in Houston," August 20, 1992, American Presidency Project, UC Santa Barbara, last accessed April 23, 2024, https://www.presidency.ucsb.edu/documents/remarks-accepting-the-presidential-nomination-the-republican-national-convention-houston.

34. George H. W. Bush, "Remarks at a Rally in St. Louis," October 30, 1992, American Presidency Project, UC Santa Barbara," last accessed April 23, 2024, https://www.presidency.ucsb.edu/documents/remarks-rally-st-louis.

35. "Second Half Debate Transcript." October 15, 1992. The Commission on Presidential Debates, last accessed May 19, 2024. https://www.debates.org/voter-education/debate-transcripts/october-15-1992-second-half-debate-transcript/.

36. "Second Half Debate Transcript."

37. Meacham, *Destiny and Power*, 356.

38. We obtained each key event and eliminated those over which the president had little to no agency. For example, the Miller Center listed Jack Ruby's murder conviction as a key event during the Johnson administration. Because President Johnson had very little to do with Ruby's trial, this is not considered a significant domestic or foreign policy event for LBJ. After removing irrelevant events for each president, we sorted them into domestic or foreign policy categories. It also should be noted that there are instances in which Congress had to pass legislation for a foreign policy accomplishment. President Truman's Marshall Plan and the Mutual Security Act are prime examples. Because the legislation was shepherded by the administration and fulfilled a key administration priority, we code such situations as foreign policy accomplishments.

39. Philip B. K. Potter, "Lame-Duck Foreign Policy," *Presidential Studies Quarterly* 46 (2016): 849–867.

40. Office of the Historian, Department of State, "The Eisenhower Doctrine," https://history.state.gov/milestones/1953–1960/eisenhower-doctrine.

CHAPTER SIX

Modern Day Minutemen?
Public Opinion and Reserve Component Mobilization

Jessica D. Blankshain and Lindsay P. Cohn

One key arena in which Congress's power to "raise and support Armies" and the president's authority as commander in chief directly intersect is the way in which the country generates personnel for the military, in both peacetime and time of crisis. In military personnel systems, such as voluntarism, conscription, and reserve structures, we also see a key intersection between government institutions and the public—who serves in the military, how they are selected, and how they are mobilized has the potential to directly affect the lives of millions of Americans. Moreover, what the public *believes* about these things can in turn affect decision-makers' calculus about policy. This suggests an important possibility: personnel institutions can constrain the president's ability to use the military by imposing political costs or can facilitate presidential freedom of action by hiding them. A considerable amount of scholarship indicates that US public support for military operations is negatively affected by the prospect of conscription,[1] although the mechanism for that relationship is still unclear.[2] What we know less about is how the mobilization of reserve forces affects the public's attitudes toward military operations. In this chapter, we shed some light on how and why reserve mobilization affects US public opinion, and whether it may serve as a constraint on the executive or serve to facilitate executive freedom of action.

Existing research on the connection between personnel systems and public support for military action, both in the United States and internationally, has tended to focus on conscription and in particular on a dichotomy between conscript and voluntary systems. This focus limits our understanding of the US public's relationship to military personnel systems, as the United States has now relied on an all-volunteer "total" force for five decades. Despite the continued existence of the Selective Service System, few believe that a draft is likely to be reinstated for any but the most existential of military conflicts. Throughout the all-volunteer force (AVF) era, and especially in the post-9/11 era, the reserve component (consisting of the National Guard and service reserves) has been used in varying ways that dramatically affect who serves, where, and when. But far less academic attention has been paid to the public's views of reserve component mobilizations. One recent study investigating the effect of reserve component mobilization on public support for a hypothetical military action found no effect relative to use of the active-duty force only.[3] This may be unsurprising after two decades of limited public outcry over reserve-component deployments in support of operations in Afghanistan and Iraq, but it stands in stark contrast to President Lyndon Johnson's view that deployment of the reserve component to Vietnam would impose dramatic political costs on his administration.[4]

Similarly, existing research has not provided clear answers about the mechanisms underlying connections between personnel systems and public support for military action. This is important not only for understanding how different variations on personnel systems might matter, but also for understanding how elite rhetoric about military mobilizations might mediate their effect on public opinion, much as it appears to moderate gender gaps in support for war (as Childree et al. in this volume discuss). Much public and academic discourse implicitly or explicitly assumes that a primary mechanism linking personnel systems to public support for military action is "skin in the game," an individual's perception that they will be personally affected by the conflict. But empirical support for this mechanism is mixed.[5] Furthermore, Blankshain et al. find that an expectation of conscription lowers public support for a proposed military action even after controlling for its effects on perceptions of skin in the game (i.e., costs the respondent expects to bear, personally) and expected casualties.[6] This, along with clearly different effects for the draft versus reserve component mobilization (despite both of those expanding the number of people affected by the mobilization), suggests a role for norms or views about the legitimacy of various personnel systems rather than just the costs they impose. One key difference between conscription and reserve service is the degree of compulsion involved in mobilizing forces, which could affect the public's view of the legitimacy of either the mobilization or the military operation more generally.[7] Another key difference between conscription and reserve mobilization is the commonness of each type of mobilization in the post-9/11 era. Prospect theory suggests the public may use an ordinariness baseline to think about the costliness of a military mobilization. As noted above, the draft has not been used in the United States in decades, while reserve component mobilizations and deployments have become extremely common, beginning in the 1990s and accelerating after September 11, 2001.

In this chapter, we investigate mechanisms that might connect reserve mobilization to public support for conflict, particularly norms of voluntarism and perceptions of unusualness. Studying the reserve component is ideally suited to this investigation, both because it is highly relevant to current US military personnel policy and because reserve-component service is multifaceted in a way that makes it possible to untangle and highlight different aspects of personnel systems. We first briefly review the literature on possible connections between personnel policy and support for war. We then describe our experimental design and present our results. We conclude with a discussion of our findings and avenues for further research.

Literature Review: Public Views of Military Service and Mobilization

It is often argued that personnel policy affects public support for military action and that, in turn, changes to personnel policy can be used to constrain military adventurism. For example, in arguing for a refocus on the checks the founders placed on military adventurism, Lt. Col. Paul Yingling wrote in 2010, "Imposing conscription, mobilizing National Guard and reserve forces, raising taxes and cutting domestic spending to pay for military expenditures will be politically unpopular."[8] He directly connects this unpopularity to governmental constraint: "If members of Congress had to impose conscription and fully mobilize the National Guard, they might have been more skeptical of the case for war."[9] But somewhat undermining Yingling's argument is the fact that at that point the National Guard had been playing a significant role in overseas conflicts for years, with little public push-back.[10]

There is evidence that conscription reduces the American public's support for a hypothetical military action.[11] But even this relationship is not straightforward. Benjamin Fordham, for example, finds that wartime actually increases the popularity of the draft,[12] Pickering finds that states with conscription are no less likely to engage in war,[13] and Horowitz, Simpson, and Stam find that states with conscription both suffer and accept more casualties than those with volunteer forces.[14]

Most of the work on public support for military action assumes that public support is shaped by the expected costs and benefits of a potential action,[15] implying that any policy that raises costs should (ceteris paribus) lower public support. But we know that individuals' perceptions of the costs and benefits associated with the conflict may not reflect an objective reality. For example, prospect theory tells us that people perceive costs and benefits relative to the status quo.[16] In the context of military mobilizations, this means that the public may perceive costs from a military action only if the action requires a significant change in the way the public thinks of mobilization.

Individuals may also consider the costs of military action not only in absolute terms but also in the context of norms about the fairness or appropriateness of the costs. The public may, for example, be more comfortable with servicemembers being deployed overseas when they know those individuals volunteered for military service.[17] There is also evidence that the public cares about the fairness of the distribution of the costs associated with a conflict.[18]

Our experiment is an attempt to test directly for these additional mechanisms connecting personnel systems and public support for military action in order to understand how the public responds to reserve mobilization and how elite rhetoric about mobilization might shape these responses. We think it is important to understand these dynamics because they are believed to have effects on the circumstances under which a president could undertake a major military operation. In theory, the more a form of personnel mobilization creates public awareness and concern, the more constrained a president would be. But presidents are also aware of this and are likely to resist or evade laws designed to create public opinion costs, or limit public awareness of the less appealing aspects of the mobilization.

American Political Culture and Norms about Military Service

Why might Americans be less supportive of a military operation involving conscription or other forms of coercion, even apart from any expectations they might have of paying any personal price or of the overall size of the conflict? The US experience with military establishments is complex, but one steady trend is a general distaste for coercion in favor of voluntarism.[19] The debate among the founders beginning in 1783 and continuing for at least the next three decades was whether to have any federal force of regulars at all or to rely entirely on the state-based militia forces in times of need,[20] but both of these options were predicated on an idea of voluntarism, not coercion. The Federalists—Washington, Hamilton, and Adams, among others—generally won this debate, creating a small, but regular, standing federal force of volunteers.[21] While the concept of a militia of universal white male obligation remained an ideal for many—especially men like Jefferson and Madison—the reality was that militia forces generally consisted of volunteers, anyway, and after about 1795, they fell into disrepair in most states until after the Civil War.[22] Up until the Civil War, the normal mode of raising manpower was for the federal government to issue calls for volunteers for short service terms. These calls were sometimes answered by individuals, often by whole units of state organized militia.[23]

During the Civil War, both the United States and the Confederacy used a form of conscription at the "national" level, but it was designed primarily to encourage voluntary enlistment, and it lasted only a year or two.[24] In the twentieth century, the United States implemented drafts for World War I, World War II, and the Cold War (for this last, beginning in 1948 and encompassing both the Korean War and the Vietnam War). In only two of these instances (the two World Wars) was the US draft total, in the sense that voluntarism was actually disallowed for the duration of the conflict. This was done so that all manpower—military, industrial, agricultural, and public service—could be centrally controlled and coordinated. At least in the twentieth century, the United States has never actually inducted more than a quarter of those registered with the draft.[25]

As the war in Vietnam drew to a close, the policy question confronting Nixon was whether to maintain a peacetime draft, as the US had done in 1948 to 1949 and from 1953 to 1964, or return to the traditional model of voluntary regulars supplemented by reserves and a draft in times of need. The main empirical question was, Could the United States maintain the large standing military now considered indispensable with volunteers alone at an acceptable cost? The scale would be entirely new. Nixon and his advisory commission, made up primarily of economists, determined that it could. As Ronald Krebs has argued, "the AVF was the authentic expression of how the liberal state would meet the demands of national security."[26] The way this was going to be accomplished was with more reliance on the federal reserves and National Guard instead of on conscription. If the Guard and reserves were made complementary to the active component, instead of largely replicating the structures and capabilities of the active force, then the US could still field a large and capable force but without relying on conscription and at a lower cost than a standing force of the same size.[27]

In short, the preference of the US public has always been for voluntarism over coercion. The public has tolerated drafts when they feel they are necessary for national security and when the system appears decently fair, but for the most part they are content to let individuals choose their own form of participation in the national endeavor.[28] The biggest change over time has been the growing willingness of US citizens to tolerate an enormous standing defense establishment and to pay for its maintenance. Voluntarism is as old as the Republic itself.

In the AVF era, when recruiting has become a perennial concern, attention has shifted from the coercive nature of the institution to the motivations of (and *perceived* motivations of) individual service members: are they motivated by patriotism, by obligation, or by self-interest?[29] Ronald Krebs and Robert Ralston categorize four possible types of servicemember motivation based on whether motivation is intrinsic or extrinsic and whether individuals have a high or low degree of choice in joining the military. Individuals may be motivated by patriotism (intrinsic, high choice), civic duty (intrinsic, low choice), pay and benefits (extrinsic, high choice), or escaping desperate circumstances (extrinsic, low choice).[30] Krebs, Ralston, and Rapport found that US public support for military deployments was significantly shaped by public beliefs about why people had joined the military.[31] Specifically, they argue that public support emerges from a "logic of consent" in which members of the public who believe people join the military out of a sense of duty or patriotism also tend to believe that members of the military themselves will support the deployment, and therefore they, the public, also support the deployment. Those who believe people join the military mainly for the pay and benefits or out of a sense of desperation tend to believe the servicemembers are not supportive of the mission, and thus the public are also less supportive.

Prospect Theory, Framing, and the Status Quo

Prospect theory, first articulated by Daniel Kahneman and Amos Tversky, argues that the way a decision is framed, and particularly the reference point used, has a significant effect on the decision-maker's choice.[32] This framework has often been applied to foreign policy decision-making, particularly looking at leaders' decisions to initiate conflicts.[33] It has also been applied to public support for war, in particular the framing of policy objectives as either preventing losses or seeking gains,[34] and to civil-military relations and the extent to which different framing may be responsible for divergent civilian and military views.[35] In the context of military mobilizations, prospect theory suggests that people will perceive the costs or benefits of a mobilization relative to some reference point, rather than in some objective, abstract way.

Absent manipulation, for most individuals the reference point for military mobilizations is likely to be the current "status quo" personnel system, to the best of that individual's knowledge. So, for instance, if the individual is at least somewhat aware that the reserve component has been deployed frequently for the past several decades, they are unlikely to perceive such a mobilization as costly. If, on the other hand, they know that there has not been a draft in decades and are told there will now be one, they are likely to perceive this change as costly or disruptive, which may reduce their support for the military action itself. Thus in today's US context of an operational versus strategic reserve component—one that is regularly used in overseas operations, rather than a "break glass in case of emergency" backup force—we would expect the public to view reserve component mobilizations as a part of everyday life rather than a significant disruption.[36]

Hypotheses

Based on the existing literature, we expect that manipulating perceptions of the reserve component will affect public support for a proposed military action involving mobilizing the reserve component. In particular, we hypothesize that

> H1: Emphasizing the voluntary nature of service in the reserve component will increase support for military action, while emphasizing the coercive nature of reserve component mobilization will decrease support for military action.
>
> H2: Emphasizing that reserve component use is a normal part of military operations today will increase support for military action, while emphasizing that the reserve component was traditionally used only for major conflicts will decrease support for military action.

In addition, we hypothesize that our treatment effects may be moderated by an individual's existing knowledge about the US military and its employment. We are attempting to manipulate what people believe about how voluntary and how normal reserve mobilization is, so we expect people with high levels of military knowledge will have stronger priors and be less affected by our (somewhat subtle) manipulation.

> H3: The effects expected in H1 and H2 will be conditional on an individual's existing knowledge about the US military and its personnel policies. Individuals with high knowledge will be less likely to be affected by our treatments.

Finally, we hypothesize that emphasizing the voluntary or coercive aspect of reserve component mobilization might have spillover effects, altering subjects' beliefs about why people join the military in general.

> H4: Emphasizing the voluntary nature of service will make subjects more likely to believe people join the military for "high choice" reasons, and possibly, following Krebs, Ralston, and Rapport,[37] for intrinsic reasons as well.

In addition to these hypotheses, we also examine whether our treatments seem to have a direct effect on subjects' support for military action, or rather operate through their effect on expectations of the personal or aggregate costs of the operation[38] or the likely success of the operation.[39]

Experimental Design

To test our hypotheses, we administered a survey experiment to a sample of 1,194 US subjects recruited through Lucid. Lucid is a survey sampling service that uses quota sampling to produce samples matched to the demographics of the US population on age, gender, ethnicity, and geographic region. Research has shown that experimental effects observed in Lucid samples largely mirror those found using probability-based samples.[40]

Our survey was administered from June 28 to June 29, 2021. Before beginning the experiment, subjects were asked a standard array of demographic questions covering their gender, education, income, and political views. Overall, the sample was 47 percent male, 74 percent white, 34 percent Republican, and 51 percent Democrat.[41] The median age was forty-three, and 38 percent of our sample had at least a four-year college degree. According to US Census Bureau estimates for 2019, the US population is approximately 49 percent male, 76 percent white, and 32 percent of those age twenty-five and older have a bachelor's degree or higher. Pew Research estimates that as of 2018, US adults were 39 percent Republican and 48 percent Democrat, with these numbers relatively stable over the previous decade.[42] This suggests that our sample is largely representative of US adults.

We also asked whether subjects or their close friends or family members were serving or had ever served in the military. Fifty-two percent of subjects reported no close connection to military service. Fifteen percent reported that they themselves had served, while 34 percent reported a connection only through a close friend or family member's service. Splitting the numbers differently, 15 percent reported a current connection to military service, while 33 percent reported a connection only through previous service.[43] This suggests our sample slightly overrepresents veterans, given that they make up a little less than 10 percent of the general population.[44] Our sample probably slightly underrepresents the population with a close friend or family member who has served. As of 2011, Pew reported that 61 percent of respondents had an immediate family member (a more restrictive definition than close friend or family member) who was a veteran.[45] While that number has certainly declined in the last ten years, it is unlikely to have declined more than ten percentage points.[46] We do not believe these differences will significantly affect our results as we control for connection to the military in our models.

All subjects read a short vignette about a possible use of the US military adapted from one used by Michael Horowitz and Matthew Levendusky:[47] "A country has attacked its neighbor, an ally of the United States. Our ally has asked the U.S. to send troops to help their military repel the attack. The President is considering sending the U.S. military to defend our ally." This type of operation is generally considered highly legitimate by the American public and therefore likely to generate high levels of support.[48]

Subjects were then assigned to one of six experimental conditions designed to influence perceptions about the nature of the mobilization that would provide troops for this military action. In five conditions, subjects were informed, "To provide the necessary troops, the U.S. military will rely on the current all-volunteer active-duty force and will also mobilize the National Guard and reserve forces." In one condition, this is all the information they received. The four treatments were designed to take advantage of the nuances of reserve-component service to highlight the relevant dimensions of mobilization policies—voluntarism and commonness—without lying to subjects.

Two treatments were designed to influence perceptions of voluntarism among servicemembers in the reserve component. To emphasize the voluntary nature of reserve service, the voluntarism treatment added, "The National Guard and reserve forces are comprised of Americans who volunteer for part-time service in the armed forces in addition to their regular jobs." Conversely, to emphasize the coercive nature of mobilization, the coercion treatment added, "The National Guard and reserve forces are comprised of Americans who serve in the military part-time in addition to their regular jobs. If they are mobilized, they must comply with the order or they risk facing disciplinary action."

Two treatments were designed to influence perceptions of whether deploying the reserve component is common or uncommon. The common treatment added, "The National Guard and reserve forces have been mobilized frequently over the past three decades to provide forces for overseas operations, including in Bosnia, Iraq, and Afghanistan." The uncommon treatment added instead, "Historically, the National Guard and reserve forces were mobilized for overseas use only 'in case of emergency' when there were not enough active-duty troops available."

A sixth condition informed subjects, "To provide the necessary troops, the U.S. military will rely on the current all-volunteer active-duty force. The military will not mobilize the National Guard and reserve forces." This condition allows us to attempt to replicate Blankshain, Cohn, and Kriner's finding that mobilization of the reserve component does not significantly affect public support for a military action relative to employing only active-duty troops.[49] No conditions mentioned the possibility of a military draft.

Experimental Results

Public Support for Military Action

Our primary outcome of interest is support for the hypothetical military action. After reading the scenario with the accompanying personnel condition, subjects were asked, "Should the President send American troops to defend our ally and fight the invading country?" We recorded responses on a four-point scale: Definitely should send troops, Should send troops, Should not send troops, Definitely should not send troops. From these responses, we also created a simple binary variable for supporting sending the troops. Overall, 76 percent of subjects supported sending troops to aid the United States' ally. Within each category (send or not) a majority of subjects chose the more moderate option on the scale. 47 percent of subjects said the president "should send troops," while 29 percent said the president "definitely should send troops." Eighteen percent of subjects said the president "should NOT send troops," while only 6 percent said the president "definitely should NOT send troops."

As treatments were randomly assigned, we first directly compared support for the military action across treatment groups.[50] Figure 6.1 shows support for sending troops (using the binary measure) by condition with 95 percent confidence intervals for the active duty only versus baseline reserve component mobilization treatments. Consistent with Blankshain, Cohn, and Kriner,[51] we find no significant difference in means between active duty only (74% support) and reserve component mobilization treatments (78% support).

Figure 6.2 shows support for sending troops (using the binary measure) by condition with 95 percent confidence intervals for the five reserve component mobilization treatments. None of the voluntarism or commonness conditions significantly shift support from the reserve component

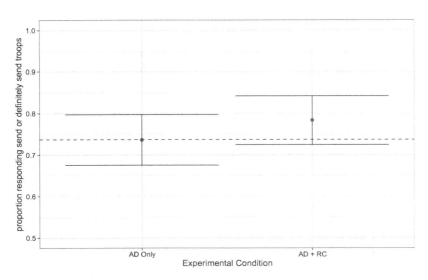

FIGURE 6.1. Average Support for Military Action — Active Duty vs. Reserve Mobilization
Note: I-bars present 95 percent confidence intervals.

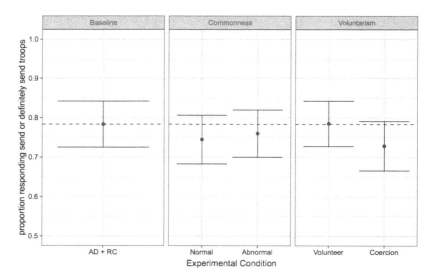

FIGURE 6.2. Average Support for Military Action by Reserve Mobilization Condition
Note: I-bars present 95 percent confidence intervals.

mobilization baseline, as confirmed by difference in means t-tests. The lowest level of support is in the coercion treatment (73%), while the highest level of support is in the volunteer (79%), with the normal (75%) and abnormal (76%) conditions in between.

To more fully explore possible experimental effects with demographic controls in place, column one of table 6.1 shows a logistic regression model using the binary measure of support for sending troops as the dependent variable, dummy variables for the treatments as the primary independent variables,[52] and a range of demographic controls. As suggested by the simple comparison of means, none of the coefficients on the treatments are significant. The relationships between demographic controls and support are largely as expected—Republicans and Democrats are more likely to support military action than are independents, and men are more likely to support military action than women (as discussed by Childree et al. in this volume). Education is also correlated with support for action. Those without a personal connection to the military are less likely to support the military action.[53]

We next directly compared the volunteer versus coercion and normal versus abnormal conditions (rather than comparing all conditions to the reserve mobilization baseline). A simple t-test for difference in means

TABLE 6.1. **Personnel Policies and Support for Military Action**

	Support for Sending Troops (binary)	
	(1)	(2)
Active Duty Only	−0.181	−0.227
	(0.244)	(0.263)
Volunteer	0.052	0.130
	(0.253)	(0.272)
Coercion	−0.316	−0.419
	(0.245)	(0.264)
Normal	−0.125	−0.229
	(0.249)	(0.266)
Abnormal	−0.140	−0.132
	(0.249)	(0.268)
Personally Affected		0.195***
		(0.074)
Expected Casualties		−0.108**
		(0.044)
Expected Success		0.914***
		(0.105)
Intrinsic Motivation		0.357**
		(0.159)
High Choice Motivation		0.134
		(0.170)
Republican	0.837***	0.461**
	(0.199)	(0.219)
Democrat	1.030***	0.612***
	(0.188)	(0.208)
Male	0.388***	0.224
	(0.145)	(0.155)
Age	0.004	0.006
	(0.004)	(0.005)
Education	0.098**	0.058
	(0.047)	(0.050)
White	−0.043	−0.107
	(0.169)	(0.182)
Military Knowledge	−0.051	−0.010
	(0.109)	(0.121)
No Military Connection	−0.550***	−0.359**
	(0.147)	(0.159)
Constant	0.119	−2.846***
	(0.342)	(0.542)
Observations	1,194	1,194

Note: Logit models. Reserve component mobilization baseline is the omitted experimental condition.
* $p<0.1$, ** $p<0.05$, *** $p<0.01$

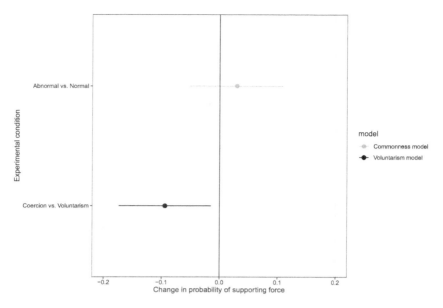

FIGURE 6.3. Direct Comparison of Voluntarism and Commonness Conditions
Note: Horizontal bars present 95 percent confidence intervals.

shows no significant difference in either case, although in the coercion versus volunteer case the 95 percent confidence interval on the difference in means ranges from -0.03 to 0.14, with the volunteer treatment generating higher support. For ease of coefficient interpretation, we use a linear model with a range of controls to directly compare only two conditions of interest. The coercion condition does significantly decrease support relative to the volunteer condition, while there is no significant difference between the normal and abnormal conditions, as shown in figure 6.3.

In summary, H1—that emphasizing the voluntary versus coercive aspect of reserve service will increase support for military action—is somewhat supported by our experimental data. H2—that emphasizing the normal versus abnormal nature of reserve component use will increase support for military action—is not supported by our experimental data.

Manpower System Knowledge

We further hypothesize (H3) that knowledge of military personnel systems will moderate the effects of our treatments because those with higher levels of knowledge will have stronger priors about reserve service. To assess our subjects' prior knowledge of military personnel systems we asked a series of three factual questions about the US military before exposing subjects to our hypothetical scenario. These questions were designed to be challenging. The first factual question asked subjects to choose the best description of the National Guard from among three plausible answers: "A U.S. military service similar to the Army or the Navy," "A state-based component of the U.S. military that can be placed under federal control," or "A U.S. government agency that conducts law enforcement and search and rescue operations." The correct answer was option two. The second factual question asked subjects to identify conflicts from a list (World War I, World War II, Korea, Vietnam, the Gulf War, Afghanistan, and Iraq) in which the US used a military draft, and the third asked subjects to identify conflicts from the same list in which the US mobilized and deployed the reserve component.

Overall, these questions proved difficult for our subjects. Forty-seven percent of subjects answered zero questions correctly, 40 percent answered exactly one question correctly, and 13 percent answered two questions correctly. No subjects answered all three questions correctly. The highest success rate was on defining the National Guard: 45 percent of respondents correctly chose "a state-based component of the U.S. military that can be placed under federal control." Subjects had some knowledge of the history of US military mobilization and knew more about the draft than about reserve component use. Twenty-one percent of subjects correctly identified the conflicts in which the US used a draft (WWI, WWII, Korea, and Vietnam, but not the Gulf War, Afghanistan, or Iraq). By comparison, only one subject correctly answered that the US deployed the reserve component in all conflicts except Vietnam.[54] Figure 6.4 shows the percentage of subjects who believed the United States used each type of personnel system in each conflict.[55] To be scored as "correct" on one of these questions, a subject had to answer correctly for all seven conflicts. From these responses, we created a binary variable equal to 1 if a subject answered *any* of our three knowledge questions correctly and zero otherwise. Regression analysis indicates that in our data, Republicans, men, older subjects, and those with more education were more likely to have some knowledge of US military personnel, while those without a personal connection to the military were less likely to have any knowledge of US military personnel. Preexisting knowledge of personnel systems was not correlated with support for sending troops.

We find no evidence that preexisting knowledge moderated our treatment

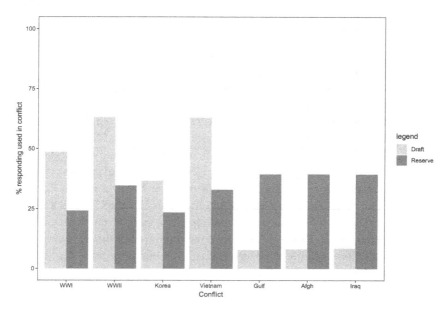

FIGURE 6.4. Subjects' Beliefs about Historical Use of US Military Servicemembers

effects in the way we expected (H3). Figure 6.5 replicates the treatment effects plot from figure 6.2 with subjects broken into three subgroups based on how many questions they answered correctly—zero, one, or two. The confidence intervals in the high-knowledge group are wide given the small number of subjects in that category. As indicated in the plots, none of our experimental conditions significantly affected support for military action among subjects who answered all three factual questions incorrectly. Among those who answered one question correctly, the difference in support among those in the volunteer versus coercion treatments is marginally significant, with a 95 percent confidence interval on the difference in means ranging from -0.02 to 0.25. The difference between the normal and abnormal conditions is similarly marginally significant but in the opposite direction than was hypothesized, with a 95 percent confidence interval ranging from -0.26 to 0.00. For the high knowledge group—those answering two questions correctly—the differences between conditions are again insignificant, although in the expected direction. In summary, H3 is not supported—our experimental conditions did not have a greater effect on those with less prior knowledge of military personnel systems.

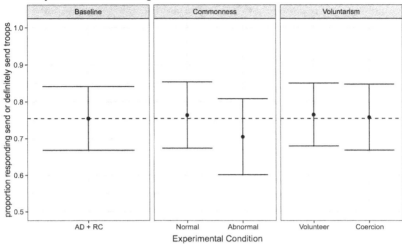
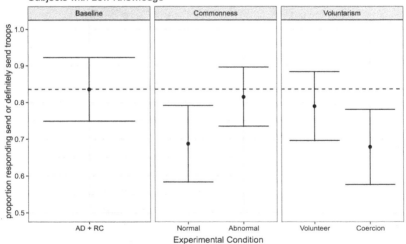

FIGURE 6.5. Treatment Effects by Knowledge Level
Note: I-bars present 95 percent confidence intervals.

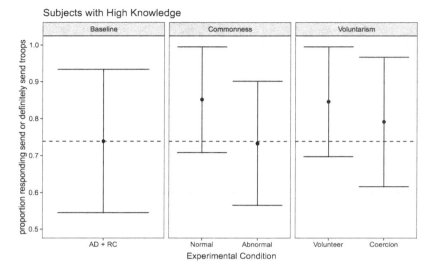

FIGURE 6.5. (*continued*)

Perceptions of Servicemember Motivations

Finally, we hypothesize (H4) that our experimental conditions emphasizing the voluntary or coercive nature of reserve component service could have spillover effects on subjects' perceptions of service member motivations more generally. As shown in figure 6.6, across all reserve mobilization conditions subjects were most likely to select pay and benefits and patriotism as the most common servicemember motivations, with lack of other opportunities as the least popular choice. We further aggregated subject choices into intrinsic (civic duty or patriotism) versus extrinsic (pay and benefits or lack of options) and high choice (pay and benefits or patriotism) versus low choice (civic duty or lack of options). Figure 6.7 shows that subjects in the coercion versus volunteer experimental conditions did not differ significantly in their choice of intrinsic versus extrinsic or high choice versus low choice motivations, contradicting H4. This suggests that beliefs about what motivates men and women to join the US military are relatively durable, at least with respect to somewhat subtle experimental manipulation. As shown in table 6.1, those who believed servicemembers joined primarily for intrinsic reasons were more likely

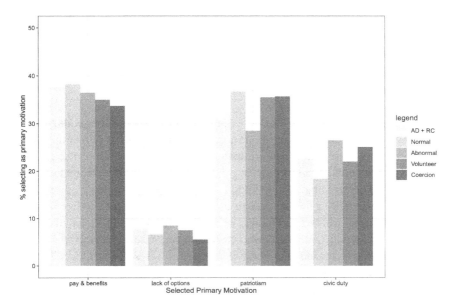

FIGURE 6.6. Perceptions of Servicemember Motivations by Experimental Condition

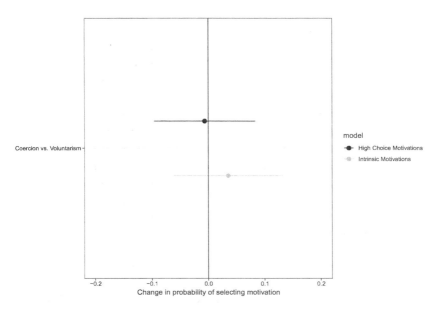

FIGURE 6.7. Treatment Effects of Coercion vs. Volunteer Condition on Servicemember Motivations

Note: Horizontal bars present 95 percent confidence intervals.

to support the conflict, while the high choice variable had no significant effect, consistent with Krebs, Ralston, and Rapport.[56]

Alternative Explanations

It is possible that rather than affecting subjects' support for military action directly through signals about norms of voluntarism or perceptions of commonness, our conditions are instead sending signals about the likely costs and benefits of the conflict. In particular, these conditions might signal something about subjects' likelihood of being personally affected by the conflict, expected aggregate casualties from the conflict, or the likelihood the US military will be successful in its mission. Previous studies have found that, all else equal, higher expected casualties decrease support for military action[57] while increased likelihood of success increases support for military action.[58] The relationship between expectations of personal connection to the conflict and support for the conflict is not straightforward.[59]

As shown in table 6.2, none of our experimental conditions significantly affect perceptions of personal cost (relative to the reserve component mobilization baseline). Those in the coercion condition, however, had statistically significantly higher expectations of casualties and marginally statistically significantly higher expectations of mission success. Expected casualties are negatively correlated with support for military action, while expected success is positively correlated with military action, so the overall effect on support is ambiguous.

Column two of table 6.1 again shows a logistic regression model with support for sending troops (binary) as the dependent variable, with the addition of variables for subjects' post-treatment expectation that they or a loved one would be personally affected, for total casualties, for mission success, and for why people join the military. As expected, the coefficient on expected casualties is negative and statistically significant, while the coefficient on expected success is positive and statistically significant. The coefficient on expectations of being personally affected is statistically significant and positive—that is, those who expected that they or a friend or family member would be personally affected by the conflict were more likely to support sending troops. It is important to note that this is a direct measure of subjects' expectations of the prospective conflict.[60] This result contradicts much conventional wisdom but supports earlier findings that there is not a straightforward negative relationship between "skin in the game" and support for military action.[61]

TABLE 6.2. **Treatment Effects on Expected Costs and Benefits of Action**

	Dependent variable:		
	Personally Affected	Expected Casualties	Expected Success
Active Duty Only	−0.012	0.120	0.133
	(0.182)	(0.179)	(0.199)
Volunteer	0.200	0.263	−0.223
	(0.181)	(0.179)	(0.196)
Coercion	−0.237	0.357**	0.373*
	(0.185)	(0.178)	(0.205)
Normal	0.097	0.155	0.204
	(0.184)	(0.182)	(0.201)
Abnormal	−0.080	0.268	0.071
	(0.184)	(0.178)	(0.200)
Republican	0.151	−0.171	1.019***
	(0.168)	(0.169)	(0.181)
Democrat	0.313**	−0.122	1.082***
	(0.159)	(0.159)	(0.170)
Male	0.344***	−0.057	0.492***
	(0.108)	(0.105)	(0.119)
Age	−0.023***	−0.003	0.004
	(0.003)	(0.003)	(0.004)
Education	0.184***	0.067**	0.073*
	(0.035)	(0.033)	(0.038)
White	0.072	0.243*	0.235*
	(0.127)	(0.125)	(0.138)
Military Knowledge	−0.395***	−0.022	−0.028
	(0.082)	(0.078)	(0.089)
No Military Connection	−0.688***	−0.037	−0.374***
	(0.110)	(0.105)	(0.120)
Observations	1,194	1,194	1,194

Note: Ordered logit models. Reserve component mobilization baseline is the omitted experimental condition.
* $p<0.1$; ** $p<0.05$; *** $p<0.01$

Conclusion

Overall, our results confirm that the US public is not particularly concerned about reserve component mobilization or attentive to military personnel policies as a whole, meaning two of the mechanisms long assumed to be constraining probably are not. The "skin in the game" theory does not work the way many pundits think it does. The US public does, however, seem to care about consent and dislikes coercion in the military context. Public support for military operations is clearly linked to expectations of overall costs, likelihood of success, and likely also legitimacy of the policy objective. But support may also be affected by perceptions of the legitimacy of how personnel are generated.

More specifically, we find some support for the hypothesis that the US public is less supportive of military action when they believe people are being mobilized for military service against their will. Several of our subjects made this logic explicit in response to an open-ended prompt asking how friends or family members might be affected by the conflict, with one responding, "I wouldn't care because the[y] shouldn't have joined the military in the first place," and another noting, "[I] think that they could be sent but that is also what was known when they signed up." Some of our data indicate that the idea of coercion is connected in the minds of the public with both an expectation of higher casualties and a perception of greater national commitment (thus more likely success). Surprisingly, emphasizing the historical "break glass in case of emergency" role of the reserve component does not trigger similar expectations.

The significance of intrinsic as opposed to high-choice motivations supports Krebs, Ralston, and Rapport's argument that the public cares, in particular, whether servicemembers themselves support the action they will be involved in.[62] The fact that none of our treatments affected people's beliefs about motivation to serve indicates that those beliefs may be fairly strongly held and probably connected to political ideology, as Krebs and Ralston find.[63] There is also the possibility of endogeneity at play—individuals may be more likely to attribute intrinsic motivations to servicemembers when primed to think about their role in a highly legitimate type of mission that they are already likely to support.

We find no evidence that Americans are particularly attuned to the current personnel policy "status quo," which indicates that their perceptions of cost are not likely to be affected by ideas of what is or is not "normal." It is possible, however, that conceptions of consent and of commonness are linked through assumptions about what, exactly, volunteers believe they signed up for. For example, while reserve service was previously seen as a way to get some of the status and benefits of military service while committing only one weekend a month, or even as a get out of Vietnam free card, those who join the reserve component today expect to deploy regularly.[64]

The implications of our study for the possibility of policy constraint on the executive in the post-9/11, AVF, operational reserve-era are fairly grim. Current law designates the reserves and the National Guard as the first resort when the active component requires support and the public does not feel affected or concerned by reserve mobilization. Furthermore, all the main variables affecting public support for military operations are subject to elite framing and narrative manipulation. Indeed, our findings underline how desirable it may be for politicians to emphasize the voluntary nature of service when they need to buttress public support.

Exactly how the US public—or any other public—determines the legitimacy of their military personnel system is still not clear. Nor is the relationship between, for example, ideology, general knowledge, specific information transmitted through the media, and beliefs about legitimacy. These are all questions that will require clearer answers if we wish to better understand the mechanisms of public support for or resistance to military operations. At present, in terms of the use of the US military, the president appears to retain significant discretion. As several other contributions to this volume also indicate, the US self-narrative of individualism and voluntarism may actually help policymakers hide the costs of war.

Notes

1. Michael C. Horowitz and Matthew S. Levendusky, "Drafting Support for War: Conscription and Mass Support for Warfare," *The Journal of Politics* 73, no. 2 (April 2011): 524–534, https://doi.org/10.1017/S0022381611000119.

2. Richard R. Lau, Thad A. Brown, and David O. Sears, "Self-Interest and Civilians' Attitudes toward the War in Vietnam," *Public Opinion Quarterly* 42, no. 4 (1978): 464–483; Benjamin O. Fordham, "Historical Perspective on Public Support for the Draft: War Costs and Military Service," *Journal of Global Security Studies* 1, no. 4 (2016): 303–322; Jessica D. Blankshain, Lindsay P. Cohn, and Douglas L. Kriner, "Citizens to Soldiers: Mobilization, Cost Perceptions, and Support for Military Action," *Journal of Global Security Studies* 7, no. 4 (2022), https://doi.org/10.1093/jogss/ogac017.

3. Blankshain, Cohn, and Kriner, "Citizens to Soldiers."

4. John D. Stuckey and Joseph H. Pistorius, "Mobilization for the Vietnam War: A Political and Military Catastrophe," Army War College, 1985, https://apps.dtic.mil/dtic/tr/fulltext/u2/a521559.pdf.

5. Horowitz and Levendusky, "Drafting Support"; Fordham, "Historical Perspective"; Ronald R. Krebs, Robert Ralston, and Aaron Rapport, "Why They Fight: How Perceived Motivations for Military Service Shape Support for the Use of Force," *International Studies Quarterly* 65, no. 4 (2021): 1012–1026; Blankshain, Cohn, and Kriner, "Citizens to Soldiers."

6. Blankshain, Cohn, and Kriner, "Citizens to Soldiers."

7. Krebs, Ralston, and Rapport, "Why They Fight."

8. Paul L. Yingling, "The Founders' Wisdom," *Armed Forces Journal*, February 1, 2010, http://armedforcesjournal.com/the-founders-wisdom/.

9. Yingling, "The Founders' Wisdom."

10. Miranda Summers Lowe, "The Gradual Shift to an Operational Reserve: Reserve Component Mobilizations in the 1990s," *Military Review* 99, no. 3 (June

2019): 119–126; Jessica D. Blankshain, "Who Has 'Skin in the Game'? The Implications of an Operational Reserve for Civil-Military Relations," in *Reconsidering American Civil-Military Relations: The Military, Society, Politics, and Modern War*, ed. Lionel Beehner, Risa Brooks, and Daniel Maurer (New York: Oxford University Press, 2021), 98–100.

11. Horowitz and Levendusky, "Drafting Support."

12. Fordham, "Historical Perspective."

13. Jeffrey Pickering, "Dangerous Drafts? A Time-Series, Cross-National Analysis of Conscription and the Use of Military Force, 1946–2001," *Armed Forces & Society* 37, no. 1 (2011): 119–140.

14. Michael C. Horowitz, Erin M. Simpson, and Allan C. Stam, "Domestic Institutions and Wartime Casualties," *International Studies Quarterly* 55, no. 4 (2011): 909–936.

15. Christopher Gelpi, Peter D. Feaver, and Jason Reifler, "Success Matters: Casualty Sensitivity and the War in Iraq," *International Security* 30, no. 3 (2005): 7–46; Christopher Gelpi, Peter D. Feaver, and Jason Reifler, *Paying the Human Costs of War* (Princeton, NJ: Princeton University Press, 2009); Horowitz and Levendusky, "Drafting Support"; Fordham, "Historical Perspective"; Krebs, Ralston, and Rapport, "Why They Fight."

16. Daniel Kahneman and Amos Tversky, "Choices, Values, and Frames," *American Psychologist* 39 (1984): 341–350, https://www.proquest.com/openview/d908cbfd6937d66b0c74e4f83a34f9ec/1?pq-origsite=gscholar&cbl=60929.

17. Krebs, Ralston, and Rapport, "Why They Fight."

18. Douglas L. Kriner and Francis X. Shen, "Reassessing American Casualty Sensitivity: The Mediating Influence of Inequality," *Journal of Conflict Resolution* 58, no. 7 (October 1, 2014): 1174–1201, https://doi.org/10.1177/0022002713492638; Douglas L. Kriner and Francis X. Shen, "Conscription, Inequality, and Partisan Support for War," *Journal of Conflict Resolution* 60, no. 8 (2016): 1419–1445.

19. Eliot A. Cohen, *Citizens and Soldiers: The Dilemmas of Military Service* (Ithaca, NY: Cornell University Press, 1990).

20. William H. Riker, *Soldiers of the States: The Role of the National Guard in American Democracy* (Washington, DC: Public Affairs Press, 1957); Richard H. Kohn, *Eagle and Sword: The Beginnings of the Military Establishment in America* (New York: The Free Press, 1975); Edward M. Coffman, *The Old Army: A Portrait of the American Army in Peacetime, 1784–1898* (New York: Oxford University Press, 1986).

21. Kohn, *Eagle and Sword*.

22. It was an inefficient use of resources to try to coerce people into service because most would simply desert, and desertion levels were high enough that trying to police it was also well beyond the means of the states or the federal government. Militias were raised through a call, but if a governor could not fill his quota, there was no federal enforcement mechanism against him. Riker, *Soldiers of the States*; Kohn, *Eagle and Sword*; Jerry Cooper, *The Army and Civil Disorder: Federal Military Intervention in Labor Disputes, 1877–1900* (Westport, CT: Greenwood Press, 1980).

23. Coffman, *The Old Army*.

24. John Whiteclay II Chambers, "Conscripting Colossus: The Progressive Era and the Origin of the Modern Military Draft in the United States in World War I," in *The Military in America: From the Colonial Era to the Present*, ed. Peter Karsten, *297–311* (New York: The Free Press, 1980).

25. Authors' calculations using statistics on registrations and inductions from the Selective Service System (sss.gov), and on registration during the Vietnam War from History of the Draft—Daily Press.

26. Ronald R. Krebs, "The Citizen-Soldier Tradition in the United States: Has Its Demise Been Greatly Exaggerated?" *Armed Forces & Society* 36, no. 1 (October 1, 2009): 158–159, https://doi.org/10.1177/0095327X09337370.

27. Patrick M. Cronin, *The Total Force Policy in Historical Perspective* (Alexandria, VA: Center for Naval Analyses, 1987); M. Wade Markel et al., *The Evolution of U.S. Military Policy from the Constitution to the Present, Vol. IV: The Total Force Policy Era, 1970–2015* (Santa Monica, CA: Rand Corp, 2020).

28. Cf. Fordham, "Historical Perspective," on the general unpopularity of the draft.

29. Krebs, "The Citizen-Soldier Tradition in the United States," 162.

30. Ronald Krebs and Robert Ralston, "Patriotism or Paychecks: Who Believes What about Why Soldiers Serve," *Armed Forces & Society* 48 (2022): 25–48.

31. Krebs, Ralston, and Rapport, "Why They Fight."

32. Kahneman and Tversky, "Choices, Values, and Frames." See also Jack S. Levy, "An Introduction to Prospect Theory," *Political Psychology* 13, no. 2 (1992): 171–186.

33. Jack S. Levy, "Prospect Theory and International Relations: Theoretical Applications and Analytical Problems," *Political Psychology* 13 no. 2 (1992): 171–186.; Rose McDermott, *Risk-Taking in International Politics: Prospect Theory in American Foreign Policy* (Ann Arbor: University of Michigan Press, 2001); Rose McDermott and Jacek Kugler, "Comparing Rational Choice and Prospect Theory Analyses: The US Decision to Launch Operation 'Desert Storm,' January 1991," *Journal of Strategic Studies* 24, no. 3 (September 2001): 49–85, https://doi.org/10.1080/01402390108437845.

34. Héctor Perla, "Explaining Public Support for the Use of Military Force: The Impact of Reference Point Framing and Prospective Decision Making," *International Organization* 65, no. 1 (2011): 139–167.

35. Gregory Winger, "Prospect Theory and Civil–Military Conflict: The Case of the 1976 Korean Axe Murder Incident," *Armed Forces & Society* 43, no. 4 (2017): 734–757.

36. Blankshain, "Who Has 'Skin in the Game'?" See also Rachel Maddow, *Drift: The Unmooring of American Military Power*, 1st ed. (New York: Crown, 2012).

37. Krebs, Ralston, and Rapport, "Why They Fight."

38. Blankshain, Cohn, and Kriner, "Citizens to Soldiers."

39. Gelpi, Feaver, and Reifler, "Success Matters."

40. Alexander Coppock and Oliver A. McClellan, "Validating the Demographic, Political, Psychological, and Experimental Results Obtained from a New Source of Online Survey Respondents," *Research & Politics* 6, no. 1 (2019): 2053168018822174.

41. Throughout, Republican and Democrat categories include "leaners," subjects who initially chose "Independent" but when pressed said that they leaned toward one of the two parties. As discussed by the Pew Research Institute (1–14), leaners tend to behave like copartisans in many important respects.

42. Pew Research, "Political Independents: Who They Are, What They Think," U.S. Politics & Policy (blog), Pew Research Center, March 14, 2019, https://www.pewresearch.org/politics/2019/03/14/political-independents-who-they-are-what-they-think/.

43. Subjects were asked to check all that apply from lists describing their own and close friend or family member service. From these responses we created mutually exclusive categories for a connection through one's own service versus only through a friend or family member, and for a current connection to the military versus a connection only through previous service. So, for example, an individual who is currently serving would be given a 1 for own service, a 0 for friend or family service, a 1 for current service, and a 0 for previous service regardless of other connections reported.

44. Jonathan Vespa, "Those Who Served: America's Veterans from World War II to the War on Terror," US Census Bureau, June 2, 2020, https://www.census.gov/library/publications/2020/demo/acs-43.html; Katherine Schaeffer, "The Changing Face of America's Veteran Population," Pew Research Center, April 5, 2021, https://www.pewresearch.org/fact-tank/2021/04/05/the-changing-face-of-americas-veteran-population/.

45. Pew Research Service, 2011 "War and Sacrifice in the Post-9/11 Era," 66. https://www.pewresearch.org/social-trends/2011/10/05/war-and-sacrifice-in-the-post-911-era/.

46. As a point of comparison, from 1980 to 2018, the percentage of veterans in the US population dropped from 18 percent to approximately 7 percent. Schaeffer, "The Changing Face of America's Veteran Population."

47. Horowitz and Levendusky, "Drafting Support."

48. Bruce W. Jentleson and Rebecca L. Britton, "Still Pretty Prudent: Post-Cold War American Public Opinion on the Use of Military Force," *Journal of Conflict Resolution* 42, no. 4 (1998): 395–417; John H. Aldrich et al., "Foreign Policy and the Electoral Connection," *Annual Review of Political Science* 9 (2006): 477–502; Gelpi, Feaver, and Reifler, *Paying the Human Costs of War*.

49. Blankshain, Cohn, and Kriner, "Citizens to Soldiers."

50. One-way ANOVA cannot reject the null hypothesis of equal means across treatment groups for key demographic variables, including political party, gender, age, education, race, and connection to the military.

51. Blankshain, Cohn, and Kriner, "Citizens to Soldiers."

52. Throughout, the active duty plus reserve component control condition is the omitted category.

53. Consistent with Blankshain, Cohn, and Kriner, "Citizens to Soldiers."

54. While the US did deploy some members of the reserve component to Vietnam, President Johnson intentionally avoided a full reserve component mobilization for this conflict, and joining the National Guard or service reserves was a well-known way to avoid being sent to Vietnam. Only 7 percent of respondents answered that the reserve component was mobilized in every conflict listed, so it does not appear that a large number of respondents were confused by this technicality.

55. It does not appear that subjects simply skipped the draft and reserve use questions because they did not know the answer—for each question, only approximately 1 percent of subjects did not select any options.

56. Krebs, Ralston, and Rapport, "Why They Fight." For this specification, we used the binary variables for intrinsic and high choice motivation choices. In an alternate specification using variables for the percentage of servicemembers a subject estimated joined for each reason (with civic duty as the omitted category), those who thought a higher percentage of servicemembers joined for the pay and benefits were less likely to support sending troops, also in accordance with Krebs, Ralston, and Rapport.

57. John E. Mueller, *War, Presidents, and Public Opinion* (New York: John Wiley & Sons, 1973); Scott Sigmund Gartner and Gary M. Segura, "War, Casualties, and Public Opinion," *Journal of Conflict Resolution* 42, no. 3 (1998): 278–300.

58. Gelpi, Feaver, and Reifler, "Success Matters."

59. Lau, Brown, and Sears, "Self-Interest"; Fordham, "Historical Perspective"; Blankshain, Cohn, and Kriner, "Citizens to Soldiers."

60. To check the likely accuracy of these expectations, we checked their correlation with a number of pretreatment variables. Men were more likely to expect to be affected, as were younger and more educated subjects. Democrats were also more likely to expect to be affected. Those with more knowledge of military personnel systems were less likely to be affected. Both respondents who have themselves served and those connected to the military through a close friend or family member were more likely to expect to be personally affected than those without a military connection. The same was true for those with a current connection to military service and those with a previous connection to military service, although the magnitude of the effect of current service was larger.

61. Lau, Brown, and Sears, "Self-Interest"; Fordham, "Historical Perspective"; Blankshain, Cohn, and Kriner, "Citizens to Soldiers."

62. Krebs, Ralston, and Rapport, "Why They Fight."

63. Krebs and Ralston, "Patriotism or Paychecks."

64. Blankshain, "Who Has 'Skin in the Game'?" It should be noted that experience may differ significantly by service.

CHAPTER SEVEN

Gender and the Political Costs of War
Partisan Cues, Gender Heuristics, and the Politics of Public Opposition to War

Aaron Childree, Katherine Krimmel, Max Palmer, and Douglas L. Kriner

Wartime presidents have strong incentives to respond to public opinion. Presidents Truman and Johnson both opted not to run for reelection rather than face the voters as public sentiment turned against costly, protracted, and inconclusive wars in Korea and Vietnam. While George W. Bush won reelection in 2004, public support for the Iraq War eroded during his second term. This rising tide of public dissatisfaction helped catapult Democrats to majorities in both chambers in the 2006 midterms and aided Barack Obama's meteoric ascent to the White House in 2008. Yet precisely how the American public will respond to military conflict—and whether these dynamics have changed in the post-9/11 era—is still hotly debated.

Some scholars have argued that the level of public support varies significantly depending on the policy goals presidents pursue militarily. For example, some research finds that while Americans are innately skeptical of trying to effect internal policy change within foreign countries, they are much more likely to support the use of force when it is intimately tied to US national security interests or justified on humanitarian grounds.[1] In this volume, research by Lindsay Cohn and Jessica Blankshain shows that the personnel policies used to recruit the fighting force may also matter. Conscription significantly decreases support for war, while, somewhat paradoxically, mobilizing the National Guard and reserves has little corrosive effect on war support. This finding nicely illustrates the logic underlying policymakers' continued reliance on the all-volunteer force even during the severe manpower shortages encountered in the mid-2000s, which necessitated lengthy and costly mobilizations of the reserve component.

Other scholars have sought to understand how public support for war changes over time. While early studies suggested that American support for war inevitably wanes as casualties mount,[2] later research argues that this is not necessarily the case. For example, when political elites rally behind the commander in chief and the war effort, public support for war can remain robust even in the face of massive casualties, as witnessed in World War II.[3]

In this chapter, we focus instead on an important source of individual-level variation in support for war—gender—and we examine how the magnitude and even very existence of the gender gap can vary across conflicts and over time.[4] In so doing, we contribute to a long-standing academic literature examining the gender gap and the forces driving it by showing how the size of the gender gap is inversely proportional to the strength and accessibility of partisan heuristics. Our findings also have important practical consequences for policymakers. Over the last thirty years, women have become an electoral backbone of the Democratic Party.[5] As just one quick illustration shows, in the American National Election Study (ANES) data from 1948 through 1988, only 2 percent more women, on average, reported favoring the Democratic presidential candidate at the ballot box than did men. From 1992 through 2020, the gender gap in ANES-reported vote choice more than tripled to an average of over 7 percent. According to exit polls, women's preference for Democrats in recent presidential contests has been even greater still.[6] As such, Democratic presidents have particularly strong incentives to be responsive to the military preferences of women voters. When a significant gender gap emerges or is likely to do so, the pressure on Democratic presidents to scale back military operations or to avoid using force altogether may be significantly higher than aggregate opinion data suggests.

In the analyses that follow, we examine more than eighty thousand individual-level survey responses measuring public opinion toward the wars in Iraq and Afghanistan. The sheer volume of survey data allows us to measure differences in the magnitude of the gender gap across wars and over time within individual conflicts. Our core analyses focus on retrospective assessments of each conflict—whether respondents believed that going to war was a mistake. This question has both practical and substantive advantages. It is the most frequently and consistently fielded question across conflicts, giving us the most data over time. Moreover, past research has shown that retrospective conflict assessments are stronger predictors of vote choice than prospective assessments.[7] Thus, policymakers should be particularly attuned to the dynamics shaping voters' assessments of whether going to war was the right thing or a mistake. Both across conflicts and over time, we find strong evidence that the strength of the gender heuristic in shaping war support varies inversely with the clarity, consistency, and accessibility of partisan elite cues.

The analysis concludes with a more focused evaluation of the gender gap in assessments of the decision to withdraw from Afghanistan and President Biden's handling of it. We find that while the public widely disapproved of Biden's management of the chaotic withdrawal, women were significantly less likely to disapprove of the decision to withdraw than were men, and women were significantly more likely both to support withdrawal and Biden's handling of it. This dynamic at least somewhat mitigated the costs the president paid for making the difficult decision to end the nation's longest war and for unleashing the chaos that inevitably ensued.

What We Know ... and Don't Know about the Gender Gap

Scholars have consistently argued that women tend to be more antimilitaristic than men[8] and that this shapes their relative support for the use of force. The gender gap has been an important feature of American support for war since the advent of modern polling. A significant gender gap emerged in World War II, and it continued to characterize public support for America's less popular wars in Korea and Vietnam.[9] Even in the post–Cold War era, significant gender differences remained; indeed, the gender gap in support for the first Persian Gulf War was one of the largest yet observed.[10] While some evidence suggests smaller gender gaps for the more peacekeeping and humanitarian interventions of the Clinton years and in the immediate aftermath of the 9/11 terrorist attacks, a wealth of research has found a strong gender gap in support for the protracted wars in Iraq and Afghanistan.[11] Analyzing 965 questions pertaining to twenty-four episodes between 1982 and 2013, Eichenberg finds an average gender gap of 10 percentage points in support of military action.[12] Importantly, this gap spans the majority threshold—54 percent of men supported the use of force, on average, compared to 44 percent of women.

It is tempting to infer from this pattern that gender is a critical and enduring determinant of opinion on war, that there is a heuristic rooted in gender identity that inexorably leads men and women, on average, to different conclusions about military engagements. Contextual elements, like the conflict's purpose,[13] may inflame or dampen these differences, but the differences remain broadly consistent and significant. We argue, however, that the gender gap is considerably more limited and conditional than conventional wisdom suggests and that this has important implications for policymakers anticipating and seeking to manage the political costs of military action.

Many early studies advanced structural explanations for the gender gap. For example, some scholars argue that women's greater economic vulnerability made them prioritize butter over guns, making them intrinsically skeptical of costly military ventures.[14] Others argue that motherhood and the associated greater levels of empathy shape the foreign policy attitudes of many women, encouraging a more pacifistic approach to international affairs.[15] A third branch of thinking prioritizes the role of feminism in leading some women to embrace values fundamentally different from those of men; values that, among others, encourage pacifism.[16] Each of these perspectives predicts variation within women, depending on situation, life experience, and ideological beliefs. However, none of the approaches clearly predicts significant differences in the gender gap across cases in similar socio-political contexts or considers how gender might interact with other salient political influences to shape foreign policy preferences.

More recently, several analyses have examined how gender interacts with another critically important part of most Americans' social identity[17]—political partisanship—in forging attitudes toward military action.[18] Over the past four decades, women have increasingly affiliated with the Democratic Party,[19] which, at least since the end of the Vietnam War, has tended to embrace more dovish positions than the Republican Party. As a result, partisanship may be a critical mediating mechanism in producing the gender gap.[20] More generally, Feinstein argues that partisanship and gender interact differently across military contexts and environments, such that the gender gap expands or narrows in response to events on the ground, albeit in seemingly unpredictable ways.[21] Michael Hansen, Jennifer Clemens, and Kathleen Dolan focus on whether partisan and gender heuristics are in alignment or conflict.[22] For Democratic women, these heuristics are aligned: both their gender and their partisan identities encourage them to embrace more dovish foreign policy preferences. By contrast, Republican women are cross-pressured, as the gender heuristic impels a more dovish course, while the partisan heuristic sends a more hawkish signal. As a result, Hansen and colleagues argue that while a significant gender gap emerges in most contexts in the aggregate, the intrapartisan gender gap is stronger among Democrats than among Republicans.

Building on this foundation, we argue that the relative strength of the gender and partisan heuristics in guiding foreign policy attitude formation will vary with the clarity and consistency of the signals sent by trusted elites and with the salience of the use of force on the public agenda. When partisan elites send clear signals to an attentive public, partisan cues may overwhelm gender in shaping military policy preferences. However, when trusted elites send mixed signals or the public is not paying attention, gender may be an important available heuristic informing attitudes.

Understanding precisely how partisanship and gender interact and how this varies across contexts has important implications for policymakers. A wealth of recent scholarship has argued that domestic politics severely constrain the commander in chief's freedom of action.[23] One of the primary objectives of domestic political battles is to influence public opinion, what Louis Klarevas called the "essential domino" of military operations.[24] If gender gaps are inevitable features of American wartime opinion, then building a critical mass of support for military action will require more than simply countering the challenges offered by other political elites,[25] bolstering expectations of eventual success,[26] or minimizing American casualties.[27] For Democratic presidents in particular, a significant gender gap in support for war could be politically crippling given that women are a critical constituency within the Democratic coalition. Are gender gaps inevitable? Does minimizing them require politicians to find a way to appeal to women in the electorate *as women;* that is, will they need to understand the gender heuristic guiding public opinion on war, and convince women that military action is appropriate or inappropriate under the standard implied by this heuristic? Or can partisan heuristics in some circumstances overwhelm the power of gender heuristics and build solid support for war across genders?

Understanding the nature of gender gaps on opinion toward the use of force is also important for political leaders seeking to mobilize opposition to a military conflict. In this case, the perception of an unavoidable gender gap may inform the tactics of those opposed to the use of force, who are seeking to act as a democratic constraint on those in power. Can war critics count on a more sympathetic reception among women voters? Will sustained public criticism close the gender gap by increasing wartime opposition among men, or will it only widen it by resonating with women while having little to no impact among men?

To answer these questions, we examine the contours of the gender gap and changes in it over time across America's two post-9/11 wars: Iraq and Afghanistan. Analyzing more than eighty thousand individual-level survey responses, we find that the gender gap, while an important feature of public opinion toward war, is far from constant. Rather, the strength of the gender heuristic varies significantly with the clarity and consistency of the signals sent by political elites and the salience of the war on the public agenda.

The Intersection of Partisanship and Gender

Scholars have long sought to understand the gender gap's roots, contours, and boundary conditions. While the gap has been quite durable from a historical perspective, prior work shows that it is not entirely stable. Its size and sometimes its very presence depend on the purpose of the conflict, the type of military action, the expected result, and the degree of international support.[28] While some research has focused on cross-case variation, prior work offers little explanatory power for how the gender gap might change over the course of a protracted conflict. We argue that much of this variation, both within and across cases, can be explained by the relative importance of partisan and gender heuristics in wartime opinion formation.

Many aggregate-level analyses, including Eichenberg's study of opinion on war from 1982 to 2013[29]—the most comprehensive of its kind, to date—do not consider the impact of party identification on the gender gap. As women have become more Democratic than men since the 1980s,[30] some of the gender gap observed in the aggregate could be driven simply by the fact that women are more Democratic than men.

Several studies have explicitly considered the impact of parties;[31] however, they have done so primarily by controlling for partisan identification in a model of individual-level opinion. In most cases, the strength of the relationship between gender and war support is significantly reduced after controlling for partisanship. This suggests that partisanship is not doing all of the "work" in explaining the gender gap, but important questions remain about the relative roles that partisanship and gender play in shaping attitudes about war. Recently, scholars have become more attentive to the ways that gender and partisan identities interact.[32] However, there are still unanswered questions surrounding the dynamics of this relationship, especially the cause of changes in the size of the gender gap across conflicts and even within longer conflicts. Do partisan heuristics overwhelm gender heuristics? Is there a partisan difference—does being a Republican overwhelm gender differences, while being a Democrat does not, or vice versa? Is the gender gap exclusively a reality among women who do not have a strong partisan affiliation with one of the two major parties?

We argue that the strength of the gender heuristic will depend on the relative strength of partisan cues and a war's salience to the public agenda. When partisan cues are clear and strong and the public is attentive to them, gender will have little independent impact on support for war. However, when partisan cues are relatively weak or uninformative or when war is far from the public agenda, the gender heuristic will be a more powerful predictor of war support.

Scholars of political behavior have documented the importance of cues from trusted partisan elites in shaping public issue positions and policy preferences.[33] And given most Americans' dire lack of knowledge about foreign affairs,[34] an extensive literature shows how elite position-taking shapes public opinion on military matters.[35] A cross-partisan elite consensus yields strong and stable support for war.[36] When elites divide on questions of war and peace, public support wanes as many Americans embrace the positions advanced by trusted copartisan elites.

However, the power of elite cues is moderated by two critical factors. First, consistent with Zaller's reception axiom,[37] for elite cues to influence public opinion they must be received. Thus, the influence of elite cues on opinion formation should be stronger (and the influence of gender correspondingly weaker) when the public is paying attention and military matters are more salient to the public agenda. By contrast, when military questions are of relatively low salience, elite cues about the war may go largely unnoticed. With partisan cues being less salient, the gender heuristic should be a stronger predictor of support for war.

Second, when military policy is salient to the public agenda, the influence of elite cues on public support for war should also vary with the clarity and consistency of partisan elite signals themselves. Elite opinion leadership should be strongest when there is a cross-partisan coalition either supporting or opposing the use of force. In such conditions, Democrats and Republicans in the mass public receive trusted signals from copartisan elites advancing the same position.[38] Moreover, support from the presidential opposition party or opposition to the war from the president's partisan allies are costly signals that may be particularly credible and influential to citizens across the political spectrum.[39] As a result, in such conditions elite cues should be most influential and the gender heuristic should be weakest.

When the parties divide on questions of war and peace—often with elites of the incumbent president's party supporting the use of force and opposition party elites opposing it (though see Kreps and Kriner in this volume)—elite cues may still be influential provided that elites in each party send clear and consistent signals. In this context, public opinion should diverge sharply along partisan lines and partisan cues may again overwhelm or at least sharply diminish the importance of gender in shaping wartime opinions.[40] Here, the gender heuristic may be strongest among political independents given the lack of costly elite signals.

Finally, when elites within a party divide and take contrasting positions for and against the use of force, they send conflicting signals to their followers in the mass public. When this occurs, the gender heuristic may be more powerful among that partisan group given the mixed messages coming from trusted political elites.

In the following section, we outline precise hypotheses for the contours of the gender gap across Iraq and Afghanistan and over time as elite discourse and levels of salience vary. Our core argument is that gender gaps are not a constant feature of American public support for war. Rather, gender gaps will be greatest when wars are lower in salience. And when wars are highly salient to the public agenda, the size of the gender gap should vary depending on the clarity and consistency of elite cues sent by trusted partisan elites.

Gender, Partisanship, and the Wars in Iraq and Afghanistan

To test our theoretical argument that salience and the clarity and consistency of partisan elite cues moderate the influence of gender heuristics on wartime opinion formation, we analyze more than eighty thousand individual-level survey responses from the nation's two post-9/11 wars: Iraq and Afghanistan. The salience of war on the public agenda and the

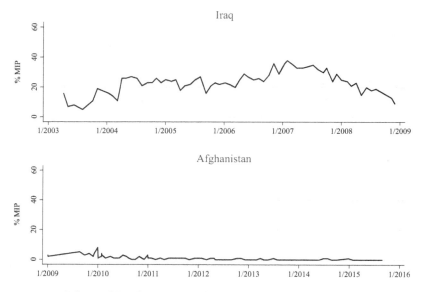

FIGURE 7.1. Salience of Wars in Iraq and Afghanistan over Time
Note: Each graph shows the percentage of Americans responding that each war was the most important problem facing the United States at the time.

clarity and consistency of partisan elite position-taking vary significantly both across the two conflicts and (at least for the clarity of partisan elite cues) temporally within them.

To generate expectations concerning when and among what subsets of the public we expect to observe a significant gender gap in support for war, we first collected data on the salience of both wars using Gallup's long-running "most important problem" time series. Figure 7.1 plots the percentage of Americans identifying the wars in Iraq and Afghanistan as the most important problem facing the country over multiple years.

The Iraq War was highly salient on the public agenda for almost its entirety. From the initial invasion in March 2003 through 2008, almost one in four Americans (23% on average) identified Iraq as the most important problem facing the nation. From 2004 through the election of Barack Obama, who campaigned on a pledge to end the conflict in the Middle East, the war in Iraq was almost always labeled the most important problem facing the country by more than 20 percent of Americans.

However, figure 7.1 reveals a much different pattern for Afghanistan. Despite its length, considerable cost, and the two waves of troop surges that almost tripled the number of American troops in theater during President Obama's first two years in office, Afghanistan never secured a strong foothold on the public agenda. Figure 7.1 begins in 2009 because prior to that year, when the incoming Obama Administration debated the war's future and greatly escalated American troop levels, the salience of the war was so low that it barely registered in public opinion polls. After the expeditious toppling of the Taliban regime in December 2001, the war quickly receded from the public agenda, replaced first by the drumbeats of war against Saddam Hussein and then the Iraq War itself. By March 2002, a Pew poll showed just 10 percent of Americans identifying the war in Afghanistan as the most important problem facing the country. And between that poll and the end of the Bush presidency, Afghanistan rarely registered in any most important problem polls.[41] Moreover, it is not simply the case that public concerns about Afghanistan are wrapped up in broader concerns about terrorism. For example, in the fall of 2009, as the Obama Administration debated its second troop surge, polls routinely showed even fewer Americans identifying terrorism as the most important problem than the Afghanistan War; adding them together would rarely push the tally into double digits. More generally, from mid-2002 through 2008 there is a remarkable paucity of public surveys asking Americans about the war in Afghanistan in any capacity.[42]

Afghanistan does appear more regularly in most important problem polling beginning in the early Obama Administration. However, pitted against the steepest economic recession since the Great Depression, the Afghanistan War gained little traction on the public agenda. On average, just over 2 percent of Americans identified the war as the most important problem from 2009 to 2010, the height of the Obama troop surges, and this topped out at 8 percent in a single poll. From 2011 through 2015, when Afghanistan ceases to appear on MIP polls with any regularity, fewer than 0.5 percent of Americans, on average, identified the war as the most important problem facing the country. This clear cross-war difference leads to our initial hypotheses:

H1: Because the war in Afghanistan was rarely highly salient to the public agenda, the gender gap should be stronger in Afghanistan than in Iraq.

H2: Moreover, because this low salience mitigates the influence of elite cues, the gender gap for Afghanistan should be roughly consistent across partisan groups.

The high public salience of the Iraq War opens the door for elite opinion leadership, which could significantly moderate the power of the gender heuristic in shaping support for war. However, the relative power of elite cues also depends on their clarity and consistency. While most Republican elites consistently backed the Iraq War and the Bush Administration's conduct of it from 2003 through 2008, the positions of many Democrats evolved over time. In fall 2002, 110 congressional Democrats voted to authorize the use of force against Saddam Hussein's regime, including the eventual 2004 Democratic presidential nominee, John Kerry, and Hillary Clinton, who would later become the clear front-runner for the 2008 nomination, while 147 Democrats voted against the authorization. As Adam Berinsky describes, this split within the party persisted in the aftermath of the invasion and continued through the 2004 nominating season as John Kerry, who voted for the war and subsequently resisted taking a clear position for or against it, defeated antiwar candidates Howard Dean and Wesley Clark.[43] Consequently, Berinsky argues that Democrats in the mass public in mid-2004 were forced to base their opinions not on a consensus of cues from trusted, copartisan elites, but by defining themselves in opposition to the supportive cues coming from President Bush. The significant support for the war from some congressional Democrats in this early stage also constitutes a costly signal that should be influential with independents.

However, over time many erstwhile Democratic supporters of the war became vocal critics, and Democrats spoke out more vigorously and unanimously against the war as the conflict progressed (or, perhaps more accurately, failed to do so).[44] By 2006, pledging to wind down a "war of choice" became official Democratic dogma and a key plank of the midterm campaign that returned Democrats to power in both the House and the Senate, triggering efforts during the 110th Congress to try to mandate a timetable for withdrawing American forces.

As elites send increasingly clear signals to their copartisans in the mass public, the partisan heuristic should begin to overwhelm the gender heuristic. This pattern of elite rhetoric generates a final set of hypotheses:

> H3: Republican elites' consistent support for the Iraq War should significantly diminish the influence of gender heuristics on support for the Iraq War throughout its course among Republicans in the mass public.
>
> H4: By contrast, because Democratic elites' position-taking on Iraq evolved over time, we expect a significant gender gap among Democrats in the mass

public in the war's earlier stages, but that this gap will diminish in later years as Democratic elites more consistently and clearly opposed the war publicly.

H5: The gender gap in support for the Iraq War should be largest among independents; moreover, because independents do not follow trusted copartisan elites, the gender gap should be stable over time, rather than vary with the clarity and consistency of elite position-taking.

Gender, Partisanship, and the Iraq War

To analyze the gender gap during the Iraq War, we collected Gallup survey data from 2004 to 2008 from the Roper Center's iPoll archive.[45] We assembled a dataset of every survey respondent from every Gallup poll in this period that included a question on the Iraq War. In particular, we focused on polls asking respondents if they viewed the Iraq War as a mistake. The wording of the question varies slightly, but is generally phrased as follows: "In view of the developments since we first sent our troops to Iraq, do you think the United States made a mistake in sending troops to Iraq, or not?" While Gallup asked other questions about the war as well, we focused on this question because it was the most commonly asked question on the war, it was asked in a generally consistent manner across the time series, and it allows for the most direct comparison to the war in Afghanistan. We treat affirmative answers to this question as a measure of opposition to the war in Iraq.

We collected data from sixty-eight Gallup surveys comprising more than sixty thousand respondents. Model 1 of table 7.1 presents a simple logistic regression, modeling opposition to the war as a function of gender, education, and age, as well as year fixed effects. Consistent with prior work on the Iraq War, we find that women are significantly more likely than are men to oppose the war and believe that the invasion was a mistake. The raw strength of the gender heuristic in the aggregate may be surprising given the high salience of the war and the sheer volume of elite cues on it. However, more nuanced analyses show that the gender gap is both smaller and more conditional than it superficially appears.

Model 2 examines to what extent the Iraq War gender gap is a function of women's greater affiliation with the Democratic Party by including a pair of partisan indicator variables. The coefficient for gender remains positive and statistically significant. However, the coefficient is substantially smaller than that observed in the first model without controls for

TABLE 7.1. **Believe US Made a Mistake Invading Iraq**

	All	All	Dem	GOP	Ind
Female	0.23**	0.10**	0.05	−0.00	0.18**
	(0.02)	(0.02)	(0.04)	(0.04)	(0.03)
Democrat		1.13**			
		(0.02)			
Republican		−1.83**			
		(0.02)			
College	0.17**	0.27**	0.62**	−0.04	0.29**
	(0.02)	(0.02)	(0.04)	(0.04)	(0.03)
Age	0.01**	0.01**	0.02**	0.01**	0.01**
	(0.00)	(0.00)	(0.00)	(0.00)	(0.00)
Constant	−0.73**	−0.70**	0.06	−2.62**	−0.38**
	(0.03)	(0.04)	(0.07)	(0.08)	(0.06)
Observations	62,756	61,149	20,593	20,200	20,356

Note: Logistic regressions with year fixed effects. Standard errors in parentheses.
* $p<0.05$, ** $p<0.01$

partisanship. First differences illustrate the magnitude of the difference. The model that fails to control for partisanship suggests a roughly 6 percent gender gap. However, more than half of this gap is due to the partisan differences between men and women. First differences show that after controlling for partisanship, the median woman is only 2 percent more likely to judge the Iraq War a mistake than the median man, all else being equal. This relatively small gender gap is at least initially consistent with H1, pending the comparison with the magnitude of the gender gap in Afghanistan.

The final three models of table 7.1 estimate separate regressions for each partisan group to examine how partisanship and gender interacted to shape Americans' assessments of the war. We hypothesized that the impact of gender is conditional on partisan messaging. When party cues are weak, gender may shape attitudes about war. When party cues are strong, however, they are likely to overpower the gender heuristic.

The gender coefficients are very small for partisans (indeed, for Republicans, the coefficient is 0.00) and do not even approach statistical significance. This null finding for Republicans is strongly consistent with H3. By contrast, for independents the relevant coefficient is strongly positive and statistically significant. This large gender gap for independents (contrasted with insignificant gender gaps for both Democrats and Republicans) is consistent with H5. The Iraq War was highly salient to the public agenda and there was no shortage of elite cues on the conflict. However, for independents neither Democratic nor Republican elites are necessarily trusted sources, and the most prominent costly signals—Democratic support for President Bush's war—waned over time. As a result, we would expect gender to be a more important heuristic for independents.

Finally, to test the over-time components of H3, H4, and H5, we estimated separate logistic regressions for each partisan group in each year of the conflict. Republican elites, led by the president, steadfastly backed the war from its outset through the Bush Administration's time in office. Given this strong, consistent partisan cue, we hypothesized that a gender gap would fail to materialize among Republicans. By contrast, Democratic elites sent conflicting cues concerning the war in its early stages, but they grew to cohere around a clear antiwar position over time. As a result, we hypothesized that a gender gap would emerge among Democrats in the war's early years, since some Democrats may have relied more on the gender heuristic in the absence of strong elite cues. However, the gender gap should close and even disappear over time as Democratic identifiers in the electorate were exposed to more consistent partisan messaging. Finally, we expected the gender gap both to be greatest and most stable among independents.

Beginning with the bottom left panel of figure 7.2, we can see that a gender gap never emerges among Republicans. Strongly consistent with H3, for each year the coefficient on the gender variable among Republicans is small, and the confidence interval around the point estimates always includes zero. By contrast, among independents (bottom right quadrant of figure 7.2) the coefficient for gender is consistently positive, and in every case except 2004 (where the 95 percent confidence interval narrowly spans zero) it is statistically significant. Consistent with H5, the gender heuristic was regularly influential among independents, who lack trusted elite cues on which to base their wartime opinions.

Finally, among Democrats (top right quadrant of figure 7.2) we find evidence that the gender gap varied substantially over time, which is mostly, though not perfectly, consistent with H4. Somewhat surprisingly, we found no evidence of a gender gap among Democrats in the polls from 2004. This was unexpected given the conflicting signals about the war sent by Democratic elites during this period. As noted previously, the gender gap was also statistically insignificant among independents in 2004. It is possible that a "rally around the flag" phenomenon, driven either by the onset of war itself or by the capture of Saddam Hussein in December 2003, dampened differences across standard political cleavages at the outset; but, as the war progressed, this effect dissipated, and heuristics

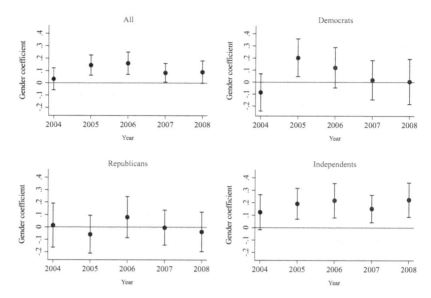

FIGURE 7.2. Coefficients on Gender by Party and Year: Iraq
Note: This figure plots coefficients on gender for twenty separate logistic regression models, one for each subgroup in each year. All models include controls for education and age. I-bars present 95 percent confidence intervals.

rooted in these cleavages gained power. In the 2005 polls, we observed a sizable gender gap among Democrats. However, this gender gap waned significantly over time. In 2006, the coefficient for gender remained positive, but it was no longer statistically significant. And in 2007 and 2008, as congressional Democrats labored very publicly to frustrate the Bush Administration's surge and prosecution of the war effort, the gender gap disappeared altogether.

Gender, Partisanship, and the War in Afghanistan

Finally, we turn to the war in Afghanistan to test H1 and H2. We compiled individual-level data from eighteen polls via the Roper Center's iPoll archive conducted between 2004 and 2015 that asked the same "mistake" question as above, this time regarding military action in Afghanistan.[46] While the question wording varied slightly in some polls, the most common wording was, "Looking back, do you think the United States made a mistake sending troops to fight in Afghanistan in 2001?" Again, this is a retrospective question that allows for the most direct comparison between Afghanistan and Iraq. Most of the polls in this analysis are from Gallup, but because of the relative paucity of public polling on the war in Afghanistan, we supplemented the Gallup polls with polling questions from other organizations that also asked the "mistake" question.[47]

In table 7.2, we present a series of logistic regressions virtually identical to those we estimated previously for Iraq. Model 1 regresses opposition to the war on gender, age, and education, and also includes year and polling outfit fixed effects. This model shows a significant gender gap in views toward the Afghanistan War. Moreover, model 2, which also controls for party identification, shows that controlling for partisanship barely diminishes the magnitude of the gender coefficient in the context of the Afghanistan War. Whereas controlling for partisanship decreased the size of the gender gap from roughly 6 percent to 2 percent in the Iraq data, estimated gender effects for the median subject are virtually identical across models with and without partisan controls for Afghanistan (on average, women are about 7% more likely to believe the Afghanistan War a mistake than men, all else being equal). The greater magnitude of the gender gap in opinions about Afghanistan than in opinions about Iraq is strongly consistent with H1.

Additionally, H2 hypothesized that the gender gap would be present and consistent across all partisan groups in the Afghanistan case. This expectation also receives robust support. Models 3–5 in table 7.2 show that while the gender gap is largest among Democrats, we see a strong and statistically significant gender gap across all three partisan groups.[48] The cross-partisan consistency of the gender gap is a clear contrast to the findings from the highly salient war in Iraq, in which gender gaps varied significantly across partisan subsets of the public.

Finally, to explore the contours of the gender gap in support for the war in Afghanistan over time, we estimated separate logistic regressions for each year and partisan group. Figure 7.3 plots the gender coefficients over time by year. Here we see that for the entire sample (upper left quadrant), the gender gap was statistically significant in every year in which polling data was available. While estimating separate regressions by party inevitably leads to smaller sample sizes and less precise estimates in some years, we still find a large positive gender coefficient in most years for all three partisan groups. By contrast, in Iraq we never observed a gender gap among Republicans and the gender gap among Democrats waned over time until it effectively disappeared by the late stages of the conflict.

TABLE 7.2. **Believe War in Afghanistan Was a Mistake, 2004–2015**

	All	All	Dem	GOP	Ind
Female	0.40**	0.37**	0.44**	0.25**	0.31**
	(0.03)	(0.03)	(0.05)	(0.07)	(0.06)
Democrat		0.31**			
		(0.04)			
Republican		−0.73**			
		(0.04)			
College	−0.28**	−0.29**	−0.23**	−0.27**	−0.40**
	(0.03)	(0.03)	(0.05)	(0.07)	(0.06)
Age	0.01**	0.01**	0.01**	0.02**	0.01**
	(0.00)	(0.00)	(0.00)	(0.00)	(0.00)
Constant	−1.70**	−1.63**	−1.08**	−3.15**	−1.52**
	(0.09)	(0.10)	(0.14)	(0.22)	(0.17)
Observations	19,636	19,636	6,553	5,854	6,670

Note: Logistic regressions with unreported year and polling outlet fixed effects. Standard errors in parentheses.
* $p<0.05$, ** $p<0.01$

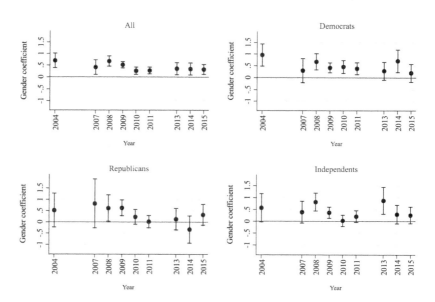

FIGURE 7.3. Coefficients on Gender by Party and Year: Afghanistan

Note: This figure plots coefficients on gender for thirty-six separate logistic regression models, one for each subgroup in each year. All models include controls for education and age as well as polling outfit fixed effects. I-bars present 95 percent confidence intervals.

A final pattern of interest concerns the first three years of the Obama Administration. During 2009, the new administration committed to two waves of troop surges that roughly tripled the number of US forces on the ground. While most Republicans largely backed the administration's moves, although some (quite loudly) criticized the administration's slow timing, multiple prominent Democrats publicly broke with the president.[49]

Because the war was of relatively low public salience throughout this period, the influence of elite cues should be muted. However, it is interesting to note that we find a statistically significant gender gap for 2009, 2010, and 2011 among Democrats during this period of elite dissension. By contrast, among Republicans and independents the gender gap is not statistically significant in either 2010 or 2011. Additional analyses show that during both the Bush and Obama Administrations, there were significant gender gaps among all three partisan groups. However, only during the Obama Administration was the gender gap significantly larger for Democrats.[50] This is at least suggestive evidence that public Democratic bickering over the war may have heightened the salience of the gender heuristic among Democrats in the mass public during Obama's first term. However, it is important to emphasize that in sharp contrast to the highly salient Iraq War, in this lower salience war we consistently observed gender gaps among all three partisan groups.

The Gender Gap during the Afghanistan Withdrawal and Its Aftermath

The preceding analyses found considerable support for our theoretical argument that the size—and even the very existence—of the gender gap varies predictably across conflicts, partisan groups, and over time with the clarity, consistency, and accessibility of partisan elite cues. The strength of the gender heuristic in shaping public support for war is inversely related to the strength of partisan heuristics. Here, we conclude our empirical analysis of the gender gap by focusing on its political ramifications for presidents in a critical case—President Biden's withdrawal of the last US forces from Afghanistan, which marked a major turning point in American foreign policy two decades after 9/11.

In February 2020, President Trump signed a deal with the Taliban that would make good on his pledge to end the war in Afghanistan and withdraw all American troops by May 1, 2021. Upon succeeding Trump,

President Biden initially delayed the American exit, but on April 14, Biden declared that he would end America's longest war by bringing the last US forces home by September 11, the twentieth anniversary of the terrorist attack that precipitated the US invasion.[51] As the American withdrawal accelerated in the late summer, Taliban forces launched a major offensive, routed Afghan government forces, and seized the capital city of Kabul in a matter of days. The gut-wrenching scenes of thousands of Afghans, many of whom collaborated with US forces and risked reprisals, storming the Kabul airport desperate to flee via the last US military flights were reminiscent of the evacuation helicopters leaving the US Embassy in Saigon almost a half century earlier.

With the benefit of hindsight, there is little doubt that the withdrawal could have been better managed and at least some of the human suffering ameliorated. However, the end result—a Taliban takeover of the country—was all but assured. This made withdrawal politically parlous. While opinion polls show that the public had little appetite for continuing the war and most Americans favored withdrawal at least in the abstract,[52] the war was never highly salient (figure 7.1), and for the better part of two decades most Americans gave little thought to the continuing conflict. Given this, the politically easy policy would have been to maintain a US troop presence, continue propping up the Afghan government, and avoid defeat long enough to pass the buck to the next president. Withdrawal—which would inevitably unleash chaos and provoke criticism when the Taliban returned—was politically a riskier proposition. However, given the critical importance of women to the Democratic electoral coalition, if women were significantly more predisposed to support ending the war and the president's handling of the withdrawal than men, it might have at least somewhat mitigated the political risks.

To examine the gender gap in public opinion about the withdrawal, we analyzed data from an ABC News/Washington Post poll in the field as the last American soldier left Afghanistan.[53] The survey asked an adult general population sample, "Which of these comes closest to your opinion regarding the withdrawal of all United States forces from Afghanistan? Would you say you support the withdrawal and approve of how (Joe) Biden has handled it, support the withdrawal but disapprove of how Biden has handled it, or oppose the withdrawal of all US forces from Afghanistan?"

To assess the gender gap in opinions about the chaotic withdrawal and President Biden's handling of it, we estimated a pair of multinomial logit models. In both, the independent variable of interest is an indicator variable for female respondents; both models also controlled for respondents' educational attainment, age, and race/ethnicity.[54] In the first model, we do not control for partisanship; in the second, we include indicators for those who identify as partisans or lean toward the Democratic and Republican parties, respectively. To ease the substantive interpretation, figure 7.4 presents how much more or less likely the average female respondent was to hold each of the three opinions than the average man, all else equal. The models confirm that President Biden's decision enjoyed significantly greater support among women than men. In the model without partisan controls, the average woman was 9 percent more likely to approve both of the decision to withdraw from Afghanistan and of Biden's handling of it than the average man. Women were also significantly less likely to oppose the decision to withdraw altogether than were men, by approximately 7 percent on average.

Moreover, as shown in the bottom panel of figure 7.4, these gender differences remain substantively and statistically significant even after controlling for partisanship. Controlling for gender differences in party affiliation, women were still about 5 percent more likely to support both the withdrawal and Biden's handling of it and 5 percent less likely to oppose withdrawal than were men, all else equal.

While not a direct test of our earlier hypotheses, these results showing a substantively large and statistically significant gender gap in Americans' assessments of the withdrawal from Afghanistan and President Biden's handling of it are broadly consistent with H1. Moreover, they speak to the potential political importance of gender gaps when they do emerge. In this case, the greater propensity of women to support withdrawal and President Biden's handling of it may have mitigated, at least somewhat, the political costs of Biden's gambit.

Discussion and Conclusions

The conventional wisdom holds that the gender gap in support for war is a consistent and pervasive feature of American politics. However, our analysis of more than eighty thousand individual-level survey responses across the nation's two post-9/11 conflicts finds that gender differences in public opinion toward military force are much more conditional than often believed. Some of the gender gap—at least in certain contexts—is the result of gender differences in partisan affiliation. In Iraq, for example,

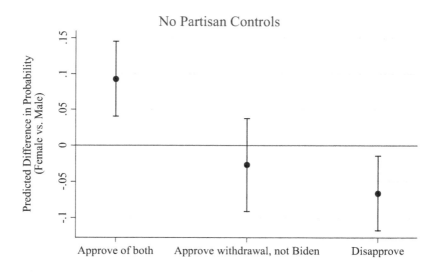
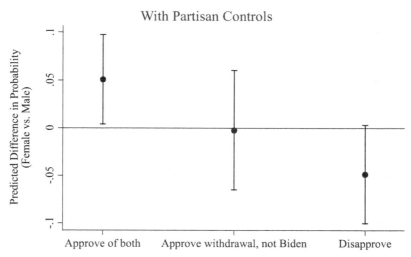

FIGURE 7.4. Marginal Effects of Gender on Afghanistan Withdrawal Assessments

Note: This figure plots the difference in the predicted probability of the average female versus male respondent holding each of the three assessments of the US withdrawal from Afghanistan. Marginal effects obtained from a multinomial logit model with controls for education, age, race, and partisan identification (lower panel only). I-bars present 95 percent confidence intervals.

controlling for partisanship more than halved the estimated effect of gender on opposition to the war. However, this is not always the case; in Afghanistan, the magnitude of the gender gap remained virtually the same in models with and without partisan controls. Instead, in Afghanistan we observed sizable and statistically significant gender gaps across partisan groups.

These results make clear that how gender and partisanship interact to shape public support for war depends critically on context. Specifically, we found that a war's salience and the clarity and consistency of partisan elite signals moderate the influence of the gender heuristic within different partisan groups in the mass public. Scholars have long shown that many Americans look to elites when forming their wartime opinions and assessments. As a result, elite cues could overwhelm and mute the influence of gender heuristics in shaping support for war. However, to be influential and accessible in citizens' minds, elite cues must be received. This is much more likely when the public is paying attention. By contrast, when a war—even a lengthy and costly one—is low on the public's list of priorities, elite cues are less accessible, and the power of gender heuristics is stronger. This is precisely what we see when comparing opinion dynamics in Iraq and Afghanistan. Although both wars were launched shortly after 9/11 and both cost thousands of US lives and (conservatively) hundreds of billions of dollars, Iraq dominated the public agenda for almost five years, while Afghanistan barely registered on Americans' list of the most important problems (figure 7.1). Accordingly, the gender gap was significantly greater in the latter than the former.

The clarity and consistency of trusted partisan elite cues over the course of a conflict also moderate the influence of gender on wartime attitudes. During periods of internal Democratic elite dissension over the Iraq War, we observed significant gender gaps among Democrats in the mass public. By contrast, more consistent Republican elite messaging prevented the emergence of a gender gap.

Many existing arguments about the mechanisms underlying the gender gap cannot explain this significant variation across conflicts, across partisan groups, and perhaps most importantly, over time within the same conflict. For example, consider arguments that gender differences in threat perception[55] drive the gender gap. This theory posits that women perceive greater threat from war than men and are also less supportive of a violent response to that threat because they have greater anxiety about possible retaliation. If this mechanism drives gender differences, there is no clear reason to expect the gender gap to vary over the course of the Iraq War. This mechanism struggles to explain variation in the gender gap over time as well as variation across partisan subgroups. Similarly, other theories suggest theoretical logics as to why the gender gap may vary across conflicts—for example, the principal policy objective of the use of force may matter, with women being more supportive of humanitarian missions than men,[56] or a lack of international support may exacerbate the gender gap.[57] While these arguments may offer insight into variation across cases, they do not offer clear expectations concerning variation in the size of the gender gap concerning an individual conflict over time. Finally, Hansen, Clemens, and Dolan posited that the alignment of ideological and gender heuristics suggests the gender gap will be stronger among Democrats than among Republicans.[58] We find evidence of this in Iraq during certain periods of the conflict but not in others. And in Afghanistan, the only suggestive evidence of a larger gender gap among Democrats is limited to periods of Democratic elite dissension during the early years of the Obama Administration. Our emphasis on the moderating role played by salience and the clarity of elite signaling better fits these patterns and pushes forward scholarly understanding of the gender gap on several fronts.

Future research might examine whether similar dynamics hold in other contexts. For example, Krebs and Ralston in this volume show significant opinion gaps in support for war across racial and ethnic lines in the US, UK, and Israel. Does the strength of racial heuristics in shaping wartime opinion similarly vary with the accessibility, clarity, and consistency of partisan elite cues? Or are racial and ethnic differences in wartime opinions more constant across contexts and over time?

Finally, our findings also have important implications for policymakers striving to maintain strong and stable public support for war as well as for politicians and activists looking to stir up opposition to a military conflict and the political costs such opposition entails.[59] Large gender gaps may superficially appear to be a challenge for wartime leaders eager to avoid political pushback. Political elites seeking to rally public opinion against the use of force may view a significant gender gap as an obstacle to building a broad coalition; or they may view it as a goal, finding a way to activate the gender heuristic to drive up wartime opposition among women who might be predisposed to oppose the use of force. However, our findings suggest that the power of gender heuristics varies significantly depending on elite discourse, particularly when wars are highly salient to the public agenda. When elites send clear and consistent messages, particularly when wars are highly salient, they can close gender gaps in attitudes toward war. Thus, our findings provide additional support for long-standing theories on the importance of elite opinion leadership,[60] while also suggesting an additional mechanism through which elite cues matter: by moderating the influence of gender on wartime opinion formation.

Strong and steady Republican elite support for the Iraq War, even when it proved far more costly in both casualties and financial costs than the Bush Administration publicly promised, prevented the emergence of a politically damaging gender gap among Republicans. From 2004 through 2008, the gender gap among Republicans was almost precisely zero with only 20 percent of male and female Republicans judging the Iraq War a mistake.[61] Even the emergence of a small gender gap among Republicans could have been politically transformative given that if sixty thousand voters in Ohio had changed their votes from Bush to Kerry it would have flipped the result of the 2004 presidential election. By contrast, amid the chaos and battling among political elites in Washington over the 2021 withdrawal from Afghanistan, the significant gender gap that emerged may have helped President Biden. The greater support for withdrawal and his handling of it among women, a core Democratic constituency, may have mitigated at least somewhat the political costs of finally pulling the plug on America's longest war.

Notes

1. Bruce W. Jentleson, "The Pretty Prudent Public—Post-Vietnam American Opinion on the Use of Military Force," *International Studies Quarterly* 36, no. 1 (1992): 49–74; Bruce W. Jentleson and Rebecca L. Britton, "Still Pretty Prudent: Post-Cold War American Public Opinion on the Use of Military Force," *Journal of Conflict Resolution* 42, no. 4 (1998): 395–417.

2. John E. Mueller, *War, Presidents, and Public Opinion* (New York: Wiley, 1973).

3. Adam Berinsky, *In Time of War: Understanding American Public Opinion from World War II to Iraq* (Chicago: University of Chicago Press, 2009).

4. For a complementary analysis of individual-level variation along race/ethnicity lines, see Ronald Krebs and Robert Ralston's chapter in this volume.

5. Janet M. Box-Steffensmeier, Suzanna De Boef, and Tse-min Lin, "The Dynamics of the Partisan Gender Gap," *American Political Science Review* 98, no. 3 (2004): 515–528.

6. Samantha Schmidt, "The Gender Gap Was Expected to be Historic. Instead Women Voted Much as They Always Have," *Washington Post*, November 6, 2020,

https://www.washingtonpost.com/dc-md-va/2020/11/06/election-2020-gender-gap-women/.

7. Christopher Gelpi, Peter Feaver and Jason Reifler, *Paying the Human Costs of War* (Princeton, NJ: Princeton University Press, 2009), 162.

8. Robert Y. Shapiro and Harpreet Mahajan, "Gender Differences in Policy Preferences: A Summary of Trends from the 1960s to the 1980s," *Public Opinion Quarterly* 50 (1986): 42–61; Pamela Johnston Conover and Virginia Sapiro, "Gender, Feminist Consciousness, and War," *American Journal of Political Science* 37, no. 4 (1993): 1079–1099; Nancy W. Gallagher, "The Gender Gap in Popular Attitudes Toward the Use of Force," in *Women and the Use of Military Force*, ed. Ruth H. Howes and Michael R. Stevenson 23–38(Boulder, CO: Lynne Rienner, 1993); Joshua S. Goldstein, *War and Gender* (New York: Cambridge University Press, 2001); Richard C. Eichenberg, "Gender Differences in Public Attitudes toward the Use of Force by the United States, 1990–2003," *International Security* 28, no. 1 (2003): 110–141.

9. Berinsky, *In Time of War*; Mueller, *War, Presidents, and Public Opinion*; Lisa Catherine Olga Brandes, "Public Opinion, International Security Policy, and Gender: The United States and Great Britain Since 1945" (PhD diss., Yale University, 1994); Miroslav Nincic and Donna J. Nincic, "Race, Gender, and War," *Journal of Peace Research* 39, no. 5 (2002): 547–568.

10. Conover and Sapiro, "Gender, Feminist Consciousness, and War"; Clyde Wilcox, Joseph Ferrara, and Dee Allsop, "Group Differences in Early Support for Military Action in the Gulf: The Effects of Gender, Generation, and Ethnicity," *American Politics Quarterly* 21, no. 3 (1993): 343–359.

11. Eichenberg, "Gender Differences."

12. Richard C. Eichenberg, "Gender Difference in American Public Opinion on the Use of Military Force, 1982–2013," *International Studies Quarterly* 60 (2016): 138–148.

13. Eichenberg, "Gender Difference."

14. Mary E. Bendyna et al., "Gender Differences in Public Attitudes toward the Gulf War: A Test of Competing Hypotheses," *The Social Science Journal* 33, no. 1 (1996): 1–22; Nincic and Nincic, "Race, Gender, and War."

15. Deborah Jordan Brooks and Benjamin A. Valentino, "A War of One's Own: Understanding the Gender Gap in Support for War," *Public Opinion Quarterly* 75, no. 2 (2011): 270–286; Sara Ruddick, *Maternal Thinking: Toward a Politics of Peace* (Boston, MA: Beacon Press, 1995).

16. Pamela Johnston Conover, "Feminists and the Gender Gap," *The Journal of Politics* 50, no. 4 (1988): 985–1010; J. Ann Tickner, *Gender in International Relations: Feminist Perspectives on Achieving Global Security* (New York: Columbia University Press, 1992); Conover and Sapiro, "Gender, Feminist Consciousness, and War."

17. Donald P. Green, Bradley Palmquist, and Eric Schickler, *Partisan Hearts*

and Minds: Political Parties and the Social Identities of Voters (New Haven, CT: Yale University Press, 2002).

18. To be sure, prior work did not ignore the importance of partisanship in shaping attitudes toward the use of force. For example, a number of individual-level analyses controlled for partisanship within regression analyses (e.g., Conover and Sapiro, "Gender, Feminist Consciousness, and War"; Brooks and Valentino, "A War of One's Own".). However, until recently few studies focused explicitly on the intersection of party and gender in opinion formation on war.

19. Box-Steffensmeier, De Boef, and Lin, "The Dynamics of the Partisan Gender Gap."

20. Yuval Feinstein, "The Rise and Decline of 'Gender Gaps' in Support for Military Action: United States, 1986–2011," *Politics & Gender* 13, no. 4 (2017): 618–655.

21. Feinstein, "The Rise and Decline of 'Gender Gaps.'"

22. Michael A. Hansen, Jennifer L. Clemens, and Kathleen Dolan, "Gender Gaps, Partisan Gaps, and Cross-Pressures: An Examination of American Attitudes toward the Use of Force," *Politics & Gender* 18, no. 1 (2020): 1–23.

23. David Clark, "Agreeing to Disagree: Domestic Institutional Congruence and U.S. Dispute Behavior," *Political Research Quarterly* 53, no. 2 (2000): 375–401; William Howell and Jon Pevehouse, *While Dangers Gather: Congressional Checks on Presidential War Powers* (Princeton, NJ: Princeton University Press, 2007); Douglas Kriner, *After the Rubicon: Congress, Presidents, and the Politics of Waging War* (Chicago: University of Chicago Press, 2010); Jack Goldsmith, *Power and Constraint: The Accountable Presidency after 9/11* (New York: W.W. Norton & Company, 2012); Helen V. Milner and Dustin Tingley, *Sailing the Water's Edge: The Domestic Politics of American Foreign Policy* (Princeton, NJ: Princeton University Press, 2015).

24. Louis Klarevas, "The 'Essential Domino' of Military Operations: American Public Opinion and the Use of Force," *International Studies Perspectives* 3 (2002): 417–437; Richard Sobel, *The Impact of Public Opinion on U.S. Foreign Policy* (New York: Oxford University Press, 2001); Eric V. Larson and Bogdan Savych, *American Public Support for U.S. Military Operations from Mogadishu to Baghdad* (Santa Monica, CA: RAND, 2005); Matthew A. Baum and Philip B. K. Potter, *War and Democratic Constraint: How the Public Influences Foreign Policy* (Princeton, NJ: Princeton University Press, 2015).

25. Richard Brody, *Assessing the President: The Media, Elite Opinion, and Public Support* (Stanford, CA: Stanford University Press, 1991); John Zaller, *The Nature and Origins of Mass Opinion* (New York: Cambridge University Press, 1992); Berinsky, *In Time of War*.

26. Eric Larson, *Casualties and Consensus: The Historical Role of Casualties in Domestic Support for U.S. Military Operations* (Santa Monica, CA: RAND, 1996); Gelpi, Feaver, and Reifler, *Paying the Human Costs of War*.

27. Mueller, *War, Presidents, and Public Opinion*; Scott Gartner and Gary Segura, "War, Casualties and Public Opinion," *Journal of Conflict Resolution* 42 (1998): 278–300.

28. Eichenberg, "Gender Differences."

29. Eichenberg, "Gender Differences."

30. Karen M. Kaufman, "The Gender Gap," *PS: Political Science and Politics* 39 (2006): 447–453; Barry C. Burden, "The Social Roots of the Partisan Gender Gap," *Public Opinion Quarterly* 72 (2008): 55–75; Box-Steffensmeier, De Boef, and Lin, "The Dynamics of the Partisan Gender Gap."

31. Notably, David Fite, Marc Genest, and Clyde Wilcox, "Gender Differences in Foreign Policy Attitudes: A Longitudinal Analysis," *American Politics Research* 18, no. 4 (1990): 492–513; Conover and Sapiro, "Gender, Feminist Consciousness, and War"; Nincic and Nincic, "Race, Gender, and War"; Brooks and Valentino, "War of One's Own."

32. Feinstein, "The Rise and Decline of 'Gender Gaps' in Support for Military Action"; Hansen, Clemens, and Dolan, "Gender Gaps, Partisan Gaps, and Cross-Pressures."

33. Geoffrey C. Layman and Thomas M. Carsey, "Why Do Party Activists Convert? An Analysis of Individual Level Change on the Abortion Issue," *Political Research Quarterly* 51 (1998): 723–750; Zaller, *Nature and Origins of Mass Opinion*; Geoffrey L. Cohen, "Party over Policy: The Dominating Impact of Group Influence on Political Beliefs," *Journal of Personality and Social Psychology* 85 (2003): 808–822; Cindy D. Kam, "Who Toes the Party Line? Cues, Values, and Individual Differences," *Political Behavior* 27 (2005): 163–182; Richard R. Lau and David P. Redlawsk, "Advantages and Disadvantages of Cognitive Heuristics in Political Decision Making," *American Journal of Political Science* 45 (2001): 951–971; Richard R. Lau and David P. Redlawsk, *How Voters Decide: Information Processing During Election Campaigns* (New York: Cambridge University Press, 2006); Jeffrey J. Mondak, "Public Opinion and Heuristic Processing of Source Cues," *Political Behavior* 15 (1993): 167–192; James Druckman, Erik Peterson, and Rune Slothuus, "How Elite Partisan Polarization Affects Public Opinion Formation," *American Political Science Review* 107 (2013): 57–79.

34. Walter Lippmann, *Public Opinion* (New York: MacMillan, 1992 [1922]); Gabriel Almond, *The American People and Foreign Policy* (New York: Praeger, 1950).

35. Brody, *Assessing the President*; Zaller, *Nature and Origins of Mass Opinion*; Howell and Pevehouse, *While Dangers Gather*; Berinsky, *In Time of War*; Douglas Kriner and Francis Shen, "Responding to War on Capitol Hill: Battlefield Casualties, Congressional Response, and Public Support for the War in Iraq," *American Journal of Political Science* 58 (2014): 157–174; Elizabeth N. Saunders, "War and the Inner Circle: Democratic Elites and the Politics of Using Force," *Security Studies* 24 (2015): 466–501.

36. Although see Sarah Kreps, "Elite Consensus as a Determinant of Alliance Cohesion: Why Public Opinion Hardly Matters for NATO-led Operations in

Afghanistan," *Foreign Policy Analysis* 6 (2010): 191–215; Douglas Kriner and Graham Wilson, "The Elasticity of Reality and British Support for the War in Afghanistan," *British Journal of Politics and International Relations* 18 (2016): 559–580.

37. Zaller, *Nature and Origins of Mass Opinion*.

38. Arthur Lupia, "Shortcuts versus Encyclopedias: Information and Voting Behavior in California Insurance Reform Elections," *American Political Science Review* 88 (1994): 63–76; Matthew Baum and Timothy Groeling, *War Stories: The Causes and Consequences of Public Views of War* (Princeton, NJ: Princeton University Press, 2009).

39. Randall L. Calvert, "The Value of Biased Information: A Rational Choice Model of Political Advice," *The Journal of Politics* 47, no. 2 (1985): 530–555; Baum and Groeling, *War Stories*.

40. For example, Gary C. Jacobson, "A Tale of Two Wars: Public Opinion on the U.S. Military Interventions in Afghanistan and Iraq," *Presidential Studies Quarterly* 40, no. 4 (2010): 585–610.

41. Afghanistan is listed in several polls before 2008 and in several more not included in figure 7.1; however, in these cases it is lumped together with Iraq, making disentangling the relative salience of the two wars impossible.

42. Douglas Kriner, "Congress, Public Opinion, and the Political Costs of Waging War," in *Congress Reconsidered*, 11th ed., ed. Lawrence Dodd and Bruce Oppenheimer (Washington, DC: CQ Press, 2017), 433.

43. Adam Berinsky, "Assuming the Costs of War: Events, Elites, and American Public Support for Military Conflict," *Journal of Politics* 69 (2007): 979.

44. Kriner and Shen, "Responding to War on Capitol Hill."

45. While the Iraq War began in 2003, we exclude polls from this year and start our analysis in 2004. Gallup used a variety of different poll questions on the war in 2003 and did not consistently ask respondents if they viewed the war as a mistake until 2004.

46. The mistake question was only asked twice before 2004 and individual-level data is not available for one of these. The last mistake poll for which individual-level data is available during the Obama presidency is a June 2015 Gallup poll.

47. Replicating all analyses using only Gallup data yields substantively similar results. The models in table 7.2 include fixed effects to account for differences across polling outfits.

48. Estimating a single model with partisan-gender interactions confirms that the gender gap for Democrats is significantly greater than for independents ($p<0.05$, two-tailed test) and marginally greater than for Republicans ($p<0.10$, two-tailed test).

49. Kriner, "Congress, Public Opinion, and the Political Costs of Waging War."

50. The gender gap was statistically significant for all three partisan groups during the Obama Administration. However, for Democrats it was significantly greater than for independents ($p<0.05$, two-tailed test). The estimated gender gap

for Democrats was greater than for Republicans, however this difference was not statistically significant.

51. Joe Biden, "Remarks by President Biden on the Way Forward in Afghanistan," April 14, 2021, https://www.whitehouse.gov/briefing-room/speeches-remarks/2021/04/14/remarks-by-president-biden-on-the-way-forward-in-afghanistan/.

52. Over-time polling data available at PollingReport.com, last accessed April 23, 2024, https://www.pollingreport.com/afghan.htm.

53. ABC News/Washington Post, "ABC News/Washington Post Poll: September 2021 (August 29-September 1), Question 4, 31118604.00003," Langer Research Associates, Cornell University (Ithaca, NY: Roper Center for Public Opinion Research, 2021). As of December 2022, this was the only poll conducted after mid-August 2021 for which individual-level data was available via the Roper Center for Public Opinion Research that asked about opinions toward the withdrawal.

54. We do so by including an indicator variable for respondents who identified as (non-Hispanic) white. Alternate specifications yield substantively identical results.

55. Leonie Huddy et al., "The Consequences of Terrorism: Disentangling the Effects of Personal and National Threat," *Political Psychology* 23, no. 3 (2002): 485–509; Leonie Huddy et al., "Threat, Anxiety, and Support of Antiterrorism Policies," *American Journal of Political Science* 49, no. 3 (2005): 593–608; Leonie Huddy, Stanley Feldman, and Erin Casese, "Terrorism, Anxiety, and War," in *Terrorism and Torture: An Interdisciplinary Perspective*, ed.: 290–312. Werner G. K. Stritzke (New York: Cambridge University Press, 2009).

56. Jentleson, "Pretty Prudent Public"; Eichenberg, "Gender Differences."

57. Eichenberg, "Gender Differences"; Brooks and Valentino, "War of One's Own."

58. Hansen, Clemens, and Dolan, "Gender Gaps, Partisan Gaps, and Cross-Pressures."

59. For example, Howell and Pevehouse, *While Dangers Gather*.

60. Brody, *Assessing the President*; Zaller, *Nature and Origins of Mass Opinion*; John Zaller, "Elite Leadership of Mass Opinion: New Evidence from the Gulf War," in *Taken By Storm: The Media, Public Opinion, and U.S. Foreign Policy in the Gulf War*, ed. David L. Palatz and W. Lance Bennett (Chicago: University of Chicago Press, 1994, 186–211); Berinsky, *In Time of War*; Kriner and Shen, "Responding to War on Capitol Hill"; Saunders, "War and the Inner Circle."

61. By contrast, among non-Republicans a simple difference in means tests shows a 6 percent gender gap over the course of the war, with 68 percent of men judging the war a mistake versus 74 percent of women.

CHAPTER EIGHT

Nondominant Communal Groups and Casualty Sensitivity

Evidence from Israel, the United Kingdom, and the United States

Ronald R. Krebs and Robert Ralston

Support for military operations hinges at least in part on people's tolerance of casualties.[1] People may, by some accounts, be willing to support even high-casualty military operations when the interests at stake are seen as vital[2] or when victory seems likely.[3] People seem to be less supportive of military operations when casualties hit closer to home — when militaries fill the ranks via broad-based conscription,[4] as opposed to voluntary recruitment,[5] and when casualties touch their local community,[6] their ethnic or racial group,[7] or their family.[8] People appear to be far more sensitive to predicted deaths in combat than they are to projected injuries.[9] It stands to reason that casualties feature centrally in people's thinking about the use of force. The costs of military operations in blood (and to a lesser extent treasure), along with their possible benefits and the likelihood of success, should all feature in a rational calculation regarding initiating, continuing, or expanding these operations. Casualties that impact our social networks are more visible and more salient and thus weigh more heavily in that calculus.

However, we know much less about whether and how categorical identities shape support for the use of force and attitudes toward casualties, separate from the distribution of war's burdens. Even the effects of gender, which have been studied more than other categorical identities, remain uncertain: although substantial research has shown that women are less supportive of military missions and more sensitive to casualties,[10] evidence from Childree, Krimmel, Kriner, and Palmer's chapter (this volume) suggests that women are not as consistently opposed to the use of force as previously thought. We know much less about how members of nondominant communal groups respond to the prospect of war, and especially to war's costs, compared to members of dominant racial and ethnic groups.

The answer has significant, and growing, implications. Many states around the globe are multiethnic mosaics, and even once relatively homogeneous nation-states are becoming increasingly ethnically, racially, and religiously diverse.[11] If growing nondominant communal populations are more likely to oppose the use of force and military deployments and are more sensitive to casualties, states will have less capacity, and leaders will be less willing, to deploy force and mobilize societal resources to that end, especially if the operations may be protracted. If they do express such sensitivity, then these nondominant communal groups could represent an important constraint on executive decision making in a wartime context.

Moreover, an increasingly polarized electorate in the United States and elsewhere has decreased politicians' incentives to appeal to the median voter and correspondingly increased their incentives to focus on mobilizing their base. As Kreps and Kriner note (this volume), a more polarized US Congress, coupled with growing partisan tribalism in the US public, may significantly erode checks on the use of force. However, it is also possible that the effects of polarization may vary greatly by party. If nondominant communal groups are more sensitive to military casualties, the political coalitions that rely heavily on such groups will find embarking on and sustaining military operations especially challenging, and they may find standoff military options, using missiles or drones, particularly appealing. In the US context, Democrats are ideologically less inclined to see military force as an effective instrument for resolving disputes and are more inclined to try diplomacy. Their coalition—more heavily constituted by a racially and ethnically diverse constellation of Americans and of women—may be more casualty sensitive (notwithstanding the findings of Childree et al., this volume). Polarization therefore may make Democrats even less inclined to embrace force—or at least to put US soldiers in harm's way. Moreover, if the military has a high operational tempo, underprivileged groups, which have historically been a common source of soldiers, may then be reluctant to volunteer for military service. The attitudes and behaviors of nondominant communal groups—racial, ethnic, and religious—can affect whether leaders embark on the use of force and whether they can sustain the effort, and nondominant groups' support for military missions and their sensitivity to battlefield casualties can be an important component of democratic accountability in wartime.

It would be tempting to explore the question purely within the United States, with its highly salient racial cleavages. But whether America's racialized attitudes translate to polities that lack America's history of slavery and its ongoing institutionalized racial discrimination or that are marked by ethnic and religious, rather than racial, cleavages is not clear. If US minority groups, and perhaps especially Black Americans, are particularly casualty sensitive, are nondominant racial, ethnic, or religious groups elsewhere? We find that they are, which raises questions about whether Black Americans' views on the use of force reflect their experience and history alone. There is a more general pattern at work.

This chapter is a first-cut slice into the question of nondominant communal groups and casualty sensitivity. Its findings derive from surveys conducted in 2018 and 2019 in the United States, the United Kingdom, and Israel to explore attitudes toward a prospective hypothetical military mission.[12] Our primary purpose, via both survey experiments and observational data, was to explore whether, and why, public beliefs about soldiers' reasoning for joining the military shape public attitudes toward the use of force and its hazards.[13] Analysis of the surveys produced a consistent and serendipitous finding. Across all three nations, being a member of a non-dominant racial or ethnic group—nonwhite in the United States and the United Kingdom and non-Ashkenazic Jew in Israel—was not consistently associated with greater opposition to the military mission, but it was consistently associated with greater sensitivity to prospective casualties. The differences in casualty sensitivity were both statistically and substantively significant: the predicted probability of Sephardic or Mizrahi Jewish respondents in Israel, nonwhite respondents in Britain, and nonwhite respondents in the United States accepting any casualties in support of the mission was, depending on the country, between 5 and 12 percent lower than among other respondents. These results proved robust to numerous model specifications and controls.

Why might nondominant racial and ethnic groups in these three advanced democracies—and perhaps around the globe—be less tolerant of casualties in a prospective military mission, but roughly equally favorable toward the mission? Because the surveys were not constructed with this research question in mind, we cannot fully evaluate all possible explanations at this time. Existing data suggest that neither distinctive communal beliefs about citizenship and military service nor racial or ethnic homophily account for the finding. It seems more likely that nondominant ethnic and racial groups' sensitivity to casualties is grounded in discrimination, which in turn produces alienation from the political community and skepticism of political efficacy. However, in the absence of further careful study and a specially designed survey, this conclusion is necessarily speculative.

The rest of this chapter proceeds in five parts. First, we review the existing literature on casualty sensitivity and on ethnicity, race, and military affairs. Second, we describe the three surveys and the key variables of interest in our study. Third, we present the findings from the three surveys. Fourth, we explore several possible explanations for these findings. In the conclusion we discuss the possibilities for future research on race and casualty sensitivity.

Military Operations and Nondominant Racial and Ethnic Groups: What We Know

The extensive literature on war and US public opinion sheds limited light on the attitudes of nondominant racial and ethnic groups toward military missions and casualties. The dominant approach to public opinion and the use of force employs a rationalist, event-driven model. Within this approach, an important set of debates has sought to parse out the relative weight of war's costs (especially casualties), its benefits (its purposes or stakes), and the likelihood of victory (that is, of achieving those benefits) in shaping opinion.[14] A complementary strain of literature has attempted to clarify when and for whom war's casualties are most salient and has found strong support for the intuitive claim that casualties that strike closer to home have a larger impact on public opinion and voter turnout.[15] Yet, while the racial identity of respondents is typically included as a control variable in existing studies, the impact of race is usually not noted in these studies even in passing. As a result, reviews of Black public opinion in the United States have commonly noted that little is known about Black Americans' attitudes toward foreign or military affairs.[16]

In contrast, general scholars of US public opinion have been skeptical that events, such as mounting casualties, shape public opinion in an unmediated way. Because most Americans are not attentive to politics in general or foreign policy in particular, their views tend to mirror, or cue off, those of trusted elites.[17] When elites are unified in their narrative of war, so is the mass public. But when elites divide, the mass public follows suit. Partisan polarization is thus more the norm than the exception in attitudes toward war. Rather than casualties shaping people's attitudes toward war, people's partisan loyalties underpin their support for war and even their perceptions of war's costs.[18] From this perspective, people's basic political predispositions can be critical, and thus ethnic attachments may be key drivers of attitudes toward conflict. Adam Berinsky finds that during World War II, children of "Axis-born" parents were less supportive of US intervention in the Second World War than were children of "Allied-born" or US-born parents.[19] In contrast to the rationalist stream of literature, this approach is at least theoretically open to the possibility that nondominant ethnic and racial groups might have predispositions that affect their views of military missions—whether rendering them leery of sending troops into battle or making them more eager to do so. However, this literature does not suggest a straightforward answer to our puzzle: why nondominant ethnic and racial groups might, across national contexts, be casualty sensitive.

We are aware of just three articles on war and US public opinion that place race at their analytical center. First, Miroslav Nincic and Donna Nincic's study of US public opinion on the Korean, Vietnam, Desert Shield, and Desert Storm conflicts finds that Black respondents have consistently been less supportive of the use of force abroad. They attribute Black respondents' opposition to their political alienation.[20] Second, Scott Gartner and Gary Segura's study of Californians during the Vietnam War finds that race is not a significant correlate of casualty sensitivity. Using eight pooled surveys of 6,300 Californians during the Vietnam War, they argue that citizens, regardless of race, were especially sensitive to the deaths of individuals from their locality regardless of the casualty's racial identity. They conclude that "members of all racial and ethnic groups react negatively to casualties, whether they share racial and ethnic traits with the casualties or not ... neither the race of the respondent nor any combination of the race of the citizen observer and race of the casualties negated the relationship between recent local casualties and support. Blacks and whites reacted more similarly than differently to racially disaggregated deaths."[21] Third, in a meta-analysis, Naima Green-Riley and Andrew Leber comprehensively collect and reanalyze existing US observational data from various polling sources from the 2000s forward, as well as several scholarly surveys and survey experiments, from the standpoint of race. They find a consistent association between being Black and being less favorable toward the use of force in both experimental and observational (Iraq and Afghanistan Wars) contexts.[22]

Yet, overall, findings on race and casualty sensitivity in US public opinion are mixed. While Gartner and Segura question the association between race and casualty sensitivity in the United States, Christopher Gelpi, Peter Feaver, and Jason Reifler note in passing that "race is a significant factor" in predicting casualty sensitivity, "with African Americans being more sensitive to casualties than Caucasians."[23] However, in earlier work, Feaver and Gelpi found that nonwhites in the United States were not more casualty sensitive when presented with prospective terrorism or realpolitik missions and that nonwhites were *less* casualty sensitive when exposed to humanitarian missions in Congo and Kosovo.[24] Green-Riley and Leber draw on seven Public Agenda Forum and Pew Research Center polls regarding the Iraq War between October 2002 and March 2008 to show that Black Americans were indeed more worried about casualties than were other Americans. They cite a 1990 poll showing that Black Americans believe that Black soldiers are more likely to die in combat, which Green-Riley and Leber attribute to the reality of Black soldiers dying in droves early in the Vietnam War. They assert that this belief has been persistent among Black Americans, and they speculate that their casualty sensitivity in the 2000s was a product of this linked-fate logic.[25]

Given how little research centers its analytical energies on nondominant ethnic and racial groups' attitudes toward military missions and casualties, this chapter's findings would be valuable even if it presented and analyzed only Americans' attitudes. But its contribution is significantly greater because it places US public opinion in a cross-national conversation. Most existing studies of public opinion on the use of force and casualties employ data from the United States alone. There are numerous exceptions that examine individual countries in isolation.[26] Examining single country cases, or single population groups within the nation, may lead one to overstate the distinctiveness of that nation and population. Regrettably, studies leveraging cross-national, comparative opinion data on public opinion and the use of force and casualties are rare in general,[27] and we are not aware of other studies that have examined nondominant communal groups' attitudes toward the use of force outside the United States. This chapter wagers that examining these diverse nations' and communal groups' experiences alongside each other yields novel insight, analytical leverage, and value.

Survey Design

The US survey was fielded September 12–21, 2018, to 2,451 US-based respondents recruited by Lucid. The Israel survey was fielded between October 27 and November 5, 2019, to 1,659 respondents via iPanel, a survey firm based in Israel. Finally, the UK study was fielded June 20–26, 2019, via Dynata to 2,448 respondents. In each country, respondents were balanced on demographic and ideological characteristics. Table 8.1 outlines comparisons of each national sample to benchmarks.

TABLE 8.1. **National Samples and Benchmarks**

Variable[1]	Israel Sample	Israel Benchmark	United Kingdom Sample	United Kingdom Benchmark	United States Sample	United States Benchmark
Gender						
Female	51%	51%	53%	51%	51%	52%
Race/Ethnicity						
White	N/A	N/A	88%	86%	72%	65%
Asian	N/A	N/A	6%	8%	N/A	N/A
Black	N/A	N/A	3%	3%	12%	12%
Hispanic	N/A	N/A	N/A	N/A	8%	15%
Ashkenazi	39%	44%	N/A	N/A	N/A	N/A
Mizrahi or Sephardi	39%	45%	N/A	N/A	N/A	N/A
Education & Age						
Education	59%	60%	65%	63%	34%	30%
Age	30–39	30–39	35–44	35–44	46	47
Religious ID						
Secular	43%	43%	N/A	N/A	N/A	N/A
Traditional	36%	36%	N/A	N/A	N/A	N/A
Religious	11%	11%	N/A	N/A	N/A	N/A
Ultraorthodox	10%	10%	N/A	N/A	N/A	N/A

Benchmarks: Israel—provided by iPanel[2]; UK—2011 Census; US—American National Election Studies 2016, Current Population Survey 2017.
Education: Israel = higher education; UK = A-level equivalent or above; US = bachelor's degree or above.
Age: Israel & UK = median; US = mean.
[1] For a fuller accounting of national samples and benchmarks, see online appendix 8.1, section 1.
[2] Noah Lewin-Epstein and Yinon Cohen, "Ethnic Origin and Identity in the Jewish Population of Israel," *Journal of Ethnic and Migration Studies*, 45, no. 11 (2019), 2118–2137.

These surveys' primary analytical purpose was to ascertain the impact of different representations of soldiers' motives for service on respondents' support for a military mission. To that end, all three surveys included an experiment. Respondents were presented with a vignette, portrayed as an edited selection from an actual news article, that described an interview with a service member awaiting deployment on a prospective military mission in either "Martesia" (US and UK) or Lebanon (Israel). An interviewed soldier—"Michael Cameron," "Luke Baker," or "Captain D"[28] in the US, UK, and Israel, respectively—explains why he joined the military (or, in Israel, signed on as an officer) and confirms that most of his battalion (or fellow officers) joined for the same reason. The vignette further claims that surveys indicate that the hypothetical soldier's/officer's reasons are typical of most service-members/officers. After reading the vignette, respondents were asked whether they favored or opposed the mission as well as questions to gauge their sensitivity to casualties. We also asked a series of follow-up questions to evaluate how the respondents perceived the hypothetical soldier/officer: his race/ethnicity, socio-economic background, willingness to undertake the mission, and political ideology. To avoid introducing post-treatment bias into the statistical analysis, respondents read all questions measuring control variables (described below) before their randomly assigned vignette. In addition, all respondents were, before the experimental treatment, asked about soldiers'/officers' reasons for enlisting/accepting a commission. In each survey, some vignettes were controls that did not prime respondents regarding the soldier's/officer's reason for service.[29]

We have described the survey experiment in some, albeit limited, detail largely to explain the context of the analyses that follow. The survey experiment does not feature directly in the core analyses, and the manipulated variable—soldier motivation—is neither this study's dependent nor independent variable. This context also makes transparent that these surveys were not fielded with questions of communal identity at their analytical center. We regret that, in that sense, we have reproduced the cardinal sin of so much research on race and foreign policy, in which race is merely a control variable, and thus we are not well positioned to explore fully its correlates or implications.

Nevertheless, the primary independent variable is whether a respondent self-identifies as a member of a nondominant racial or ethnic group. In Israel, 39 percent of respondents self-identified as Sephardic or Mizrahi Jewish,[30] 11 percent of respondents in the United Kingdom self-identified as nonwhite, and 28 percent of US respondents self-identified as nonwhite. In our analyses below, either we treat communal identification as a binary variable or we disaggregate communal identification to see if particular subgroups are driving results.

In this chapter, unlike our other work derived from this project,[31] the dependent variable of interest is casualty sensitivity. Existing studies typically measure casualty sensitivity in one of two ways. Some pose open-ended questions about specific conflicts, asking respondents to identify the highest number of casualties they would tolerate.[32] Others ask respondents if they would support the mission at a particular casualty level and, if the respondent says yes, iteratively repeat the question with a higher number of casualties until respondents either reach the maximum number of casualties offered by the researchers or no longer favor the mission.[33] We follow the latter approach.[34] The number of casualties in each country setting was tailored for reasons of external validity: in Israel, we offered respondents casualty options ranging from 0 to 15, in Britain from 0 to 100, and in the United States from 0 to 1,000.[35]

All three surveys also included a standard battery of control variables: political ideology, gender, age, level of education, and income, among others. They also included truncated versions of well-established batteries of questions from the psychological literature that gauge a respondent's disposition to "blind patriotism," "right-wing authoritarianism," and "social dominance orientation."[36] The surveys also measured respondents' hawkishness based on their preference for using military force rather than diplomacy in addressing international problems facing their country. Finally, the surveys asked respondents to use a feeling thermometer to rate how favorably they feel toward members of various institutions, including the military.

Findings

Across the three national surveys, when respondents from nondominant communal groups are asked, in generic terms, about their support for the prospective military mission—and possible casualties were not mentioned—their views do not differ systematically from those of dominant-group respondents. However, nondominant communal group respondents *are* systematically more casualty sensitive: they are significantly less likely than dominant-group respondents to favor the mission if it results in deaths among the nation's soldiers. Put differently, when the question is framed with respect to potential mounting casualties, non-dominant-group respondents' support erodes more quickly than that of dominant-group respondents.

Table 8.2 presents ordered logistic regression models in which casualty sensitivity is the dependent variable in Israel (model 1), the United Kingdom (models 2 and 3), and the United States (models 4 and 5).[37] Positive coefficients indicate more tolerance for casualties while negative coefficients indicate less tolerance—that is, greater sensitivity to casualties. The base category in the Israel model is Ashkenazi Jews, while white respondents constitute the base category in the US and UK models. All models include full batteries of psychological, political, and demographic controls.[38] As Table 8.2 shows, the coefficients for Sephardi Mizrahi and nonwhite respondents across all models are negative and statistically significant, meaning that these respondents are more sensitive to casualties than are Ashkenazi or white respondents.

The impact of nondominant communal status in these three countries is substantively significant. To assess the substantive significance of respondents' self-declared identity, we calculated the predicted probability that a respondent would favor the mission while accepting *any* casualties in each sample. In Israel, the predicted probability of Sephardi or Mizrahi respondents accepting any casualties is 36 percent, while the predicted probability among all other respondents is 48 percent.[39] In Britain, the predicted probability of nonwhite respondents accepting any casualties is 34 percent, while that among all other respondents is 39 percent. In the United States, the nonwhite predicted probability is 43 percent, while that among all other respondents is 52 percent.

Exploring Explanations

What might explain these findings? Our control variables allow us to discount two potential explanations. First, in all three countries, members of nondominant racial and ethnic groups tend to have less education and lower incomes. Perhaps their greater casualty sensitivity reflects these factors rather than their race or ethnicity. However, we control for both education and income in table 8.2. Second, at least in the United States, some nondominant racial and ethnic groups have been over-represented in the armed forces roughly since the turn to voluntary recruitment in

TABLE 8.2. Casualty Sensitivity in Israel, the United Kingdom, and the United States

Israel	(1)	United Kingdom	(2)	(3)	United States	(4)	(5)
Sephardi or Mizrachi	−0.48*** (0.12)	Nonwhite	−0.29+ (0.15)		Nonwhite	−0.26** (0.10)	
Mixed	−0.09 (0.16)	Black		0.19 (0.27)	Black/African Am		−0.20 (0.13)
Other	0.16 (0.18)	British Indian		−0.56+ (0.30)	Latinx/Hispanic		−0.36* (0.16)
		Other		−0.35 (0.29)	Asian		−0.66** (0.23)
		Asian		−0.25 (0.33)	American Indian		0.53 (0.38)
		Mixed		0.60 (0.94)	Other/None		−0.07 (0.24)
		Arab		−1.47* (0.65)			
		Other					
Additional Controls?	Yes	Additional Controls?	Yes	Yes	Additional Controls?	Yes	Yes
N	1528	N	2448	2448	N	2451	2451
pseudo R²	0.005	pseudo R²	0.0597	0.0612	pseudo R²	0.0445	0.0612

Note: Ordered Logistic Regressions with all respondents. Reference groups were white respondents in the UK and US analyses and Ashkenazi Jews in the Israel analysis. Controls in all models include the treatment variables, feelings toward the military, hawkishness, ideology, age, education, income, personal military service, gender, prior beliefs regarding soldiers/officers' motivations, and a battery of psychological dispositions (right-wing authoritarianism, social dominance orientation, blind patriotism). An additional control in the US and UK models is household military service and in Israel, religiosity. For robustness, we also ran the US analyses with party identification, obtaining similar results. Standard errors in parentheses.

+ p≤0.10, * p<0.05, ** p<0.01, *** p<0.0001

1973. Perhaps nonwhites' greater casualty sensitivity reflects their concern for family members and the reality that battlefield casualties more closely touch their lives. However, this argument's premise does not apply cross-nationally: non-dominant racial and ethnic groups are not especially over-represented in the Israeli and the British militaries.[40] Additionally, the US and UK models in table 8.2 control for having had a household member serve in the armed forces.[41]

We now present in this section four other conceivable explanations for nondominant racial and ethnic groups' greater casualty sensitivity, and we evaluate those explanations to the extent that our data allow.[42] As previously mentioned, because the surveys were not constructed with this question in mind, what follows is more searching and suggestive than definitive. We present the four candidate explanations in order not of their plausibility or persuasiveness but of their definitiveness: we start with those explanations to which our data speak most directly.

Empathy and Consent

It is plausible that casualty tolerance derives from the human capacity for empathy. Empathy involves identification with another, both cognitively and emotionally. It requires imagining how that person thinks or feels given her situation and adopting her perceptions and emotions as, to some extent, one's own. Existing studies of casualty sensitivity leverage, sometimes only implicitly, a basic feature of empathy: human beings find it easier to empathize with those who, in some measure, are similar to them.[43] Thus Americans seem to care more about battlefield casualties that hail from their local community than from the nation as a whole.[44]

However, people vary in their capacity for empathy, whether by nature or nurture or social position. Empathic individuals are especially reluctant to coerce others into unwanted behavior because they intuitively adhere to the golden rule: they would object if someone forced them to do something they did not want to do.[45] Empathy thus gives rise to what we have called elsewhere "the logic of consent": a reluctance to deploy troops on a dangerous mission when those soldiers would rather not be deployed, and greater comfort sending soldiers into harm's way when it seems likely that the soldiers themselves are supportive of the mission.[46]

In all three national surveys, we asked respondents how strongly they agreed with a statement encapsulating consent logic: "When soldiers would rather not be deployed on a mission, I am uncomfortable putting them in harm's way." Endorsing this logic is strongly associated with both opposition to military missions and sensitivity to casualties. It seems plausible that members of nondominant racial and ethnic groups, who often suffer from discrimination, may find the logic of consent especially appealing. After all, given the degree to which their life choices are often constrained by discrimination of various kinds, they may wish that others had been more considerate of their consent. Consistent with this expectation, we indeed find that non-dominant respondents in all three national samples are more likely to endorse the consent statement than are their majority counterparts. These differences in dominant and nondominant respondents' agreement with the consent statement are statistically significant. Substantively, the largest difference in mean score—around 8.5 percent—is in the United States (5.1 among nonwhites, on a 7-point scale versus 4.7 among whites); the smallest—around 4.5 percent—is in Israel (6.03 among Mizrahim and Sephardim versus 5.79 among Ashkenazim).

However, and crucially, nondominant respondents' belief in consent logic does not appear to be a significant driver of their casualty sensitivity. First, while agreement with the consent statement is associated with greater casualty sensitivity in all three countries, in Israel and the United States its inclusion in the models does not render respondents' race or ethnicity statistically insignificant, nor does it even substantially reduce the size of the coefficient. In Britain, inclusion of the consent logic variable renders respondents' race ("nonwhite") insignificant at conventional levels, but just barely ($p = 0.11$).[47] Were nondominant respondents' adherence to consent theory the reason for their high casualty sensitivity, including that variable in the regression should have a major impact on the significance of the race/ethnicity variable. Consistent with this observation, mediation analyses in each sample did not find that respondents' agreement with consent theory meaningfully mediates the relationship between race/ethnicity and casualty sensitivity.[48]

Second, if belief in consent logic were driving the finding, then members of nondominant racial and ethnic groups who endorsed that logic should be more casualty sensitive than those who did not. We therefore included a term interacting the respondents' race/ethnicity and their agreement with the consent statement. The precise behavior of the interaction term varies across the three nations under study, but in *no* case does it strongly support the consent-logic hypothesis. The strongest evidence in support of this hypothesis comes from the United States, where the interaction term is significant. As figure 8.1 shows, nonwhites who more strongly agree with the consent-logic statement are significantly more casualty sensitive—that is, they are less likely to support the portrayed military mission if it was projected to entail any casualties—than are nonwhites who strongly disagree or less strongly agree with the consent-logic statement. However, even in the United States, this claim is less significant than it appears at first glance. Notice that the top line in figure 8.1, representing white respondents, slopes downward at a much steeper angle than the bottom line, representing nonwhite respondents. In other words, in the US data, respondents from the racial/ethnic *majority group* are much *more* affected by belief in the logic of consent than are nondominant respondents. In fact, at high levels of agreement with consent logic, the distinction between white and nonwhite respondents essentially disappears—in tension with the argument that disproportionate nondominant belief in the consent logic explains their casualty sensitivity. In the United Kingdom, the impact of consent, when interacted with respondent race, is surprisingly inversely correlated with casualty sensitivity: nonwhite respondents' line, in the parallel figure, slopes significantly upward, meaning that, among nonwhite British respondents, higher levels of agreement with the consent logic are oddly associated with greater casualty tolerance. Moreover, as in the United States, white respondents in the United Kingdom are much more strongly affected by the logic of consent: their line slopes much more steeply downward, across levels of consent, eliminating the ethnoracial difference in UK casualty sensitivity (and, at the highest levels of consent, even reversing it).[49] In Israel, the interaction between Mizrahi and Sephardi identity and consent is not significant.[50]

Soldier Motivation

Related to the above logic, in our previous work we found that perceptions of soldiers' reasons for joining the military have a significant impact on respondents' support for a hypothetical mission. *Prior* to the treatment, we asked respondents the primary reason they think people join the military: pay and benefits, lack of other options, good citizenship, and patriotism. In addition, as described earlier, we exposed respondents to experimental treatments that primed them to one of these four motivations for enlistment (on these narratives of soldier motivation, see also Blankshain and Cohn, this volume). The logic of consent suggests that respondents will be most sympathetic to the plight of soldiers who they believe are extrinsically motivated and whose life choices are subject to

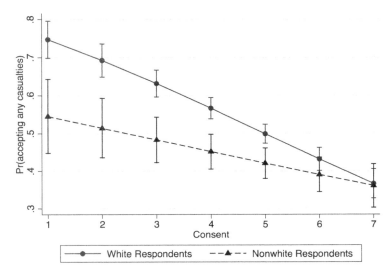

FIGURE 8.1. Predicted Probability of Tolerating Any Casualties: USA

Note: I-bars present 95 percent confidence intervals.

See online appendix 8.1, section 3, table 2 for the underlying table (appendix available at the Harvard Dataverse: https://doi.org/10.7910/DVN/OEOIM3). All other variables held at their means.

great constraint. It implies that, when respondents believe that soldiers join the armed forces for the pay and benefits that service bequeaths, and especially when respondents believe that soldiers join out of desperation to escape adverse circumstances—or when respondents are primed to view soldiers in that light—they should then be less favorable toward the mission and more casualty sensitive.[51] Across the three nations, the evidence is mixed but suggestively supportive of these hypotheses derived from the logic of consent. In Britain, belief in soldiers' desperate motives—both when previously held (in an observational analysis) and when primed (in the experimental analysis)—is associated with opposition to the mission but not with greater casualty sensitivity. The finding in the United States is even stronger: not only is that same belief, both when previously held and when primed, related to greater opposition to the mission, but prior belief in soldiers' desperation is also associated with greater casualty sensitivity.[52] In Israel, where the desperate narrative understandably has little traction with respect to either conscripted soldiers or officers, respondents' prior belief that officers are motivated by the pay and benefits of that career path is associated, in observational analyses, with less support for the mission and greater casualty sensitivity relative to respondents who believe officers join out of patriotism.

Perhaps nondominant respondents are more likely to think that people join the military out of desperation, and therefore they are more casualty sensitive. The evidence from the United States is mixed. Nonwhites are significantly more likely to say, when asked pretreatment, that soldiers primarily join the military because they have "no other options" relative only to an account emphasizing "love of country" but not compared to "pay/benefits" or "duty."[53] In addition, when nonwhites are exposed to the "no other options" treatment—that is, when the fictional soldier Michael Cameron is quoted as ascribing his enlistment to having no other way to escape his dead-end circumstances—they are much more likely to think Cameron nonwhite, but whites are much more likely to infer that as well.[54] The evidence from the British and Israeli samples is even less supportive. In the United Kingdom, when asked pretreatment about soldier motivation for enlistment, nonwhites more commonly choose patriotism rather than either of the extrinsic motivational options, and white respondents attribute enlistment to a lack of options.[55] In Israel, Mizrahi and Sephardi pretreatment views of soldier motivations do not generally diverge significantly from those of their Ashkenazi compatriots.[56] Moreover, our multivariate analyses of casualty sensitivity in table 8.2 control for respondents' pretreatment beliefs about service motivation in all three nations. This control does not render respondents' race or ethnic status statistically or substantively insignificant.

Homophily

In a wide variety of contexts, people display homophilic tendencies: they have a marked preference for individuals who are like them, notably who share one or more of their categorical identities.[57] It seems plausible that racial and ethnic homophily might be at play when it comes to casualty sensitivity as well. If racial and ethnic homophily is driving our finding, it implies not only that members of nondominant racial and ethnic groups have greater concern for the lives of their coethnics in the armed forces but also that they must believe that people of their ethnicity or race constitute a disproportionate share of prospective casualties. Both statements must be true for the homophily explanation to have merit.

Our surveys do not allow us to evaluate fully this candidate explanation: we did not ask respondents what populations they believe fill the combat ranks, and we did not conduct a survey experiment selectively priming respondents with such information or with the ethnic or racial identity of the likely casualties. The data we do have, however, suggest that racial and ethnic homophily is likely not the primary explanation for our finding. We asked respondents, post-treatment, for their perception of the racial and ethnic identity of the fictional soldier portrayed in the vignette—white or nonwhite, in the United States and United Kingdom; Ashkenazi, Mizrahi, mixed, or "impossible to tell" in Israel. In the US and UK, a majority of white and nonwhite respondents think that our fictional soldier is white, but nonwhite respondents are more likely than white respondents to think that he is nonwhite.[58] In Israel, the vast majority of respondents believe that it is impossible to tell the ethnicity of Captain D; Mizrahim and Sephardim are slightly more likely to see D as Mizrahi, but the differences across ethnicity are negligible.[59] However, controlling for respondents' post-treatment beliefs about the racial and ethnic identity of the fictional soldier or officer does not have an appreciable impact on the statistical or substantive significance of the results in any of three nations: nondominant respondents in all three countries are still more casualty sensitive.[60]

However, inserting this control mixes together nondominant respondents who believe the fictional soldier or officer a member of their communal group and those who do not. Perhaps nonwhites in the United States and United Kingdom who believe Michael Cameron or Luke Baker not white—presumptively the subset of respondents most likely to prefer individuals of their shared race or ethnicity—are especially casualty sensitive. To test this intuition, we interacted beliefs regarding the soldier's race/ethnicity and the respondent's race/ethnicity. This interaction is neither statistically nor substantively significant in the United States: nonwhite respondents in the United States who believe Michael Cameron to be nonwhite are no more casualty sensitive than nonwhite respondents who believe Cameron to be white.[61] The same is true in Israel: Sephardi or Mizrahi respondents who believe that Captain D is Mizrahi are no more casualty sensitive, though this may be because the vast majority of Israeli respondents think D's ethnicity unclear.[62] In the United Kingdom, the interaction term is not statistically significant in a simple model with no controls, but it is significant when controlling for the usual host of demographic, ideological, and psychological variables. In the latter specification, the difference is substantively significant as well: the predicted probability that a nonwhite respondent who believes Baker to be white would support the hypothetical mission with some casualties is 35 percent, while the predicted probably that a nonwhite respondent who believes Baker also to be nonwhite would support the hypothetical mission under those same conditions is just 21 percent.[63] It is therefore possible that ethno-racial homophily is at work in the UK data, but this claim should be treated with caution for two reasons: first, because the interaction term is significant only in a model with full controls; relatedly, second, because the number of nonwhite respondents who believe Baker nonwhite is very small (just 39, compared to 219 nonwhite respondents who believe Baker to be white). Overall—and consistent with existing findings—the evidence supporting the ethno-racial homophily hypothesis is weak.[64]

Nevertheless, our data is not fully dispositive with respect to ethno-racial homophily. It is possible that nonwhite respondents think Cameron or Baker white—and that Mizrahi and Sephardi respondents thought D Ashkenazi—but nevertheless believe that nonwhites constitute a disproportionate share of the armed forces or its combat arms or that nonwhites are especially likely to be deployed as cannon fodder.[65] However, while these beliefs do not logically contradict each other, they are certainly in tension. Most people find maintaining cognitively dissonant beliefs uncomfortable and would prefer to resolve the tension by bringing their perception of the fictional soldier or officer's identity in line with their general beliefs. We therefore think it reasonable to extrapolate from our analysis that ethno-racial homophily is not likely the explanation for the casualty sensitivity finding.

Political Alienation and Inefficacy

The most plausible remaining explanation—which our data do not allow us to test—is nondominant political alienation. Nondominant communal status around the world is often, but not always, associated with harmful discriminatory structures and practices. Nonwhites in the United States and the United Kingdom, and non-Ashkenazi Jews in Israel, have all historically suffered substantially at the hands of majority citizens and majority-dominated institutions, and all continue to lag behind their fellow citizens by many social, economic, and political measures. This remains true even in Israel, where Mizrahi Jews have been a major, and at times even determining, force in Israeli politics since the late 1970s. It is not surprising that nonwhites in the United States and the United

Kingdom, and Mizrahi Jews in Israel, express higher levels of alienation from the political system.[66] They are less likely to think their community's interests and needs are well-represented, and they are less likely to have confidence in their own political efficacy.[67] Again, this is somewhat surprisingly true even of Mizrahi Jews, whose impact on Israeli politics has been substantial.

One implication of the alienation hypothesis is that members of nondominant communal groups may not identify with the goals of the political community or the threats it faces. For the alienated, the nation is "you," not "us." This suggests that members of nondominant communal groups should rank lower on measures of "blind patriotism."[68] In our data, nonwhites are indeed less blindly patriotic in the United States, but race is not predictive of blind patriotism in the United Kingdom, and Mizrahi and Sephardi Jews are actually more patriotic than other Jewish Israelis.[69] If members of nondominant communal groups do not identify with the collective, they should be less supportive of the military mission, regardless of prospective casualties. Observational studies of US public opinion on war have indeed found that Black respondents have been less supportive of the use of force abroad (in the Korean, Vietnam, Desert Shield, and Desert Storm conflicts) and that respondents' political alienation is predictive of their opposition.[70] However, our cross-national data are not as supportive of the alienation hypothesis. While, in line with past research, nonwhites in the United States are consistently less favorable toward the military mission, that is not true of nonwhites in Britain, who are not statistically distinguishable from whites in this regard, and it is not true of Mizrahim and Sephardim in Israel, who are especially hawkish in general and supportive of the proposed mission in particular.[71] However, "blind patriotism" is an imperfect measure of political alienation, and we regrettably did not include in the survey any questions directly assessing respondents' alienation from the political community.

But perhaps, and crucially, nondominant respondents are especially doubtful of their own political efficacy. If they are more likely to believe that they can have little impact on the decisions leaders make, they may be especially reluctant to authorize a potentially costly military operation because they doubt their ability to influence the end of a conflict they believe is going badly. Although survey questions that seek to gauge political alienation and political efficacy are very similar, if not identical, the concepts are, we believe, distinct. Alienation speaks to one's identification with the collective. Efficacy speaks to one's capacity to shape the policies produced by the political system.[72] Either can, but need not, produce the other. Those who believe they lack efficacy may consequently disassociate from the collective, but they need not: excluded from the US political system after Reconstruction, Black Americans nevertheless sought equality and first-class citizenship, suggesting that they continued—indeed had no choice but—to identify with the polity. Those who are alienated have little desire to devote their energies to shaping policy, but they may nevertheless possess the resources and capacity to do so: they may retain *potential* efficacy. Skepticism of their political efficacy may well be driving casualty sensitivity among members of nondominant communal groups. Identifying with the political community, they can be persuaded to support military missions, especially when they are costless. But they may also fear that, if the mission goes south, they—and citizens like them—are powerless to coerce or persuade decision-makers into terminating the mission. Respondents with low perceived political efficacy may therefore demand a lower level of projected casualties before supporting the mission, as we indeed find. Unfortunately, we included no survey questions gauging respondents' sense of political efficacy.[73]

In this section, we have presented four conceivable explanations for our finding that members of nondominant communal groups in the United States, the United Kingdom, and Israel are all significantly more casualty sensitive than the general population and have evaluated these explanations to the extent that our data allow. We find little evidence that respondents' beliefs in either consent logic or soldier motivation are a significant driver of nondominant respondents' casualty sensitivity. As for ethno-racial homophily, while our existing data do not permit us to reach definitive conclusions, they suggest that homophily is not at work. Finally, we believe that nondominant political alienation and political efficacy may be plausible explanations, but current data do not allow us to test it.

Conclusion

While studies have shed light on gendered dimensions of public opinion on the use of force—including, notably, Childree et al. (this volume)[74]—scholars have only rarely and very recently focused their gaze on how other categorical identities, particularly race and ethnicity, shape how citizens think about military force. Studies of casualty sensitivity are especially uncommon. This chapter represents a preliminary attempt to fill that gap using cross-national data from Israel, the United Kingdom, and the United States. Our central finding—that, across all three country samples, members of non-dominant communal groups were systematically less likely to tolerate casualties than their dominant communal counterparts—demands explanation. If nondominant communal populations in diverse, multiethnic, societies are unsupportive of missions or are more casualty sensitive than majority groups, states and their leaders may find it difficult to legitimate the use of force abroad and engage in missions that put soldiers in harm's way. Our existing data allowed for only provisional and partial evaluation of four potential explanations: (1) empathy and consent, (2) soldier/officer motivation, (3) homophily, and (4) alienation and efficacy.

These preliminary findings have implications for policymakers' freedom of action when using force. The casualty sensitivity of nondominant communal groups likely impacts the ability of some political leaders more than others to deploy troops into potentially dangerous situations. Those whose political coalitions more heavily rely on nondominant communal groups may well be less inclined to approve military missions involving significant ground troops or to escalate existing missions that run the risk of casualties. It also follows that such political leaders, when contemplating different ways of using force, will be more tempted by those that minimize the risk of casualties for their own forces—such as missiles and air strikes (perhaps especially by remotely piloted aircraft).

In the United States today, and more generally around the world, more racially, ethnically, and religiously diverse coalitions have tended to be—and still largely are—located on the political left. Politicians on the left are more reluctant to use military force: their ideological inclinations already tilt that way, and their nondominant constituents' resentment and alienation merely reinforce that disposition. But this logic also suggests that politicians on the left face particular political constraints regarding sending ground troops into battle and should be especially attracted to offshore modes of force employment. Yet politicians on the left then confront a political and ideological dilemma: offshore modes of using force, which are often no less bloody, shift the cost of military operations onto local civilians rather than the interveners themselves.

We believe that mass opinion is more of a constraint on the use of force by democracies than some scholarly literature allows (as Blankshain and Cohn, this volume, suggest as well). True, public opinion is malleable, and people will support even military operations that involve significant casualties if the stakes are sufficiently high and the prospects of victory sufficiently bright.[75] But those caveats are important, because politicians must always think twice about whether they can persuade a critical mass of citizens that the stakes are indeed high and that the prospects of victory are in fact bright. Public opinion thus exerts its most profound effects on the use of force—sometimes for good and sometimes for ill—not because it is committed, but precisely because it is not. Uncertainty can cut both ways: it offers hope to the risk acceptant and arrogant, and it reinforces the caution and modesty of the risk averse and the humble. But the historical record is littered with politicians who overestimated their capacity to shape public opinion,[76] especially over the long haul.[77] And we suspect that the historical record is even more full of dogs that did not bark: politicians who did not use force, or who delayed using force, because they worried about their ability to move public opinion and sustain the public's support. Highly polarized political environments magnify this endemic uncertainty. When opinion is highly divided, when swaying those from the other camp seems especially unlikely, and thus when sustaining a political coalition in the face of casualties is even more difficult, politicians must be especially sensitive to the views, and casualty tolerance, of ever smaller slices of the population.

This chapter suggests several potential future directions of research. First, more work should center race and ethnicity as the focus of analysis in the study of public opinion on foreign and military policy in general and of casualty sensitivity in particular. Surveys specifically directed toward these questions would allow scholars to distinguish among conceivable explanations for the differences between the views of dominant and nondominant communal groups.

Second, our preliminary analysis disaggregating the nonwhite category in Britain and the United States suggests that there may be differences among nondominant communal groups. In Britain, British Indians and respondents who chose "other" were less likely to tolerate casualties, while Black Britons were not distinguishable in their casualty tolerance from white Britons. The same pattern holds in the United States: Black, Latino, and Asian respondents were more sensitive to casualties than were other Americans, but Native Americans' casualty sensitivity did not significantly differ from that of other American respondents. Future research should oversample nondominant communal groups to permit for adequately powered analyses of these groups.

Third, our chapter has pointed to the importance of exploring such questions using cross-national data. Few studies examine public opinion on military affairs outside the United States, and even fewer put data from different national contexts into conversation with each other. Yet the experiences of nondominant communal groups diverge across the world, and their relationships with the military vary as well. Unpacking these relationships cross-nationally would paint a richer and more diverse picture of opinion toward the use of force and casualty sensitivity.

Fourth, as countries become more diverse, right-wing parties are also becoming adept at mobilizing nondominant populations. Thus, Republicans in the United States have, in recent elections, made significant inroads with Latino voters and with Black men. Are right-wing nondominant group voters still relatively casualty sensitive or are they no more, or less, casualty sensitive than dominant-group voters or right-wing voters in general? If right-wing parties are successfully peeling off nondominant-group voters who are more casualty tolerant, the remaining nondominant-group voters of liberal-left parties are presumably even more casualty sensitive, further magnifying the effects on their political representatives. How much can elite framing by leaders of left- or right-leaning coalitions change nondominant constituents' tolerance of casualties?

Finally, nondominant communal status is not static. Do erstwhile nondominant communal groups develop different attitudes toward the use of force and casualties as they become increasingly central to the nation and its politics? Mizrahim in Israel are a particularly notable example, but it has been widely observed that the United States will, within the next twenty to twenty-five years, become a majority minority nation. Centering race and ethnicity in the study of public opinion on the use of force opens a range of heretofore unexplored questions of great significance for democratic accountability in wartime.

Notes

1. John E. Mueller, *War, Presidents, and Public Opinion* (New York: Wiley, 1973).

2. Bruce W. Jentleson, "The Pretty Prudent Public: Post Post-Vietnam American Opinion on the Use of Military Force," *International Studies Quarterly*, 36, no. 1 (March 1992): 49–74; Bruce W. Jentleson and Rebecca L. Britton, "Still Pretty Prudent: Post-Cold War American Public Opinion on the Use of Military Force," *Journal of Conflict Resolution*, 42, no. 4 (1998): 395–417.

3. Peter D. Feaver and Christopher Gelpi, *Choosing Your Battles: American Civil-Military Relations and the Use of Force* (Princeton, NJ: Princeton University Press, 2004); Christopher Gelpi, Peter Feaver and Jason Reifler, *Paying the Human*

Costs of War: American Public Opinion and Casualties in Military Conflicts (Princeton, NJ: Princeton University Press, 2009).

4. Michael C. Horowitz and Matthew S. Levendusky, "Drafting Support for War: Conscription and Mass Support for Warfare," *Journal of Politics*, 73, no. 2 (April 2011): 524–534.

5. James Burk, "The Changing Moral Contract for Military Service," in *The Long War: A New History of U.S. National Security Policy Since World War II*, ed. Andrew J. Bacevich (New York: Columbia University Press, 2007), 444; David R. Segal, *Recruiting for Uncle Sam: Citizenship and Military Manpower Policy* (Lawrence: University Press of Kansas, 1989).

6. Scott L. Althaus et al., "When War Hits Home: The Geography of Military Losses and Support for War in Time and Space," *Journal of Conflict Resolution*, 56, no. 3 (June 2012): 382–412; Douglas L. Kriner and Francis X. Shen, "How Citizens Respond to Combat Casualties: The Differential Impact of Local Casualties on Support for the War in Afghanistan," *Public Opinion Quarterly*, 76, no. 4 (January 2012): 761–770.

7. Scott Sigmund Gartner and Gary M. Segura, "Race, Casualties, and Opinion in the Vietnam War," *The Journal of Politics*, 62, no. 1 (February 2000): 115–146.

8. Scott Sigmund Gartner, "Ties to the Dead: Connections to Iraq War and 9/11 Casualties and Disapproval of the President," *American Sociological Review*, 73, no. 4 (August 2008): 690–695.

9. Tanisha Fazal, "Life and Limb: New Estimates of Casualty Aversion in the United States," *International Studies Quarterly*, 65, no. 1 (2021): 160–172.

10. Richard C. Eichenberg, "Gender Difference in American Public Opinion on the Use of Military Force, 1982–2013," *International Studies Quarterly*, 60, no. 1 (March 2016): 138–148; Richard C. Eichenberg, *Gender, War, and World Order: A Study of Public Opinion* (Ithaca, NY: Cornell University Press, 2019).

11. International Organization on Migration, *World Migration Report 2020* (Geneva: International Organization on Migration, 2020).

12. These surveys were designed with the assistance of David Blagden (University of Exeter), Aaron Rapport (University of Cambridge), and Shaul Shenhav (Hebrew University of Jerusalem).

13. For analysis of data from the US, see Ronald R. Krebs and Robert Ralston, "Patriotism or Paychecks: Who Believes What About Why Soldiers Serve," *Armed Forces & Society* 48, no. 1 (2022): 25–48; Ronald R. Krebs, Robert Ralston, and Aaron Rapport, "Why They Fight: How Perceived Motivations for Military Service Shape Support for the Use of Force," *International Studies Quarterly* 65, no. 4 (2021): 1012–1026.

14. Mueller, *War, Presidents, and Public Opinion*; Jentleson, "Pretty Prudent Public"; Jentleson and Britton, "Still Pretty Prudent"; Feaver and Gelpi, *Choosing Your Battles*; Gelpi, Feaver, and Reifler, *Paying the Human Costs of War*. Other

entries in this debate include, among others, William A. Boettcher and Michael D. Cobb, "'Don't Let Them Die in Vain': Casualty Frames and Public Tolerance for Escalating Commitment in Iraq," *Journal of Conflict Resolution* 53, no. 5 (October 2009): 677–697; William A. Boettcher and Michael D. Cobb, "Echoes of Vietnam? Casualty Framing and Public Perceptions of Success and Failure in Iraq," *Journal of Conflict Resolution* 50, no. 6 (2006): 831–854; James Burk, "Public Support for Peacekeeping in Lebanon and Somalia: Assessing the Casualties Hypothesis," *Political Science Quarterly* 114, no. 1 (Spring 1999): 53–78; Richard C. Eichenberg, "Victory Has Many Friends: U.S. Public Opinion and the Use of Military Force, 1981–2005," *International Security* 30, no. 1 (2006): 140–177; Scott Sigmund Gartner and Gary M. Segura, "War, Casualties, and Public Opinion," *Journal of Conflict Resolution*, 42, no. 3 (1998): 278–300; Scott Sigmund Gartner, "The Multiple Effects of Casualties on Public Support for War: An Experimental Approach," *American Political Science Review*, 102, no. 1 (2008): 95–106; Patricia L. Sullivan, "Sustaining the Fight: A Cross-Sectional Time-Series Analysis of Public Support for Ongoing Military Interventions," *Conflict Management and Peace Science* 25, no. 2 (2008): 112–135; Erik Voeten and Paul R. Brewer, "Public Opinion, the War in Iraq and Presidential Accountability," *Journal of Conflict Resolution* 50, no. 6 (2006): 809–830.

15. Horowitz and Levendusky, "Drafting Support for War"; Althaus et al., "When War Hits Home"; Kriner and Shen, "How Citizens Respond to Combat Casualties"; Scott Sigmund Gartner et al., "All Politics Are Local: Local Losses and Individual Attitudes toward the Vietnam War," *Journal of Conflict Resolution* 41, no. 5 (1997): 669–694; Gartner, "Ties to the Dead"; Andrew F. Hayes and Tereas A. Myers, "Testing the 'Proximate Casualties Hypothesis': Local Troop Loss, Attention to News, and Support for Military Intervention," *Mass Communication and Society* 12, no. 4 (2009): 379–402; Tiffany C. Davenport, "Policy-Induced Risk and Responsive Participation: The Effect of a Son's Conscription Risk on the Voting Behavior of His Parents," *American Journal of Political Science* 59, no. 1 (2015): 225–241; David Karol and Edward Miguel, "The Electoral Cost of War: Iraq Casualties and the 2004 U.S. Presidential Election," *The Journal of Politics* 69 (2007): 633–648.

16. Robert C. Smith and Richard Seltzer, *Contemporary Controversies and the American Racial Divide* (Lanham, MD: Rowman & Littlefield, 2000); David L. Leal, "American Public Opinion toward the Military," *Armed Forces & Society* 32, no. 1 (2005): 123–138; Melissa V. Harris-Lacewell, "Political Science and the Study of African American Public Opinion," in *African American Perspectives on Political Science*, ed. Wilbur C. Rich (Philadelphia: Temple University Press, 2007), 120–121; Naima Green-Riley and Andrew Leber, "Whose War is it Anyway? Explaining the Black-White Gap in Support for the Use of Force Abroad," *Security Studies* 32, no. 4-5 (2023): 811–845.

17. John Zaller, *The Nature and Origins of Mass Opinion* (New York: Cambridge University Press, 1992); John Zaller, "Strategic Politicians, Public Opinion,

and the Gulf Crisis," in *Taken By Storm: The Media, Public Opinion, and U.S. Foreign Policy in the Gulf War*, ed. W. Lance Bennett and David L. Paletz (Chicago: University of Chicago Press, 1994), 250-274.

18. Adam J. Berinsky, "Assuming the Costs of War: Events, Elites, and American Public Supoort for Military Conflict," *Journal of Politics* 69, no. 4 (2007): 975-997; Adam J. Berinsky, *In Time of War: Understanding American Public Opinion from World War II to Iraq* (Chicago: University of Chicago Press, 2009).

19. Berinsky, *In Time of War*, 8.

20. Miroslav Nincic and Donna J. Nincic, "Race, Gender, and War," *Journal of Peace Research* 39, no. 5 (2002): 547-568. For other research noting that Black Americans have been more opposed to conflict abroad, see Sidney Verba et al., "Public Opinion and the War in Vietnam," *American Political Science Review* 61, no. 2 (1967): 317-333; Gartner et al., "All Politics Are Local"; Val Burris, "From Vietnam To Iraq: Continuity And Change In Between-Group Differences in Support For Military Action," *Social Problems* 55, no. 4 (2008): 443-479; Katherine Tate, *What's Going On?: Political Incorporation and the Transformation of Black Public Opinion* (Washington, DC: Georgetown University Press, 2010); Rachel Allison, "Race, Gender, And Attitudes Toward War in Chicago: An Intersectional Analysis," *Sociological Forum* 26, no. 3 (2011): 668-691.

21. Gartner and Segura, "Race, Casualties, and Opinion in the Vietnam War," 138.

22. Green-Riley, Naima, and Andrew Leber. "Whose War is it Anyway? Explaining the Black-White Gap in Support for the Use of Force Abroad." *Security Studies* 32, no. 4-5 (2023): 811-845.

23. Gelpi, Feaver, and Reifler, *Paying the Human Costs of War*, 14. Our own analysis of the data underlying both Gelpi (2005) and Kriner and Shen (2014) suggests that minorities—especially Black respondents—are more casualty sensitive in these studies. See Christopher Gelpi, Peter D. Feaver, and Jason Reifler, "Success Matters: Casualty Sensitivity and the War in Iraq," *International Security* 30, no. 3 (Winter 2005/2006): 7-46; Douglas L. Kriner and Francis X. Shen, "Reassessing American Casualty Sensitivity: The Mediating Influence of Inequality," *Journal of Conflict Resolution* 58, no. 7 (October 2014): 1174-1201. See online appendix 8.2 for replication details from both studies.

24. Feaver and Gelpi, *Choosing Your Battles*, 125.

25. Green-Riley and Leber, "Whose War is it Anyway?"

26. Among the many exceptions examining public opinion on the use of force outside the United States, see, on Australia, Charles Miller, "Re-examining the Australian Public's Attitude to Military Casualties: Post-heroic or Defeat-phobic?" *Australian Journal of International Affairs* 68, no. 5 (2014): 515-530. On Canada, Jean-Christophe Boucher, "Evaluating the Trenton Effect: Canadian Public Opinion and Military Casualties in Afghanistan (2006-2010)," *American Review of Canadian Studies* 40, no. 2 (2010): 237-258; Scott Fitzsimmons et al., "Canadian

Public Opinion about the Military: Assessing the Influences on Attitudes toward Defence Spending and Participation in Overseas Combat Operations," *Canadian Journal of Political Science* 47, no. 3 (2014): 503–518. On China, see Mark S. Bell and Kai Quek, "Authoritarian Public Opinion and the Democratic Peace," *International Organization* 72, no. 1 (2018): 227–242. On Germany, see Harald Schoen, "Personality Traits and Foreign Policy Attitudes in German Public Opinion," *Journal of Conflict Resolution* 51, no. 3 (2007): 408–430; Alexander Jedinger and Matthias Mader, "Predispositions, Mission-Specific Beliefs, and Public Support for Military Missions: The Case of the German ISAF Mission in Afghanistan," *International Journal of Public Opinion Research* 27, no. 1 (2015): 90–110. On Israel, see Asher Arian, *Security Threatened: Surveying Israeli Opinion on Peace and War* (New York: Cambridge University Press, 1996). On Russia, see Theodore P. Gerber and Sarah E. Mendelson, "Casualty Sensitivity in a Post-Soviet Context: Russian Views of the Second Chechen War, 2001–2004," *Political Science Quarterly* 123, no. 1 (2008): 39–68. On the United Kingdom, see Jason Reifler et al., "Foreign Policy Beliefs in Contemporary Britain: Structure and Relevance," *International Studies Quarterly* 55, no. 1 (2011): 245–266; Ben Clements, "A Micro-Level Analysis of Support in Britain for the War in Afghanistan," *British Journal of Politics and International Relations* 16, no. 2 (2014): 230–250; Rachael Gribble et al., "British Public Opinion after a Decade of War: Attitudes to Iraq and Afghanistan," *Politics & Gender*, 35, no. 2 (2015): 128–150.

27. For cross-national, comparative opinion data on public opinion and the use of force, see Hank C. Jenkins-Smith et al., "Foreign and Domestic Policy Belief Structures in the U.S. and British Publics," *Journal of Conflict Resolution* 48, no. 3 (2004): 287–309; Ebru Ş. Canan-Sokullu, "Domestic Support for Wars: A Cross-Case and Cross-Country Analysis," *Armed Forces & Society* 38, no. 1 (2012): 117–141; Robert Johns and Graeme A. M. Davies, "Democratic Peace or Clash of Civilizations? Target States and Support for War in Britain and the United States," *Journal of Politics* 74, no. 4 (2012): 1038–1052; Philip Everts and Pierangelo Isernia, *Public Opinion, Transatlantic Relations, and the Use of Force* (London: Palgrave MacMillan, 2015); Richard C. Eichenberg and Richard J. Stoll, "The Acceptability of War and Support for Defense Spending: Evidence from Fourteen Democracies, 2004–2013," *Journal of Conflict Resolution* 61, no. 4 (2017): 788–813; Timothy B. Gravelle et al., "The Structure of Foreign Policy Attitudes in Transatlantic Perspective: Comparing the United States, United Kingdom, France and Germany," *European Journal of Political Research* 56, no. 4 (2017): 757–776; Eichenberg, *Gender, War, and World Order*, chapter six; Timothy B. Gravelle et al., "The Structure of Foreign Policy Attitudes among Middle Power Publics: A Transpacific Replication," *Australian Journal of International Affairs* 75, no. 2 (2021): 217–236.

28. The Israel survey centered on an officer rather than a soldier because pilot studies found insufficient variation in the motives that Israelis ascribed to soldiers, even those who volunteered for special units. The fictional officer was not named

except by initial for purposes of verisimilitude. Israeli newspaper articles are not permitted by law to reveal the names of interview subjects currently serving in the Israel Defense Forces.

29. In the US survey, these vignettes varied the objective of the prospective mission. However, we found that the impact of soldiering narratives did not vary significantly across missions. Consequently, subsequent surveys in the United Kingdom and Israel did not introduce treatments that varied the mission type.

30. The Israel survey enrolled only non-Arab/non-Palestinian respondents. With rare exceptions, Arab/Palestinian citizens of Israel do not serve in the Israel Defense Forces, and we thus expected them to be unresponsive to the larger survey's primary variable of interest: representations of soldier motivation. Recruiting sufficient Arab/Palestinian respondents in Israel is, furthermore, expensive. However, given this chapter's focus on racial and ethnic identity, that choice proved regrettable. While Arab/Palestinian citizens of Israel would surely be less supportive of the prospective mission, in which Lebanese citizens and Hizballah fighters might die, they might be more tolerant of casualties among Israeli soldiers and officers because few of their coethnics/conationals would be at risk of death or injury in combat.

31. Krebs and Ralston, "Patriotism or Paychecks"; Krebs, Ralston, and Rapport, "Why They Fight."

32. Boettcher and Cobb, "'Don't Let Them Die in Vain'."

33. Gelpi, Feaver, and Reifler, *Paying the Human Costs of War*.

34. Critics have argued that individual casualty tolerance, measured in this fashion, should not be relied upon as the sole indicator of an individual's support for war. They have also pointed out that respondents likely lack an accurate understanding of potential casualties in given military campaigns. For such criticism, see Adam J. Berinsky and James N. Druckman, "Review: Public Opinion Research and Support for the Iraq War," *The Public Opinion Quarterly* 71, no. 1 (Spring 2007): 126–141. However, even if the critics are right and this measure of casualty tolerance is flawed with respect to external validity, our puzzle—the persistent disparity between nondominant and dominant communal groups with respect to their self-projected casualty sensitivity—remains internally valid and puzzling.

35. See online appendix 8.1, section 2, for histograms with the distribution of each country's casualty sensitivity measure.

36. Alain van Hiel and Ivan Mervielde, "Explaining Conservative Beliefs and Political Preferences: A Comparison of Social Dominance Orientation and Authoritarianism," *Journal of Applied Social Psychology* 32, no. 5 (2002): 965–976.

37. The results are also robust to different modelling strategies, such as using negative binomial regressions and treating the data as count data. See online appendix 8.1, section 3, table 18.

38. The coefficients are also significant in the absence of controls.

39. In all the models reported in this paragraph, casualty sensitivity was binary. Controls were included for demographic variables (education, income, personal

military service, gender, and age) and some political variables (hawkishness, ideology, and feelings toward the military). The Israel models also included a control for religiosity. The US and UK models also included a control for household military service. Other variables were held at their means.

40. If anything, members of nondominant communal groups are still underrepresented in the UK military overall, especially at the higher ranks: see "UK Armed Forces Biannual Diversity Statistics: 1 April 2020," Ministry of Defense, last updated December 17, 2020, https://www.gov.uk/government/statistics/uk-armed-forces-biannual-diversity-statistics-2020/uk-armed-forces-biannual-diversity-statistics-1-april-2020; Anthony King, "Decolonizing the British Army: A Preliminary Response," *International Affairs* 97, no. 2 (2021): 443–461.

41. We do not control for household military service in Israel because there is no meaningful variation in our data due to the draft among Jewish Israelis.

42. We acknowledge that there may be no single explanation across national contexts. It is possible, even likely, that different explanations carry different weight in different countries, given their unique histories and ethno-racial legacies and ongoing dynamics. However, this chapter proceeds from the premise that there are commonalities in the experience of nondominant citizens that may account for this cross-national finding. Its quest for a common explanation derives from that premise. Thanks to Ben Fordham for pressing us on this point in the initial project workshop in January 2021.

43. Eric J. Vanman, "The Role of Empathy in Intergroup Relations," *Current Opinion in Psychology* 11 (October 2016): 59–63; Marius C. Vollberg and Mina Cikara, "The Neuroscience of Intergroup Emotion," *Current Opinion in Psychology* 24 (2018): 48–52.

44. Althaus et al., "When War Hits Home"; Kriner and Shen, "How Citizens Respond to Combat Casualties."

45. C. Daniel Batson, "Empathy and Altruism," in *The Oxford Handbook of Hypo-Egoic Phenomena*, ed. Kirk Warren Brown and Mark R. Leary (Oxford: Oxford University Press, 2017); Nancy Eisenberg and Janet Strayer, eds., *Empathy and Its Development, Cambridge Studies in Social and Emotional Development* (Cambridge: Cambridge University Press, 1987); Eric L. Stocks and David A. Lishner, "Empathy and Altruism," in *Oxford Research Encyclopedia of Psychology* (October 24, 2018).

46. Krebs, Ralston, and Rapport, "Why They Fight."

47. See online appendix 8.1, section 3, table 1.

48. See online appendix 8.1, section 4, figures 1–3.

49. See online appendix 8.1, section 4, figure 4. However, the number of non-white respondents in the UK sample is small—just over 250, compared to 2,190 whites—complicating our capacity to draw firm conclusions from this data.

50. See online appendix 8.1, section 3, table 16.

51. Krebs, Ralston, and Rapport, "Why They Fight."

52. Krebs, Ralston, and Rapport, "Why They Fight."

53. Krebs and Ralston, "Patriotism or Paychecks."

54. Interestingly, the gap between white and nonwhite respondents' perception of Cameron's race is greatest when he is quoted as attributing his joining the military to the pay and benefits of service. See online appendix 8.1, section 3, table 3.

55. White respondents were also more likely to endorse a pay-and-benefits account of service and less likely to attribute service to good citizenship, but these coefficients did not achieve conventional levels of significance. For relevant crosstabs and multivariate analysis, see online appendix 8.1, section 3, tables 4 and 5.

56. See online appendix 8.1, section 3, table 6.

57. Miller McPherson et al., "Birds of a Feather: Homophily in Social Networks," *Annual Review of Sociology*, 27 (2001): 415–444.

58. See online appendix 8.1, section 3, table 7 and 8 for US and UK data, respectively.

59. See online appendix 8.1, section 3, table 9. This finding must be treated with great caution, since the critical cell (Mizrahi respondents who believed Captain D was Mizrahi) contained just fourteen respondents.

60. See online appendix 8.1, section 3, tables 10–12.

61. See online appendix 8.1, section 3, table 10.

62. See online appendix 8.1, section 3, table 12.

63. See online appendix 8.1, section 3, table 11.

64. Gartner and Segura, "Race, Casualties, and Opinion in the Vietnam War."

65. As suggested by Green-Riley and Leber, "Whose War is it Anyway?"

66. Benjamin I. Page and Robert Y. Shapiro, *The Rational Public: Fifty Years of Trends in Americans' Policy Preferences* (Chicago: University of Chicago Press, 1992), 177–182, 285–320; David L. Weakliem and Casey Borch, "Alienation in the United States: Uniform or Group-Specific Change?," *Sociological Forum* 21, no. 3 (2006): 415–438.

67. Harrell R. Rodgers, "Toward Explanation of Political Efficacy and Political Cynicism of Black Adolescents: An Exploratory Study," *American Journal of Political Science* 18, no. 2 (1974): 257–282; Paul R. Abramson, *Political Attitudes in America: Formation and Change* (San Francisco: W. H. Freeman and Company, 1983), 150–151; Robert C. Smith and Richard Seltzer, *Race, Class, and Culture* (Albany: State University of New York Press, 1992), 33; Paula McClain and Joseph Stewart, *Can We All Get Along? Racial and Ethnic Minorities in American Politics*, 3rd ed. (Boulder, CO: Westview Press, 2002); Jennifer L. Merolla et al., "Descriptive Representation, Political Efficacy, and African Americans in the 2008 Presidential Election," *Political Psychology* 34, no. 6 (2013): 863–875.

68. The blind patriotism index is comprised of an additive index of three questions. Respondents were asked, on a seven-point scale, whether they agreed or disagreed with the following three statements: (1) "There is too much criticism of the [country] in the world, and we its citizens should not criticize it"; (2) "I would support my country right or wrong"; (3) "I believe that [country] policies are almost

always the morally correct ones." See Robert T. Schatz et al., "On the Varieties of National Attachment: Blind Versus Constructive Patriotism," *Political Psychology* 20, no. 1 (1999): 151–174.

69. See online appendix 1, section 3, tables 13–15 for details.

70. Nincic and Nincic, "Race, Gender, and War"; Green-Riley and Leber, "Whose War is it Anyway?"

71. Had the survey in the United States oversampled communal minorities, we might have been able to leverage the well-established variation in alienation across these communal groups. However, because the current sample sizes are far too small, we are not willing to place any credence in the reported variation in casualty sensitivity among Asian Americans, Latino Americans, Black Americans, and Native Americans.

72. This conception of political efficacy aligns closely with "internal" political efficacy: "beliefs about one's own competence to understand, and to participate effectively in politics." It is possible that alienation—identification with the collective—is associated with "external" efficacy: "beliefs about the responsiveness of governmental authorities and institutions to citizen demands." See Richard G. Niemi et al., "Measuring Internal Political Efficacy in the 1988 National Election Study," *American Political Science Review* 85, no. 4 (1991): 1407–1413, quotes at 1408, 1412.

73. We asked respondents about their warmth toward particular political institutions, which might serve as a proxy for external efficacy and alienation. However, including respondents' feeling thermometer with respect to the national parliament did not have significant effects on casualty sensitivity in any country and little-to-no-effect on the statistical or substantive significance of respondents' race. See online appendix 8.1, section 3, table 17.

74. See also Eichenberg, "Gender Difference in American Public Opinion on the Use of Military Force, 1982–2013"; Eichenberg, *Gender, War, and World Order*; Joslyn Barnhart et al., "The Suffragist Peace," *International Organization* 74, no. 4 (2020): 633–670.

75. Jentleson, "Pretty Prudent Public"; Gelpi, Feaver, and Reifler, *Paying the Human Costs of War*.

76. George C. Edwards III, *On Deaf Ears: The Limits of the Bully Pulpit* (New Haven, CT: Yale University Press, 2003); George C. Edwards III, *The Strategic President: Persuasion and Opportunity in Presidential Leadership* (Princeton, NJ: Princeton University Press, 2009); Ronald R. Krebs, *Narrative and the Making of U.S. National Security* (Cambridge: Cambridge University Press, 2015).

77. Matthew A. Baum and Tim Groeling, *War Stories: The Causes and Consequences of Public Views of War* (Princeton, NJ: Princeton University Press, 2010).

CHAPTER NINE

"Hand-to-Hand Combat"

Bureaucratic Politics and National Security

Andrew Rudalevige

If war is politics by other means, bureaucratic politics might be another kind of war. A rather nasty kind, if former CIA Director and Defense Secretary Leon Panetta has it right: asked to describe the Pentagon's relationship with the White House staff, he replied it was like "hand-to-hand combat."[1] But the fighting goes beyond a single trench. Scholars Daniel Farber and Anne Joseph O'Connell, for instance, portray "agencies as adversaries" engaged in "constant battles, between and within " those agencies.[2] Robert Hunter's book about his service on the National Security Council staff borrows from Shakespeare to describe his travels "into the breach!" (And more than once.)[3]

Even those participants in the foreign policy process less inclined to martial metaphor use phrases like "permanent struggle" (Henry Kissinger) or "unending contest" (McGeorge Bundy) to describe the relationship between the president and the wider executive branch.[4] Elsewhere Kissinger talks about the tendency of "the various elements of the bureaucracy [to] make a series of nonaggression pacts" to keep decisions out of presidential hands[5]—indeed, analogies to statecraft appear frequently in attempts to summarize the workings of the federal establishment. Harold Seidman and Robert Gilmour argue that the executive branch is not hierarchical so much as "an alliance" or "a confederation of sovereigns."[6] Francis Rourke frames relations between the president and the bureaucracy as "diplomacy" and not prone to relaxed negotiation: one State Department official, quoted in a foreign policy textbook, comments that "it has long been easier for us to deal with the Russians than to produce agreements with our own Defense Department."[7] In short, even in foreign and national security policy—long posited as the easiest arena wherein presidents work their will—implementation is rarely a simple matter of presidential command.

Presidents themselves confirm this, often in self-pitying tones. "I agree with you," John F. Kennedy reportedly told one confidant, "but I don't know if the government will"—a sentiment echoed six decades on when Donald Trump, asked about a policy initiative, replied, "I didn't do it.... I don't know anything about it. It's the administration." Franklin Roosevelt complained that the Navy was like a "feather bed" that, once punched, simply sprang back to its original shape. George W. Bush carped to an Egyptian opposition leader that "I too am a dissident in Washington. Bureaucracy in the United States does not help change." Barack Obama grew frustrated with how "the foreign policy bureaucracy could slow-walk, misinterpret, bury, badly execute, or otherwise resist new directions from a president."[8]

Such consistent lamentation is surely inconsistent with recent claims to a unitary executive that assumes the seamless translation of presidential preferences into policy outputs. But it fits comfortably with the simple fact of a constitutional structure premised on preventing the unilateral exercise of power. The system of intertwining branches of government grants each the standing to check their counterparts, amplified by the internal fragmentation of those branches. While less formally divided by the Constitution than the legislative branch, the executive branch is very much a "they," not an "it." Each element of the executive has its own preferences and interests, goals that may diverge from the president's, and resources for achieving them (or, at the least, for preventing someone else from achieving *theirs*), and each normally possesses more information than its political overseers about the substantive concerns within its jurisdiction. Further, the very nature of organizational behavior limits the range of options available for governmental action and presidential choice. The president can order off the bureaucratic menu but only slowly create a new dish from scratch.[9]

While the growth of the administrative state and especially its national security components has surely increased presidential capacity in absolute terms, empowerment has not been a linear function. The larger the "state," the more agencies and personnel, the harder the challenge of coordination and communication across a diffuse bureaucracy—something the September 11, 2001, attacks demonstrated in tragic fashion. When presidential efforts to solve those problems layer a new "counter-bureaucracy" over existing organizational sprawl, unintended new management burdens may be the result.[10]

Thus to the roster of domestic checks on the chief executive we must add the executive branch itself. Bureaucratic control is a holy grail of sorts and like that relic out of mortals' reach.

What follows lays out these themes as developed in political science and public administration, using examples from postwar history generally and concluding with a more extended case study of the United States' twenty years in Afghanistan from 2001 to 2021. It is not meant to assess the absolute strength of the presidency so much as remind us that the very features that produced that strength can impose their own constraints. To be sure, as Rebecca Ingber shows in her chapter, the bureaucracy has actively expanded presidential power, not least by articulating legal rationales that maximize executive authority in foreign affairs at the expense of other actors, particularly Congress. Rarely will an executive branch lawyer decide that the president has less power rather than more.[11] However, essential features of bureaucratic politics ensure that presidents will nonetheless struggle to wield that power effectively. Presidential experience in foreign affairs since 9/11 serves as a reminder that the Constitution, no matter how urgent the faith of its unitarian adherents, produces polytheistic governance.

Bureaucracies and Bargaining

In 2018, once and future attorney general William Barr stated bluntly in a memo to Justice Department officials that "constitutionally, it is wrong to conceive of the President as simply the highest officer within the Executive branch hierarchy. He alone *is* the Executive branch."[12] This claim had an immediate, instrumental purpose (seeking to protect Donald Trump from indictment), but also reflected a long effort by advocates of presidential power to define "the executive power" vested in the president by Article II of the Constitution as an exclusive "zone of autonomy."[13] A slightly less personalized version can be found as early as the 1937 Brownlow Report to Franklin Roosevelt, holding that "the constitutional principle of the separation of powers ... places in the President, and the President alone, the whole executive power of the Government of the United States."[14] Different expositions of "unitary executive" theory have distinct visions of the content of that executive power (Barr's was far more robust than Brownlow's), but their lowest common denominator is that presidents have control of the executive branch: its preferences should entirely coincide with theirs.[15]

This credo is dubious even in theory. James Madison's *Federalist* essays clarify that the pure separation of powers associated with "the celebrated maxim of the celebrated Montesquieu" is a recipe for tyranny. Instead, the branches need to have overlapping powers so that they can actually check and balance one another.[16] Back in 1838, the Supreme Court held that while of course "the executive power is vested in a President,"

> it by no means follows that every officer in every branch of that department is under the exclusive direction of the President. Such a principle, we apprehend, is not and certainly cannot be claimed by the President.... [I]t would be an alarming doctrine that Congress cannot impose upon any executive officer any duty they may think proper which is not repugnant to any rights secured and protected by the Constitution.[17]

As Richard Neustadt would put it 125 years later, the US system is not one featuring a separation of powers but "separated institutions *sharing* powers."[18] In this view, the presidential office, as strictly defined by the Constitution, is obstructed rather than omnipotent.[19]

That is certainly true in practice, and especially so in the era of the modern administrative state. The New Deal, World War II, the Cold War (and its warmer interludes), the Great Society, and the regulatory explosions of the 1970s built up a huge federal establishment. By the 1980s, some went to far as to argue the bureaucracy now challenged Congress and the president "for hegemony in the national political system," competing "on equal, and sometimes superior, terms" to those political actors.[20]

If that conclusion seems extreme, it did not go dramatically beyond the broader school of public administration research traced above. By 1973, Morton Halperin and Arnold Kanter had produced an edited volume of readings on American foreign policy centered on "a bureaucratic perspective," driven by "the assumption that the predominant sources of a nation's behavior in the international arena are the organizations and individuals in the executive branch who are responding to opportunities for, and threats to, the maximization of their diverse interests and objectives."[21]

Epitomized by Graham Allison's appraisal of the Cuban Missile Crisis, originally published in 1971, scholars in this camp noted various aspects of bureaucratic politics that limited the presidential command and control posited by their predecessors going back to Brownlow and even Woodrow Wilson. Allison's *Essence of Decision* saw American government acting as the "conglomerate of semi-feudal, loosely allied organizations" far more frequently than as a singular rational actor.[22] In this view, presidents certainly have clear legal and constitutional advantages in dealing with others in the executive branch. But they find themselves in the position of a ruler of a far-flung empire nominally under centralized control whose constituent states are both de facto autonomous most of the time and also provide much of what the ruler's capitol needs for its very subsistence. Even books taking the opposite tack in their choice of title concede the case by their very existence, for instance with how-to books by longtime practitioners guiding presidents toward *Presidential Command* or *Presidential Control of Foreign Policy*.[23] Without their advice, they fear, the result will be *How the Bureaucracy Makes Foreign Policy*.[24]

This literature is too sprawling to sum up in its entirety here, but it generally agrees on at least three structural features of the executive branch that shape this relationship: (1) its size and fragmentation; (2) the "principal-agent" challenges posed by information asymmetry and goal divergence between the president and executive agencies; and (3) the nature of organizational behavior, driven by bureaucratic standard operating procedures.[25]

Not a Singular Noun

Back in 1937, organization theorists identified a public executive's optimal "span of control" at a maximum of four people.[26] The number of people at least nominally working for the president is not four, but four million.

This vast cast of characters is spread across fifteen cabinet departments (with 173 bureaus within them) and nearly eighty agencies outside those departments, including independent regulatory commissions created precisely to resist hierarchical political control.[27] Each has its own bespoke incentives and resources, and sometimes a lot of them: Secretary of Defense James Mattis liked to quip that if the Pentagon were its own country, its GDP would rank seventeenth in the world.[28] And policy problems, from environmental protection to various aspects of foreign affairs, are frequently split across the jurisdictions of multiple agencies. Even within the fifteen-hundred-person strong Executive Office of the President, coordination problems arise; while this problem is largely left aside below, it is worth keeping in mind that "presidential control [is] not a unified enterprise but coalitions of different offices competing for influence."[29]

Obviously the president's relationship with executive agencies *is* quite different from that of legislators or judges. Presidents have real advantages of "unity" relative to Congress; relative to the courts, they can rely on a first-mover advantage and the reactive nature of judicial intervention. Presidents bargain with the bureaucracy from a distinctive vantage point, as chief executive. They reside atop the formal hierarchy and have a clear claim to powers of command derived from the vesting clause and beyond—powers that, as Ingber stresses, are self-perpetuated by executive branch lawyers' parsing of Constitution, statute, and history. Still, as the references to intrabranch "combat" that opened the chapter imply, presidents themselves rarely assume frictionless interaction within the executive branch, nor see it as a monolithic entity. Thus in practice (and I would argue even in theory), presidential control over the bureaucracy is constrained by collective action and transaction-cost concerns issues arising within the executive branch itself.

Indeed, pluralism emerges even in what we often think of as a pure form of unilateralism, the formulation and issuance of presidential directives such as executive orders (EOs). Recent research shows that a plurality of executive orders originate not in the White House but in the agencies, with the Departments of Defense and State serving as the top two EO producers.[30] Further, most proposed EOs, including those drafted by the president's immediate staff, are subject to significant interagency bargaining over their content and even over their issuance. For instance, in 1986 Secretary of Defense Caspar Weinberger personally wrote to Ronald Reagan's budget director to complain about a pending order proposed by the Department of Commerce granting export administration powers to, well, itself. The Pentagon objected, Weinberger said, "given the unprecedented nature of the authorities it confers on the Secretary of Commerce over critical national security and foreign policy issues." He demanded an interagency meeting and provided a "preliminary point paper outlining some of Defense's most serious concerns" to serve as its "focal point." The Office of Management and Budget convened such a meeting; in it, neither agency was willing to back down. Ultimately the State Department proposed a face-saving compromise in which the dispute was referred to a National Security Council working group, a venue likely to favor DoD. Indeed, the proposal expired there. DoD does not always win, though; numerous agencies objected to a 1966 Office of Emergency Preparedness (OEP) proposal that would have assigned numerous functions to the Pentagon. The OEP director backed down: "because of the issues raised by the agencies, a decision on the assignment is not appropriate at this time."[31] In another case from the Kennedy administration, different parts of the Pentagon were in conflict with another: the Navy held up issuance of an EO dealing with Guam until overridden by the Office of the Secretary of Defense's civilian leadership, then leaked its displeasure to congressional allies in hopes of reversing the decision.[32]

As in these historical examples, bureaus' objections can delay or deep-six proposed orders, but the underlying dynamic is simply a matter of math. As Jeffrey Pressman and Aaron Wildavsky demonstrated, increasing the number of actors required to sign off on a decision can postpone that decision considerably even when none of the signers are intent on delay.[33] The executive order research cited above shows that adding one additional agency to the review of an EO, all else equal, adds five days to the formulation process.[34] Agency input often improves the substantive quality of an EO, to be sure (the role of bureaucratic expertise is emphasized in the next section) but it also highlights the management challenge facing presidents in coordinating an unwieldy executive branch around their priorities. Here, as elsewhere, the actions of government may be "outcomes" rather than proactive decisions, as Allison puts it: "outcomes in the sense that what happens is not chosen as a solution but rather results from compromise, coalition, competition, and confusion among government officials who see different faces of an issue" and use their resources to bargain to consensus.[35]

Principal-Agent Problems

Those agency resources are key to another impediment to presidential control of the bureaucracy, often framed in terms of the "principal-agent" relationship imported from studies of contracting in economics. The basic question is one that occurs frequently in real life: how to buy services from someone who knows more about what they are providing than you do, without getting cheated? For instance, if I know little about how cars work (sad but true), a mechanic who would like to make extra money can take advantage of my relative ignorance to sell me expensive but unnecessary repairs ("this vehicle will never pass inspection without a new gold-plated alternator filter gauge . . .").

As Richard Waterman and Kenneth Meier's useful overview of the literature observes, the key dimensions to this relationship are goal divergence and information asymmetry. The principal wants to make sure that the agent acts in the principal's interest despite knowing more and wanting different things. As the gaps in preferences and information widen and narrow, what is required to enforce that will vary too. A wide range of structures and contracts can result.[36]

Applying this to president and agency rests on substantive expertise as the bureaucracy's coin of the realm. "The President knows a hell of a lot of things," as Nixon told his press secretary in 1973, but it is impossible for any single person to track the government-wide details of policymaking. (More bluntly, as Nixon continued, "but does he know what the Christ some dumb assholes are going to do?"[37]) Indeed, political decisionmakers have incentives to provide bureaucrats with discretion and autonomy sufficient to cultivate their specialized competence. "That expertise is something that is valued by political principals," Sean Gailmard and John Patty note, is "a foundational presumption" of their research.[38] Without it, presidents will be lost in a fog of uncertainty about the likely outcome of a policy proposal someone is trying to sell them.[39] The key commodity supplied by agencies is information, some of it raw, some of it refined, about the causes and effects of policy problems and potential solutions.[40]

A large literature assesses how advising systems might be structured to ensure those systems convey crucial information to the president in a timely fashion.[41] The institution of central clearance, housed in the Executive Office of the President, is what economist Oliver Williamson called a "governance structure" with this function: it is a centrally-run peer-review mechanism created to help presidents reduce the costs arising from their bounded rationality, the strategic opportunism of their departmental bargaining partners, and that pervasive state of uncertainty.[42] But for present purposes it is enough to note the likely information asymmetry between president and bureaucracy, an imbalance that will vary in degree by issue area, and perhaps diminish over the span of a presidential term, but will rarely be entirely absent. The inherited gap may be particularly large for presidents without past exposure to national security policymaking—which is most of them in recent decades. In the wake of the Bay of Pigs debacle, John F. Kennedy lamented, "You always assume that the military and intelligence people have some secret still not available to ordinary mortals."[43] In the postwar era perhaps only Dwight Eisenhower could take on the defense bureaucracy wholly on its own ground. Ike, of course, had been a military careerist dating from his arrival at West Point in 1911 and rose to become a five-star general, overseeing D-Day and serving as NATO's first supreme commander.

At the other end of the spectrum was Donald Trump, the only president in US history to have held no elective or appointed public office, including military service, before entering the White House. As one of his own close advisers noted, Trump "was at times dangerously uninformed," even about highly salient historical events like Pearl Harbor.[44] This spotty knowledge of world affairs alarmed even his bureaucratic agents, given his propensity to "fire off tweets without any sort of process beforehand."[45] Six months after he took office, in July 2017, the Defense Department, supported by State, Treasury, the National Economic Council (NEC), and the CIA scheduled a long session to provide a "tailored tutorial on the state of the world"—what one officer called "Commander in Chief 101" or, as a White House aide put it, a course in "remedial president-ing."[46] The meeting, held in the Pentagon's august National Military Command Center (known as "the Tank") quickly became infamous, "a debacle for those who had organized it."[47] Efforts by Defense Secretary James Mattis, Secretary of State Rex Tillerson, and NEC director Gary Cohn to give Trump a sense of historical American commitments and the costs and benefits of current policies were met with hostility. From "gentle lesson" the meeting veered into a confrontation that "so thoroughly shocked the conscience of military leaders that they tried to keep it a secret."[48] Longtime Trump observer Maggie Haberman observes that "Trump knew that he was being told something he did not fully comprehend, and ... shouted down the teachers," attacking US troops as mercenaries and their commanders as "losers," "dopes," and "babies."[49] Tillerson's pithy summary of the president's performance soon went viral: "he's a fucking moron," said the secretary of state.[50]

If nothing else, the Tank confrontation rather violently revealed goal divergence between Trump and his foreign policy agencies, whether about alliances, free trade, or the American presence in Afghanistan and beyond.[51] But goal divergence between principal and agent can arise from a variety of dynamics. "What bureaucrats want" is a matter of longstanding debate. "To do no work," was William Niskanen's answer, framed rather more politely as a theory of "slack."[52] Anthony Downs's taxonomy identified five different bureaucratic types, from "Climbers" to "Zealots" to "Statesmen," each with different "utility maximization" functions.[53] Marissa Golden posits that careerists are driven by a combination of such traits, including self-interest, professionalism, role perception, and agency socialization.[54] James Q. Wilson classifies the actions of agency personnel, and then agencies themselves, according to their tasks, the nature and clarity of their goals, and the transparency of their efforts' outputs and outcomes.[55]

We don't need to adjudicate these perspectives in order to identify two key attributes of the president-agency relationship. first is the simple fact that agencies have more than one boss; they have, in the jargon, "multiple principals." The president is chief executive, true, but numerous other actors hold institutional sway over bureaucratic behavior. Indeed, the concept of "iron triangles" prominent in the twentieth-century interest-group literature did not include the president at all, placing industry groups and congressional subcommittees at the other two vertices. Even expansion to a model of "issue networks" did not wholly displace the idea of bureaucracies "captured" by the industries they are supposedly regulating.[56]

Congress, of course, creates the organizations of the executive branch in the first place, and has what Herbert Kaufman called an "awesome arsenal" of tools for influencing bureaucratic views.[57] For instance, legislators can shape agency preferences and direct agents' behavior through the annual budget process or authorizing legislation. And past statute has present consequence. Trump Homeland Security Secretary John Kelly told legislators that if they didn't like "the laws they've passed and we are charged to enforce," they should amend the statute books. "Otherwise," Kelly said, "they should shut up and support the men and women on the front lines."[58] The sentiment applies to presidents too. As an Eisenhower deputy secretary put it, "Congress . . . enacts the laws, and [when] you come into office as a Presidential appointee, you take an oath of office to administer the laws of the United States. And until . . . Congress changes those laws, there is a definite limit as to how far you can go as part of the [president's] arm of the government."[59]

That limit can (and should) prevail even on national security issues topping a president's priority list. A dramatic example came in March 2004, when George W. Bush's surveillance program, codenamed "Stellar Wind," was reviewed by the Justice Department's Office of Legal Counsel (OLC). Attorneys there had concluded that the program, as originally authorized by the president some years before, went well beyond its lawful bounds. The 2001 legal opinion signing off on the program, Deputy Attorney General James Comey told Vice President Dick Cheney, "was so bad as to be 'facially invalid.' "[60] In response, Bush's chief of staff and his

White House counsel sought to go over Comey's head. They drove to the hospital room where Attorney General John Ashcroft was in postoperative intensive care; quickly Comey and DOJ staff, including FBI director Robert Mueller, converged on the room as well. As the showdown progressed, Ashcroft—though (as Mueller saw it) "feeble, barely articulate, clearly stressed"—repeated the department's legal doubts and endorsed Comey's authority.[61] Even then, Bush himself planned to reauthorize the program over DOJ's objections. He backed down only when the entire senior leadership of the department threatened to resign in public protest of such a move. "Tell Jim [Comey] to do what needs to be done to get this to a place where Justice is comfortable," Bush finally ordered.[62]

Of course, as this episode indicates, the meaning of the law can be contested. As a result, the courts serve as another important principal for federal agencies, interpreting the scope of bureaucratic discretion under statute and whether their exercise of authority is reasonable or capricious.[63] In other cases, presidential policymaking pits one agency against another, seeking amenable analysis. The NATO intervention in Libya in 2011 is a reminder that statutory interpretation is a product available through an intra-administrative market for legal advice. As the War Powers Resolution clock ticked away on that operation, most of the president's national security lawyers (including OLC and the Pentagon) seemed to think that US involvement would have to be dialed back, perhaps providing logistic support for NATO attacks but withdrawing from offensive operations. However, the White House counsel and State Department legal adviser developed what journalist Charlie Savage termed "a very aggressive interpretation" of the War Powers Resolution.[64] They argued that the Libya operation did not constitute hostilities under the terms of the War Powers Resolution, and therefore that law and its limits simply did not apply at all.

Second, agencies' statutory grounding and ongoing missions mean they naturally develop lasting independent institutional preferences. Battles over turf are constant, partly as a generic bureaucratic quest for autonomy, partly to secure resources and policy outcomes that empower or disfavor a particular agency.[65] The well-known "law" that "where you stand depends on where you sit" predicts that one's position on a given issue stems from the organizational position you hold.[66] As Leslie Gelb, who served in the State and Defense Departments, commented, "I have generally found that staffers from the Department of State or Defense or from the Central Intelligence Agency behave very differently if they are moved to the White House. They become far more conscious of Presidential stakes and interests."[67] This was the logic behind making Richard Nixon's short-lived "supersecretaries" members of the White House staff even as they also served a department.[68]

In the national security context, Francis Rourke suggests intrastate analogs for the observation that "war made the state, and the state made war." As Rourke argues, "War may well be a tonic for state organizations charged with responsibility for waging it, and the goals of these organizations may lead them to pursue it even when it has disastrous consequences of the welfare of their own nation."[69] The Vietnam War, he notes, was not a policy choice the military made. But once political actors had committed the United States to fighting it, the military acquired interests in its continuation and enlargement—among them, huge increases in funding, combat experience leading to career advancement in the officer corps, and even the less tangible badge of institutional pride. Likewise, even as the Iraq War lost public and political support, the military generally favored expansion over withdrawal. Two decades after that war began, the then chair of the Joint Chiefs, Admiral Mike Mullen, was asked by an interviewer about the 2006 decision to implement a surge strategy: "did anyone in the Pentagon argue . . . at that moment, the thing to do actually is to stop. This is not going well, stop digging?" Mullen's response was succinct: "No. No, no. Not from my perspective."[70]

That agencies have their own perspectives and preferences is fundamental to adherents of the "deep state"; Trump White House aide Steve Bannon actually took heart from the Tank meeting, since he wanted the president to understand that "the apparatus has a mind of its own."[71] But we don't need to deepen the state to see organizations as having goals distinct from the president's preferences. The nature of institutional dynamics produce just that.

Organizational Process

The nature of bureaucratic organizations itself can shape policy, not through overt lobbying or bargaining but simply by the way relevant agencies function and how that constrains the choices of higher-level decisionmakers. Christopher Hill identifies a number of important bureaucratic dynamics with regard to foreign policy, ranging from the inherent risk-aversion of public agencies to the way policy problems are categorized in ways that match the extant organizational structure.[72] Placing a problem for resolution within a specific structure affects the nature of its resolution.

As one State Department official commented, "Problems become regional largely because we force them into regional frameworks due to our bureaucratic arrangements, and this often conceals too much. For example, there is really no such thing as 'East Asia' except as we choose to lump countries together."[73] When it comes to coordinating policy, it also matters that the Defense Department and State Department carve up the globe into distinct and incompatible divisions and the Pentagon's regional combatant commanders have far more authority and autonomy than any local ambassador.[74]

Along those lines, perhaps the most crucial aspect of organizational process is the creation of, and reliance on, standard operating procedures (SOPs): formal rules that dictate how an organization will act or react to a given input. Hill says flatly that bureaucracies "cannot work" without SOPs; Henry Kissinger called their creation the very "purpose of bureaucracy."[75] If functioning well, these procedural routines match up neatly with the problems that actually arise the most frequently and are relevant to solving them. But even then they impose limits on policy choice. Like a piece of software that requires a university to adopt a particular policy governing, say, course registration—because the policy must track what the software can do—SOPs serve up a certain set of options from which a decision-maker can select. Another analogy is a restaurant menu, with available meals limited to those listed (and themselves derived from the mission of the establishment and expertise of the kitchen staff). Presidents cannot drop by the Justice Department and place an order for a quarantine of Cuba; they need to go to the Navy. And when they do, they may find that the recipe dates from the War of 1812.[76] To be served a dish more relevant to 1962, John F. Kennedy found, required a good deal of managerial effort. Meanwhile, Nikita Khrushchev's hope to prevent the United States from discovering the missiles in Cuba before they were operational foundered on another SOP. The missile construction sites were identifiable from high-altitude grainy photographs because they were arranged exactly as they would have been on the Soviet steppe, uncamouflaged in open fields.[77] Other examples include 1950s Air Force rules that called for placing strategic bases overseas, with closely concentrated facilities. The idea was to reduce costs and flight times, but the procedure made those bases hugely vulnerable to an enemy's first strike. Even in October 1962, the US military's build-up procedure led to hundreds of aircraft lined up wingtip to wingtip on airfields within range of the medium-range missiles in Cuba.[78]

In short, even high-quality SOPs guide decision-making into certain preset channels. Others, even if responsive, may be suboptimal. And of course problems may arise that have no SOP ready to activate. Agencies may even seek to discourage their creation. In the lead-up to the Iraq War, for instance, postwar planning was actively resisted by Secretary of Defense Donald Rumsfeld, who also sought to undermine efforts elsewhere in the government to think through the logistics of occupation and transition. The subsequent Coalition Provisional Authority was notoriously unsuccessful in making up for that lost time.[79]

Twenty Years Past 9/11: Is Foreign Policy Different?

The dynamics explored above are consistent across the American bureaucratic landscape Indeed, the wave of bureaucratic politics literature noted and cited in this essay is largely inspired by and devoted to foreign policy, where presidents have long been thought most autonomous.[80] To be sure, the September 11, 2001, attacks led to institutional changes centralizing presidential authority and certainly to enhanced congressional delegation of power in that regard. But even in the post-9/11 world, presidents' clear structural advantages vis-à-vis Congress in driving foreign policy does not eliminate their own collective action problems within the executive branch nor grant them unalloyed authority over its denizens.

Theories of a unitary executive, likewise, serve as an important legal rationale as presidents seek to fend off efforts by Congress to influence the bureaucracy or legislate constraints on presidential attempts to do so. Still, even when successful in demanding deference they do not address fundamental principal-agent issues within the executive branch.[81] That is to say: even if claims of a unitary executive pare away multiple principals (a fair-sized "if"), the problems of the remaining principal themselves remain. The three categories tracked above may even be exacerbated in the world of foreign policy. One key post-9/11 effort to centralize authority was the 2004 creation of a Director of National Intelligence (DNI) to coordinate the eighteen agencies within the intelligence community (IC) and improve connections between the IC and law enforcement. But this effort was itself a compromise providing a "case study in American power politics" and thus left room for bureaucratic maneuvering, if on a newly landscaped playing field.[82] "Intelligence chiefs clash over turf," the headlines exclaimed in 2009 when CIA director Leon Panetta resisted DNI

Dennis Blair's effort to place his own personnel in foreign embassies.[83] As one analyst observed at the time, statutory language gave the DNI "few tools to fight through the bureaucratic tangles," including insufficient budget authority to truly consolidate lines of authority. He had in fact "simply inherited his grandmother's furniture," and even that was short a chair or two after Obama sided with Panetta.[84]

As noted, nearly twenty agencies comprise the intelligence community, and a 2011 *Washington Post* study identified forty-six federal bureaus engaged in national security work.[85] But that's not new: a Brookings Institution study from the mid-1960s delineating "the characteristics of the [foreign policy] system" noted that its "agencies and agents" had already expanded not only quantitatively ("more people, more organizational subdivisions, much larger budgets") but qualitatively. The field now encompassed many other executive agencies with international dimensions to their bailiwicks, including Treasury, Commerce, Agriculture, Labor, and NASA.[86] Sixty years later we could now add many more, from the DNI to the Department of Homeland Security to the Department of Energy to even the Environmental Protection Agency. And in terms of sheer numbers, there are upward of 830,000 civilian employees on the Defense payroll alone, plus 1.3 million uniformed personnel. The heft of the executive branch is part of the president's absolute power, but size is a double-edged sword and using that power to achieve desired results may be only a relative feat.[87]

In part this is because of the previously noted prominence of SOPs across the branch; as two-time Secretary of Defense Donald Rumsfeld put it, "large organizations especially favor practices they have already mastered, even if those practices ... are outdated."[88] But the structural challenges of principal-agent relations are also amplified in international affairs. National security expertise is particularly specialized, ramping up information asymmetry between the intelligence community and their Oval Office customers. The then director of national intelligence, Michael McConnell, warned the incoming Obama Administration that it was "easy to get misled or sidetracked if you didn't know about the hardware, personnel, special language, rituals, protocols and traditions" of the IC.[89] Further, the moral authority of the uniform is hard for lifetime civilians to surmount. As discussed below, the Obama aides pondering the Afghanistan surge could perhaps relate to Kennedy State Department appointee Chester Bowles's comment that "when a newcomer enters the field and finds himself confronted by the nuances of international questions, he becomes an easy target for the military-CIA-paramilitary type answers which are often in specific logistical terms which can be added, subtracted, multiplied, or divided."[90]

Yet even those experienced in the field may be stymied. Rumsfeld, when he returned to the helm of the Pentagon in 2001, complained about senior officials' firm resistance to the "transformation" he sought. With a blizzard of short "snowflake" memos, he aimed to reassert civilian control over what he felt had become unconstrained military "privilege."[91] Yet his efforts, as they progressed through the Afghanistan and Iraq Wars, ultimately led to a "revolt of the Generals" and his own resignation in November 2006. "Why," even sympathetic observers asked, "did Rumsfeld fail?" One reason, AEI's Thomas Donnelly concluded, was that he had not been able to remake the "corporate culture of the professional American military" or the "preferred American way of war."[92]

Goal divergence is enhanced by the key role of military contracting to economies across the country, a half-trillion dollar annual enterprise both concentrated in huge corporations (Lockheed-Martin alone won $45.7 billion in contracts in 2022) and dispersed in politically advantageous ways (the *Washington Post* study above found nearly two thousand private companies at ten thousand locations across the country with some role in counter-terrorism.)[93] As Richard Hanania notes, "There is no industry that has so much to directly gain or lose based on government decisions," nor as many resources to lobby for those decisions.[94] The military-industrial complex lives on.

For scholars like Michael Glennon, in fact, the Madisonian institutions of the presidency, Congress, and the courts have long been supplanted by the (Harry) "Trumanite" organizational architecture that emerged in the postwar era to safeguard American security. The national security state has incentives to inflate threats, in part to avoid blame if too little is done; it is reactive rather than proactive; it tends toward conformity and the continuation of existing policies even when they serve little present purpose. DNI McConnell's advice above—which continued with his urging the president to "put people in charge who have lived in that world. It's different from anything else"—is for Glennon both truism and huge problem.[95] "The United States," he concluded (fifteen years after the 9/11 attacks), "has moved beyond a mere imperial presidency to a bifurcated system—a structure of double government—in which even the President now exercises little substantive control over the overall direction of U.S. national security policy."[96]

Twenty Years in Afghanistan

Glennon's motivating example is the surprising continuity of the war in Afghanistan across the George W. Bush and Obama Administrations. As Defense Secretary Robert Gates wrote of Obama, "For him, it's all about getting out."[97] Yet he did not succeed in doing so. Nor did Donald Trump, who was even more vocally opposed to continued intervention. Joe Biden finally did so—but only in a chaotic manner that hamstrung the administration's nascent reputation for coordinated competence.

It is perhaps worth closing the chapter, then, with an extended examination of successive presidents' efforts to extract the United States from Afghanistan. The American military presence there was of course a direct consequence of the 9/11 attacks but played out in ways far beyond that for two full decades.[98] Bureaucratic resistance played an important role in pushing back against efforts by Obama, Trump, and Biden to de-escalate and ultimately conclude that front of the "forever wars."

Obama

Barack Obama took office as an early opponent of the Iraq War. But he stressed he wasn't against all wars, just "dumb wars."[99] He saw Iraq as a distraction from the fight against al-Qaeda centered in Afghanistan, a mission that had stalled as resources and attention were diverted to Baghdad. Osama bin Laden remained at large after his escape from US forces at Tora Bora in December 2001, and a comprehensive study of the war at the tail end of the George W. Bush Administration concluded that "we're not losing, but we're not winning," citing little unified strategy or even command across the thirty-eight thousand US troops, plus twenty-nine thousand allied forces, dispersed across the country. Endemic problems of governance and corruption, an increasing Taliban insurgency, poorly-trained Afghan security forces, and (at best) a lack of cooperation from neighboring Pakistan all contributed to what was at best a high-casualty holding pattern.[100]

Upon taking office, Obama moved quickly to approve an additional seventeen thousand combat troops and four thousand trainers for the Afghan theater. At a meeting two days after his inauguration, Gates and Gen. David McKiernan, then the commanding officer in Afghanistan, had asked for thirty thousand, supported by the entire national security cabinet. As Obama noted in his memoirs, only Vice President Joe Biden had misgivings, warning the president expressly about information asymmetry: "Maybe I've been around this town too long, but one thing I know is when these generals are trying to box in a new president," Biden told Obama. The president recalled: "He brought his face a few inches from mine and stage-whispered, 'Don't let them jam you.'"[101] Ultimately DoD conceded the revised number was sufficient for the immediate, still ill-defined, mission.[102]

But pressure for a full-bore "Afghan surge," parallel to the 2007–2008 effort in Iraq, continued. Two new reviews of the situation were commissioned in quick succession, one by longtime national security aide Bruce Riedel and then one by Gen. Stanley McChrystal, who replaced McKiernan in May. Riedel's recommendations were not unambitious, but McChrystal's agenda quickly supplanted them, presenting Obama with a request for another forty thousand troops. The goal was to shift strategy from discrete counterterrorism missions to a nationwide counterinsurgency campaign designed to provide security to the wider population—a "bait and switch," Obama thought.[103] In McChrystal's assessment, the Karzai regime was on the cusp of falling to the Taliban. "Proper resourcing will be critical," the general wrote. "The campaign in Afghanistan has been historically under-resourced and remains so today.... [It is] operating in a culture of poverty [and] requires more forces."[104]

A classic process of bureaucratic bargaining ensued, as Kevin Marsh's research tracks in some detail.[105] Leon Panetta, then CIA director, noted that "the options were infinite in theory, limited in practice."[106] Pressed to give the White House more than one option, McChrystal produced three, but in the classic Washington style of "giving ... one choice and making it look like three."[107] The revised proposal offered increases of ten thousand and eighty-five thousand troops as alternatives to the forty thousand figure. But the military promised that Afghanistan would fall back into extremist hands if the ten thousand option were chosen—and given the twenty-one thousand already newly deployed, the eighty-five thousand would have meant an unsustainable increase of more than one hundred thousand troops in 2009 alone.

Panetta wryly concludes that the debate "took too long and was too public, especially given that ... it was destined to end pretty much where the military wanted it to end."[108] Obama was new, had no military experience, and was vulnerable to just the kind of "jamming" Biden had warned about. The status quo was untenable; the military promised a solution; even the State Department supported more troops.[109] And the pressure rose as an array of generals made their case through leaks, in congressional testimony, and even (in McChrystal's case) in a *60 Minutes* interview. Ultimately, after a process that dragged into November, Obama approved an increase of thirty thousand troops, but with a two-year timetable that Obama demanded the military literally sign on to. National Security Council (NSC) staff, he wrote, "had persuaded me that having the Pentagon brass look me in the eye and commit to an agreement laid out on paper was the only way to publicly avoid their publicly second-guessing my decision if the war went south. It was an unusual and somewhat heavy-handed gesture, one that no doubt grated on Gates and the generals and that I regretted almost immediately. A fitting end, I thought, to a messy, difficult stretch for my administration."[110]

One might have expected the direct, personal involvement of the president to have tilted outcomes in his preferred direction. But as Marsh notes, "Obama found himself largely ordering what the military and other pro-surge advocates had pressured him to do.... Obama made the final decision, but his decision was constrained by the menu of choices presented to him by his advisers. This menu of choices was itself the product of bureaucratic politics."[111]

Nor did US involvement end after the two years agreed upon. In a January 2011 meeting, when asked how long the nation-building process would last and how much it would cost, the American ambassador to Afghanistan said ten to fifteen years, at $6–8 billion per year.[112] Obama rejected this, and in June declared the US was meeting its goals and could begin a gradual withdrawal of perhaps ten thousand troops per year. Troop levels scaled back to seventy-seven thousand by the 2012 election and to forty-six thousand a year later. But despite a May 2014 announcement that troops would leave completely by the end of 2016, in the fall of 2015 Obama was convinced that the security situation required a continued presence. The size of that presence was increased in July 2016 given "precarious" conditions.[113] Ultimately, Obama left office with 8,400 troops still in Afghanistan.

Trump

Donald Trump's prepresidential Twitter feed left little doubt about his policy preferences regarding the war in Afghanistan. "Afghanistan is a complete waste! Time to come home!" he proclaimed in 2012.[114] On his first day as president, in the reviewing stands for his inaugural parade,

Trump repeated the sentiment. "Get out of Afghanistan," he told new Defense Secretary Mattis and Joint Chiefs chair Joseph Dunford.[115]

Mattis and Dunford were taken aback. "To the generals," Peter Baker and Susan Glasser write, "Trump was the third straight president who seemed to want to leave the military on the hook for failing to win an Afghan war that the politicians never really committed to."[116] Mattis, one of his deputies recounts, thought Afghanistan was "fundamentally a winnable proposition" if all-party negotiations could be enforced, and that "stepping away from another international commitment—one the U.S. led—could be viewed as a further erosion of America's global influence."[117] Dunford's take upped the ante, warning Trump that immediate withdrawal would lead to domestic attacks, even on the Mall of America.[118] For his part, new national security adviser H. R. McMaster (yet another general) felt a "do-over" in Afghanistan was required after the Taliban had simply waited out Obama's expired surge and pushed to send twelve thousand more troops; he felt his job "was to prevent the debacle of leaving," one of McMaster's aides said.[119]

Trump at first replied that "we need to get out of there. We're paying too much money and getting nothing in return," adding in January 2018 that "seriously, who gives a shit about Afghanistan?"[120] Yet by the fall of 2017, he had approved sending more than 5,600 additional soldiers there. In a televised speech on August 21, he said that "I share the American people's frustration" with the war and that "my original instinct was to pull out. . . . But all my life I've heard that decisions are much different when you sit behind the desk in the Oval Office."[121] Thus after "stud[ying] Afghanistan in great detail and from every conceivable angle" he had concluded, "with my Cabinet and generals," that the US could not withdraw without leaving a vacuum quickly filled by terrorists. Trump stressed that "conditions on the ground, not arbitrary timetables, will guide our strategy from now on. America's enemies must never know our plans or believe they can wait us out."[122]

Part of that decision was a matter of timing, coming as it did in the wake of Trump's "fire and fury" comments regarding North Korea and his endorsement of a white supremacist march in Charlottesville, Virginia. At that stage, Trump's bargaining capital, vis-à-vis the entire national security establishment, was low.[123] But the generals had also cannily framed the escalation as the antidote to Obama's ticking clock for withdrawal, playing on Trump's disdain for his predecessor.[124] In the aftermath, they praised Trump's status-quo-plus policy to the skies: "fundamentally different," "a game-changer," said Gen. John W. Nicholson from Kabul. The biggest change was Trump's authorization for an escalated bombing campaign, which, while aimed at the Taliban, also led to greatly increased civilian casualties (and subsequent Taliban recruiting success).[125]

The softening of presidential decision-making by bureaucratic massage took various forms. One tactic was, as one Trump official recalls, the "time-honored DOD planning dance," which in asking for a wide range of alternate options "just kind of stretches things out, and stretches things out, and stretches things out."[126] Trump's next confirmed Secretary of Defense, Mark Esper, took a similar tack: "I would ask some questions and give some initial feedback, anything from 'I understand what you want to do' or 'I don't think that makes sense, but I owe you a formal recommendation once I've done my homework....' The president had a short attention span.... Chances were he'd forget about it for three or four months."[127] That allowed the Pentagon to stick to the National Defense Strategy, "a document they fully believed Trump hadn't bothered to read."[128]

Esper's successor, Christopher Miller, took the reverse approach, describing in great detail the technical means of achieving what Trump said he wanted. Asked, for instance, if US air power could destroy Iran's nuclear program, the answer was yes—with massive, repeated airstrikes and substantial American casualties. "I would play the f—-ing madman," he told reporter Jonathan Karl, getting even "more provocative than" Trump to make him "dial it down.... They're like, 'Yeah, I was f—-ing crazy, but that guy's batshit.' "[129]

Sometimes, though, the menu was trimmed, requested plans were not provided. For instance, the Pentagon resisted withdrawing troops from Syria or providing plans for military strikes on North Korea.[130] Another version of this followed Trump's sudden tweet barring transgender soldiers from service, which the Pentagon considered "ill-informed and ill considered."[131] (Despite the tweet's wording, DoD had not been consulted; perhaps not coincidentally, it came shortly after the Tank meeting.) Mattis refused to accept the tweet as a presidential directive and demanded formal guidance. When that was issued, he put in place a six-month comprehensive review headed by one of his deputies. Eventually Trump got a modified version of his preferred policy, but not until early 2019.[132] Bureaucratic unity in most of these cases was quite remarkable. As a forty-year veteran of the State Department, Daniel Fried, observed: "I've seen Washington where State and Defense were at odds. I've seen Washington where State and NSC were at odds. I've never seen Washington where State, NSC, and Defense were all in one place, with a couple of exceptions, and the president was in another place."[133]

But Trump continued to push against the Afghanistan (and Russian, and NATO, and South Korean, and . . .) consensus. By the end of 2018, Mattis had resigned in the wake of another unannounced Trump declaration about troop withdrawal (this time in Syria), noting a long list of disagreements with the president. In a White House meeting in early 2019, Trump complained that "I gave our generals all the money they wanted. They didn't do such a great job in Afghanistan . . . I'm not happy with what he's [Mattis] done in Afghanistan."[134]

By then, negotiations had opened with a Taliban delegation in Qatar. This had long been resisted, not least when coalition allies held more leverage, but preliminary talks began in the fall of 2018, notably excluding the Afghan government.[135] A tentative deal fell apart when Trump sought to invite the Taliban delegation to the presidential retreat at Camp David, prompting huge public and congressional blowback. But by February 2020, having survived his first impeachment trial, Trump signed off on a deal withdrawing all US troops from Afghanistan by May 2021, having lost all "patience for the careful PowerPoint presentations or patronizing lectures from the Pentagon about why doing so would be a disaster."[136]

Even then the Pentagon resisted a rapid drawdown of the 8,600 troops still in Afghanistan, worried about continued support for the Afghan army; Esper argued levels should stay close to five thousand through November.[137] Even as the Taliban finally met with the Afghan government, it escalated its demands while continuing its military operations (though not against US forces). On October 7, 2020, Trump overturned the negotiations by tweeting that all troops should be home by Christmas. A "strategic mistake," Esper thought, and far from "conditions-based"—not to mention "logistically impossible" and with an "odious psychological effect on our Afghan partners."[138] Working with Secretary of State Mike Pompeo and Joint Chiefs chair Mark Milley, Esper avoided issuing formal orders based on the tweet; a memo to the president argued that the Taliban had not lived up to their side of the bargain and that "strategic patience" was needed.[139]

After his electoral defeat, though, Trump fired Esper. And two days later, on November 11, he issued a one-page memo directing that all US forces were to be withdrawn from Afghanistan by January 15, 2021. Brand new as acting defense secretary, Miller had heard nothing about this; nor had Milley; nor had Robert O'Brien, the national security adviser; nor

White House counsel. It had been drafted by Trump's thirty-one-year old director of personnel, Johnny McEntee—as *Axios* later put it, part of an "off-the-books operation by the commander in chief himself," fighting back against classic bureaucratic techniques that would "delay key decisions by disputing that strategic meetings had led to consensus, insist the process was still ongoing, and leak apocalyptic scenarios to the media."[140] Even so, confronted in the Oval Office by an angrily united front of Miller, Milley, and O'Brien, Trump backed down. Ultimately about 3,500 troops remained in Afghanistan as Trump left office.[141]

Biden

Joe Biden first visited Afghanistan in 2002 as a US Senator with three decades of legislative service already under his belt, including a stint as chair of the Senate Foreign Committee. As noted above, during his two terms as Obama's vice president he was deeply involved in the 2009 Afghanistan surge debates and a strong voice for a much smaller US footprint focused on counterterrorism. Even before his inauguration, Obama sent Biden (and vice presidential foreign policy adviser Antony Blinken) to the region. Biden came away concerned about Pakistan's relationship with the Taliban, about the corruption endemic in the Afghan government, and especially about the undefined nature of the American mission. "This has been on autopilot," he told Obama upon his return.[142]

In 2021, as president—with Blinken as the new secretary of state—Biden retained his suspicion that Afghanistan was, as he had told Obama, "a dangerous quagmire."[143] His instinct was that the US had accomplished what it could by 2011, when bin Laden was finally killed. Honoring Trump's deal with the Taliban risked the return of Afghanistan to Taliban rule; reneging on it meant propping up the Afghan government indefinitely; and negotiations between the two had broken down. Instead, twenty-five NSC meetings over two months ensued, what Bob Woodward and Robert Costa called "one of the most wide-ranging policy reviews ever held."[144] Biden grilled the national security players for detailed intelligence estimates— indeed, for more certainty than could be plausibly proffered—returning again and again to the expected utility of different options. The Pentagon continued to push to keep at least a small force in the country. But Blinken and national security adviser Jake Sullivan wound up "running the Pentagon," said one official in the discussions.[145] Biden said in March that the 2020 deal was "not very solidly negotiated"—after all, while the

Taliban committed to preventing other terrorist organizations from residing or training in Afghanistan, the US withdrawal was not conditioned on the Taliban's own reduction of violence or any negotiations with the Afghan government itself. Even so the president also disavowed any "intention to stay there for a long time."[146]

Ultimately, Biden overruled the military and opted for full withdrawal, albeit at a slower pace than Trump had demanded—by the twentieth anniversary of the September 11 attacks. His long experience gave him the confidence and standing to do so, even aside from his long-held preferences. "War in Afghanistan was never meant to be a multigenerational undertaking," the president said on April 14. "After twenty years of valor and sacrifice, it's time to bring those troops home."

The president accelerated the timetable even as worries grew about the future stability of Afghanistan: in early July, as the massive Bagram Air Base was transferred to Afghan forces, he announced that the US military mission would end on August 31. Biden had repeatedly expressed confidence in the Afghan government and its huge (on paper) army while downplaying the prospect of an ascendant Taliban. But both faiths, or intelligence estimates, proved misplaced. From May to July more than half of Afghanistan's four hundred districts came under Taliban control, and by August half of the country's provincial capitals had fallen as well. On August 15 Blinken stated the obvious, "We've seen that force has been unable to defend the country, and that has happened more quickly than we intended."[147] That same day the Taliban began entering Kabul, and Afghan president Ashraf Ghani fled the country.

American forces retained control of the city's airport and began a substantial airlift. The administration touted its success in evacuating some 124,000 people by the end of August. But the operation was necessarily chaotic, with thousands braving Taliban lockdowns to mill outside the airport, begging for escape from the new regime. The situation turned from desperation to horror on August 26 when suicide bombers affiliated with ISIS detonated in the crowd, murdering 170 Afghans and 13 US servicemen. A retaliatory drone attack three days later—a "righteous strike," said General Milley —wound up making matters worse, killing not the bombing's masterminds but ten civilians, seven of whom were children.

While in July Biden said the 1975 withdrawal from Vietnam was "not at all comparable"—"there's going to be no circumstance where you see people being lifted off the roof"—the final days in Kabul were indeed reminiscent of the fall of Saigon. Perhaps that was the military's standard operating procedure for concluding endless wars. Certainly no SOP for "withdrawal" seems to have been developed during the two decades in Afghanistan, perhaps because the military had not expected ever to need one. Nor did intelligence estimates of the Afghanistan government's own capacities prove accurate. Ultimately the chaotic evacuation scenes inflicted damage on the Biden Administration's reputation for foreign policy expertise—the president, not the national security establishment, took the blame. (Efforts to place that blame on Biden's predecessor, while not entirely without merit, did not change this calculus.)[148] The administration gambled that the perceptual and policy benefits of finally extricating the US from Afghanistan would outweigh those costs.

Accountable Expertise?

Richard Neustadt famously portrayed Harry Truman envisioning a frustrated Dwight Eisenhower in the Oval Office: Ike would "say 'do this! Do that!' *And nothing will happen.*" Neustadt's own take on the matter, developed as a midcentury White House aide, was to warn against the "illusion" that "administrative agencies comprise a single structure, 'the' executive branch, where presidential word is law, or ought to be." More recently, public administration scholars have put the question in terms of "transactional authority" rather than "principal authority" in defining presidential relations with the wider bureaucracy.[149]

This chapter has addressed both points: the frequently plural nature of the executive branch and the transactions, and transaction costs, imposed upon the president as a result. But it remains unclear whether we should admire, or decry, these bureaucratic constraints on presidential power. There are conflicting normative dynamics at play, constant tensions between electoral accountability and specialist expertise.[150]

On the one hand, we value substantive knowledge and rightly want it to govern policymaking, partitioning the "right" result off from partisanship and subjecting it to a sort of intrabranch peer review. Former solicitor general Neal Katyal goes so far as to argue that a "well-functioning bureaucracy contains agencies with differing missions and objectives that intentionally overlap to create friction."[151]

We also question presidential control of bureaucracy because we fear personal impulse. Peter Rodman puts it nicely: "one part of our brain seems to side with the permanent government," at least when the president is not

Lincolnesque.[152] We may cheer for a "resistance" preventing initiatives we don't like, especially when these are matters of life and death, war and peace—indeed, David Rothkopf subtitles his book on the Trump years "how the deep state saved the nation." Scholar-practitioner Kori Schake argues that the Trump Pentagon's recalcitrance to give the president offensive war plans for Korea is "a perfect example of the legitimate use of the distributed powers in the American government to slow something down and prevent a dangerous action, by simply using the powers extant in a bureaucracy."[153]

When presenting factual evidence is treated as disloyalty, that becomes all the more tempting. And the unwillingness of military leaders to countenance Trump's explorations of the Insurrection Act in 2020 and early 2021 is, indeed, admirable.

We should hope, though, that January 6, 2021, was a dramatically distant outlier. Because we must also hope that elections are held on the basis that the person thereby chosen will set executive branch policies: "democratic legitimacy is also democratic accountability."[154] When Rex Tillerson complained that White House staffers were micromanaging his department—"I feel like I have four secretaries of state"—Jared Kushner's response had some merit. "Well," said the president's son-in-law, "if you were doing the policies that the president actually wanted, then there would only be one secretary of state and we'd all be working for you. The problem is that you're doing shit that's against what the president wants."[155] Obama, thinking about the Afghanistan surge, made a similar if less petulant point. He claimed never to have questioned the motives of the military actors with whom he butted heads, but observed that "men like [Admiral] Mullen were creatures of the system to which they'd devoted their entire adult lives—a U.S. military that prided itself on accomplishing a mission once started, without regard to cost, duration, or whether the mission was the right one to begin with." After 9/11, Obama continued, "basic policy decisions ... had been steadily farmed out to the Pentagon and the CIA" to the point that it was "hard for [Defense Secretary Gates] to see that what he dismissed as politics was democracy as it was supposed to work.... Maybe it wasn't Gates's job to think about those things," Obama concluded, "but it was mine."[156]

Yet—on yet another hand—as Francis Rourke acidly noted, "criticism of bureaucracy can ... serve the same function in the United States that it has in the Soviet Union—as a device by which blame for failures in policy can be shifted from political to administrative elites—from a party that can do no wrong to a bureaucracy that is often made to seem as though it can do no right."[157] It is clear that managing the executive branch—that is, melding expertise and accountability in a way that benefits the polity—is a key aspect of the president's job. It is the electorate's job to make sure they elect a president capable of doing it.

Notes

1. Leon Panetta, interview with the author, August 9, 2016.

2. Daniel A. Farber and Anne Joseph O'Connell, "Agencies as Adversaries," *California Law Review* 105, no. 5 (2017): 1378.

3. Robert E. Hunter, *Presidential Control of Foreign Policy: Management or Mishap?* (New York: Praeger, 1982), 44. The erudite readers of this book will hardly need reference to *Henry V*, Act III, Scene 1.

4. Or in Kissinger's case between the bureaucracy and "great statesmen," a.k.a. himself. Henry Kissinger, *White House Years* (Boston: Little, Brown, 1979), 39; McGeorge Bundy, *The Strength of Government* (Cambridge: Harvard University Press, 1968), 37. Bundy was assistant to the president for national security under John F. Kennedy; Kissinger held that post under Richard Nixon and was secretary of state under Nixon and Gerald Ford.

5. Henry Kissinger, "Domestic Structure and Foreign Policy," *Daedalus* 95, no. 2 (Spring 1966): 510.

6. Harold Seidman and Robert Gilmour, *Politics, Position, and Power: From the Positive to the Regulatory State*, 4th ed. (New York: Oxford University Press, 1986), 78.

7. Francis E. Rourke, *Bureaucracy, Politics, and Public Policy*, 3rd ed. (Boston: Little, Brown and Company, 1984), 130; Howard J. Wiarda, *American Foreign Policy: Actors and Processes* (New York: HarperCollins College Publishers, 1996), 198. A Clinton-era foreign policy practitioner quoted in Wiarda's textbook says he "would much rather have to deal with the murderous factions in the former Yugoslavia than to go across town to deal with his counterparts in another U.S. government agency." See Wiarda, *American Foreign Policy*, 8.

8. FDR quoted in Richard E. Neustadt, *Presidential Power and the Modern Presidents* (New York: Free Press, 1990), 37; Obama's comment is from his memoir *A Promised Land* (New York: Crown, 2020), 312. Others quoted in Andrew Rudalevige, *By Executive Order: Bureaucratic Management and the Limits of Presidential Power* (Princeton, NJ: Princeton University Press, 2021), 25.

9. The "menu" analogy is developed in Graham T. Allison and Philip Zelikow, *Essence of Decision: Explaining the Cuban Missile Crisis*, 2nd ed. (New York: Longman, 1999).

10. The phrase "counter-bureaucracy" comes from Richard Nathan, *The Plot That Failed* (New York: Wiley, 1975), 45; George Krause, "Organizational Com-

plexity and Coordination Dilemmas in U.S. Executive Politics," *Presidential Studies Quarterly* 39, no. 1 (March 2009), 74–88. More broadly, see Michael Glennon, *National Security and Double Government* (New York: Oxford University Press, 2015).

11. Indeed, in other contexts I have noted the Justice Department's Office of Legal Counsel's tendency to cite itself, relying on its own past opinions as if they came from an independent source of authority. See, e.g., Andrew Rudalevige, "Authorizing Military Force, Twenty Years After 9/11," *Bipartisan Policy Review* 3 (March 2022): 22–26.

12. Memorandum from Bill Barr to Deputy Attorney General Rod Rosenstein and Assistant Attorney General Steve Engel, "Mueller's 'Obstruction' Theory," June 8, 2018, quoted in Donald Ayer, "Why Bill Barr is So Dangerous," *The Atlantic*, June 30, 2019, https://www.theatlantic.com/ideas/archive/2019/06/bill-barrs-dangerous-pursuit-executive-power/592951/.

13. The phrase comes from a Justice Department brief in 2004. Quoted in (and for a more detailed discussion see) Andrew Rudalevige, "'On My Own': George W. Bush, the Unitary Executive, and Unilateral Action," in *43: Inside the George W. Bush Presidency*, ed. Michael Nelson et al. (Lawrence: University Press of Kansas, 2022), 114.

14. Quoted in John A. Rohr, *To Run a Constitution* (Lawrence: University Press of Kansas, 1986), 137.

15. Graham G. Dodds, *The Unitary Presidency* (New York: Routledge, 2020).

16. See especially *Federalist* nos. 47 and 48. Madison assures readers he is merely interpreting Montesquieu correctly, not contradicting him. (Presumably one should not contradict the "celebrated"!)

17. *Kendall v. United States ex Rel. Stokes*, 37 U.S. (12 Pet.) 524 (1838).

18. Neustadt, *Presidential Power and the Modern Presidents*, 29.

19. Jeffrey Crouch, Mark J. Rozell, and Mitchel A. Sollenberger, *The Unitary Executive Theory* (Lawrence: University Press of Kansas, 2020).

20. Lawrence C. Dodd and Richard L. Schott, *Congress and the Administrative State* (New York: Macmillan, 1986), 2. See also the useful review in Krause, *Two-Way Street: The Institutional Dynamics of the Modern Administrative State* (Pittsburgh, PA: University of Pittsburgh Press, 1999), chapter 1.

21. Morton H. Halperin and Arnold Kanter, eds., *Readings in American Foreign Policy: A Bureaucratic Perspective* (Boston: Little, Brown, 1973), 3.

22. Graham T. Allison, *Essence of Decision: Explaining the Cuban Missile Crisis* (Boston: Little, Brown, 1971), 67. See also the earlier reference to the book's second edition, updated with Philip Zelikow in 1999. Halperin likewise argued that the executive branch could not be treated as "a single individual with a single purpose and an ability to control completely his actions." See Morton Halperin, with the assistance of Patricia Clapp and Arnold Kanter, *Bureaucratic Politics and Foreign Policy* (Washington, DC: Brookings Institution, 1974), 311.

23. Peter Rodman, *Presidential Command* (New York: Knopf/Borzoi, 2009); Robert E. Hunter, *Presidential Control of Foreign Policy: Management or Mishap?* (New York: Praeger, 1982). See also Halperin's chapter entitled "Presidential Control" in *Bureaucratic Politics and Foreign Policy*.

24. David Howard Davis, *How the Bureaucracy Makes Foreign Policy* (Lexington, MA: D.C. Heath, 1972); see also Richard Hanania, *Public Choice Theory and the Illusion of Grand Strategy: How Generals, Weapons Manufacturers, and Foreign Governments Shape American Foreign Policy* (New York: Routledge, 2022), which "focuses on the state itself, specifically the military and the rest of the national security bureaucracy, as an important interest group in its own right" (5).

25. See the works just cited as well as, inter alia, Alan A. Altshuler, ed., *The Politics of the Federal Bureaucracy* (New York: Dodd, Mead and Co., 1968); I.M. Destler, *Presidents, Bureaucrats, and Foreign Policy: The Politics of Organizational Reform* (Princeton, NJ: Princeton University Press, 1972); Roger Hilsman, *The Politics of Policy Making in Defense and Foreign Affairs* (New York: Harper & Row, 1971).

26. Kenneth J. Meier and John Bohte, "Span of Control and Public Organizations," *Public Administration Review* 63 (January 2003): 62.

27. See David E. Lewis and Jennifer L. Selin, *Sourcebook of United States Executive Agencies*, 2nd ed. (Washington, DC: Administrative Conference of the United States, 2018), 2n3, 5–6, 10. An even larger population of agencies comes from the General Service Administration's *USA.gov* website, which lists more than six hundred separate governmental organizations. See Lewis and Selin, *Sourcebook*, 12. The total includes civilian employees, uniformed service members, and postal workers.

28. Guy M. Snodgrass, *Holding the Line: Inside Trump's Pentagon with Secretary Mattis* (New York: Sentinel, 2021), 47–48.

29. Lisa Schultz-Bressman and Michael P. Vandebergh, "Inside the Administrative State: A Critical Look at the Practice of Presidential Control," *Michigan Law Review* 105 (October 2006), 93; and see 68–69, 91. See also Krause, "Organizational Complexity."

30. See Andrew Rudalevige, *By Executive Order: Bureaucratic Management and the Limits of Presidential Power* (Princeton, NJ: Princeton University Press, 2021), from which this section is largely drawn; estimates of EOs linked to specific agencies can be found in table 4.5 on page 106.

31. Rudalevige, *By Executive Order*, 193–194.

32. Rudalevige, *By Executive Order*, 201–202.

33. Jeffrey L. Pressman and Aaron Wildavsky, *Implementation*, 3rd ed. (Berkeley: University of California Press, 1984), 118–119.

34. Rudalevige, *By Executive Order*, 153. Further, a multivariate survival model shows a significant difference ($p<0.01$) between "time to issuance" for EOs at the 10th percentile of jurisdictional crossover and those at the 90th percentile (161).

35. Graham Allison, "Conceptual Models and the Cuban Missile Crisis," *American Political Science Review* 63 (September 1969), 708.

36. Richard Waterman and Kenneth Meier, "Principal-Agent Models: An Expansion?" *Journal of Public Administration Research and Theory* 8, no. 2 (1998): 173–202.

37. To be fair, this is about the Watergate scandal. See Nixon to Ron Ziegler, May 14, 1973, in Stanley Kutler, *Abuse of Power* (New York: Free Press, 1997).

38. Sean Gailmard and John W. Patty, *Learning While Governing: Expertise and Accountability in the Executive Branch* (Chicago: University of Chicago Press, 2013), 55. See also Kathleen Bawn, "Political Control versus Expertise: Congressional Choices about Administrative Procedures," *American Political Science Review* 89 (1995): 62–73; David Epstein and Sharyn O'Halloran, *Delegating Powers: A Transaction Cost Politics Approach to Policy Making under Separate Powers* (New York: Cambridge University Press, 1999); John D. Huber and Charles R. Shipan, *Deliberate Discretion? The Institutional Foundations of Bureaucratic Autonomy* (New York: Cambridge University Press, 2002); Gary J. Miller and Andrew B. Whitford, *Above Politics: Bureaucratic Discretion and Credible Commitment* (New York: Cambridge University Press, 2016); William G. Resh, *Rethinking the Administrative Presidency* (Baltimore, MD: Johns Hopkins University Press, 2015).

39. Gailmard and Patty, *Learning While Governing*, chapter 5; Andrew Rudalevige, "The Structure of Leadership: Presidents, Hierarchies, and Information Flow," *Presidential Studies Quarterly* 35, no. 2 (June 2005): 333–360.

40. For an interesting discussion framed in "commodity" terms, see Davis, *How the Bureaucracy Makes Foreign Policy*, chapter 2.

41. For a review, see Rudalevige, "The Structure of Leadership."

42. Rudalevige, *By Executive Order*, chapter 2.

43. Quoted in *Kennedy and the Bay of Pigs*, Kennedy School of Government Case C14-80-279 (1998): 19.

44. Quoted in Philip Rucker and Carol Leonnig, *A Very Stable Genius: Donald J. Trump's Testing of America* (New York: Penguin, 2020), 169.

45. Maggie Haberman, *Confidence Man: The Making of Donald Trump and the Breaking of America* (New York: Penguin, 2022), 308. She adds that "Cohn believed that Trump's problems with foreign policy stemmed from a lack of understanding about the globe's interconnectedness and the importance of the post–World War II international order to it" (309–10).

46. Rucker and Leonnig, *Very Stable Genius*, 131; military aide and White House staffer both quoted in David Rothkopf, *American Resistance: The Inside Story of How the Deep State Saved the Nation* (New York: PubicAffairs, 2022), 108; Cohn called it "Allies 101," quoted in Peter Baker and Susan Glasser, *The Divider: Trump in the White House* (New York: Doubleday, 2022), 114.

47. Baker and Glasser, *The Divider*, 115.

48. Rucker and Leonnig, *Very Stable Genius*, 131, 139.

49. Haberman, *Confidence Man*, 310–311. See too Rucker and Leonnig, *Very Stable Genius*, who note that "Trump appeared peeved by the schoolhouse vibe but also allergic to the dynamic of his advisers talking at him" given a "ricocheting attention span" (133, and see 135–136).

50. Quoted in Rucker and Leonnig, *Very Stable Genius*, 138; Haberman, *Confidence Man*, 311; Baker and Glasser, *The Divider*, 116.

51. Whether that divergence arose from presidential ignorance, as Tillerson and the rest assumed, or from presidential principles, as Trump aide Steve Bannon believed, is a question whose answers are observationally equivalent for present purposes.

52. William A. Niskanen, *Bureaucracy and Representative Government* (Chicago: Aldine-Atherton, 1971); for a review of the wider "slack" literature see Paul Gary Wyckoff, "The Simple Analytics of Slack-Maximizing Bureaucracy," *Public Choice* 67 (1990): 35–47.

53. Anthony Downs, *Inside Bureaucracy* (Prospect Heights, IL: Waveland Press, 1994 [1967]), 81, and see chapters 8–9.

54. Marissa Martino Golden, *What Motivates Bureaucrats: Politics and Administration during the Reagan Years* (New York: Columbia University Press, 2000), 11–13, which also provides a useful summary of older arguments in economics and public administration along these lines. See too Zachary Oberfeld, *Becoming Bureaucrats: Socialization at the Front Lines of Government Service* (Philadelphia: University of Pennsylvania Press, 2014).

55. James Q. Wilson, *Bureaucracy* (New York: Basic Books, 1989).

56. For a discussion of these models, see Jeffrey M. Berry, *The Interest Group Society*, 3rd ed. (New York: Longman, 1997), 194ff.

57. Herbert Kaufman, *The Administrative Behavior of Federal Bureau Chiefs* (Washington, DC: Brookings Institution, 1981), 164. See also Morris fiorina, *Congress: Keystone of the Washington Establishment*, 2nd ed. (New Haven: Yale University Press, 1989); Wilson, *Bureaucracy*, chapter 13.

58. Devlin Barrett, "DHS Secretary Kelly says Congressional Critics Should 'Shut Up' or Change Laws," *Washington Post*, April 18, 2017, https://www.washingtonpost.com/world/national-security/dhs-secretary-kelly-says-congressional-critics-should-shut-up-or-change-laws/2017/04/18/8a2a92b6-2454-11e7-b503-9d616bd5a305_story.html.

59. Eisenhower deputy agriculture secretary True Morse oral history, quoted in Andrew Rudalevige, *Managing the President's Program* (Princeton, NJ: Princeton University Press, 2002), 21.

60. See James Comey, *A Higher Loyalty* (New York: Flatiron Books, 2018), 87, and see 82–84.

61. Comey, *A Higher Loyalty*, 90, quoting Mueller's notes on the meeting, and see 87–90.

62. Comey, *A Higher Loyalty*, 98; see too Charlie Savage, *Power Wars*, rev. ed. (Boston: Back Bay Books, 2017), 190–193.

63. Readers are referred to the extensive literature on the *Chevron* doctrine and, more recently, on the "major questions doctrine."

64. Savage, *Power Wars*, 645.

65. On autonomy, see Wilson, *Bureaucracy*; Halperin, *Bureaucratic Politics and Foreign Policy*.

66. See Allison and Zelikow, *Essence of Decision*, 307; the 1999 discussion reduces the causal force of what the first edition called "Miles' Law."

67. Leslie Gelb, "Muskie and Brzezinski: The Struggle over Foreign Policy," *New York Times Magazine*, July 20, 1980, https://www.nytimes.com/1980/07/20/archives/muskie-and-brzezinski-the-struggle-over-foreign-policy-foreign.html.

68. Mordecai Lee, *Nixon's Super-Secretaries: The Last Grand Presidential Reorganization Effort* (College Station: Texas A&M Press, 2012).

69. Rourke, *Bureaucracy and Foreign Policy*, 9. The phrase is Charles Tilly's.

70. Transcribed from NPR, *Morning Edition*, March 20, 2023, https://www.npr.org/2023/03/20/1164641676/after-iraq-mullen-wants-to-prevent-future-presidents-from-launching-a-war-of-cho. There was significant debate, however, over the scope and speed of expansion; for instance, the then Iraq commander George Casey favored a much smaller surge and a faster transition of responsibility to the Iraqi military. See Michael Gordon, "Troop 'Surge' Took Place Amid Doubt and Debate," *New York Times*, August 31, 2008, https://www.nytimes.com/2008/08/31/washington/31military.html.

71. Quoted in Baker and Glasser, *The Divider*, 117.

72. Christopher Hill, *Foreign Policy in the Twenty-first Century*, 2nd ed. (New York: Palgrave Macmillan, 2016), 109–112.

73. Quoted in William Bacchus, *Foreign Policy and the Bureaucratic Process* (Princeton, NJ: Princeton University Press, 1974), 296.

74. Dana Priest, "A Four Star Foreign Policy?" *Washington Post*, September 28, 2000, https://www.washingtonpost.com/archive/politics/2000/09/28/a-four-star-foreign-policy/f9779938-7a88-449f-9f55-84ab020abbd7/; see also Mackenzie Eaglen, "Putting Combatant Commanders on a Demand Signal Diet," War on the Rocks, November 9, 2020, https://warontherocks.com/2020/11/putting-combatant-commanders-on-a-demand-signal-diet/.

75. Hill, *Foreign Policy*, 110; Kissinger, "Domestic Structure and Foreign Policy," 507. See also Christopher M. Jones, "Bureaucratic Politics and Organizational Process Models," Oxford Research Encyclopedia of International Studies, November 2017, https://oxfordre.com/internationalstudies/view/10.1093/acrefore/9780190846626.001.0001/acrefore-9780190846626-e-2.

76. "We've been doing this since the days of John Paul Jones," Admiral George Anderson reportedly snapped at Secretary of Defense Robert McNamara. See Walter Poole, "How Well Did the JCS Work?" *Naval History* 6, no. 4 (December

1992), https://www.usni.org/magazines/naval-history-magazine/1992/december/how-well-did-jcs-work.

77. Allison and Zelikow, *Essence of Decision*, 207–208.

78. Bruce L.R. Smith, "Strategic Expertise and National Security Policy," *Public Policy* 13 (1964): 69–108; Allison and Zelikow, *Essence of Decision*, 237–238; James M. Lindsay, "TWE Remembers: The OAS Endorses a Quarantine of Cuba (Cuban Missile Crisis, Day Eight)," *Council on Foreign Relations*, October 23, 2012, https://www.cfr.org/blog/twe-remembers-oas-endorses-quarantine-cuba-cuban-missile-crisis-day-eight.

79. Robert Draper, *To Start a War* (New York: Penguin, 2020); James Fallows, *Blind into Baghdad* (New York: Vintage, 2006).

80. For a review, see Paul E. Peterson, "The President's Dominance in Foreign Policy Making," *Political Science Quarterly* 109, no. 2 (Summer, 1994), 215–234.

81. Thanks to Doug Kriner for suggesting this formulation.

82. Michael Allen, *Blinking Red: Crisis and Compromise in American Intelligence after 9/11* (Dulles, VA: Potomac Books, 2013), xi; the DNI was created in the 2004 Intelligence Reform and Terrorism Prevention Act (P.L. 108–458).

83. "Intelligence Chiefs Clash over Turf," CBS News, May 27, 2009, https://www.cbsnews.com/news/intelligence-chiefs-clash-over-turf/.

84. Marc Ambinder, "An Intelligence Turf War or Just Unfinished Business," *The Atlantic*, May 28, 2009, https://www.theatlantic.com/politics/archive/2009/05/an-intelligence-turf-war-or-just-unfinished-business/18433/; see also Morton Halperin and Priscilla Clapp, with Arnold Kanter, *Bureaucratic Politics and Foreign Policy*, 2nd ed. (Washington, DC: Brookings Institution, 2006), 328–329.

85. Glennon, *National Security and Double Government*, 16; for the original data see Dana Priest and William Arkin, *Top Secret America: The Rise of the New American Security State* (Boston: Little, Brown, 2011).

86. Burton M. Sapin, *The Making of United States Foreign Policy* (Washington, DC: Praeger/Brookings Institution, 1966), 16.

87. This figure is an estimate for 2023. Congressional Research Service, "Defense Primer: Department of Defense Civilian Employees," IF11510 version 7, updated February 6, 2023. Available at https://sgp.fas.org/crs/natsec/IF11510.pdf

88. Donald Rumsfeld, *Known and Unknown: A Memoir* (New York: Sentinel/Penguin, 2011), 294.

89. This is Bob Woodward's paraphrase of McConnell's advice, in Woodward, *Obama's Wars* (New York: Simon & Schuster, 2010), 56.

90. Bowles notes from Cabinet Meeting of April 20, 1961, Office of the Historian, U.S. Department of State, https://history.state.gov/historicaldocuments/frus1961-63v10/d158. Or as Arthur Schlesinger put it in a 1998 interview, "Here we were, a bunch of ex-college professors sitting around faced by this panoply of the Joint Chiefs of Staff, Allen Dulles, a legendary figure, and Dick Bissell, the man who invented and promoted the U-2. It was rather difficult even to open one's

mouth sometimes, in the face of these guys." Quoted in Lars Schoultz, *That Infernal Little Cuban Republic* (Chapel Hill: University of North Carolina Press, 2011), 152.

91. Donald Rumsfeld, *Known and Unknown: A Memoir* (New York: Sentinel/Penguin, 2011), 290–295. See too Rodman, *Presidential Command*, 242–244.

92. Thomas Donnelly, "Why Did Donald Rumsfeld Fail?" *Armed Forces Journal* (January 1, 2007), https://www.aei.org/articles/why-did-donald-rumsfeld-fail/. It is perhaps worth noting that in a theater where Rumsfeld's preferred "light footprint" model was followed, it arguably led to the failure to capture al-Qaeda and Taliban leaders at Tora Bora in late 2001. See Sarah Burns, *The Politics of War Powers* (Lawrence: University Press of Kansas, 2019), 218.

93. Priest and Arkin, *Top Secret America*; Rebecca Thorpe, *The American Warfare State: The Domestic Politics of Military Spending* (Chicago: University of Chicago Press, 2014); "Top Hundred Defense Contractors 2022," Defense and Security Monitor, February 22, 2023, https://dsm.forecastinternational.com/wordpress/2023/02/22/top-100-defense-contractors-2022/.

94. Hanania, *Illusion of Grand Strategy*, 53. And after all, "money is policy": see Gordon Adams and Cindy Williams, *Buying National Security: How America Plans and Pays for Its Global Role and Safety at Home* (New York: Routledge, 2010), 1.

95. Woodward, *Obama's Wars*, 56.

96. Michael Glennon, *National Security and Double Government* (New York: Oxford University Press, 2015), 7, and see 24–28.

97. Robert Gates, *Duty: Memoirs of a Secretary at War* (New York: Knopf, 2014).

98. Even this is truncated, of course, given US support for Afghan mujahideen forces fighting the Soviets after the USSR invaded Afghanistan in 1979.

99. Christi Parsons and W.J. Hennigan, "President Obama, Who Hoped to Sow Peace, Instead Led the Nation in War," *Los Angeles Times*, January 13, 2017, https://www.latimes.com/projects/la-na-pol-obama-at-war/.

100. Bob Woodward, *Obama's Wars* (New York: Simon & Schuster, 2010), 40–44. See too Craig Whitlock, *The Afghanistan Papers: A Secret History of the War* (New York: Simon & Schuster, 2021).

101. Barack Obama, *A Promised Land* (New York: Crown, 2020), 318–319.

102. See Woodward, *Obama's Wars*, 95–96, on the "incomplete math" the Pentagon originally offered.

103. Obama, *Promised Land*, 432.

104. Stanley McChrystal, *Commander's Initial Assessment* (Kabul, Afghanistan: Headquarters, NATO International Security Assistance Force, 2009), 20.

105. Kevin Marsh, "Obama's Surge: A Bureaucratic Politics Analysis of the Decision to Order a Troop Surge in the Afghanistan War," *Foreign Policy Analysis* 10 (July 2014): 265–288.

106. Leon Panetta, with Jim Newton, *Worthy Fights* (New York: Penguin, 2014), 250.

107. Panetta, *Worthy Fights*, 253.

108. Panetta, *Worthy Fights*, 255.

109. Hillary Rodham Clinton, the secretary of state, strongly supported the surge—perhaps for the same reasons Panetta notes.

110. Obama, *Promised Land*, 443.

111. Marsh, "Bureaucratic Politics," 285.

112. Panetta, *Worthy Fights*, 287.

113. Associated Press, "A timeline of U.S. troop levels in Afghanistan since 2001," *Military Times*, July 6, 2016, https://www.militarytimes.com/news/your-military/2016/07/06/a-timeline-of-u-s-troop-levels-in-afghanistan-since-2001/.

114. Jacob Pramuk, "What Trump Said About Afghanistan Before He Became President," CNBC.com, August 21, 2017, https://www.cnbc.com/2017/08/21/what-trump-said-about-afghanistan-before-he-became-president.html.

115. Baker and Glasser, *The Divider*, 105.

116. Baker and Glasser, *The Divider*, 115.

117. Snodgrass, *Holding the Line*, 123–124.

118. Baker and Glasser, *The Divider*, 115.

119. Baker and Glasser, *The Divider*, 108; they also report (112) that Steve Bannon claimed McMaster's first preference was fifty thousand new troops.. Baker and Glasser further argue (165-166) that "McMaster's determination to talk the president out of withdrawing from Afghanistan was perhaps his biggest misreading of Trump," and quote a State Department official on McMaster's effort to "convert" Trump on this score: "He would wake up, go into the Oval, right into the buzzsaw, right into the wood-chipper. And, God bless him, he'd get up the next day and walk into the wood-chipper again."

120. Quoted in Snodgrass, *Holding the Line*, 79, 168.

121. Donald Trump, "Remarks by President Trump on the Strategy in Afghanistan and South Asia," August 21, 2017, https://trumpwhitehouse.archives.gov/briefings-statements/remarks-president-trump-strategy-afghanistan-south-asia/. Here, interestingly, endorsing the notion of positionality over personality, Trump and Obama echo each other. Obama wrote in 2020 that his campaign positions were "from the cheap seats.... These were my wars now." Obama, *Promised Land*, 314.

122. Trump, "Remarks by President Trump."

123. See Baker and Glasser, *The Divider*, 124.

124. Craig Whitlock, *The Afghanistan Papers: A Secret History of the War* (New York: Simon & Schuster, 2021), chapter 19.

125. Whitlock, *The Afghanistan Papers*.

126. Quoted in Rothkopf, *American Resistance*, 115.

127. Quoted in Jonathan Karl, *Betrayal: The final Act of the Trump Show* (New York: Dutton, 2021), 160–161.

128. Jonathan Swan and Zachary Basu, "Trump's War with His Generals," Axios, May 16, 2021, https://www.axios.com/2021/05/16/off-the-rails-trump-military-withdraw-afghanistan.

129. Quoted in Karl, *Betrayal*, 167.

130. Rothkopf, *American Resistance*, 106. See also Baker and Glasser, *The Divider*, 110, who note that Mattis and Dunford felt that giving Trump the fullest range of options risked him picking the objectively worst one. This angered McMaster, at NSC, who thought they were withholding information from the president. He wasn't wrong. On Syria, see Jonathan Swan and Zachary Basu, "Trump's War with His Generals.".

131. Snodgrass, *Holding the Line*, 85.

132. Wesley Morgan, "All the Ways Mattis Tried to Contain Trump," Politico, December 20, 2018, https://www.politico.com/story/2018/12/20/how-mattis-tried-to-contain-trump-1049741.

133. Quoted in Baker and Glasser, *The Divider*, 199.

134. Quoted in Snodgrass, 307.

135. See Whitlock, *Afghanistan Papers*, chapter 21. As Baker and Glasser note, "Trump was so eager to come to terms that he cut the Afghan government itself out of the negotiations altogether," Baker and Glasser, *The Divider*, 424.

136. Baker and Glasser, *The Divider*, 425. See, too, John Bolton, *The Room Where It Happened* (New York: Simon & Schuster, 2020), chapter 13, for example pages 435–443.

137. Mark T. Esper, *A Sacred Oath: Memoirs of a Secretary of Defense during Extraordinary Times* (New York: William Morrow, 2022), 613.

138. Esper, *Sacred Oath*, 614–616.

139. Esper, *Sacred Oath*, 619.

140. Jonathan Swan and Zachary Basu, "Trump's War with His Generals"; Bob Woodward and Robert Costa, *Peril* (New York: Simon & Schuster, 2021).

141. Trump's order was for 2,500, but about 1,000 Special Forces also remained in the country. See Whitlock, *Afghanistan Papers*.

142. Woodward, *Obama's Wars*, 72.

143. Lara Seligman et al., "How Biden's Team Overrode the Brass on Afghanistan," Politico, April 14, 2021, www.politico.com/news/2021/04/14/pentagon-biden-team-overrode-afghanistan-481556.

144. Woodward and Costa, *Peril*, 337.

145. Quoted in Seligman et al., "Biden's Team."

146. Brian Naylor and Diaa Hadid, "U.S. May Miss Deadline for Withdrawing Troops From Afghanistan, Biden Says," National Public Radio, March 17, 2021, https://www.npr.org/2021/03/17/978106035/biden-says-u-s-may-miss-deadline-for-withdrawing-troops-from-afghanistan.

147. "Secretary Antony J. Blinken with Jake Tapper of State of the Union on CNN," U.S. Department of State, August 15, 2021, https://www.state.gov/secretary-antony-j-blinken-with-jake-tapper-of-state-of-the-union-on-cnn/.

148. Trump national security adviser John Bolton wrote that "the full effects of the deal may not become apparent until after Trump leaves office. But there

should be no mistaking this reality: Trump will be responsible for the consequences, politically and militarily," Bolton, *Room Where it Happened*, 443. In April 2023, the Biden White House released an executive summary of a longer report on the Afghanistan withdrawal that placed the blame on the problematic deal with the Taliban the Trump Administration had negotiated and endorsed; for a link and critique, see Madiha Afzal, "Commentary: What the Biden Administration's Report on the Afghanistan Withdrawal Gets Wrong," Brookings Institution, May 5, 2023, https://www.brookings.edu/blog/order-from-chaos/2023/05/05/what-the-biden-administrations-report-on-the-afghanistan-withdrawal-gets-wrong/.

149. Richard E. Neustadt, *Presidential Power and the Modern Presidents* (New York: Free Press, 1990), 10, 33 (emphasis in the original); Daniel Carpenter and George A. Krause, "Transactional Authority and Bureaucratic Politics," *Journal of Public Administration Research and Theory* 25 (2014): 5–25.

150. For a useful discussion of this tension, see Steven Skowronek, John Dearborn, and Desmond King, *Phantoms of a Beleaguered Republic: The Deep State and the Unitary Executive* (New York: Oxford University Press, 2021)

151. Neil Kumar Katyal, "Internal Separation of Powers: Checking Today's Most Dangerous Branch from Within," *Yale Law Journal* 115 (2006), 2317.

152. Peter Rodman, *Presidential Command* (New York: Knopf/Borzoi, 2009), 3.

153. Quoted in Rothkopf, *American Resistance*, 106.

154. Rodman, *Presidential Command*, 8.

155. Baker and Glasser, *The Divider*, 159.

156. Barack Obama, *A Promised Land* (New York: Crown, 2020), 319, 435, 436, 437.

157. Francis Rourke, *Bureaucracy and Foreign Policy* (Baltimore: Johns Hopkins University Press, 1972), 6.

CHAPTER TEN

War Powers, the "Deep State," and Insurrection

Rebecca Ingber

Throughout the Trump Administration, the then-president openly lamented the power of the so-called deep state, a shadowy bureaucracy that he professed was thwarting his domestic and foreign policy agendas. On Twitter (now X) alone, Trump used the phrase thirty times to decry bureaucratic obstruction, whether real or imagined.[1] So great was the alleged reach of the "deep state" that it even extended to questions of war and peace. Cato Institute senior fellow Doug Bandow blamed savvy bureaucrats for sidestepping the wishes of the commander in chief in an article titled "The Deep State Thwarted Trump's Afghanistan Withdrawal."[2] But it was not just Trump and his cavalry hawking the idea that faceless bureaucrats were undermining his presidency; the "deep state" concept resonated broadly with the American public. A 2018 Monmouth poll asked whether respondents believed the deep state is real, having first defined it as "the possible existence of a group of unelected government and military officials who secretly manipulate or direct national policy." More than two in three Americans said the deep state either definitely (27%) or probably (47%) exists.[3]

But where is the dividing line between a democratically unaccountable deep state and the normal friction that exists in any large organization, in this case between the career bureaucracy and the politically elected principals? One of the earliest conceptions of bureaucracy, from Max Weber, designates government agencies as efficient and rational ways to organize the administration of the state. A byproduct of that organizational structure, often conceived as a plus, is consistency and continuity. The career bureaucracy, the thousands of government officials who remain in their jobs as political appointees come and go, provides a steadying hand on the rudder that helps keep the ship afloat and on an even keel, but can be frustrating for any president. For an iconoclastic executive, it can prove stifling.

The complex realities of bureaucratic resistance and executive branch aggrandizement also lend cover to simplistic, false, and dangerous fears of a deep-state conspiracy. Careful parsing about the legitimacy or risks of bureaucratic constraints gives way in the popular narrative to the sexier "deep state" espoused by the former president, Trump, and his supporters.[4] Efforts to confront these fears, in turn, often go too far, praising the idea of a deep state or even urging that career bureaucrats rise up and "resist" the sitting president in an effort to undermine his policy objectives.[5]

The reality is more nuanced and more mundane, but nevertheless still dangerous. The bureaucracy, seated in the executive branch, but also created and empowered by Congress, has long helped entrench executive power as a whole at the expense of Congress. It also serves as a constraint on the individual president or his advisers, sometimes on behalf of Congress. As Rudalevige shows in his chapter, bureaucratic resistance has significantly shaped many presidential foreign policy decisions in the post-9/11 landscape, in key instances skewing policy away from presumed presidential preferences. On balance, however, the bureaucracy's role in codifying and expanding presidential power in foreign affairs is as significant or more so than is the check it exercises on individual presidents.

Two mechanisms are of paramount importance. First, the very existence of a career bureaucracy and the constraint it exercises—which, considering the complexity of modern government, is essential to Congress's ability to extend its oversight capabilities into the far reaches of the executive—also mollifies Congress and makes executive aggrandizement palatable. Legislators are more ready to defer to any given president knowing that technocratic actors motivated more by foreign policy and military expertise than by politics are superintending the executive's policies. Second, and perhaps even more importantly, the norms and institutional prerogatives of that bureaucracy lead it to assert and then protect increasing claims to power for the president. Bureaucrats have strong incentives and norms that lead them to seek or craft and then reaffirm legal interpretations that maximize executive power. Efforts to roll back extraordinary precedents routinely fail as even presidents who pledged to do so and other political appointees arrive in their new positions to face offices and legacy policies that have long relied upon these same precedents. The end result is a ratcheting effect in which executive power increases cumulatively, a process that is aided and abetted by the bureaucracy itself.

Focusing on the events of January 6, 2021, and the longstanding practice of executive branch war powers, this chapter draws upon my prior scholarship on bureaucratic resistance and executive branch legal decision-making to examine the duality of the executive branch bureaucracy in constraining the president while expanding the power of the presidency.[6] While the attack of January 6 on the US Capitol is a fantastical, extraordinary snapshot in time, it affords important insights into the strength and resilience of bureaucratic checks in the face of unprecedented threats. The insurrection was a violent assault on our governing institutions, but in stark contrast to 9/11, the president in this case did not take action to repel that threat. Rather, he prompted and promoted it, leaving the bureaucracy to muddle through to protect our political institutions without clear direction from its own politically-elected head.

This case affords unique insight into the bureaucracy's capacity to check a presidential power grab of the most extreme sort. In so doing, it seeks to answer a paradox of January 6: How did the executive branch bureaucracy prove vital to securing the election and preventing a coup d'état while simultaneously answering to the person at the crux of that attempted coup—the president himself? The events of January 6, extreme as they were, bring into stark relief how essential the institutional constraints and normal operation of the executive branch bureaucracy are to the continued functioning of our democracy. In that regard, the events that day help mediate debates about how the federal branches of government operate: whether the president is constrained by law; whether the tripartite framework of the president, courts, and Congress act as the set of checks and balances that the framers intended; and whether the bureaucracy has become an essential piece of that equation.

The second case study, the longstanding practice of war powers inside the executive branch, is a story of business as usual. The executive branch's process for wartime decision-making, its expansive claims to unilateral power, and even most of its wartime acts fly so far beneath the radar that if you plucked a person from the street and said, "How concerned are you about the president's claims to unilateral war powers?" they might easily respond, "What war?" But the very mundaneness of this process, the very fact that it flies under the radar, enables this steady accrual of executive power. The executive branch practice of war powers demonstrates how these institutional constraints and norms of governance also promote a lopsided tilt of ever-increasing power to the executive branch itself, an executive branch run by a president who might once again seek to abuse that power.

These two features of the bureaucracy are symbiotic. The existence of one creates space for the other. The knowledge that bureaucratic constraints exist permits the other branches to delegate and defer to the president as an entity even when they fear the president as a person. Hence, the existence of bureaucratic constraints on the president allows the other branches to abdicate some of their own responsibility to check that institution themselves. Yet internal constraints alone will eventually prove insufficient without the external forces of the courts and Congress to support, empower, and legitimize them.

Bureaucracy and Insurrection

Throughout the course of the 2020 election, and leading up to the events of January 6, 2021, scholars, current and former government officials, the press, and other government watchers engaged in a near-constant drumbeat of speculation with respect to whether the then president Trump might order US forces to interfere in the US election on his behalf and how those forces might respond if ordered to do so.[7] The level of anxiety was so significant that former *and current* Department of Defense and military officials, including all of the living former defense secretaries, spoke out—either to provide assurance that the military would not interfere or to warn off anyone who might have an inclination to do so.[8]

These concerns were potent. If senior Pentagon officials had conspired with the president to install him in power for a second term and beyond, there would not have been much recourse to stop them. A few years prior, this would have seemed a far-fetched scenario. But so too would a sitting president calling for a reversal of the election, pressuring local state officials to change the vote, and sending violent supporters to march on the Capitol, not to mention those supporters breaching the barricades to hunt down members of Congress and the vice president, calling for their heads.[9] Each of these events would have seemed a fantastical fiction had we not watched it happen live before our eyes. And thus, in light of the shattering of many expectations about the normal functioning of government, it would have been irresponsible to assume the worst could never happen. Nevertheless, there was still, for many, a powerful urge to believe that some things would continue to work as normal, and that the senior ranks of the US military would never turn on democracy. That all living former secretaries of defense felt the need to warn them off doing so was bone chilling.

These statements from current and former military and others, either promising not to interfere in the election or warning off others from doing so, surely brought some measure of comfort to those who had raised concerns. But this posture of total noninterference also carried some risks that went unaddressed. Historically, presidents have deployed US military forces domestically in emergency contexts when local forces were insufficient, or when they could not rely on the fidelity of local forces to the rule of law and justice for all under their jurisdiction.[10] Placing categorical constraints on the military's ability to operate domestically might have been prudent in light of the threat posed by the then sitting president himself, but it also could have meant leaving vulnerable people without recourse in the hands of those who intended them harm. This is a conundrum that is unresolved. If local forces are insufficient or untrustworthy, infiltrated with extremists, we must turn to federal forces to protect the vulnerable and the institutions under threat. If federal forces cannot be trusted, the uncomfortable truth is that we do not have a Plan C.

The events of January 6 brought this conundrum into sharp relief. The Capitol police quickly became overwhelmed by the violent mob, which breached the perimeter they had established and soon gained entry to the building, and yet there was little response for hours from the usual source of backup power, the federal government.[11] Many raised questions about the federal government's failure to send in troops immediately to quell the violence, suggesting that perhaps the Trump Administration had held them back for nefarious purposes.[12] Former acting secretary of defense Chris Miller faced heated questions in congressional testimony; none of it clarified a shocking timeline in which approximately four hours passed between Miller's awareness of the situation at the Capitol and the arrival of the National Guard.[13]

It remains an open question whether any members of the Trump Administration sought to curtail or in fact stymied the response to the insurrection at the Capitol.[14] But it is quite plausible that the precise opposite dynamic was also at play: that in the runup to that terrifying moment, the city, the Capitol police, members of Congress, and even Pentagon leadership itself had been reluctant to rely on help from the military precisely because they did not trust the commander in chief.[15]

Ultimately, the forces formally under his command were necessary to securing the Capitol.[16] Whatever the initial holdup in getting troops to the Capitol, the National Guard ultimately arrived at 5:20 p.m. and with the Metropolitan and Capitol police reestablished a secure perimeter and enabled the election certification process to continue that night.[17] In the days and weeks that followed, the US military stationed troops outside of US agencies to protect them from extremists who had been inspired and incited by the sitting US president, their commander in chief.[18] FBI agents hunted down leads and Department of Justice prosecutors filed charges against the president's supporters who, answering his call, rallied to DC and charged the Capitol.[19] The executive branch bureaucracy, from the heads of agencies to the line officials, kicked into gear to combat the crisis that had been set ablaze and condoned by the president himself.[20] Bureaucratic actors, from agencies across the executive branch and ultimately answering to the president, were necessary to prevent President Trump from undermining the electoral process and later to investigate and pursue justice against those who sought to do so on his behalf.

The executive branch bureaucracy, acting in accordance with longstanding practical precedent and under legal authorities put into place by both Congress and the executive itself, including the president and his most immediate appointees, was ultimately responsible and *essential* to the undermining of that president's, Trump's, explicit goal—the overturning of the election—and thus essential to the protection of the American system of government. Did the bureaucracy save the American Experiment from the president? And if so, what stands between the bureaucracy saving democracy from an autocrat and the bureaucracy installing an autocrat? The next section will discuss the real constraints the bureaucracy places on the US president along with the constraints on the bureaucracy itself.

Executive Branch Bureaucracy as a Constraint on the President

The Trump Administration provided fertile soil for debates about the role of the executive branch bureaucracy in the separation of powers. As Trump came to power and throughout his administration, many who feared what he might do with the vast powers of the presidency at his disposal searched for means of reining him in. The options were limited.

Significant powers have accreted in the executive branch in modern history.[21] Congress, for its part, has not only acquiesced to presidents' aggrandizement, in many cases it has passed the laws creating those powers and handing them over.[22] The courts have been a mixed bag at best. But certainly, in the national security space, where much of the concern about presidential power tends to bubble up, the courts have been highly deferential to presidents' unilateral exercises of power.[23]

Perhaps for lack of alternatives, many Trump critics and presidential power watchers writ large landed on hopes that the executive branch bureaucracy might provide that constraint. Social media platforms were suddenly awash in references to a #Resistance.[24] New social media accounts cropped up purporting to represent disaffected civil servants within the government.[25] Nongovernmental organizations sought ways to promote avenues for civil service workers to distinguish service to their country and law from service to the president.[26] And many scholars hailed accounts of disobedience among the civil service, in some cases exhorting career bureaucrats to resist by providing a road map for doing so.[27]

The incoming president Trump and his supporters, for their part, decried the possibility of constraint from within, and painted the bureaucracy in broad terms as an illegitimate "deep state" seeking to undermine his presidency.[28] By using the term *deep state*, they drew upon a term that has historically been used—often in conspiratorial terms—to describe a group of unelected actors, often in the military or intelligence community, holding the reins of power in lieu of the legitimate government. It has long been used in Turkey and elsewhere, both by critics outside of government as well as by government officials, as a means of stoking fear or support for their own agendas.[29] But deep-state rhetoric is a comparatively recent import to discussions about bureaucracy in the United States.

Here, its use is intended to evoke images of an organized cabal of faceless bureaucrats pulling the strings of government in lieu of the elected president, thus undermining his power as well as the will of the American electorate.[30]

Some scholars have endorsed descriptions of American government similar to the deep-state view, whether or not they employ the rhetoric.[31] Others have redefined the term, applying it to the US bureaucracy without necessarily embracing the full thrust of its original import. For example, Jack Goldsmith has acknowledged the benefits along with the rationale behind bureaucratic resistance to Trump, nevertheless positing significant risks in empowering what he terms "the 'Deep State' in the United States."[32] To Goldsmith, the US ""deep state" . . . is not nearly as sinister as in authoritarian countries" but includes "the US intelligence and related national security bureaucracies endowed with extraordinary powers of secret intelligence collection (or access to the fruits of that intelligence)" and which historically abused that power.[33]

Ironically, the "deep state" portrayal of the executive branch bureaucracy decried by President Trump and his surrogates bears some significant similarities to the full-throated #Resistance image embraced by his critics. But neither accurately reflects the real power or constraint embodied by the executive branch bureaucracy. Deep-state rhetoric itself has often been quite messy, used to cast aspersions in broad brushstrokes on just about anything that presidents or their supporters wanted to denigrate as stymying his agenda or undermining his leadership. That rhetoric was often particularly inapposite during the Trump era, during which the people primarily standing in the way of the president's agenda or disparaging his administration in the press were most typically his own politically appointed advisers.[34]

But there are more fundamental flaws with both the deep-state and the #Resistance accounts of bureaucratic action. First, both theories are heavy-handed and lack a clear vision for where to draw the line between legitimate and illegitimate activity. Even an aggressive unitary executive theory viewing all executive power as flowing from and beholden to the president alone must account for the fact that civil servants, foreign service and military officers, and other bureaucratic actors, including the president's own political appointees, are not cyborgs; *any* theory of bureaucratic legitimacy or illegitimacy must account for the countless micro decisions and actions bureaucrats must take each day, including simply asking questions or raising concerns, all of which might change the course of executive action.[35] Nor are these thousands of bureaucratic actors organizationally united; to the contrary, they are dispersed throughout agencies and offices that answer to political actors who themselves have independent perspectives and agendas.[36] At all levels, these actors are often more likely to be stymied from the sides—by their counterparts in other offices and agencies—than from above or below.[37]

More fundamentally, as I have discussed extensively in *Bureaucratic Resistance and the National Security State*, these accounts insufficiently address both the formal authority bureaucrats hold *and* the functional constraints on their power to act.[38] As a result, neither the "deep-state" nor the #Resistance account can help us understand the events of January 6: why the bureaucracy was necessary to securing the election certification process after the attack on the Capitol and yet failed to prevent that attack.

In fact, bureaucrats have significant formal authority to act in many ways that result in resistance to the president's agenda.[39] They may and do ask questions, raise concerns, insist on following the law and ethical obligations, refuse to falsify evidence to suit a policy agenda, seek out help from executive branch offices or congressional officials, or, if it comes to it, resign, all within their formal authorities. I use the term *formal* to connote authorities that derive from conventional, democratically accountable sources such as Congress (e.g., through statutory delegations and statutory protections), and the president (through subdelegations and allocations of power) as well as those that derive from judicial doctrines that allocate certain forms of power to bureaucrats.[40]

There also exist significant functional constraints on bureaucrats' ability to act, which "deep-state" and #Resistance accounts both underestimate or fail to consider altogether. Bureaucrats face constraints on their sphere of activity not merely—or, in most cases, not ever—from the president himself, but from every single direction, from immediate superiors, more distant superiors, colleagues, and counterparts in other agencies. Bureaucratic actors face vertical constraints on action from their managers and other superiors up the organizational chart.[41] They also face horizontal constraints, from hard resistance from counterparts in other agencies to the group think and professional culture of their own offices.[42] And they face constraints from external sources as well—from the other branches, foreign counterparts, and civil society.[43]

As a result, bureaucrats often find their actions heavily circumscribed by practical hurdles, even when they hold formal authority to act. This runs contrary to much conventional wisdom, which presumes that bureaucrats have and exercise the practical ability to act well beyond their formal authority to do so. Both the deep-state and #Resistance rhetoric adopt and rely upon these assumptions, which also infiltrate popular perceptions of bureaucrats. As a result, observers outside the executive branch—or even high-level actors such as the president—who lack the specific details surrounding an event or knowledge of the legal framework under which actors are operating, may misinterpret the products of mundane, normal bureaucratic activity as instead the acts of deep-state operatives involved in transgressive resistance. Similarly, both deep-state and #Resistance accounts grossly overestimate the ability of the bureaucracy to chart a new course of action at odds with that of the president's will.

The events of January 6 highlight both the understated formal authority of bureaucrats to act, including to resist, as well as the functional constraints on their actually doing so. One specific event from January 6 highlights how bureaucratic resistance is often misunderstood from outside perspectives, and formal authority in particular is often underestimated. In the midst of the attack, then acting defense secretary Chris Miller announced that he and the chairman of the Joint Chiefs of Staff, Mark Milley, had "just spoke[n] separately with the Vice President and with Speaker Pelosi, Leader McConnell, Senator Schumer and Representative Hoyer about the situation at the U.S. Capitol. We have fully activated the D.C. National Guard to assist federal and local law enforcement as they work to peacefully address the situation. We are prepared to provide additional support as necessary and appropriate as requested by local authorities. Our people are sworn to defend the constitution and our democratic form of government and they will act accordingly."[44] Some analysts immediately took this explicit mention of the vice president and the absence of any mention of the president to suggest that the defense secretary and the chairman of the Joint Chiefs were acting without authority or else under some authority of the vice president, a "de facto invocation of the Twenty-Fifth Amendment."[45] Others worried that the military might be going rogue.[46] If so, the consequences of such a breakdown would be dire. While sending in US troops to save legislators from mob violence might have been essential in this particular scenario, if they had done so against orders or without authority, might that set a precedent from which we might never return? Military forces acting outside of the chain of command could have presented the true constitutional crisis that the Trump Administration was always threatening yet never quite managing to realize.

And yet, this too was not the constitutional crisis it might have appeared. The reality in this case as in many others was, if not mundane, then at least not a total breakdown in the chain of command. The power to call up the DC National Guard has long been delegated by the president to the secretary of defense, who further delegated it to the secretary of the army.[47] The secretary of defense and secretary of the army were thus fully empowered, by the president himself, to activate the guard. Pence was never in the chain of command and did not have any authority to order the guard to deploy. Instead, he was likely on the call along with the leaders of Congress perhaps to provide some political cover, but mainly because he was there, at the Capitol, as president of the Senate, calling for help alongside congressional leadership as *one of the victims of the attack*.

What was unusual in this case was not an overstepping of *formal* authority by bureaucratic actors but rather the way that these actors exercised their discretion in acting on that authority. In addition to the still-unexplained delays in getting troops to the Capitol, it also appears that no one affirmatively chose, as a matter of discretion, to call the president to advise him on the unfurling situation or to request his guidance.[48] Had they done so, and had President Trump *ordered* them to stand down, such an order would have undercut the authorities discussed above. The secretary of defense and those under him might have obeyed the order and stood down, leaving the Capitol overrun, legislators and the vice president in hiding, obstructing the election certification process, and quite possibly leading to many more casualties. Or they might have refused his order. That would have raised a perhaps unprecedented question: whether an order to stand down, in contrast to an order to act, could itself ever be an unlawful order. Of course, from what we currently know, former president Trump did not provoke that particular crisis and it seems his own advisers may have avoided it simply by never asking him.

These are the formal authorities. What of the functional constraints on bureaucrats that stand in the way of their taking the reins themselves? Other aspects of the events of January 6 that have come to light in the weeks and months since also highlight the limits on the functional powers of bureaucrats to act, including constraints on their ability to act in contravention to the will of the president and other political actors. In recent testimony to Congress, Department of Homeland Security (DHS) and Federal Bureau of Investigation (FBI) officials sought to justify why they had not issued threat assessments or intelligence bulletins in advance of January 6, alerting law enforcement officials to the threat that was developing, apparently in plain view on social media.[49] FBI and DHS officials told Congress that their collection efforts were hindered by the difficulty in distinguishing "constitutionally protected speech" from other threats.[50] The rules are set forth in executive branch guidelines promulgated under Executive Order 12333 and prohibit "engaging in intelligence activities ... for the sole purpose of monitoring activities protected by the First Amendment."[51] Leadership failures likely also played a role, as well as the complexity of navigating potential threats from a source that was generally aligned with the president. In fact, one FBI field office actually did issue a warning, but it was not "escalated"—government-speak for raising the matter with higher-level officials to get the attention of the powers that be and force an issue onto the agenda.[52]

This is not an account of a deep state wielding the reins of power in lieu of elected leadership, or even of individual rogue actors disobeying their orders. This is a description of bureaucrats at various levels of government from the top down wielding the formal authorities granted to them by elected officials from both the executive and Congress. Moreover, these are authorities that could be reclaimed and in some cases were, such as the Pentagon's order to DC National Guard chief William Walker, constraining his power to deploy the National Guard without additional supervisory steps from the secretary of the army.[53] These formal authorities grant power to actors throughout the bureaucracy to act in ways that at times may be or appear to be in contravention of the sitting president's own agenda, and that at least appears to have been the case with the events surrounding January 6.

This is also an account of the practical constraints on bureaucrats' abilities to act. Bureaucrats are constrained not only in their ability to counteract a president bent on pursuing a given path but also at times in their ability to take action, even action they deem important, in the absence of direction. It is thus also a story of bureaucrats not taking actions that they had authority to take, and which might have effectively prevented some of this catastrophe, either because they lacked clear direction from above or received the message that such actions would be unwelcome.

Executive Branch Bureaucracy as Entrencher of Executive Power: The Case of War Powers

The description of the dynamics of constraint on the president discussed above are only a partial account of the role the executive branch bureaucracy fulfills in the separation of powers. That role is complicated still further by a feature of the bureaucracy that receives decidedly less airtime but is extremely consequential. In addition to providing some constraint on the person of the president, often through the design of Congress, the bureaucracy also operates to entrench executive power vis-à-vis Congress and the courts. Some of the features of the bureaucracy that lead to accretion in the executive have been well plumbed: the modern bureaucracy has greater resources, in particular personnel, and in turn has developed greater expertise and access to information—especially classified information—that exponentially exceed that of Congress.[54] Congress, for its part, has played a decisive role in not only permitting but in many respects even creating this aggregation of resources and expertise in the executive branch.

There are, however, other features of executive branch decision-making that serve to aggrandize and entrench executive power that fly further under the radar and as a result—in contrast to congressional decisions to create and fund agencies through legislation—have less connection to preferences made through democratic processes. These include executive-branch decision-making guided by norms favoring consistency and institutional protection, legal interpretation via a lens favoring executive power, and litigation-driven decision-making, which prioritizes defense of past action. These are each features of executive-branch decision-making and lawyering that Congress generally lacks. The executive-branch bureaucracy does not have a true counterpart pushing back from the other branch; it is largely a one-sided fight. The war powers context exacerbates the information and expertise asymmetries between Congress and the executive and along with them the dynamics of congressional acquiescence, judicial deference, and an executive branch inclined to fill as much space as possible. It thus provides a useful lens through which to examine this phenomenon.[55]

Norms

Executive branch norms, their virtues, and their thrashing by the recent presidential administration have been the subject of much recent discussion and scholarship.[56] A primary focus has been the critical and long-standing norm against the politicization of prosecutorial and investigative decisions, which the Trump administration notoriously and repeatedly violated.[57] But there are numerous other norms of executive branch lawyering that extend the norm against politicized prosecution into other areas of legal decision-making, inclining the executive branch as a whole toward retention of the status quo, protection of institutional prerogative, and entrenching claims of executive power. When presidents and their political leadership are already inclined toward aggressive claims of executive power, some of these norms might operate as a soft constraint. But such constraints only function in administrations that follow them, and interests in expanding power often go hand in hand with a willingness to flout some internal norms that might stand in the way.[58] These norms are therefore most significant in entrenching power in presidential administrations not otherwise inclined to do so. Presidents who rise to power with the intention of confronting the power aggrandizement of their predecessors and reinstating processes of good governance are most susceptible to executive branch forces that operate instead to expand and protect that power.[59] For this reason, the upward climb of presidential claims to power is rarely ratcheted back from the inside.

A president that comes to power on the heels of an administration seen to have overly politicized prosecutorial or investigatory decisions might overcompensate by reestablishing an even stronger buffer between his White House and his Justice Department. President Obama, for example, succeeded an administration plagued by scandals of politicized firings of US attorneys and reports of a secret "war council" of lawyers created to circumvent normal process and rubber stamp White House positions.[60] He also campaigned against the aggressive claims to power wrapped up in the Bush Administration's "War on Terror." Yet his administration quickly adopted many of the legal positions of his predecessor, including those regarding whom the president could detain indefinitely at Guantanamo and abroad without any further legislation necessary from Congress.[61]

The reasons for this continuity are overdetermined, but they include the kid gloves with which the Obama White House often treated Justice Department decision-making, even on matters of major policies in which the president was deeply invested. The legal positions the prior administration had given to the court were not scrapped; they formed the template from which the incoming administration started to work.[62] Instead of doing away with the military commission system installed by George W. Bush and then backed by Congress, the Obama Administration decided to retain the power for the president, proposed a few changes to the legislation, and went forward with the prosecutions within that system, despite Obama's earlier plan to try the 9/11 attackers in federal courts and despite the fact that this meant kickstarting the commissions with the prosecution of someone who had been a child at the time of his capture.[63] The new administration faced hurdles to reversing course in that case because of internal executive branch interpretations of new statutory rules enacted in response to political interference by the prior administration in the work of career prosecutors.[64]

When the legal question at issue is one of executive power vis-à-vis Congress or the courts, executive branch norms zealously favor protection of the president's institutional power even when the sitting president does not seek it. Executive power and protection of the presidency, once claimed, is rarely ceded back. Thus, for example, the Biden Department of Justice continued to argue the position claimed by the Trump Administration that the then president Trump was acting within his "scope of employment" under the Westfall Act when accusing a woman of falsifying a rape claim against him.[65] Despite then-candidate Biden's criticism of the Department of Justice taking on Trump's defense in that case, once he had taken office, Biden's own Justice Department argued that the defense was necessary because the case "implicate[d] the institutional interests of the federal government."[66] In the war powers space, the Biden Department of Justice recently filed a brief refusing to refute a Trump Administration claim that detainees at Guantanamo Bay lacked due process rights in litigation, despite the reported views of their client agencies—the Defense Department, State, and intelligence agencies—that they should acknowledge such rights in the brief.[67]

This one-way ratchet plays out consistently outside of litigation as well. The Office of Legal Counsel (OLC) is a small office of lawyers inside the Department of Justice that provides legal guidance to the president and the executive branch. OLC was the focus of significant legal scandals during the first few years in the Bush Administration's war on terror. This played out most notoriously in the context of a series of "Torture Memos" the office secretly issued to justify the administration's severe and, in some cases, tortuous treatment of military detainees.[68] But the Bush OLC also issued other extreme memoranda, in particular one asserting a unilateral right for the president to use force without congressional approval against groups, even if unconnected to 9/11, to prevent and deter future, indeterminate, attacks and another justifying invasion of a sovereign nation (Iraq) on the basis of a flexible set of factors that did not require an attack or even a high probability of attack on the United States.[69]

Legal Interpretation

A significant source of executive branch aggrandizement and power entrenchment is the regular process of legal interpretation by government lawyers, which the executive branch employs in the tens of thousands.[70] In the war powers space in particular, where courts rarely issue merits decisions, these lawyers often operate as both advocate and judge.[71] In that dual role, they are both seeking a particular outcome for their client and self-judging the limits on what they can sanction. The result is not the rubber stamping of executive action that some assume, but nevertheless an incremental expansion of claims to power and steady protection of that power. This effect requires no bad faith; most of these lawyers consistently engage in the practice of difficult and careful lawyering to help their clients enact their policies within legal bounds. But the very practice of lawyering itself, and the mixed context of litigation and ex-ante guidance in which government lawyering takes place, involves features—the building on precedent, the zealous advocacy, the protection of client flexibility, the memorializing of yeses but not noes—that lean toward the slow aggrandizement of claims to power. When there is no external pushback, and the war powers space rarely affords much, this is a one-way ratchet.[72]

The Office of Legal Counsel in the Department of Justice provides a useful platform through which to analyze this phenomenon, both because of its importance in deciding significant questions of executive power and because of its practice of memorializing in writing and in many cases publishing its opinions.[73] OLC's mandate to provide legal advice to the president and agencies is a delegation from the Attorney General, whose responsibility for doing so is established in the Judiciary Act of 1789.[74]

Government lawyers often wear two hats.[75] They are advocates for their clients, of course, but the government is not just any client and government lawyers have a moral and ethical responsibility to ensure the government does not overstep the law. In settling legal disputes between agencies, in taking responsibility for whether or not to sanction government actions, and above all, in seeking to impose their "best view," OLC lawyers in particular may appear to take on a "quasi-judicial" function as well.[76] Under OLC's own best practices guidelines, "OLC must provide advice based on its best understanding of what the law requires—not simply an advocate's defense of the contemplated action or position proposed by an agency or the Administration."[77] Their view of the law is, by necessity and design, influenced by their ultimate goal of aiding their client.[78] But they also must at times say "no." Yet government lawyers are not actually judges; they do not in fact sit at a distance, outside the administration, in impartial judgment. They can never replace the role of an external arbiter for two critical reasons that undergird the executive's incremental power aggrandizement.

The first of these is the most clear-cut. While government lawyers have a special responsibility beyond that to their clients, they nevertheless understand their role is to help their clients achieve their goals.[79] Thus, when working within an interpretive gray space—where many of the legal questions that reach OLC tend to lie—OLC lawyers will not necessarily take it upon themselves to carve out new legal constraints but rather will interpret the existing, possibly ambiguous, legal rules in a light favorable to their clients.[80] This means that when necessary to provide a binary response, they will likely err on the side of yes, but they also may prophylactically try to keep their clients from getting in trouble by steering them off from risky ventures even when they might be able to legally justify them.[81] That general desire of lawyers to have their clients stand back from the line (an instinct not shared by *all* lawyers[82]) tempers, at least somewhat, the feature of government lawyering that favors interpreting the law in a light most favorable to one's clients. But it connects to a second feature of government lawyering that over time has a significant effect on ratcheting claims to power.

This second feature is the tendency of government lawyers and other bureaucratic actors to enshrine only that legal guidance affirmatively sanctioning action. Like Article III judges, government lawyers often enshrine their legal guidance in writing. But Article III judges, who operate outside the executive in their own coequal branch of government, memorialize their legal opinions in writing without regard for whether they have sanctioned or enjoined a particular action. The noes are enshrined along with the yeses.

Government lawyers take a different approach, stemming in part from their risk-aversion. They do *tell* their clients "no." But they are less inclined to memorialize these noes in writing, much less publish them. They may not even have to tell their clients no if they are able to steer them off from risky behavior and channel their policies into safer waters before nearing the line. OLC's practice is, after all, to "avoid giving unnecessary advice, such as where it appears that policymakers are likely to move in a different direction."[83] This is sensible lawyering. Yet the result is that the yeses become memorialized, while the noes are left to the particulars of memory and oral history. This means that the outer limits on the sphere of government-lawyer sanctioned activity are up for grabs time and again, while the grants of permission are there to be picked up and built upon by a future attorney.[84] The result: internal government legal opinions build on one another over time, as generations of government lawyers deploy and extend legal justifications to new circumstances, rarely hitting redlines as they do, and even more rarely narrowing or dialing back what has already been legally blessed.[85]

One can watch the incremental creep of claims to power play out in published executive branch legal opinions. For example, in the context of military intervention abroad, OLC crafted a legal test in 1994 for when a president might use force abroad for humanitarian purposes without receiving specific congressional authorization.[86] That 1994 opinion asserted that whether a deployment of US troops abroad should be construed as "a 'war' in the constitutional sense"—and thus infringe on Congress's authority to declare war—turned on a consideration of its "nature, scope, and duration."[87] OLC's full determination that the president held authority to act without further authorization from Congress turned on "a combination of three factors": statutory evidence of Congress's support, satisfaction of the War Powers Resolution, and meeting this "nature, scope, and duration" test.[88] Moreover, in determining that the deployment's "nature, scope, and duration" would not constitute "'war' in the constitutional sense," the OLC memorandum relied upon several underlying factors, including that it was undertaken "with the full consent of the legitimate government of the country" and in accordance with a UN Security Council resolution.[89] In fact, the opinion stated that "there can thus be no question but that the deployment [to Haiti] is lawful as a matter of international law."[90] OLC also factored in "the limited antecedent risk that United States forces would encounter significant armed resistance or suffer or inflict substantial casualties as a result of the deployment," and "other aspects of the planned deployment, including the fact that it would not involve extreme use of force, as for example preparatory bombardment."[91]

Over the years, some or all of these limiting factors dropped out in subsequent opinions sanctioning unilateral force by the president. A year after the Haiti deployment, OLC found that "a proposed deployment of approximately 20,000 ground troops to enforce a peace agreement in Bosnia and Herzegovina also was not a 'war,' even though this deployment involved some 'risk that the United States [would] incur (and inflict) casualties.'"[92] In 2011, again acting in accordance with a UN Security resolution, the Office sanctioned force in Libya.[93] This time, the Office softened its stance on whether a "war in the constitutional sense" would be outside the president's Article II authority, calling it instead a "*possible* constitutionally based limit on this president['s] authority to employ military force in defense of important national interests."[94] In considering whether the case met the "nature, scope, and duration" test, the Libya memorandum asserted that the operations served "a limited and well-defined mission in support of international efforts to protect civilians and prevent a humanitarian disaster"—a claim that understated what ultimately became an effort to oust the sitting government.[95] The opinion also acknowledged that "it might not be true here that 'the risk of sustained military conflict was negligible,'" thus softening that prong of the test as well.[96]

Finally, in 2017 and again in 2018, OLC under the Trump Administration relied on this string of opinions to use force in Syria.[97] In this case, the use of force was neither authorized by a UN Security Council resolution, nor by consent of the Syrian government, and was in clear violation of international law. OLC also acknowledged risk to personnel and of further escalation, thus again severing some of the factors that had constrained prior opinions.[98] It is not clear today what key constraints remain on the OLC test for when the president may unilaterally use force abroad. This incremental exercise plays out across the war powers space. Executive-branch lawyers have, through legal interpretation, not only expanded claims to the president's constitutional authority to act unilaterally, but also the president's statutory authority to act in accordance with various congressional Authorizations to Use Military Force.[99]

These two features, zealous advocacy and its memorialization, build on one another. Government lawyers may try to steer their clients within legally safe boundaries, but in doing so they tend to avoid enshrining legal limits in writing. And when pushed to do so, they interpret the law in the best light for their clients, building on years of legal opinions doing just that, and memorializing those decisions for the government lawyers who follow them. Without externally imposed limits and challenges—which are rare in the war powers space—the result is ever-increasing power.

Litigation-Driven Decision-Making

A third mechanism of executive aggrandizement that warrants mention is the effect on government legal positions of the context in which many legal decisions arise for the government. As I have explored in past scholarship, the way a matter arises for decision within the government affects every aspect of that decision-making process: the players involved, their roles, who holds the pen, who holds final decision-making authority, how the issues are framed, the contextual biases in which they are considered, and the values that are prioritized.[100] All of this informs the substantive outcome.[101] Different triggers—which I have elsewhere termed "interpretation catalysts"—prompt different processes, and thus different interpretation catalysts are likely to prompt different substantive outcomes.[102]

Decision-making, including legal decision-making, may be triggered by infinitely varied mechanisms: from the need to respond to a sudden attack to a report coming due before a treaty body. Some triggers occur with greater frequency than others; lawsuits against the government are at the top of this list. Such lawsuits often have the effect of channeling other ongoing decision-making processes into the defensive litigation process. That process has certain features that tilt very heavily toward making aggressive claims of executive power. Among them, career litigators deep within the Department of Justice generally run the process and hold the pen, often working off old briefs as templates, and they tend to view their institutional role as defenders of executive power. There is a strong bias against reversing the positions taken in litigation, based in part in a view that doing so might undermine the strength of the government's standing in court generally; thus positions once taken tend to stick. And in arriving at those positions in the first place, the litigation posture means that the contextual biases of the decision-making process favor zealous defense of past executive action, even actions of questionable legality or merit taken by a former president.

Consider, for example, the recent decision by the Department of Justice not to acknowledge due process rights for detainees at Guantanamo, discussed above.[103] The reported contrary positions of the relevant client agencies—in particular the agency holding the detainees, Department of Defense, as well as other agencies with a significant stake in the question, such as the State Department and the intelligence agencies—suggest that had the question arisen in a non-litigation context, the outcome would have been different.[104]

In areas where the courts tend to defer to the executive's positions or fail to reach the merits entirely, as is often the case in the war powers space, the executive branch's legal position in litigation is essentially the final word on the matter. And because of the fire-drill nature of much executive branch decision-making in the war powers space, these decisions tend not to be revisited internally. Thus the defensive, executive-power-favoring litigation posture that was intended as an opening bid in adversarial litigation becomes the entrenched executive-branch position and, as a result of congressional inaction and judicial deference, the law of the land.

This conglomeration of proclivities—defense of presidential action, memorialization of legal guidance sanctioning executive action, institutional memory loss of guidance raising legal concerns, and institutional norms favoring consistency and protection of executive flexibility—combine to create an incremental ratcheting up and then entrenching of claims to executive power. Moreover, these are features, buttressed by a vast career bureaucracy, that the other branches lack. The result is a one-way staircase toward an executive less and less checked by the other purportedly coequal branches.

Executive Power and Presidential Control

How can the executive-branch bureaucracy act as both a constraint on the president and a protector of presidential power? The answer lies in a distinction of terminology. Two very different forms of the presidency and of power are at issue in these dynamics. We can call them executive power and presidential control, as I have elsewhere identified and discussed in depth.[105] Executive power, as I employ the term, is the strength of the executive branch of government as a whole vis-à-vis the other branches. This is the form of power most formally relevant to the traditional separation of powers. It is the form of power at issue in debates over presidential encroachment on Congress's constitutional responsibility to declare war.

Presidential control, by contrast, is the ability of the president personally and through political subordinates to direct and drive the agenda and policies of the executive branch more broadly. This type of power is the subject of Elena Kagan's "Presidential Administration" and scholarship more broadly concerning itself with the unitary executive theory of government, though that latter theory at times bleeds into theories of executive power for those who deem the concept a rallying cry for an all-powerful president.[106] While rhetoric varies dramatically among presidents, with some praising the career bureaucracy and some railing against the "deep state," all presidents seek to and do exert control, though never perfect control, over the bureaucracy as a means of promoting their administration's agenda. Their advancement of their goals depends largely on the extent to which they are successful in doing so.

Presidents, along with their political advisers, also come into office with their own perspectives on the relationship between the branches, governed by their own ideologies, experiences, and politics. Many have already served in Congress and may have come of political age with an institutional proclivity toward the legislative branch. There are partisan differences, as well, on the merits of congressional delegation of de facto lawmaking to a vast and increasingly powerful executive branch, and these differences generally turn on the substance at issue. At least in theory, Republicans tend to favor granting the president significant war-making capabilities and less power to regulate business, and Democrats tend to fall the other way. If presidential and partisan leanings immediately materialized in executive branch action, therefore, executive claims to power in each area might swing wildly administration to administration. Republicans might cede much of their regulatory authority back to Congress and Democrats might cede their war-making authority. We might even find some equilibrium between the branches as a result of these pendulum swings by changing presidential administrations.

Yet with rare exceptions, we do not in fact see much swing from presidential administration to administration in terms of claims to ever increasing executive power.[107] In the war powers space, our focus here, presidents that rise to power on campaign promises to rein in executive wartime overreach typically see those priorities soften once they are exercising that power themselves. Perhaps more surprisingly, Congress as a whole does not itself act inclined to assert or protect its constitutional prerogatives in the war powers space and others.

Daryl Levinson and Richard Pildes in their seminal work, "*Separation of Parties, Not Powers*," have recognized that the Madisonian ideal of checks and balances among the branches may simply not match reality.[108] In their view, the culprit, as recognized by Justice Jackson in Youngstown,[109] is the two party system, the result of which is that "the practical distinction between party-divided and party-unified government rivals in significance, and often dominates, the constitutional distinction between the branches in predicting and explaining interbranch political dynamics."[110] Levinson and Pildes's theory may well account for some of Congress's actions toward the president, in particular Congress's acquiescence to the president's agenda during times of unified government (though see chapters by both Tama and by Kreps and Kriner in this volume assessing the conditions in which congressional pushback to presidential foreign policy can occur across party divides and even in periods of unified government).[111] But it does not account for the unbalance between the president and Congress in their relative claims to power. Levinson acknowledges elsewhere that individual members of Congress may simply find it politically beneficial to leave foreign policy and war powers to the president.[112] And the president, in turn, may find it politically necessary to assume responsibility where Congress declines to exercise it.

But politics is not the only reason Congress has increasingly ceded power over war and foreign affairs to the president. There is a significant institutional reason that the president assumes and retains power at the expense of Congress: the work of the entrenched executive branch bureaucracy. The features I discuss in this chapter that lead the executive branch to reach for power and protect it once claimed are features that Madison expected of all the branches but that all but one lack. The result is not a balance of powers but rather an increasingly lopsided power-sharing arrangement.

Nevertheless, the result of this aggrandizement of power in the executive branch is not entirely the imperial president the framers feared. The person of the president does not wield perfect control over the executive-branch bureaucracy, and thus the power that accrues in it is not entirely theirs alone. This is the question of presidential control. As a result, the bureaucracy can simultaneously serve to aggrandize and entrench the president's power vis-à-vis the other branches and act as a constraint on that president's ability to act alone.

That the president does not directly and immediately wield all the power that inheres in the executive branch does not mean that some deep state cabal is doing so in their stead. There is no organizer and wielder of the executive power to rival that of the president's administration. Nevertheless, while not unitary or sentient, the executive branch bureaucracy has genuine force and is replete with institutional norms and proclivities and biases; on the whole its influence can be charted and predicted. And while the career bureaucracy is unelected, it is not lacking in formal, politically legitimate authority. In fact it is created and empowered by both Congress and the president, the very political entities whose power it also checks.

Conclusion

As this discussion of the modern history of war powers practice and the case study of January 6, 2021, demonstrate, executive branch power dynamics cannot be satisfactorily explained by a "deep state" or a #Resistance approach to bureaucracy and the separation of powers. The bureaucracy is not some invisible hand wielding the reins of power in lieu of the politically elected leadership; nor can it alone save us from politically elected leadership should the president seek total power. The career bureaucracy does provide some constraint on all presidents, including would-be tyrants. And when it operates in conjunction with the other branches, specifically Congress, their combined efforts may be both necessary and sufficient to rein in attempts at autocracy. But constraint on the president is not the bureaucracy's sole function in the separation of powers, and it is offset by its service to the steady expansion and entrenchment of executive power. Indeed, while the bureaucracy regularly constrains individual *presidents*, on the whole it has served more as a bulwark of presidential war power than as a check on the *presidency* over the course of the last half century.

Presidential power in military affairs has grown considerably in the years since 9/11 — indeed this accrual had begun decades before — and the bureaucracy has played an often unappreciated but critical role in abetting and codifying this expansion. Each president since George W. Bush has called to varying degrees for rolling back at least some of the precedents of his predecessors. And yet, once in office the institutional engine hums along uninterrupted; the inexorable ratcheting upward of presidential power continues unabated. The executive-branch bureaucracy will continue to foster the steady accretion of power in the executive for as long as it finds no counterpart in Congress to push it back.

Notes

1. Data from the *Trump Twitter Archive* using the search term "Deep State." *Trump Twitter Archive*, last accessed April 25, 2024, https://www.thetrumparchive.com/?searchbox=%22%5C%22deep+state%5C%22%22.

2. Doug Bandow, "The Deep State Thwarted Trump's Afghanistan Withdrawal," *The American Conservative*, May 20, 2021, https://www.theamericanconservative.com/the-deep-state-thwarted-trumps-afghanistan-withdrawal/.

3. Monmouth University Polling Institute, "Monmouth University Poll, Question 45, USMONM.031918.R34," Monmouth University Polling Institute, Cornell University (Ithaca, NY: Roper Center for Public Opinion Research, 2018), Survey question.

4. See below at notes 28–30 and accompanying text.

5. See below at notes 24–27 and accompanying text.

6. See generally Rebecca Ingber, "Bureaucratic Resistance and the National Security State," *Iowa Law Review* 104 (2018): 139; Rebecca Ingber, "The Obama War Powers Legacy and the Internal Forces That Entrench Executive Power," *American Journal of International Law* 110 (2016): 680 [hereinafter Obama War Powers Legacy]; Rebecca Ingber, "Co-Belligerency," *The Yale Journal of International Law* 42 (2017): 67; Rebecca Ingber, "International Law Constraints as Executive Power," *Harvard International Law Journal* 57 (2016): 49; Rebecca Ingber, "Congressional Administration of Foreign Affairs," *Virginia Law Review* 106 (2020): 395.

7. See, for example, Robert S. Taylor, "Contingency Planning for Presidential Interference with the Election," *Lawfare*, August 4, 2020, https://www.lawfareblog.com/contingency-planning-presidential-interference-election; Lolita C. Baldor, "Top General Says No Role for Military in Presidential Vote," *Associated Press*, August 28, 2020, https://apnews.com/article/virus-outbreak-election-2020-ap-top-news-politics-racial-injustice-a979ad8beceacd77c692e42448cf7b82; Dakota S. Rudesill, "Preventing a Military Decision About Who Won a Disputed Election," Just Security, October 29, 2020, https://www.justsecurity.org/73047/preventing-a-military-decision-about-who-won-a-disputed-election; Ryan Goodman and Steve Vladeck, "The Untold Power of Bill Barr to Direct US Military Forces in Case of 'Civil Unrest,'" *Just Security*, June 9, 2020, https://www.justsecurity.org/70672/the-untold-power-of-bill-barr-to-direct-us-military-forces-in-case-of-civil-unrest; Deborah Pearlstein, "Preparing the Public for a Contested Election," *Just Security*, July 14, 2020, https://www.justsecurity.org/71352/preparing-the-public-for-a-contested-election; Rosa Brooks, Opinion, "What's the Worst That Could Happen?" *Washington Post*, September 3, 2020, https://www.washingtonpost.com/outlook/2020/09/03/trump-stay-in-office/?arc404=true. *Cf.* Cole Blum, "Overwhelming Opposition to the Trump Administration's Attempts to Militarize Protest Response," *Human Rights First*, June 9, 2020, https://www.humanrightsfirst.org/resource/overwhelming-opposition-trump-administration-s-attempts-militarize-protest-response (aggregating responses by former DoD officials to Trump's threats to deploy the military against domestic protests).

8. See, for example, Ashton Carter et al., "All 10 Living Former Defense Secretaries: Involving the Military in Election Disputes Would Cross into Dangerous Territory," *Washington Post*, January 3, 2021, https://www.washingtonpost.com/opinions/10-former-defense-secretaries-military-peaceful-transfer-of-power/2021/01/03/2a23d52e-4c4d-11eb-a9f4-0e668b9772ba_story.html. It has since been reported that Liz Cheney orchestrated the defense secretary op-ed "because she was so worried about what Trump might do." Susan B. Glasser, "Forced to Choose Between Trump's 'Big Lie' and Liz Cheney, the House G.O.P. Chooses the Lie," *New Yorker*, May 6, 2021, https://www.newyorker.com/news/letter-from-bidens-washington/forced-to-choose-between-trumps-big-lie-and-liz-cheney-the-house-gop-chooses-the-lie. *Cf.* Taylor, *above at* note 4; Robert Burns, "Milley Says He Was Wrong to Accompany Trump on Church Walk during George Floyd Protests," *Military Times*, June 11, 2020, https://www.militarytimes.com/news/your-military/2020/06/11/milley-says-he-was-wrong-to-accompany-trump-on-church-walk-during-george-floyd-protests.

9. "What Trump Said to Supporters on Jan. 6 Before their Capitol Riot," *The Wall Street Journal*, January 12, 2021, https://www.wsj.com/articles/what-trump-said-to-supporters-on-jan-6-before-their-capitol-riot-11610498173; Greg Miller, Greg Jaffe, and Razzan Nakhlawi, "A Mob Insurrection Stoked by False Claims of Election Fraud and Promises of Violence Restoration," *Washington Post*, January 10,

2021, https://www.washingtonpost.com/national-security/trump-capitol-mob-attack-origins/2021/01/09/0cb2cf5e-51d4-11eb-83e3-322644d82356_story.html; Martin Pengelly, "'Hang Mike Pence': Twitter Stops Phrase Trending After Capitol Riot," *Guardian*, January 10, 2021, https://www.theguardian.com/us-news/2021/jan/10/hang-mike-pence-twitter-stops-phrase-trending-capitol-breach.

10. Lindsay P. Cohn and Steve Vladeck, "The Election and the Military," *Lawfare* (November 2, 2020), https://www.lawfareblog.com/election-and-military; "The Posse Comitatus Act and Related Matters: The Use of the Military to Execute Civilian Law," Congressional Research Service, November 6, 2018, https://fas.org/sgp/crs/natsec/R42659.pdf; Scott R. Anderson and Michel Paradis, "Can Trump Use the Insurrection Act to Deploy Troops to American Streets?," *Lawfare*, June 3, 2020, https://www.lawfareblog.com/can-trump-use-insurrection-act-deploy-troops-american-streets.

11. US Senate, "Examining the U.S. Capitol Attack: A Review of the Security, Planning, and Response Failures on January 6," at 3–4, 2021, https://www.rules.senate.gov/imo/media/doc/Jan%206%20HSGAC%20Rules%20Report.pdf [hereinafter *Senate Report*].

12. Meghann Myers and Howard Altman, "This is Why the National Guard Didn't Respond to the Attack on the Capitol," *Military Times*, January 7, 2021, https://www.militarytimes.com/news/your-military/2021/01/07/this-is-why-the-national-guard-didnt-respond-to-the-attack-on-the-capitol (quoting an anonymous "former Trump cabinet member" as demanding an investigation into the attack, implying that Trump had installed Acting Secretary of Defense Chris Miller for "nefarious reasons."); Dave Goldiner and Chris Sommerfeldt, "'Stunned': D.C. National Guard Chief Says Pentagon Brass Delayed Deployment During Capitol Riot for over Three Hours," *Daily News*, March 3, 2021, https://www.nydailynews.com/news/politics/us-elections-government/ny-capitol-riot-national-guard-senate-hearing-20210303-vs7ymgkdrbckppluusnbvr2tde-story.html (discussing some officials' blame of Trump administration officials for the delay).

13. *The Capitol Insurrection: Unexplained Delays and Unanswered Questions: Hearing Before the H. Comm. on Oversight & Reform*, 117th Cong. (2021) (testimony of Christopher C. Miller, Former Acting Secretary, Department of Defense) [hereinafter *Miller Testimony*]. There are diverging accounts on what caused the delay in sending the National Guard, which was stationed down the street, to the Capitol during the attack. DC National Guard chief William Walker testified that at 1:49 p.m., he "received a frantic call from then chief of U.S. Capitol Police, Steven Sund, where he informed me that the security perimeter at the Capitol had been breached by hostile rioters." *Examining the January 6th Attack on the U.S. Capitol, Part II: Before the S. Comm. on Homeland Sec. & Governmental Affs. and the S. Comm. on Rules & Admin.*, 117th Cong. 3 (2021) (statement of William J. Walker, Commanding General, District of Columbia National Guard) [hereinafter *Walker Written Statement*]. He "immediately" alerted Army leadership, and then

had the Guardsmen prepared, loaded onto busses, and moved closer to the Capitol, so that they would be prepared once he received authorization to mobilize. *Id.* at 4. That authorization, according to Walker, did not arrive until 5:08 p.m. *Id.* On the Pentagon side, Miller asserts that he approved the "activation and mobilization of the full D.C. National Guard" at 3:00 p.m. *The Capitol Insurrection: Unexplained Delays and Unanswered Questions: Before the H. Comm. on Oversight and Reform*, 117th Cong. 8 (2021) (statement of Christopher C. Miller, Former Acting Secretary of Defense, Department of Defense) [hereinafter *Miller Written Statement*]. Robert Salesses, senior official performing the duties of the Assistant Secretary of Defense, testified that "mobilization" only included sending the National Guard to the armory, not deploying them to the Capitol. *Examining the January 6th Attack on the U.S. Capitol, Part II: Before the S. Comm. on Homeland Sec. & Governmental Affs. and the S. Comm. on Rules & Admin.*, 117th Cong. (2021) (testimony of Robert Salesses, Assistant Secretary of Defense, Homeland Defense and Global Security Department of Defense) [hereinafter *Salesses Testimony*]. Authorization to deploy the National Guard to the Capitol was not given by Miller until 4:32 p.m. *Examining the January 6th Attack on the U.S. Capitol, Part II: Before the S. Comm. on Homeland Sec. & Governmental Affs. and the S. Comm. on Rules & Admin.*, 117th Cong. 6 (2021) (statement of Robert Salesses, Assistant Secretary of Defense, Homeland Defense and Global Security Department of Defense) [hereinafter *Salesses Written Statement*]. There was yet a further delay that remains unaccounted for: Miller's 4:32 p.m. authorization to Army Secretary McCarthy was not communicated to Walker until 5:08. *Walker Written Statement, supra* note 10, at 4. During his testimony, Miller maintained that he acted with "sprint speed" and that any criticism of the Pentagon's actions during the attack were grounded in politics and a lack of understanding of how the military operates. *Miller Written Statement, supra* note 10, at 8–11. This appears to conflict with Walker's testimony that he had the National Guard waiting on busses in anticipation of the need for quick action, and that once he received authorization, had them at the Capitol in approximately twelve minutes. *Walker Written Statement, supra* note 10, at 4. When asked to account for the thirty-six minutes delay by Congressman Ro Khanna, Miller did not offer a response. *Miller Testimony, supra* note 10. Salesses similarly could not account for the 4:32 p.m. to 5:08 p.m. delay and admitted that there were communication failures. *Salesses Testimony, supra* note 10. Whatever the reason, a total of three hours and nineteen minutes passed between Sund's initial call to Walker and Walker's receipt of approval from the Pentagon. *Walker Written Statement, supra* note 10, at 4.

14. There is evidence that at least some officials in relevant positions at the Pentagon acted bizarrely that day. On January 8, the Department of Defense released a timeline of the events that transpired during the Capitol attack in preparation for a congressional hearing. Department of Defense, untitled, last accessed June 25, 2020, https://media.defense.gov/2021/jan/11/2002563151/-1/-1/0

/planning-and-execution-timeline-for-the-national-guards-involvement-in-the-january-6-2021-violent-attack-at-the-us-capitol.pdf [hereinafter *DoD Timeline*]. However, the timeline did not exactly match subsequent testimony and news reports. The DoD timeline states that authorization to mobilize the National Guard was given at 3:04 p.m., but it does not distinguish mobilization to the armory and actual deployment to the Capitol, giving the appearance that the DoD responded quicker than it did. *Id*. The timeline further does not account for the delay between the 3:04 p.m. authorization to mobilize, the 4:32 authorization to deploy, and the subsequent communication of that authorization from Army Secretary McCarthy to DC National Guard chief Walker at 5:08. *Id*. There were other conflicting accounts from DoD leadership in the days that followed. Lieutenant General Charles Flynn, Michael Flynn's brother, was among the army leaders on the 2:22 p.m. call when Sund requested support, yet he was not included in the DoD timeline, and he repeatedly denied that he was involved until later admitting it to the Post. *Id*. See also Dan Lamothe, Paul Sonne, Carol D. Leonnig, and Aaron C. Davis, "Army Falsely Denied Flynn's Brother was Involved in Key Part of Military Response to Capital Riot," *Washington Post*, January 22, 2021, https://www.washingtonpost.com/national-security/flynn-national-guard-call-riot/2021/01/20/7f4f41ba-5b4c-11eb-aaad-93988621dd28_story.html. There were also conflicting reports on the restrictions the secretary of defense placed on the National Guard in the days leading up to January 6. Walker testified that in the leadup to January 6, he was denied certain authorities he deemed "standard"—namely the authority to employ a "Quick Reaction Force" (QRF) or "to move Guardsmen supporting MPD to move from one traffic control point to another"—requiring instead that he would need to seek additional approval from the secretary of the Army to do so. *Walker Written Statement*, *supra* note 10, at 3. See also *Senate Report*, *supra* note 8, at 80. Walker described the order as "unusual," testifying that he had never encountered such restrictions in his nineteen years of service and noting that he had received immediate approval during the protests of the summer of 2020. *Walker Written Statement*, *supra* note 10, at 3. Miller's written statement to Congress asserted that his "order gave General Walker full discretion to employ the QRF to respond quickly as needed based on the situation, subject only to the secretary of the Army's requirement that General Walker provide him with a 'concept of operations'—a reasonable and normal requirement in deploying a QRF that could be met in a matter of seconds with an oral briefing." *Miller Written Statement*, *supra* note 10, at 7. Miller's live testimony muddied the waters further. He stated that he had not placed restrictions on the deployment of the QRF, but had only issued "guidance that [he] wanted to be involved." *Miller Testimony*, *supra* note 10. He stated in his live testimony that "Walker had full authority to deploy" at 3:09 p.m., yet this conflicted with his written statement and responses he made in earlier live testimony that his approval was contingent on receiving and approving a "concept of operation," which he did at 4:32 p.m. *Miller Testimony*, *supra* note 10; *Miller Written Statement*, *supra* note 10 at 7.

15. In fact, in testimony to Congress, former acting secretary of defense Chris Miller suggested this risk factored into his reticence to deploy forces to the Capitol, though he simultaneously blamed the "media" for "heighten[ing]" his own concerns through "commentary ... about the possibility of a military coup or that advisors to the President were advocating the declaration of martial law." *Miller Written Statement, supra* note 10, at 5 (stating that "[n]o such thing was going to occur on my watch but these concerns, and hysteria about them, nonetheless factored into my decisions regarding the appropriate and limited use of our Armed Forces to support civilian law enforcement during the Electoral College certification. My obligation to the Nation was to prevent a constitutional crisis. That, in addition to the limited request from the Mayor for D.C. National Guard deployment distanced from the Capitol, is why I agreed only to deploy our Soldiers in areas away from the Capitol, avoiding amplifying the irresponsible narrative that your Armed Forces were somehow going to be co-opted in an effort to overturn the election.").

16. *Senate Report, supra* note 8, at 26.

17. *Walker Written Statement, supra* note 10, at 4.

18. See, for example, Dan Lamothe, "As Troop Levels Swell in D.C., National Guard Commander Says He Believes He Has City Officials' Trust," *Washington Post*, January 16, 2021, https://www.washingtonpost.com/national-security/national-guard-dc-inauguration/2021/01/16/c46256ee-5835-11eb-89bc-7f51ceb6bd57_story.html; Howard Altman, "Up to 21,000 National Guard Troops Now Authorized in DC for Biden Inauguration," *Military Times*, January 14, 2021, https://www.militarytimes.com/news/your-military/2021/01/14/national-guard-dc-presence-will-swell-to-26000-for-biden-inauguration; photograph of Troops Stationed Outside Department of State, January 2021, on file with author.

19. "Capital Breach Cases," Department of Justice, last accessed June 24, 2021, https://www.justice.gov/usao-dc/capitol-breach-cases; Katie Benner and Adam Goldman, "Justice Dept. Pursues at Least 150 Suspects in Capitol Riot," *New York Times*, January 15, 2021, https://www.nytimes.com/2021/01/11/us/politics/capitol-riot-justice-department-investigation.html.

20. On the evening of January 6, 2021, in the aftermath of the violent attack on the Capitol, President Trump tweeted: "These are the things and events that happen when a sacred landslide election victory is so unceremoniously & viciously stripped away from great patriots who have been badly & unfairly treated for so long. Go home with love & in peace. Remember this day forever!" Donald Trump (@realdonaldtrump), *Trump Twitter Archive*, January 6, 2021, https://www.thetrumparchive.com and on file with author.

21. See Jack Goldsmith, *Power and Constraint: The Accountable Presidency After 9/11* (New York: W.W. Norton & Company, 2012), at 31–33. See generally Richard Posner and Adrian Vermeule, *The Executive Unbound: After the Madisonian Republic* (New York: Oxford University Press, 2010); David Dyzenhaus, *The Constitution of Law: Legality in a Time of Emergency* (Cambridge: Cambridge University Press, 2006).

22. See generally Adrian Vermeule, *Law's Abnegation: From Law's Empire to the Administrative State* (2016).

23. See Vermeule, *Law's Abnegation*; Harold Hongju Koh, "Why the President (Almost) Always Wins in Foreign Affairs: Lessons of the Iran-Contra Affairs," *The Yale Law Journal* 97, no. 7 (1988): 1255, 1305; David Rudenstine, *The Age of Deference: The Supreme Court, National Security, and the Constitutional Order* 3 (New York: Oxford University Press, 2016); Eric A. Posner, "Deference to the Executive in the United States After September 11: Congress, the Courts, and the Office of Legal Counsel," *Harvard Journal of Law & Public Policy* 35, no. 1 (2012): 213, 215; Eric A. Posner and Adrian Vermeule, *Terror in the Balance: Security, Liberty, and the Courts* 3 (New York: Oxford University Press, 2007) ("When national emergencies strike, the executive acts, Congress acquiesces, and courts defer.").

24. Juliet Eilperin, Lisa Rein, and Marc Fisher, "Resistance from Within: Federal Workers Push Back Against Trump," *Washington Post*, January 31, 2017, https://www.washingtonpost.com/politics/resistance-from-within-federal-workers-push-back-against-trump/2017/01/31/c65b110e-e7cb-11e6-b82f-687d6e6a3e7c_story.html?utm_term=.9a16aa0d20ae.

25. See, for example, @ALT_DOJ, *Twitter*, https://twitter.com/alt_doj?lang=en (last visited May 25, 2021) (calling itself "[t]he unofficial 'Resistance' DOJ.") Also, "Why this U.S. Civil Servant Runs a Rogue Twitter Account Against Trump," CBC Radio, April 27, 2017, https://www.cbc.ca/radio/thecurrent/the-current-in-washington-april-27-2017-1.4086913/why-this-u-s-civil-servant-runs-a-rogue-twitter-account-against-trump-1.4086924: "There are now at least 50 so-called 'alternative' government Twitter accounts that say they are run by government staffers, tweeting out criticism of Trump and even leaked information."). See also, discussing various "resistance" measures, Rebecca Ingber, "An Ode to the Career Bureaucracy," *Take Care*, January 10, 2018, https://takecareblog.com/blog/an-ode-to-the-career-bureaucracy.

26. See, for example, "*About*," Uphold the Oath, last accessed June 20, 2021, https://upholdtheoath.org/about. Uphold the Oath describes itself as "a digital grassroots project that celebrates America's federal civil servants and encourages them to publicly reaffirm their commitment to the ideals listed in the oath of office."

27. See, for example, Jennifer Nou, "Bureaucratic Resistance from Below," *Yale Journal on Regulation*, Notice & Comment, November 16, 2016, https://www.yalejreg.com/nc/bureaucratic-resistance-from-below-by-jennifer-nou. Nou describes the methods of "resistance" available to civil servants, including "slow down," "build[ing] a record," "leak[ing] [information]," "enlist[ing] internal inspectors general," "su[ing] the agency," and "resigning," noting that the mechanisms come at a cost and that "[t]here are thorny legal and moral questions about whether and when this is a good idea.; Jennifer Nou, "Civil Servant Disobedience," *Chicago-Kent Law Review* 94 (2019): 349, 379–380. Nou extols the virtues while acknowledging some risks to civil service "resistance."

28. See, for example, Donald J. Trump (@realDonaldTrump), *Trump Twitter Archive*, last accessed September 15, 2019, 2:20 p.m., https://www.thetrumparchive.com/?searchbox=%22%5C%22deep+state%5C%22%22: "I am fighting the Fake (Corrupt) News, the Deep State, the Democrats, and the few remaining Republicans In Name Only (RINOS, who are on mouth to mouth resuscitation), with the help of some truly great Republicans, and others. We are Winning big (150th Federal Judge this week)!" Donald J. Trump (@realDonaldTrump), *Trump Twitter Archive*, September 6, 2018, 7:19 a.m., https://www.thetrumparchive.com/?searchbox=%22%5C%22deep+state%5C%22%22: "The Deep State and the Left, and their vehicle, the Fake News Media, are going Crazy — & they don't know what to do. The Economy is booming like never before, Jobs are at Historic Highs, soon TWO Supreme Court Justices & maybe Declassification to find Additional Corruption. Wow!" Donald J. Trump (@realDonaldTrump), *Trump Twitter Archive*, October 17, 2019, 11:06 p.m., https://www.thetrumparchive.com/?searchbox=%22%5C%22deep+state%5C%22%22: "Tonight, we forcefully condemn the blatant corruption of the Democrat Party, the Fake News Media, and the rogue bureaucrats of the Deep State. The only message these radicals will understand is a crushing defeat on November 3, 2020! #KAG2020." Jonathan Lemire features statements by Trump supporters such as Newt Gingrich, Sean Spicer, and Sean Hannity decrying a "deep state" seeking to undermine or, in the words of Sean Hannity, "destroy" the President; "Trump White House Sees "Deep State" Behind Leaks, Opposition," *Associated Press*, March 14, 2017, https://apnews.com/article/donald-trump-ap-top-news-sean-spicer-politics-363ccdba946548bf-a4b855ae38d1797a. Hayley Miller quotes Senior White House Advisor Stephen Miller as stating that a "deep state operative" was behind the Ukraine story, and warning of a "deep state" threat to "democracy"; "Fox News' Chris Wallace Lashes Out at Stephen Miller: 'Enough with the Rhetoric,'" *HuffPost*, September 29, 2019, https://www.huffpost.com/entry/fox-news-chris-wallace-stephen-miller_n_5d90d8c0e4b0e9e7604e677c. Lee Moran quotes several tweets by the former President during his presidency calling the executive branch bureaucracy a "deep state"; "Donald Trump's Old Tweets About the 'Deep State' Are Coming Back to Haunt Him," *Huffpost*, September 20, 2018, 4:38 a.m., https://www.huffpost.com/entry/donald-trump-deep-state-lie_n_5ba35119e4b069d5f9cff523.

29. See, for example, Ryan Gingeras, "Last Rites For a 'Pure Bandit': Clandestine Service, Historiography and the Origins of the Turkish 'Deep State,'" *Past & Present* 206, no. 1 (2010): 151; Ryan Gingeras, "How the Deep State Came to America: A History," *War on the Rocks*, February 4, 2019, https://warontherocks.com/2019/02/how-the-deep-state-came-to-america-a-history.

30. Jonathan Lemire, "Trump White House."

31. See, for example, Michael J. Glennon, *National Security and Double Government* (New York: Oxford University Press, 2015, arguing that political control over government by the president and Congress is a "myth," which conceals the true operation of government by bureaucrats; Jonathan Turley, "The Rise of the Fourth

Branch of Government," *Washington Post*, May 24, 2013, https://www.washingtonpost.com/opinions/the-rise-of-the-fourth-branch-of-government/2013/05/24/c7faaad0-c2ed-11e2-9fe2-6ee52d0eb7c1_story.html, asserting that "[o]ur carefully constructed system of checks and balances is being negated by the rise of a fourth branch," which "represents perhaps the single greatest change in our system of government since the founding" while the actual elected politicians "act like mere bystanders to the work of government." Glennon later clarified his view with respect to the Trump Administration, stating that he did not view Trump as powerless against the executive branch bureaucracy. See Leon Neyfakh, "Can the 'Secret Government' Save Us?" *Slate*, November 14, 2016, https://slate.com/news-and-politics/2016/11/can-the-secret-government-save-us-from-donald-trump.html.

32. Jack Goldsmith, "Paradoxes of the Deep State," in *Can It Happen Here?* ed. Cass Sunstein (New York: Dey Street Books, 2018), 105.

33. Goldsmith, "Paradoxes of the Deep State."

34. Quinta Jurecic, "DAG Rosestein Appoints Robert Mueller as Special Counsel," *Lawfare*, May 17, 2017, https://www.lawfareblog.com/dag-rosenstein-appoints-robert-mueller-special-counsel; Miles Taylor, "I Am Part of the Resistance Inside the Trump Administration," *New York Times*, September 5, 2018, https://www.nytimes.com/2018/09/05/opinion/trump-white-house-anonymous-resistance.html, an op-ed by formerly anonymous, and now-named former, Department of Homeland Security chief of staff member describing the alleged work of many Trump appointees to "preserve our democratic institutions while thwarting Mr. Trump's more misguided impulses until he is out of office." Mark Landler and Maggie Haberman describe acts taken by Trump-appointed officials to try to contain his behavior, including reportedly removing from his desk a letter authorizing withdrawal from the trade agreements with South Korea and NAFTA; "Jim Mattis Compared Trump to 'Fifth or Sixth Grader,' Bob Woodward Says in Book," *New York Times*, September 4, 2018, https://www.nytimes.com/2018/09/04/us/politics/woodward-trump-book-fear.html?module=Uisil. Nick Wadhams and Saleha Mohsin report that former US national security advisor John Bolton ordered aid released to Ukraine, possibly against the president's wishes; "State Department Freed Ukraine Money Before Trumps Says He Did," *Bloomberg*, November 9, 2019,https://www.bloomberg.com/news/articles/2019-11-09/state-department-freed-ukraine-money-before-trump-says-he-did?embedded-checkout=true. Paul Sonne, Josh Dawsey and Missy Ryan reported that former Defense Secretary Jim Mattis resigned after Trump—disregarding advice from Mattis and others—decided to withdrawal troops from Syria and Afghanistan; "Mattis Resigns After Clash with Trump over Troop Withdrawal from Syria and Afghanistan," *Washington Post*, December 20, 2018, https://www.washingtonpost.com/world/national-security/trump-announces-mattis-will-leave-as-defense-secretary-at-the-end-of-february/2018/12/20/e1a846ee-e147-11e8-ab2c-b31dcd53ca6b_story.html. Carter,

supra note 5, including, among the signatories, former secretary of defense Mark Esper, who served under Trump from 2019–2020.

35. Among those scholars who share a "unitary executive" theory of presidential control over the executive branch, there are more and less aggressive versions of the theory. Some, like Gary Lawson, posit that all executive action is the president's, her appointees are her appendages, and that, as a result, the president may nullify agency actions of which she does not approve. Gary Lawson, "The Rise and Rise of the Administrative State," *Harvard Law Review* 107, no. 6 (1994): 1231, 1244. For others, the "unitary executive theory" is narrowly tailored to an argument about removal power over officers, which they see as falling within the president's plenary powers. See generally Richard A. Epstein, "Executive Power in Political and Corporate Contexts," *University of Pennsylvania Journal of Constitutional Law* 12 (2010): 277.

36. See, for example, US Government Manual, "The Government of the United States," last accessed June 29, 2021, https://www.usgovernmentmanual.gov/ReadLibraryItem.ashx?SFN=Myz95sTyO4rJRM/nhIRwSw==&SF=VHhnJrOeEAnGaa/rtk/JOg==; US Department of State, "Department of State Organizational Chart," 2021, https://www.state.gov/wp-content/uploads/2021/06/DOS-Org-Chart-May-2021.pdf; Department of Defense, "Organizational and Management of the Department of Defense 5–11," 2019, https://fas.org/irp/agency/dod/org-man.pdf; Office of the Director of National Intelligence, "U.S. National Intelligence An Overview" (2013), https://www.odni.gov/files/documents/USNI%202013%20Overview_web.pdf.

37. See generally Ingber, "Bureaucratic Resistance and the National Security State."

38. Ingber, "Bureaucratic Resistance and the National Security State."

39. Ingber, "Bureaucratic Resistance and the National Security State," 175–181.

40. Ingber, "Bureaucratic Resistance and the National Security State," 173–197.

41. Ingber, "Bureaucratic Resistance and the National Security State," 190–193.

42. Ingber, "Bureaucratic Resistance and the National Security State," 193–195.

43. Ingber, "Bureaucratic Resistance and the National Security State," 195–197.

44. Christopher Miller, "Statement by Acting Secretary Miller on Full Activation of D.C. National Guard," US Department of Defense, January 6, 2021, https://www.defense.gov/Newsroom/Releases/Release/Article/2464427/statement-by-acting-secretary-miller-on-full-activation-of-dc-national-guard.

45. See, for example, Bill Kristol (@BillKristol), Twitter, January 6, 2021, 5:06 p.m., https://twitter.com/BillKristol/status/1346941194316754951?s=20; Kristol states, in a tweet with three siren emojis, "Amazing statement by the Secretary of Defense. Note whom Secretary Miller and Chairman Milley did NOT speak to: President Trump. We have had something close to the de facto invoking of the 25th amendment."

46. See, for example, Jamie Dupree (@JamieDupree), Twitter, January 6, 2021, 5:14 p.m., https://twitter.com/jamiedupree/status/1346943293171658755; the Capitol

Hill reporter wrote, "This is nuts. The Acting Secretary of Defense acknowledging that he and the Joint Chiefs Chairman did not discuss deploying the National Guard with President Trump—but rather with VP Pence and Congressional leaders."

47. Exec. Order No. 11,485, 3 C.F.R. 143 (1970); "*About Us*," DC National Guard, last accessed June 20, 2021, https://dc.ng.mil/About-Us. See also 32 U.S.C. § 1.

48. Intriguingly, later reports suggest that at least in then acting secretary of defense Chris Miller's account, he had cleared the use of the National Guard with the president the day prior, and that *the President himself* had suggested the potential need for significant troops. Adam Ciralsky, "'The President Threw Us Under the Bus': Embedding with Pentagon Leadership in Trump's Chaotic Last Week," *Vanity Fair*, January 22, 2021, https://www.vanityfair.com/news/2021/01/embedding-with-pentagon-leadership-in-trumps-chaotic-last-week?utm_source=twitter&utm_medium=social&utm_campaign=onsite-share&utm_brand=vanity-fair&utm_social-type=earned.

49. *Senate Report*, *supra* note 8, at 30–36.

50. *Senate Report*, 32n168, citing DHS Briefing to the Committees, March 1, 2021.

51. Exec. Order No. 12,333, 3 C.F.R. § 200 (1982); "Office of Intelligence and Analysis Intelligence Oversight Program and Guidelines," US Department of Homeland Security, January 19, 2017, https://www.dhs.gov/sites/default/files/publications/office-of-intelligence-and-analysis-intelligence-oversight-program-and-guidelines.pdf.

52. *Examining the January 6th Attack on the U.S. Capitol, Part II: Before the S. Comm. on Homeland Sec. & Governmental Affs. and the S. Comm. on Rules & Admin.*, 117th Congress. 2 (2021), statement of Jill Sanborn, Assistant Director Counterterrorism Division, Federal Bureau of Investigation; *Examining the January 6th Attack on the U.S. Capitol: Before the S. Comm. on Homeland Sec. & Governmental Affs. and the S. Comm. on Rules & Admin.*, 117th Cong. (2021), testimony of Robert J. Contee III, Acting Chief of Police, Metropolitan Police Department of the District of Columbia.

53. *Walker Written Statement*, *supra* note 10, at 3; *Senate Report*, *supra* note 8, at 70, 80–83.

54. Oona A. Hathaway, "National Security Lawyering in the Post-War Era: Can Law Constrain Power?" *UCLA Law Review* 68 (2021): 2, 25, noting the "relatively limited number of lawyers in Congress with clearance to examine classified matters"; Ann Koppuzha, "Secrets and Security: Overclassification and Civil Liberty in Administrative National Security Decisions," *Albany Law Review* 80 (2017): 501, 512–513; Vicki Divoll, "The "Full Access Doctrine": Congress's Constitutional Entitlement to National Security Information from the Executive," *Harvard Journal of Law & Public Policy* 34 (2011): 493, 525–527.

55. For further exploration of several of the mechanisms I discuss in this section, considered through the case study of the Obama Administration's approach to war powers, see Ingber, "Obama War Powers Legacy," *supra* note 3.

56. See, for example, Daphna Renan, "Presidential Norms and Article II," *Harvard Law Review* 131, no. 8 (2018): 2187.

57. Bruce A. Green and Rebecca Roiphe, "May Federal Prosecutors Take Direction from the President?" *Fordham Law Review* 87, no. 5 (2019): 1817.

58. As but one example, the George W. Bush Administration flouted normal procedures for receiving legal guidance as a means of ensuring legal advice that would support its aggressive executive power positions; in order to do so, it established what became known as a "War Council"—a subset of likeminded lawyers who could be counted upon to sanction the president's policies outside normal channels. See, for example, Jack Goldsmith, *The Terror Presidency: Law and Judgment Inside the Bush Administration* (New York: W. W. Norton, 2009).

59. See, for example, Ingber, "Obama War Powers Legacy," *supra* note 3.

60. See, for example, Ingber, "Obama War Powers Legacy"; *The Investigation into the Removal of Nine U.S. Attorneys in 2006: Hearing Before the H. Comm. on the Judiciary*, 110th Cong. (2008), statement of Glenn A. Fine, Inspector General, US Department of Justice.

61. See, for example, Respondents' Memorandum Regarding the Government's Detention Authority Relative to Detainees Held at Guantanamo Bay, *In re* Guantanamo Bay Detainee Litig., No. 05–1509, 2008 U.S. Dist. Lexis 86147, (D.D.C. October 24, 2008).

62. Compare the legal authority to detain proffered in the Bush Administration's briefs at the end of 2008 with the new standard the Obama Administration put forward in its brief of March 13, 2009. The former: "An 'enemy combatant' is an individual who was part of or supporting Taliban or al Qaeda forces, or associated forces that are engaged in hostilities against the United States or its coalition partners. This includes any person who has committed a belligerent act or has directly supported hostilities in aid of enemy armed forces." Boumediene v. Bush, 579 F. Supp. 2d 191, 196 (D.D.C. 2008), citing Government's Brief Statement of the Legal Basis for Detention of Petitioners, Boumediene v. Bush, 579 F. Supp. 2d 191 (D.D.C. 2008) (No. 04–1166). The latter: In addition to those responsible for the 9/11 attacks or harboring them, "[t]he President also has the authority to detain persons who were part of, or substantially supported, Taliban or al-Qaida forces or associated forces that are engaged in hostilities against the United States or its coalition partners, including any person who has committed a belligerent act, or has directly supported hostilities, in aid of such enemy armed forces." Respondents' Memorandum Regarding the Government's Detention Authority Relative to Detainees Held at Guantanamo Bay, *In re* Guantanamo Bay Detainee Litig., 787 F. Supp. 2d 5 (D.D.C. 2011) (Nos. 08–442, 05–0763, 05–1646, 05–2378). There were other changes in the briefs, in particular their discussion of the underlying

authorities, but the main substantive change to the detention standard itself was the addition of the word "substantially" before "supported."

63. Charlie Savage, "Accused 9/11 Mastermind to Face Civilian Trial in N.Y.," *New York Times*, November 13, 2009, https://www.nytimes.com/2009/11/14/us/14terror.html; Charlie Savage, "U.S. Wary of Example Set by Tribunal Case," *New York Times*, August 27, 2010, https://www.nytimes.com/2010/08/28/us/28gitmo.html.

64. These were rules that Congress enacted to protect detainees from politicized prosecution, which the Obama Administration interpreted as also creating hurdles to *aiding* the detainees. Charlie Savage, *Power Wars: The Relentless Rise of Presidential Authority and Secrecy*, New York: Little, Brown, 2017, 317–319; Unlawfully Influencing Action of Military Commission and United States Court of Military Commission Review, 10 U.S.C. § 949b(a)(2): "No person may attempt to coerce or, by any unauthorized means, influence— ... (C) the exercise of professional judgment by trial counsel or defense counsel."

65. Reply Brief of Appellant United States of America, Carroll v. Trump, Nos. 20–3977, 20–3978 (2d Cir. June 7, 2021).

66. Carroll v. Trump, Nos. 20–3977, 20–3978 (2d Cir. June 7, 2021), at 1.

67. Charlie Savage, "Biden Administration Punts on Due Process Rights for Guantánamo Detainees," *New York Times*, July 9, 2021, https://www.nytimes.com/2021/07/09/us/politics/guantanamo-detainees-due-process.html, discussing the positions taken in a brief still under seal.

68. Memorandum from John C. Yoo, Deputy Assistant Attorney Gen., Office of Legal Counsel, to William J. Haynes II, Gen. Counsel of the Dep't of Def., Re: Military Interrogation of Alien Unlawful Combatants Held Outside the United States, (March 14, 2003); Memorandum from Jay S. Bybee, Assistant Attorney Gen., Office of Legal Counsel, to Alberto R. Gonzales, Counsel to the President, Re: Standards of Conduct for Interrogation Under 18 U.S.C. 2340–2340A, (August 1, 2002); Memorandum from Jay S. Bybee, Assistant Attorney Gen., Office of Legal Counsel, to William J. Haynes II, Gen. Counsel, Dep't of Def., Re: The President's Power as Commander in Chief to Transfer Captured Terrorists to the Control and Custody of Foreign Nations (March 13, 2002); Memorandum from Jay S. Bybee, Assistant Attorney Gen., Office of Legal Counsel, to William J. Haynes II, Gen. Counsel, Dep't of Def., Re: Potential Legal Constraints Applicable to Interrogations of Persons Captured by U.S. Armed Forces in Afghanistan (February 26, 2002); Memorandum from Jay S. Bybee, Assistant Attorney Gen., Office of Legal Counsel, to Alberto R. Gonzales, Counsel to the President, Re: Status of Taliban Forces Under Article 4 of the Third Geneva Convention of 1949 (February 7, 2002); Memorandum from Jay S. Bybee, Assistant Attorney Gen., Office of Legal Counsel, for Alberto R. Gonzales, Counsel to the Pres. and William J. Haynes II, Gen. Counsel of the Dep't of Def., Re: Application of Treaties and Laws to al Qaeda and Taliban Detainees (January 22, 2002).

69. *The President's Constitutional Authority to Conduct Military Operations Against Terrorists and Nations Supporting Them*, 25 Op. O.L.C. 188 (2001); *Authority of the President Under Domestic and International Law to Use Military Force Against Iraq*, 26 Op. O.L.C. 143, 152 (2002).

70. David Fontana places the number at twenty thousand; "Executive Branch Legalisms," *Harvard Law Review* 126, no. 1 (2011): 21. See also "Federal Workforce Data," Office of Personnel Management, March 2021, https://www.fedscope.opm.gov/employment.asp; filter by Occupation, White Collar, Legal and Kindred, categorizing just the number of "general attorneys" in the executive branch at over forty thousand.

71. See, for example, US Department of Justice, "Memorandum for Attorneys of the Office: Best Practices for OLC Legal Advice and Written Opinions," July 16, 2010, https://www.justice.gov/sites/default/files/olc/legacy/2010/08/26/olc-legal-advice-opinions.pdf [hereinafter "BEST PRACTICES FOR OLC"]; OLC "is frequently asked to opine on issues of first impression that are unlikely to be resolved by the courts—a circumstance in which OLC's advice may effectively be the final word on the controlling law."

72. See generally Ingber, "Obama War Powers Legacy," *supra* note 3.

73. The OLC library of published opinions can be found here: Office of Legal Counsel, "*Opinions*," US Department of Justice, last accessed June 20, 2021, https://www.justice.gov/olc/opinions-main.

74. Judiciary Act of 1789, ch. 20, 1 Stat. 73; "And there shall also be appointed a ... attorney-general for the United States ... whose duty it shall be to ... give his advice and opinion upon questions of law when required by the President of the United States, or when requested by the heads of any of the departments."

75. See generally Randolph D. Moss, "Executive Branch Legal Interpretation: A Perspective from the Office of Legal Counsel," *Administrative Law Review* 52, no. 4 (2000): 1303; Bob Bauer, "The National Security Lawyer, In Crisis: When the 'Best View' of the Law May Not Be the Best View," NYU School of Law, Public Law Research Paper No. 17–08, 2017, https://papers.ssrn.com/sol3/papers.cfm?abstract_id=2931165#references-widget.

76. Mary B. DeRosa, "National Security Lawyering: The Best View of the Law as a Regulative Ideal," *Georgetown Journal of Legal Ethics* 31, no. 2 (2018): 277, 288. Some would like to see an office of executive branch government lawyers take on an even more formal judicial-like role. Bruce Ackerman, *The Decline and Fall of the American Republic*, Cambridge, MA: 2010, 146.

77. See "Best Practices for OLC," 1.

78. *Id.* 2, "OLC's analyses may appropriately reflect the fact that its responsibilities also include facilitating the work of the Executive Branch and the objectives of the President, consistent with the law. As a result, unlike a court, OLC will, where possible and appropriate, seek to recommend lawful alternatives to Executive Branch proposals that it decides would be unlawful."

79. Dawn E. Johnsen, "Faithfully Executing the Laws: Internal Legal Constraints on Executive Power," *UCLA Law Review* 54, no. 6 (2007): 1559, 1581, explaining that OLC is not a "disinterested arbiter" and viewing its mandate as "help[ing] the President achieve desired policies in conformity with the law."

80. See generally Jack Goldsmith, "Executive Branch Crisis Lawyering and the 'Best View,'" *Georgetown Journal of Legal Ethics* 31, no. 2 (2018): 261.

81. See generally Richard H. Pildes, "Law and the President," *Harvard Law Review* 125, no. 6 (2012): 1381.

82. See Michael V. Hayden, Director of the Central Intelligence Agency, CIA Director's Address at Duquesne University Commencement, May 4, 2007. "At a confirmation hearing a couple of years ago, one of the senators asked if I would respect American civil liberties in carrying out my intelligence tasks. I, of course, said that I would. I also told him that I had a duty to play aggressively 'right up to' the line. Playing back from the line protected me but didn't protect America. I made it clear I would always play in fair territory, but that there would be chalk dust on my cleats"; cited in Jamil N. Jaffer, "The Ethics of National Security Lawyering: A Response to Jeh Johnson," *Yale Law & Policy Review* 31, no. 1 (2012): 173, 179, n. 21).

83. "Best Practices for OLC," 3.

84. Ingber, "Obama War Powers Legacy.,"

85. There are, by contrast, numerous examples of government positions that impose new limits on government action as a matter of *policy*. The 2013 Presidential Policy Guidance released by the Obama Administration to regulate lethal targeting operations outside "areas of active hostilities" is one good example. Exec. Office of the President, "Procedures for Approving Direct Action Against Terrorist Targets Located Outside the United States and Areas of Active Hostilities," 2013, https://www.justice.gov/oip/foia-library/procedures_for_approving_direct_action _against_terrorist_targets/download#:~:text=This%20Presidential%20Policy%20 Guidance%20(PPG,areas%20of%20active%20hosti%20lities.

86. *Deployment of United States Armed Forces into Haiti*, 18 Op. O.L.C., 173, 179 (1994).

87. *Deployment of United States Armed Forces into Haiti*, 18 Op. O.L.C., 173.

88. *Deployment of United States Armed Forces into Haiti*, 18 Op. O.L.C.

89. *Deployment of United States Armed Forces into Haiti*, 18 Op. O.L.C., 177–179, 178n7.

90. *Deployment of United States Armed Forces into Haiti*, 18 Op. O.L.C., 178n7.

91. *Deployment of United States Armed Forces into Haiti*, 18 Op. O.L.C., 179.

92. *Authority to Use Military Force in Libya*, 35 Op. O.L.C., 20, 9 (2011) (quoting *Proposed Deployment of United State Armed Forces into Bosnia*, 19 Op. O.L.C. 327, 333 (1995)).

93. *Authority to Use Military Force in Libya*, 35 Op. O.L.C. 20 (2011).

94. *Authority to Use Military Force in Libya*, 35 Op. O.L.C., 8 (emphasis added).

95. *Authority to Use Military Force in Libya*, 35 Op. O.L.C., 4.

96. *Authority to Use Military Force in Libya*, 35 Op. O.L.C., 13.

97. *April 2019 Airstrikes Against Syrian Chemical-Weapons Facilities*, 42 Op. O.L.C., 1 (2018).

98. *April 2019 Airstrikes Against Syrian Chemical-Weapons Facilities*, 42 Op. O.L.C.

99. See, for example, Authorization for Use of Military Force, Pub. L. No. 107–40, 115 Stat. 224 (2001);,codified at 50 U.S.C. § 1541 (2012). Rebecca Ingber, "*Legally Sliding into War*," *Just Security*, March 15, 2021, https://www.justsecurity.org/75306/legally-sliding-into-war.

100. Rebecca Ingber, "Interpretation Catalysts and Executive Branch Legal Decisionmaking," *The Yale Journal of International Law* 38, no. 2 (2013): 359, 366–377.

101. Ingber, "Interpretation Catalysts and Executive Branch Legal Decisionmaking."

102. Ingber, "Interpretation Catalysts and Executive Branch Legal Decisionmaking."

103. See *supra* note 64.

104. *Id.*

105. I define and discuss these terms in depth in Ingber, "Obama War Powers Legacy," 685–687.

106. Elena Kagan, "Presidential Administration," *Harvard Law Review* 114 (2001): 2245. See also discussion of "unitary executive" theory, *supra* note 32.

107. Views will differ on the extent to which Republican and Democrat administrations have varied significantly in their war powers practice in modern times. Most notoriously, the George W. Bush Administration's OLC issued two extremely expansive war powers opinions. See *supra* text accompanying note 66. But the Obama Administration did not withdraw them. Moreover, that administration itself took quite controversial steps in the war powers realm, including prosecuting the conflict in Libya without congressional authorization, deploying the use of drones broadly, and interpreting the 2001 AUMF to include authorization to use force against ISIS.

108. Daryl J. Levinson and Richard H. Pildes, "Separation of Parties, Not Powers," *Harvard Law Review* 119, no. 8 (2006): 2311.

109. Youngstown Sheet & Tube Co. v. Sawyer, 343 U.S. 579 (1952).

110. Levinson and Pildes, "Separation of Parties, Not Powers," 2315.

111. Levinson and Pildes, "Separation of Parties, Not Powers," 2338.

112. Daryl J, Levinson, "Empire-Building Government in Constitutional Law," *Harvard Law Review* 118, no. 3 (2005): 915, 955.

CHAPTER ELEVEN

A Post-GWOT Syndrome?
Institutional Response, Public Opinion, and the Future of US Foreign Policy

Sarah E. Kreps and Douglas L. Kriner

More than four decades after the United States watched Saigon fall after a costly decade-long war, an even longer American conflict in Afghanistan came to a similar end, with civilians being the ultimate casualty, racing for safety amid a chaotic, hasty withdrawal. The precipitous collapse of the Afghan army and government in the face of a Taliban onslaught led tens of thousands of Afghani citizens, many of whom had collaborated openly with American forces, to flock to Kabul International Airport, the last toehold of the US military presence in the country. While US intelligence agencies had warned the administration of the deteriorating situation on the ground as the American withdrawal accelerated in the summer of 2021, they utterly failed to predict the speed and totality of the collapse.[1] As a result, the world watched in horror as news outlets broadcast images of military transport planes jam-packed with fleeing civilians. Most gut-wrenching of all was video showing desperate Afghans clinging to the transport planes themselves as they took off, with at least two falling from the sky to their deaths.[2] The parallels to the fall of Saigon and the desperate evacuations from the roof of the US embassy with civilians clinging to the helicopters were obvious. America's longest war ended in much the same ignominious fashion as its erstwhile longest war.

Vietnam triggered shockwaves throughout the American political system. The imperial presidencies of Lyndon Johnson and Richard Nixon were replaced with an era of "congressional resurgence."[3] After the Paris

Peace Accords, Congress barred funding for any future combat operations in Vietnam and placed a ceiling on the number of US troops that it could station in the country. The move essentially blocked the Ford Administration's efforts to enforce the terms of the accords and defend South Vietnam, even preventing it from resuming airstrikes, which led Henry Kissinger and other hawks to place the blame for "losing" Vietnam squarely at the foot of Congress. The congressional resurgence also had broader effects on Cold War strategy and efforts to contain Communist expansion. The Tunney and Clark amendments in 1975–1976 precluded the Ford Administration from sending covert assistance to anti-Communist forces in Angola, and the Boland amendments of the 1980s made illegal the Reagan Administration's efforts to provide covert aid to the Nicaraguan Contras. In the latter case, the Reagan Administration then worked to circumvent the legislative constraints by parsing the language in the Boland amendments to conclude that it could still control US Contra policy through the National Security Council, triggering an interbranch battle and constitutional crisis that ultimately threatened Reagan's survival in office.[4]

More broadly, policymakers and scholars alike spoke of a "Vietnam syndrome" in which the American public had become so scarred by the experience in Vietnam that it had become reluctant to support any major US military intervention unless plainly and inextricably tied to defending core national interests.[5] The Reagan Administration, in particular, viewed this mindset as a fundamental threat to America's position on the world stage and took small steps to reassert American military power with interventions that were decidedly modest in scale, such as the invasion of Grenada. Moreover, with the Weinberger Doctrine—named after the Defense Secretary who declared that the US should only resort to force when vital national interests are at stake, when the political and military objectives are clear, and when there exists "some reasonable assurance" that the use of force will enjoy broad public and congressional support—the administration openly accepted the political reality that presidential flexibility in foreign affairs was constrained.[6] Only the twin shocks of the end of the Cold War and the fantastic success of the modernized American blitzkrieg in the first Persian Gulf War broke this fundamental dynamic and set the stage for the extended military response to the terrorist attacks of September 11, 2001.

Two decades later, after the conclusion of the Global War on Terror (GWOT), or at least the parts that directly involved US personnel deployed abroad en masse, what has happened to the domestic political constraints on US foreign policy? In this concluding chapter, we reexamine the nature of both the formal institutional and the informal political checks on presidential conduct of military policy more than twenty years after 9/11. We first take a summary view of the institutional response to post-9/11 presidential power grabs—or the relative lack thereof. We then analyze observational survey data about mass attitudes in the United States to examine the broader question of whether America has witnessed the emergence of a "post-GWOT syndrome"—an instinctive reluctance to avoid the entanglements of the preceding two decades—by tracking the extent of isolationist sentiments and mapping these views onto those of political elites. Finally, we discuss the implications of the transformed post-GWOT political environment for the future conduct of US foreign policy.

Institutional Response

While some scholars warned that the tangible impact of the congressional resurgence after Vietnam was less than meets the eye,[7] on almost any metric the formal institutional response to presidential overreach and the disastrous policy choices it enabled in the years after the 9/11 attacks was far more feeble. Perhaps nowhere is this distinction clearer than in congressional efforts to revisit and revise its own role in authorizing disastrous wars. Two years before the Paris Peace Accords, Congress repealed the Gulf of Tonkin Resolution, removing the imprimatur of legislative sanction for the fighting. While the move was undoubtedly more symbolic than substantive and American forces would continue fighting and dying in Southeast Asia for years to come, it set the stage for more concrete efforts to curtail presidential power. A series of amendments between 1969 and 1973 cut off funds for military operations first in Laos and Thailand, then in Cambodia, and finally in Vietnam itself. In 1973, Congress passed, over President Nixon's veto, the War Powers Resolution, which sought to check the president's capacity to deploy US troops abroad for extended periods without congressional authorization. Finally, through measures from amendments precluding the use of funds to aid anti-Communist rebels in Angola to the Church Committee's uncovering systematic abuses of the intelligence community and covert operations, Congress pushed back against presidential supremacy in the foreign policy arena.[8]

By contrast, in March 2023 the Senate finally voted to repeal the 2002 Authorization to Use Military Force (AUMF) against Iraq, as well as a 1991 precursor that authorized the first Gulf War. Even this purely symbolic congressional reassertion prompted stark criticism from leading opponents, including Senate Minority Leader Mitch McConnell, who warned that repeal would undermine executive flexibility to respond to emerging and protean security threats.[9] Even though the Senate bill would leave unscathed the 2001 AUMF, which administrations have interpreted so broadly as to justify military force in theaters never anticipated by its drafters, including in the Philippines, Niger, and Kenya, the measure died in the House.[10]

Similarly, while Congress has always been more reactive than proactive in foreign affairs, the aftermath of the protracted and costly wars in Iraq and Afghanistan failed to change the underlying dynamic. As Fordham shows in his chapter, members stand to gain little from opposing ex ante presidential policies that later prove costly. As such they have strong incentives to withhold judgment until things unfold. President Obama pointed to this very dynamic when he explained the logic for deciding not to enforce his "red line" and order strikes against the Assad regime for its use of chemical weapons. Instead Obama decided, surprisingly, to first ask for congressional authorization. Without forcing members to go on record via an authorization vote, "Congress will sit on the sidelines, snipe. If it works, the sniping will be less. If it doesn't, a little more."[11]

To be sure, such ex post pushback—and presidential anticipation of it and the political costs it can impose—can be effective. President Obama openly admitted that it entered his decision calculus and encouraged him not to respond. This, in turn, opened the door for greater Russian intervention and eventually its formal entry into the war to prop up Assad in 2015.[12] However, twenty years of war, tens of thousands of American soldiers killed or wounded, and trillions of dollars spent have done little to incentivize Congress to exert a more proactive brake on military adventurism.

The bureaucratic response to the GWOT thus far has also erected fewer impediments to military adventurism than the response to Vietnam in the military and defense establishment. After Vietnam, core bureaucratic elements of the national security state spearheaded doctrinal changes that circumscribed presidential freedom of action as commander in chief. The lessons of Vietnam, at least as perceived by many in the defense and military establishment, first informed the Weinberger Doctrine and then the follow-on Powell Doctrine, both of which created strong norms that the United States should only use force when certain political conditions are met, and then it should do so overwhelmingly. But as Walter LaFeber has argued, almost immediately after its greatest triumph, the swift coalition victory and subsequent exit from Iraq in the 1990–1991 Gulf War, the Powell Doctrine began to unravel. The end of the Cold War and the emergence of a series of humanitarian crises in Africa, the Balkans, and beyond led the Clinton Administration to articulate a different and more expansive vision for the proper exercise of American military might.[13] And then the 9/11 attacks allowed Dick Cheney, Donald Rumsfeld, and Paul Wolfowitz to dispatch with the Powell Doctrine altogether and pursue first a small-footprint war with uncertain ultimate aims in Afghanistan and then a war for overt regime change with no clear exit strategy in Iraq.[14]

As Ingber shows in her chapter, the very norms that guide executive branch lawyering routinely produce opinions that bolster and even expand executive power. This was perhaps never truer than in the immediate aftermath of 9/11. For example, when Congress refused to include the Bush administration's preferred language authorizing it "to deter and preempt any future acts of terrorism or aggression against the United States," Bush went to the Office of Legal Counsel to execute an end-run around the legislature. OLC obliged and argued that Congress could not—either through the new AUMF or through the War Powers Resolution—"place any limits on the President's determinations as to any terrorist threat, the amount of military force to be used in response, or the method, timing, and nature of the response. These decisions, under our Constitution, are for the President alone to make."[15] Subsequent opinions by OLC walked back some of its most extraordinary claims of unfettered presidential authority over the conduct of military affairs made in the immediate aftermath of 9/11.[16] However, by the early 2010s, the legal bureaucracy within the executive branch was once again issuing opinions that dramatically expanded presidential power. In a pair of opinions by OLC and the State Department, the Obama Administration unilaterally determined that the US military intervention in Libya did not reach the threshold of "hostilities" as defined by the War Powers Resolution and therefore the administration need not abide by the resolution's withdrawal clock absent congressional authorization.[17]

Moreover, when the bureaucracy has most successfully constrained presidential freedom of action in military affairs in recent years it has primarily focused on thwarting presidential efforts to wind down longstanding wars. As Rudalevige discusses in his chapter, this dynamic was perhaps most prominent in the fierce resistance to President Trump's efforts to follow-through on his campaign pledge and bring the war in Afghanistan to an end. But even before then, the strategic leak of General Stanley McChrystal's pessimistic assessment—which asserted that failure to surge more troops into Afghanistan would lead to mission failure—tied President Obama's hands and all but forced him to acquiesce to the request for more troops.[18] Thus, in stark contrast to the Clinton Administration, when the military and defense establishment resisted, often strenuously, the president's desire to use force in a range of settings to pursue humanitarian objectives,[19] bureaucratic resistance in more recent years has focused more on frustrating presidential efforts to de-escalate or end post-9/11 military commitments.[20]

In sum, the institutional response to twenty years of inconclusive war has been mostly notable for its absence. While scholars continue to debate the relative influence of the congressional resurgence after Vietnam, it certainly looks more sweeping and impactful when compared to the virtual nonresponse of Congress to the dramatic developments of the two decades since 9/11. Exactly what "lessons" the defense establishment will ultimately draw from twenty years of at-best inconclusive and at-worst utterly disastrous war in Iraq and Afghanistan, and whether these will either constrain or perversely empower future presidents, is unclear. Yet, it is notable that thus far there is little evidence that the national security establishment has broadly embraced something akin to the "lessons of Vietnam" that hamstrung presidential freedom of action in military matters for almost two decades.

Congress can still increase the political costs of failed or risky foreign policies for presidents, and an entrenched and invested bureaucracy may still chafe against presidential efforts to move policy in new directions. These checks may not be any weaker than they were before 9/11; however, there is little reason to believe they have been strengthened despite the disastrous results produced by presidential policies—aided and abetted by extraordinary claims of unilateral authority to set foreign policy—over the last twenty years.

Widening Fractures within the Parties?

While there is little evidence that Congress has become any more willing to take a proactive role in shaping military affairs today than it was before 9/11, ex post congressional pushback can still be politically costly. Indeed, President Obama readily acknowledged this when he decided not to authorize retaliatory strikes in Syria unilaterally but instead first sought congressional sanction. Obama did not believe he required congressional authorization to order strikes; his statement announcing the decision made clear that he believed he possessed sufficient constitutional authority to go it alone.[21] Rather, Obama was sensitive to the political costs of moving without Congress—and he anticipated the intense criticism he would almost certainly face from congressional Republicans, armed with committee gavels and subpoena power, should the strikes fail to achieve their desired aim.[22]

Perhaps the most important finding of research challenging the old imperial presidency paradigm is that the strength of the congressional check on presidential power in foreign affairs varies with the strength of the opposition party in the legislature. Particularly in an era of ever-intensifying partisan polarization and contestation, we would expect this dynamic only to have strengthened. And indeed, partisanship remains an important driver of the frequency and intensity with which Congress uses many of the tools in its arsenal to raise the political costs of a given policy course for the president. Consider the congressional response to the calamitous withdrawal of the last American troops from Afghanistan. As the chaotic final days unfolded, many members of Congress, including a not-insignificant number of Democrats, vocally criticized the Biden Administration for its failure to anticipate the Afghan government's collapse and the disastrous implementation of the final withdrawal.[23] And yet, formal oversight of the withdrawal was largely muted. Democrats could only lose by holding embarrassing hearings and politically damaging a copartisan president, and they used their control of the gavels to limit this fallout. By contrast, the return of a Republican majority to the House following the 2022 midterms unleashed House investigators eager to shine a light on the administration's failings. Early hearings featured devastating testimony from a marine injured in the Abbey Gate terrorist attack[24] and subpoenas for classified documents sent by diplomats in Kabul to the White House in the summer of 2021.[25]

However, both presidents Obama and Trump also faced pushback from members of their own party when they strayed too far from partisan orthodoxy. And there is at least suggestive evidence within both parties of widening ideological gaps between more interventionist and isolationist wings. As Kreps and Kriner showed in their chapter, the strongest pushback to President Obama's troop surges in Afghanistan in 2009 came not from opposition party Republicans but from dovish left-wing Democrats who opposed the move on ideological, not partisan, grounds. Similarly, when President Obama ordered American military intervention in Libya in 2011 along with NATO allies, he enjoyed strong support from some members of both parties, including Senators John Kerry (D-MA) and John McCain (R-AZ). However, in an example of what Tama calls "antipresidential bipartisanship" in his chapter, Obama also faced stiff resistance from both sides of the aisle. While partisan incentives likely explain most of the Republican resistance, the split within the Democratic Party speaks to the growing willingness of many ideological doves to push back against the use of force even when ordered by a copartisan president. In the House, a resolution (H.J. Res 68) authorizing military action in Libya introduced by Alcee Hastings (D-FL) was easily defeated, with seventy Democrats joining all but eight Republicans to vote no. The same day, a second bill (H.R. 2278) that would have cut off funding for military operations in Libya unless expressly authorized by Congress also failed. However, 36 House Democrats joined 144 Republicans voting in favor of the funding cut-off, while 89 Republicans and 149 Democrats voted no.

This series of votes again speaks to Congress's reluctance to genuinely assert itself in directing foreign affairs. Legislators were perfectly willing to refuse to authorize the use of force but were unwilling to actually use the power of the purse to cut off funds for military operations. As Obama would later note, Congress's preferred modus operandi is to wait and see and blame the president should things fail to go according to plan. However, presidents value the political cover that congressional authorizations afford.[26] And while congressional sniping may not translate into concrete legislation legally compelling the president to change course, it can be both politically and militarily costly, as administrations from Reagan through Obama have openly acknowledged.

President Trump also faced criticism from segments of his own party when he strayed too far from orthodox Republican foreign policy ideas. For example, Trump sparred with Congress over the policy response to Russian interference in the 2016 election, which Trump avidly denied (except when he alleged Russia interfered to help his opponent).[27] In 2017, bipartisan majorities in both chambers passed legislation imposing sanctions on Russia for its malicious actions. And to guard against presidential interference, Congress expressly forbade Trump from unilaterally lifting the measures. Trump initially signaled his intention to refuse to comply with the mandate to impose sanctions, but he backed down in the face of bipartisan outcry on Capitol Hill.[28]

Republicans also split, particularly early in the administration, over one of President Trump's signature campaign pledges: to end the war in Afghanistan. While at first military and national security advisers successfully parried the president's attempts to accelerate the American withdrawal, in December 2018 Trump reversed course and announced the withdrawal of seven thousand US troops, roughly half the residual force still in the country. The announcement caught the Afghan government off guard and came just hours after Defense Secretary James Mattis said he would resign over disagreements with the president concerning Afghanistan.[29] Many prominent Republicans, including Senate Majority Leader Mitch McConnell, criticized the move as jeopardizing national security, and in early February the Republican-controlled Senate passed an amendment explicitly opposing a precipitous withdrawal from both Afghanistan and Syria, where American forces were battling the Islamic State. Forty-six Republicans broke with the president and voted aye, while four voted no. Democrats evenly split on the measure, with twenty-seven voting to oppose withdrawal and twenty-five voting against the measure.

To be clear, partisanship was still an incredibly powerful force in shaping congressional responses to the withdrawal. When President Trump signed a peace deal with the Taliban in February 2020 setting an early 2021 deadline for US withdrawal, most Republicans fell in line. Future House Speaker Kevin McCarthy publicly praised Trump and rallied most of the caucus behind him. Liz Cheney (R-WY) led the charge against the deal; but while many in the GOP caucus grumbled in private, few joined Cheney's efforts to express their serious concerns publicly. One Republican privately acknowledged to reporters, "This seems like a pretty crummy deal. If this were an Obama deal, we would be crushing him for it."[30] And true to form, when President Biden executed the agreement (albeit after first delaying the scheduled final withdrawal), many of the same Republicans who praised withdrawal under Trump lambasted Biden for it. Illinois Republican Adam Kinzinger railed against his colleagues' U-turn: "You can't be going out there and saying, 'This war was worthless and we need to bring the troops home' in May, and now hitting Biden for doing just that ... There's no shame anymore."[31]

The Republican flip-flopping during Trump's presidency and the longstanding split within Democratic ranks on Afghanistan from the surges forward speak to the widening fissures within both parties on questions regarding the proper use of American military might. Democrats have long struggled with intraparty tensions on foreign policy. The party nearly cleaved itself in two at the 1968 convention between its pro- and antiwar wings, and it has continued to grapple with intraparty tensions on questions of military policy—and the attendant electoral angst they could produce (including embarrassing photos of Democratic presidential candidates in tanks to "prove" their martial bona fides)[32]—ever since. The aftermath of 9/11 may have temporarily tilted the balance toward a more aggressive foreign policy stance. Every Democrat save one, California's Barbara Lee, voted for the 2001 AUMF. However, a year later 126 House Democrats voted against the 2002 Iraq AUMF, despite immense political and electoral pressure to support a popular commander in chief. Eighty-one House Democrats and twenty-nine of fifty Senate Democrats voted for it. And liberal Democrats led the opposition to escalation in Afghanistan, even under a Democratic president.

By contrast, particularly after the Vietnam War, Republicans were reliably more hawkish and unified on foreign affairs. Ronald Reagan ran in 1980 advocating a more muscular military posture that would exorcise the demons of Vietnam. Following the 1983 US invasion of Grenada, Reagan declared that the days of the United States turning its swords into plowshares and hoping others would follow had passed. "Our days of weakness are over. Our military forces are back on their feet and standing tall."[33] While Reagan's muscular foreign policy manifested itself in decidedly less than major military interventions, the first Gulf War under President George HW Bush demonstrated the unparalleled capabilities of the US military in a post-Cold War world. And George W. Bush sought to harness this awesome power in campaigns of "shock and awe" to remake the Middle East in America's image.

While most Republican politicians continued to embrace hawkish positions on Afghanistan and the war on terror generally even after Bush's exit, the election of Donald Trump and his "America First" platform seriously challenged the GOP's ideological orthodoxy. Commentators gasped when on the eve of the South Carolina Republican primary Trump called the Iraq War "a big, fat mistake" and blamed Bush for destabilizing the Middle East at the cost of $2 trillion and thousands of American lives.[34] But Republican voters agreed with Trump and he carried all but three counties and won all fifty delegates in the state.[35] Following Trump's electoral victory, the party's foreign policy establishment sought to moderate the political neophyte's impulses by surrounding him with more orthodox advisers such as Jim Mattis, H. R. McMaster, and John Bolton. Ultimately, each resigned or was fired.

Although it is still perhaps too early to tell, there is strong evidence that an isolationist turn among an important branch of the Republican Party—one that hearkens back to the party's past under Mr. Republican Robert Taft—will outlast Trump. While it is easy to dismiss the rantings of the likes of Marjorie Taylor Greene (who compared aiding Ukraine to the war in Iraq and warned that the former has brought us to the precipice of World War III), isolationist views have clearly gained traction among many political and media elites on the right.[36] In the immediate aftermath of Russia's invasion, isolationist opposition to aiding Ukraine was a distinctly minority position within the caucus. However, many establishment Republicans such as John Bolton warned that isolationism was like a virus that threatened to spread through a significant part of the Republican body politic.[37] Bolton's warning proved prophetic as the pressure on wavering Republicans to choose sides grew considerably as President Trump's bid for the 2024 Republican nomination accelerated. In his first town hall of the nascent primary campaign in May 2023, Trump blasted Ukraine aid and the alleged free-riding of our European allies, and he refused to say whether he would continue supporting Ukraine as president and even if he wanted Ukraine to win.[38] Pushing back against criticism of Trump's bombastic and falsehood-ridden town hall performance, senior campaign adviser Jason Miller retorted, "understandably, this [i.e., Trump's] vision is not shared by the failed warmongers, political losers and career bureaucratic hacks—many of whom he fired or defeated—who have created all of America's problems." Hammering home the former president's anti-militarist bona fides, Miller concluded that Trump had "an entire term with no new wars, and he's ready to do it again."[39] By April 2024, Trump's antipathy to Ukraine aid had captured a majority of the GOP House caucus as 112 Republicans voted against legislation to aid Ukraine while only 101 voted for the desperately needed funds.[40]

Perhaps the most important implications of these widening intraparty fissures for the nature of domestic checks on presidential authority in foreign affairs is that future presidents may face greater resistance to aggressive military policies in unified government than in the past. Presidents will almost certainly continue to have greater leeway when their partisan allies hold sway on Capitol Hill. However, the likelihood and intensity of congressional pushback may increasingly also depend on the relative strength of more dovish elements within both parties and the ideological orientations of the members who wield the most agenda power within the legislature. Since Vietnam, Democratic presidents have always had more to worry about from their party's left-flank; this may be even more true in the post-GWOT era, particularly on issues like Israel-Palestine that introduce additional cleavages into the Democratic ranks. Given Trump's iron grip on the party, it is unlikely that even growing isolationist sentiment within the Republican caucus would exercise a significant check on Trump should he win a second term and pursue a more muscular foreign policy. However, the reenergization of an isolationist wing within the Republican Party that Trump helped catalyze and accelerated could well hamstring a future, more establishment Republican President. Finally, the growth of the isolationist wing of the Republican Party could also serve to further complicate the decision calculus of Democratic presidents by reducing the prospects for support from across the aisle should they pursue a more aggressive foreign policy posture.

A Post-GWOT Syndrome?

Public opinion and real and anticipated changes in public willingness to support the use of force are a key mechanism in most studies asserting the continued importance of domestic political checks on presidential freedom of action in foreign affairs.[41] Congressional criticism can erode public support for war and the president's waging of it.[42] And members of Congress, in turn, respond to the proclivities and foreign policy predispositions of the American public. Indeed, Jentleson's study of public opinion shows that after Vietnam, the public's views tracked and thus—given the bottom-up influence of the public in a democracy—reinforced the prescription of the Weinberger Doctrine that emphasized interventions directed toward core security interests.[43]

In the aftermath of Vietnam, it was widely assumed that after three costly and protracted wars in a little more than thirty years the American people had lost their stomach for large-scale interventions.[44] Has public opinion on fundamental questions of foreign policy changed dramatically since 9/11? Going beyond the discussion above, which leaned on contributions from the volume and historical examples, here we look at the contemporary period and particularly at trends over the last twenty years with an eye toward prognostication, examining public attitudes to assess possible future policy directions.

Since 1956, the American National Election Study (ANES) has asked a question measuring isolationist sentiments. Respondents are asked whether they agree or disagree with the following statement: "This country would be better off if we just stayed home and did not concern ourselves with problems in other parts of the world." To assess changes in isolationist sentiment over time and how it varies across partisan groups we estimated a logit regression with partisan-year interactions. The model also controls for gender, age, race/ethnicity, and educational attainment.

Figure 11.1 presents the predicted probability of the median Republican, Democrat, and independent supporting an isolationist foreign policy posture by year.[45] Several trends stand out. First, among both Democrats and Republicans we see evidence generally consistent with the premise of a "Vietnam syndrome." In 1976, in the first survey following the conclusion of the Vietnam War, isolationist sentiment surged among both Democrats and Republicans. Moreover, isolationist sentiments—while a minority view among supporters of both parties—was generally much higher through the 1980s than it had been before Vietnam, with the exception of 1980, which may be a result of the Iranian Revolution and hostage crisis.

After 9/11, isolationist sentiment declined significantly among Republicans. In 2000—the year that George W. Bush campaigned against nation building abroad—the median Republican had a roughly one in four chance of saying the United States would be better off if it remained disengaged from the world's problems. In 2002 and 2004, that figure fell to just 0.13. Among Democrats, there was a similar, though smaller, drop in isolationist sentiment after 9/11. However, this decline was short-lived. By 2008, isolationist sentiments had returned to or even exceeded their pre-9/11 levels among both parties in the mass public. In 2012, both the median Democrat and the median Republican had roughly a one in three chance of embracing isolationism—the highest in the fifty-plus year timeline.

This shift in attitudes is even more pronounced among independents. Interestingly, we see very little evidence of a post-Vietnam increase in isolationism among Americans who did not back either of the major political parties. Throughout the 1970s and 1980s, the predicted probability of the median independent holding isolationist foreign policy views ranged between 0.20 and 0.25. Similarly, we see little evidence of a major shift in views after the terrorist attacks of September 11. The estimates for 2002 are virtually identical to 2000, and there is little change in the subsequent two surveys as well. However, by 2012 isolationist sentiment had surged among independents, with the median independent now being almost equally likely to express isolationist versus more interventionist

A POST-GWOT SYNDROME? 351

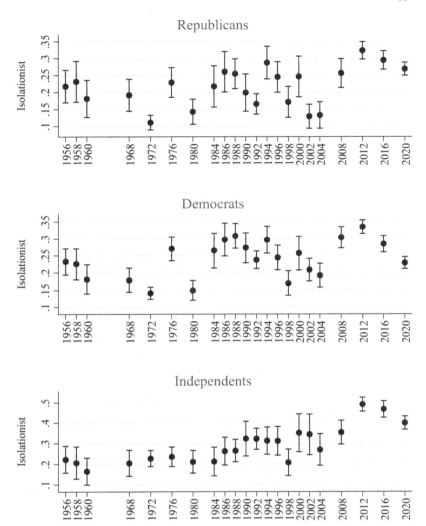

FIGURE 11.1. Isolationist Sentiment by Party, 1956–2020
Note: Predicted probability of median respondent expressing support for isolationism. I-bars present 95 percent confidence intervals.

foreign policy preferences. From 2012 to 2020, independents have been significantly more likely to embrace isolationism than either Democrats or Republicans, all else equal.

While isolationism—at least on this metric—remains a minority position among the American public, there is strong evidence of a popular backlash against aggressive, interventionist foreign policies in the wake of the protracted, immensely costly in blood and treasure, and ultimately inconclusive central fronts of the war on terror. Indeed, recent levels of support for isolationist sentiments observed in the ANES data exceeds that observed after Vietnam. This provides additional insight into at least one, oft-overlooked aspect of Donald Trump's political appeal—his incredibly blunt challenge to foreign policy orthodoxy, particularly on the right but also on the left. From the moment Trump rode down the golden escalator to announce his candidacy in August 2015, his campaign was high on personality and charisma but short on issue specificity, with a few exceptions. Trump clearly articulated a tough-on-immigration platform, pledging to build a wall across the border with Mexico. Decidedly less orthodox for a Republican, Trump also pledged a more isolationist turn in American foreign policy. He expressed open disdain for many international commitments and alliances, pledged to put America First, and promised to end the "stupid wars" of his predecessors.[46]

While foreign policy concerns are rarely highly salient in peacetime elections, the analyses in figure 11.1 show evidence of a clear surge in isolationism among Republicans and independents in the lead-up to the 2016 election. There is evidence that Trump capitalized on these shifts. In the primaries, Trump performed particularly well with voters who held isolationist positions generally, as well as on the specific issues of Syrian refugees and trade.[47] In the general election, Trump's opponent voted for the Iraq War in the Senate and advocated as secretary of state for a major escalation of the war in Afghanistan, tripling the number of troops there in 2009 to 2010. While demonstrating the impact of foreign policy on voting patterns is exceedingly difficult, Republican candidates lost ground electorally in communities that suffered the highest casualty rates in a series of elections in the mid-2000s.[48] Trump returned many voters in these communities to the Republican fold in 2016, significantly improving on Romney's 2012 performance in high-casualty states and counties.[49]

More generally, the rise in isolationist sentiment in the second decade after 9/11 suggests a potentially powerful political constraint on presidential flexibility in military affairs. After twenty years of costly and inconclusive warfare, a significant share of Americans—and particularly electorally pivotal independents—are skeptical of aggressively interventionist foreign policies. This increased popular baseline also creates opportunities for more isolationist politicians to arise, gain traction, and erode public support even further. If policymakers after Vietnam showed heightened sensitivity to the need to cultivate congressional and public support before using force abroad, then the incentives should be even stronger in the contemporary period.

An important difference between such informal political checks and institutional ones is that the former set is more ephemeral. In his fifth letter, the anti-Federalist writer Cato warned that "opinions and manners are mutable and may not always be a permanent obstruction against the encroachments of government."[50] However, until there is a significant change in the underlying political environment, presidents have strong incentives to anticipate the possibility of popular backlash to large-scale military deployments not immediately tied to vital national interests that risk incurring clearly visible costs in lives and treasure.

Constraints and Opportunities

At both the elite and mass level, there is evidence of a significant backlash against the failed policies that produced the costly and inconclusive war on terror and a resurgence of isolationist sentiment. At least in the contemporary political environment, this shift has greatly raised the political costs presidents should expect to pay if they choose to pursue a post-9/11 style large-scale, extended-duration deployment of US troops to advance a foreign policy objective. There are strong reasons to believe that a significant share of the public is predisposed to be skeptical of any such venture. Moreover, while presidents have long had to anticipate resistance from members of the opposition party, the growth of more dovish or even isolationist wings in both parties increases the prospect of bipartisan congressional pushback that could prove politically costly.[51] Even though the formal institutional checks on presidential freedom of action remain weak, the political checks against bold foreign policy gambits may be significantly strengthened twenty years after 9/11.

However, presidents still enjoy broad political latitude to pursue a range of foreign policy objectives provided they can do so in ways that attract little public scrutiny and therefore remain removed from the public agenda. The willingness of members of Congress and the public alike to continue to support massive levels of military spending greatly aid presidential flexibility in this regard.

While more Americans may be skeptical of interventionist foreign policies today than even in the aftermath of Vietnam, this rise in isolationist sentiment has not given rise to a concomitant demand for cuts in military spending. Since 1980, the ANES has asked respondents their opinions on whether military spending should be increased or decreased.[52] To assess changes in support for military spending cuts since 9/11 and how they compare with earlier shifts, we estimate a logit regression with partisan-year interactions. The model also controls for gender, age, race/ethnicity, and educational attainment.

Figure 11.2 presents the predicted probability of the median Republican, Democrat, and independent supporting military spending cuts by year. As we would expect, throughout the 1980s Democrats were more likely to support military spending cuts than Republicans, though not overwhelmingly so. With the end of the Cold War and the promise of a peace dividend, support for defense cuts increased significantly among both Democrats and Republicans with the median Democrat being more likely than not to support military spending cuts, and the median Republican having over a 0.40 predicted probability of doing so. But then as the 1990s progressed, support for military spending cuts decreased among both Democrats and Republicans alike. While support for defense spending cuts has risen slightly since 2000 among Democrats, it remains lower than it was in the late 1980s and early 1990s. Among Republicans, support for military spending cuts has remained roughly flat since 2000, far below its levels even in the 1980s as President Reagan spearheaded a massive increase in military spending. Finally, among independents support for military spending cuts has also been mostly flat since 2000. Moreover, the level of support for spending cuts throughout the last twenty years is far lower than it was in the 1980s and 1990s.

Similarly, there is little serious appetite for significant cuts in defense spending in Congress, even in an era of intense budgetary fights on Capitol Hill that have repeatedly brought the United States to the brink of default. Even the most ardent voices championing a more restrained role for the United States in the world are not calling for significant reductions in military spending.[53]

Broad public and elite support for maintaining large defense budgets gives presidents great latitude to pursue a range of foreign policy objectives through alternate means that do not require massive and extended deployments of US troops overseas, such as Operations Enduring and Iraqi Freedom. Dramatic advances in drone warfare and related technologies allow presidents to project power across the globe with little to no risk to US forces, which helps keep their political visibility low.[54]

This dynamic also allowed the Biden Administration to lead a massive assistance program to Ukraine and in so doing to counter Russian expan-

A POST-GWOT SYNDROME?

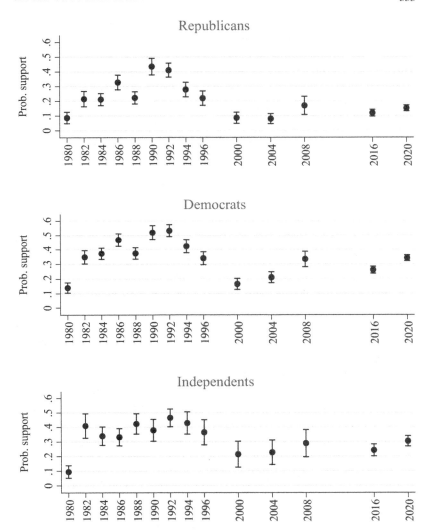

FIGURE 11.2. Support for Cutting Defense Spending by Party, 1980–2020
Note: Predicted probability of median respondent expressing support for cutting defense spending. I-bars present 95 percent confidence intervals.

sionism while also sending a signal of US resolve to China should it move against Taiwan. In the first year after the Russian invasion, the United States sent more than $75 billion to Ukraine, with more than $40 billion of that total being military assistance.[55] While growing opposition in the Republican House significantly delayed the 2024 aid package—at tangible cost to the Ukrainian war effort[56]—both chambers eventually passed the legislation overwhelmingly, paying little credence to those who warned about the significant monetary cost. Perhaps equally telling and important, despite its massive scale the administration's efforts to aid Ukraine continue to fly largely under the political radar. For example, from August 2022 through April 2024, the war in Ukraine never topped 2 percent in Gallup's surveys of public beliefs about the most important problem facing the United States.[57] Conditional on indirect American involvement and a war in Ukraine far removed from the public consciousness, the political pressure to change course will remain minimal.

* * *

The terrorist attacks of 9/11 provided an exogenous shock that allowed President George W. Bush to launch some of the boldest and most massive military strikes in American history. After twenty years of fighting, thousands of US soldiers dead, tens of thousands wounded, and trillions of dollars spent, the wars in Iraq and Afghanistan have finally come to an end. But despite the wars' staggering costs, failure to achieve their desired ends, and widespread public disillusionment, the extent to which the developments of the last twenty years have produced a chastened, more constrained presidency are debatable.

At least since World War II, the most important and influential checks on presidents' freedom of action as commander in chief have been political rather than institutional. The almost complete absence of any serious institutional response to the disastrous presidential policies of the last two decades ensures this will continue to be the case in a post-GWOT era. Nevertheless, the informal political checks on presidential military adventurism may be strengthened. In the contemporary political environment, presidents contemplating significant deployments of US troops abroad have had strong incentives to proceed with caution. In 2017, an ambush led to the deaths of four Army Green Berets in Niger and became a political liability for President Trump. To insulate themselves from political pushback, presidents of both parties have made increasing recourse to new types of limited interventions to project power while avoiding risk to uniformed American personnel. Technologies such as drones, which avoid these political liabilities, can, as President Obama admitted, lead an administration to "view drone strikes as a cure-all for terrorism"[58] because they insulate presidents from these costs.[59] As Jack Goldsmith and

Matthew Waxman have observed, candidate Obama had campaigned on ending the Bush Administration's onerous deployments, but faced with the political need to be seen as strong on counterterrorism, as president he increasingly relied on a "quick-and-dirty expression of military and covert power" through cyber, drones, and special operations that gave the president considerable latitude in his foreign policy.[60]

These two sets of factors—the end of long and costly wars on the one hand and ways to shield the American people from the costs of projecting power on the other—act in countervailing ways. The specter of the former serves as a vivid reminder that aggressive exercise of executive authority in the military arena can come at a steep political cost. The latter gives American presidents greater possible reach combined with a capacity to minimize the prospects for political pushback. Interestingly, confronted with this transformed post-GWOT reality, both Presidents Trump and Biden have leaned into versions of a similar agenda. For Trump it was "Make America Great Again," for Biden it is "Made in America." While the two presidents have clearly articulated different visions for America's role in the world, neither has advanced an agenda that emphasizes the projection of American military might and tests the boundaries of executive and legislative authority in the same way as Presidents Bush and Obama. That is not to say that either administration has shied away from combative foreign policies. The Biden Administration has shepherded billions of dollars in aid to Ukraine, despite Russian saber-rattling that doing so threatens a wider war with NATO. And both the Biden and Trump Administrations pursued hard lines toward China, seeking to counter China's rising power on multiple fronts.[61] However, in sharp contrast with their immediate predecessors, neither Trump nor Biden has shown much inclination to consider the massive and extended deployment of US troops in combat situations to pursue their foreign policy goals.

Moreover, it is notable that after the considerable partisan rancor that long characterized the political debate in Washington over the war in Iraq,[62] both Trump and Biden have succeeded in securing broad, if far from absolute, levels of bipartisan support for their aggressive policies first toward China and now under Biden toward Russia (though as noted this has eroded considerably but not completely in the face of Trump's increasing attacks on aiding Ukraine and the mounting pressure on other Republicans to take sides). Bipartisanship does not itself ensure wise policies, and in fact it may create a false sense of security that ushers in a different type of problem: cross-partisan elite support may stifle public debate over policies that are costly and ultimately counterproductive, as it did in the aftermath of 9/11.

The most intense political fault lines in contemporary American politics fall largely along cultural battle lines.[63] Surveys consistently show Americans are more divided on cultural than economic issues.[64] And twenty years after 9/11, foreign policy concerns are far removed from the everyday concerns of most voters, even as the US spends hundreds of billions of dollars on proxy wars in the face of mounting budget deficits. Given this reality, foreign policy may be one area where presidents have opportunities to cultivate bipartisan support and secure tangible policy victories.[65] However, should future presidents push too far and try like their post-9/11 predecessors to effect change at bayonet point, they risk political backlash and costs from multiple fronts.

Notes

1. Julian Barnes, "Intelligence Agencies Did Not Predict Imminence of Afghan Collapse, Officials Say," *New York Times*, August 18, 2021, https://www.nytimes.com/2021/08/18/us/politics/afghanistan-intelligence-agencies.html.

2. "Kabul Airport: Footage Appears to Show Afghans Falling from Plane after Takeoff," *The Guardian*, August 16, 2021, https://www.theguardian.com/world/2021/aug/16/kabul-airport-chaos-and-panic-as-afghans-and-foreigners-attempt-to-flee-the-capital.

3. James Sundquist, *The Decline and Resurgence of Congress* (Washington, DC: Brookings Institution Press, 1981).

4. For a more complete discussion, see Douglas Kriner, *After the Rubicon: Congress, Presidents, and the Politics of Waging War* (Chicago: University of Chicago Press, 2010), 39–42.

5. George Herring, "The 'Vietnam Syndrome' and American Foreign Policy," *The Virginia Quarterly Review* 57 (1981): 594–612; Marvin Kalb, "It's Called the Vietnam Syndrome and It's Back," *Brookings*, January 22, 2013, https://www.brookings.edu/articles/its-called-the-vietnam-syndrome-and-its-back/.

6. For further discussion of the Weinberger Doctrine and its six tests, see Eric Alterman, "Thinking Twice: The Weinberger Doctrine and the Lessons of Vietnam," *The Fletcher Forum* 10 (1986): 93–109.

7. Barbara Hinckley, *Less Than Meets the Eye: Foreign Policymaking and the Myth of the Assertive Congress* (Chicago: University of Chicago Press, 1994).

8. For an extended discussion of congressional efforts in this era, see Julian Zelizer, *Arsenal of Democracy: The Politics of National Security from World War II to the War on Terrorism* (New York: Basic Books, 2009).

9. Ali Zaslaw and Jeremy Herb, "Senate Votes to Repeal Iraq War Power Authorizations, 20 Years After US Invasion," CNN.com, March 29, 2023, https://edition.cnn.com/2023/03/29/politics/senate-vote-aumf/index.html#:~:text=The%20White%20House%20also%20backed,been%20updated%20with%20additional%20developments.

10. Andrew Rudalevige, "The Obama Administrative Presidency: Some Late-Term Patterns," *Presidential Studies Quarterly* 46 (2016): 868–890, 883–885. Tim Kaine, "Kaine statement on 19th Anniversary of 2001 AUMF, Drone Strike Authorities in Kenya," September 18, 2020, https://www.kaine.senate.gov/press-releases/kaine-statement-on-19th-anniversary-of-2001-aumf-drone-strike-authorities-in-kenya.

11. Barack Obama, "The President's News Conference with Prime Minister John Fredrik Reinfeldt of Sweden in Stockholm, Sweden," September 4, 2013, https://www.presidency.ucsb.edu/documents/the-presidents-news-conference-with-prime-minister-john-fredrik-reinfeldt-sweden-stockholm.

12. Jiri Valenta and Leni Friedman Valenta, "Why Putin Wants Syria," *Middle East Quarterly* 23 (2016): 1–17.

13. Sarah Kreps, *Coalitions of Convenience: American Military Interventions after the Cold War* (New York: Oxford University Press, 2011).

14. Walter LaFeber, "The Rise and Fall of Colin Powell and the Powell Doctrine," *Political Science Quarterly* 124, no. 1 (2009): 71–93.

15. Memorandum from John Yoo, Deputy Assistant Attorney General to Deputy Counsel to the President, "The President's Constitutional Authority to Conduct Military Operations Against Terrorists and Nations Supporting Them," September 25, 2001, (emphasis added), http://perma.cc/X3DF-2LFY.

16. Jack Goldsmith, *The Terror Presidency: Law and Judgement Inside the Bush Administration* (New York: W.W. Norton and Company, 2007); Jack Goldsmith, *Power and Constraint: The Accountable Presidency After 9/11* (New York: W.W. Norton and Company, 2013).

17. Louis Fisher, "Military Operations in Libya: No War? No Hostilities?" *Presidential Studies Quarterly* 42, no. 1 (2012): 176–189; Trevor Morrison, "Libya, 'Hostilities,' the Office of Legal Counsel, and the Process of Executive Branch Legal Interpretation," *Harvard Law Review* 124 (2011): 62–74.

18. Risa Brooks, "Paradoxes of Professionalism: Rethinking Civil-Military Relations in the United States," *International Security* 44, no. 4 (2020): 7–44.

19. Kenneth Campbell, "Once Burned, Twice Cautious: Explaining the Weinberger-Powell Doctrine," *Armed Forces and Society* 24, no. 3 (1998): 357–374.

20. Risa Brooks, Jim Golby, and Heidi Urben, "Crisis of Command: America's Broken Civil-Military Relationship Imperils National Security," *Foreign Affairs* 100 (2021): 64–75.

21. Barack Obama, "Statement by the President on Syria," August 31, 2013, https://obamawhitehouse.archives.gov/the-press-office/2013/08/31/statement-president-syria.

22. For an extended discussion of the complicated political dynamics in play, see Kenneth Mayer, "Executive Power in the Obama Administration and the Decision to Seek Congressional Authorization for a Military Attack against Syria: Implications for Theories of Unilateral Action," *Utah Law Review 4* (2014): 821–824.

23. Aaron Blake, "Democrats Offer Some Harsh Reviews of Biden on Afghanistan," *Washington Post*, August 17, 2021, https://www.washingtonpost.com/politics/2021/08/17/democrats-offer-some-harsh-reviews-biden-afghanistan/.

24. Deirdre Walsh, "An Inured Marine Gives Searing Testimony on the Chaotic Withdrawal from Afghanistan," NPR.com, March 8, 2023, https://www.npr.org/2023/03/08/1161890168/house-republicans-hearing-withdrawal-afghanistan-biden.

25. Shannon Crawford, "House Republicans Ramp Up Investigation into Afghanistan Withdrawal," ABCNews.com, March 28, 2023, https://abcnews.go.com/Politics/house-republicans-ramp-investigation-afghanistan-withdrawal/story?id=98179889.

26. Douglas Kriner, "Obama's Authorization Paradox: Syria and Congress' Continued Relevance in Military Affairs," *Presidential Studies Quarterly* 44 (2014): 309–327.

27. Lauren Egan and Jonathan Allen, "Trump Accuses Hillary Clinton of Colluding with Russia as Crowd Chants 'Lock Her Up,'" NBC News, October 11, 2018, https://www.nbcnews.com/politics/politics-news/trump-accuses-hillary-clinton-colluding-russia-crowd-chants-lock-her-n918836.

28. For an extended discussion, see Douglas Kriner and Eric Schickler, "The Resilience of Separation of Powers? Congress and the Russia Investigation," *Presidential Studies Quarterly* 48, n. 3 (2018): 436–455.

29. Thomas Gibbons-Neff and Mujib Mashal, "U.S. to Withdraw about 7,000 Troops from Afghanistan, Officials Say," *New York Times*, December 20, 2018, https://www.nytimes.com/2018/12/20/us/politics/afghanistan-troop-withdrawal.html.

30. Lara Seligman and Daniel Lippman, "Top Allies Press Trump to Keep Some U.S. Forces in Afghanistan," Politico, March 3, 2020, https://www.politico.com/news/2020/03/03/top-allies-trump-forces-afghanistan-119694.

31. Reid Epstein and Catie Edmondson, "On Afghanistan, G.O.P. Assails the Pullout it Had Supported Under Trump," *New York Times*, September 1, 2021, https://www.nytimes.com/2021/09/01/us/politics/republicans-afghanistan-withdrawal-support.html.

32. Helmut Norpoth and Bruce Buchanan, "Wanted: The Education President Issue Trespassing by Political Candidates," *Public Opinion Quarterly* 56, no. 1 (1992): 87–99.

33. Ronald Reagan, "Address to the 42d Session of the United Nations General Assembly in New York, New York," *The American Presidency Project*, ed. Gerhard Peters and John T. Woolley, last accessed April 24, 2024, https://www.presidency.ucsb.edu/node/253782.

34. "Read the Full Transcript of the Ninth Republican Debate in South Carolina," *Time.com*, February 16, 2016, https://time.com/4224275/republican-debate-transcript-south-carolina-ninth/.

35. "South Carolina Primary Results," *New York Times*, September 29, 2016, https://www.nytimes.com/elections/2016/results/primaries/south-carolina.

36. Stuart Rothenberg, "Ukraine, Putinism, Isolationism, and the GOP," *Roll Call*, February 27, 2023, https://rollcall.com/2023/02/27/isolationism-putinism-and-the-gop/.

37. John Bolton, "Containing Isolationism," *National Review*, January 23, 2023, https://www.nationalreview.com/magazine/2023/01/23/containing-isolationism/.

38. "Transcript of CNN's Town Hall with Former President Donald Trump," CNN.com, May 11, 2023, https://edition.cnn.com/2023/05/11/politics/transcript-cnn-town-hall-trump/index.html.

39. Shane Goldmacher et al., "Trump's Second-Term Goal: Shattering the Norms He Didn't Already Break," *New York Times*, May 11, 2023, https://www.nytimes.com/2023/05/11/us/politics/trump-2024-cnn-town-hall.html.

40. Roll Call 151, H.R. 8035, April 20, 2024, https://clerk.house.gov/Votes/2024151.

41. William Howell and Jon Pevehouse, *While Dangers Gather: Congressional Checks on Presidential War Powers* (Princeton, NJ: Princeton University Press, 2007); Kriner, *After the Rubicon*.

42. Howell and Pevehouse, *While Dangers Gather*; Matthew Baum and Timothy Groeling, "Crossing the Water's Edge: Elite Rhetoric, Media Coverage, and the Rally-round-the-flag Effect," *Journal of Politics* 70 (2008): 1065–1085; Adam Berinsky, *In Time of War: Understanding American Public Opinion from World War II to Iraq* (Chicago: University of Chicago Press, 2009).

43. Bruce Jentleson, "The Pretty Prudent Public: Post Post-Vietnam American Opinion on the Use of Force," *International Studies Quarterly* 36, no. 1 (March 1992): 49–73.

44. For a discussion of this perceived general reticence to support force, and particularly military actions that would result in significant numbers of US casualties, see Christopher Gelpi, Peter Feaver, and Jason Reifler, "Success Matters: Casualty Sensitivity and the War in Iraq," *International Security* 30, no. 3 (2006): 7–46.

45. Because those who "lean" toward one party or the other usually express opinions and exhibit political behaviors similar to those of self-declared partisans, our partisan indicators include leaners. John Petrocik, "Measuring Party Support: Leaners Are Not Independents," *Electoral Studies* 28, no. 4 (2009): 562–572.

46. Joseph Nye Jr., "The Rise and Fall of American Hegemony from Wilson to Trump," *International Affairs* 95, no. 1 (2019): 63–80.

47. Rachel Marie Blum and Christopher Sebastian Parker, "Trump-ing Foreign Affairs: Status Threat and Foreign Policy Preferences on the Right," *Perspectives on Politics* 17, no. 3 (2019): 737–755. For an analysis of the association between holding isolationist opinions and voting for Trump in the general election, see Kyle

Dodson and Clem Brooks, "All by Himself? Trump, Isolationism, and the American Electorate," *The Sociological Quarterly* 63, no. 4 (2022): 780–803.

48. Douglas Kriner and Francis Shen, "Iraq Casualties and the 2006 Senate Elections," *Legislative Studies Quarterly* 32, no. 4 (2007): 507–530; Christian Grose and Bruce Oppenheimer, "The Iraq War, Partisanship, and Candidate Attributes: Variation in Partisan Swing in the 2006 U.S. House Elections," *Legislative Studies Quarterly* 32, no. 4 (2007): 531–557; Scott Gartner and Gary Segura, "All Politics are Still Local: The Iraq War and the 2006 Midterm Elections," *PS: Political Science & Politics* 41, no. 1 (2008): 95–100.

49. Douglas Kriner and Francis Shen, "Battlefield Casualties and Ballot-Box Defeat: Did the Bush-Obama Wars Cost Clinton the White House?" *PS: Political Science and Politics* 53, no. 2 (2020): 248–252.

50. "Cato V," *New York Journal*, November 22, 1787, https://archive.csac.history.wisc.edu/Cato_V(1).pdf.

51. On the importance of same-party criticism, see Matthew Baum and Timothy Groeling, "Shot by the Messenger: Partisan Cues and Public Opinion Regarding National Security and War," *Political Behavior* 31 (2009): 157–186.

52. The question is measured on a seven-point scale. For our analyses, we create a dichotomous dependent variable coded 1 for respondents who chose one of the three values below the mid-point (i.e., decrease spending) and 0 otherwise. This eases substantive and allows us to examine support for decreasing military spending by party over time.

53. The Trump Administration was notoriously inconsistent on this question. After pushing for significant increases in defense spending in its first two years, Trump called the defense budget "crazy" and pushed for cuts before reversing course and calling for further increases. James Miller and Michael O'Hanlon, "Quality over Quantity: US Military Strategy and Spending in the Trump Years," *Brookings*, 2019, https://www.brookings.edu/articles/quality-over-quantity-u-s-military-strategy-and-spending-in-the-trump-years/.

54. John Kaag and Sarah Kreps, *Drone Warfare* (New York: John Wiley & Sons, 2014).

55. Jonathan Masters and Will Merrow, "How Much Has the U.S. Sent Ukraine?" *Council on Foreign Relations*, February 22, 2023, https://www.cfr.org/article/how-much-aid-has-us-sent-ukraine-here-are-six-charts.

56. Daniel Fried, "Renewed US Assistance Opens a Path to Success, If Ukraine's Friends Move Fast," Atlantic Council, April 20, 2024, https://www.atlanticcouncil.org/blogs/new-atlanticist/renewed-us-assistance-opens-a-path-to-success-if-ukraines-friends-move-fast/.

57. Gallup, "Most Important Problem," https://news.gallup.com/poll/1675/most-important-problem.aspx.

58. Barack Obama, "Remarks by the President at the National Defense University," May 23, 2013, https://obamawhitehouse.archives.gov/the-press-office/2013/05/23/remarks-president-national-defense-university.

59. John Kaag and Sarah Kreps, "Drones and Democratic Peace," *The Brown Journal of World Affairs* 19, no. 2 (Spring/Summer 2013): 97–109.

60. Jack Goldsmith and Matthew Waxman, "The Legal Legacy of Light-Footprint Warfare," *Washington Quarterly* 39, no. 2 (2016): 7–21.

61. Robert Sutter, "Domestic Politics, Congress, and U.S. Hardening to China," *Georgetown Journal of Asian Affairs* 8 (2022): 37–46.

62. On the sharp partisan divides over Iraq, see Gary Jacobson, "Perception, Memory, and Partisan Polarization on the Iraq War," *Political Science Quarterly* 125, no. 1 (2010): 31–56; Douglas Kriner and Francis Shen, "Responding to War on Capitol Hill: Battlefield Casualties, Congressional Response, and Public Support for the Iraq War," *American Journal of Political Science* 58, no. 1 (2014): 157–174.

63. Testifying to the power of culture war issues, recent research shows that whereas the conventional wisdom holds that voters normally align their policy preferences with their partisan political identities, recent research shows that many Americans have changed their partisan affinities to match their culture war orientations. Paul Goren and Christopher Chapp, "Moral Power: How Public Opinion on Culture War Issues Shapes Partisan Predispositions and Religious Orientations," *American Political Science Review* 111, no. 1 (2017): 110–128.

64. Lydia Saad, "Americans More Divided on Social Than Economic Issues," *Gallup.com*, June 24, 2021, https://news.gallup.com/poll/351494/americans-divided-social-economic-issues.aspx.

65. The logic here echoes that advanced by Potter and Dictus, who find that presidents have strong incentives to turn to foreign policy following midterm defeats that make domestic policy accomplishments significantly less likely.

Acknowledgments

The ideas at the core of this book came out of conversations between someone who studies foreign policy and wanted to understand its domestic determinants or constraints and someone who studies domestic politics and wanted to understand its foreign policy consequences. Sarah and Doug began talking about their respective research and teaching and realized that there were enough similarities to make a collaboration fruitful and differences to offer new contributions to the other's subfields. This project is the result of conversations that led to a grant proposal, a workshop, a journal special issue, and finally this coedited volume on the interplay between domestic politics and foreign policy.

We extend our thanks to all those who have contributed to the completion of this volume. Without their support, expertise, and dedication this project would not have been possible.

First and foremost, we appreciate the esteemed contributors whose chapters have enriched this volume with diverse perspectives and scholarly analyses. Your expertise and commitment to advancing knowledge in the field of international relations and domestic politics are commendable.

We are indebted to the editorial team at the University of Chicago Press for their guidance, professionalism, and support throughout the publication process. Special thanks to Chuck Myers, who saw initial promise in the project, and Sara Doskow, who shepherded the project through to completion.

We also extend our thanks to the Stand Together Trust for their grant to study the separation of powers in wartime. In particular, we thank Andrew Byers for his support of the project and his participation at the September 2022 workshop in New York City on the role of domestic checks in foreign policy decision making.

Finally, we dedicate this volume to our spouses, Gustavo and Jill, and Sarah's kids, Luke and Sebastian, who are like nephews to Uncle Doug and Aunt Jill. We look forward to many more adventures together.

Thank you all for your contributions and support.

Sarah Kreps and Douglas Kriner

Index

Page numbers in italics refer to figures and tables.

Abbey Gate terrorist attack, 344
ABC News, 220
abortion, 152–53, *165*, *167–68*
Abu Ghraib, 118
Adams, John, 179
Afghanistan: Biden and, 3, 18, 28, 204, 219–21, 225, 278, 284–86, 297n148, 344, 346; bipartisanship and, 79; bureaucratic politics and, 264, 270, 276–87, 295n98, 296n119, 297nn147–48; Bush and, 2, 42–43, 51–52, 66, 211, 225, 278, 347, 356; casualties and, 356; communal groups and, 236; cost of war and, 280, 356; drones and, 11–13, 285; foreign policy and, *168*, 338, 344, 346; gender and, 203–4, 207, 209–25; Ghani and, 285; Kabul International Airport and, 220, 338; manpower system knowledge and, 189; Obama and, 11, 28, 42–43, 49–56, 61–63, 66–67, 211, 224, 276–78, 281, 284, 287, 296n121, 341–45; opposition and, 106–8, 128, 130; partisanship and, 40–43, 49, 51–67, 73n71, 74nn77–79; presidential powers and, 1, 3, 8–13, 17–18, 23, 26, 28; public opinion and, 203–4, 207, 209–25; research methodology on, 52–67, 73n71, 73nn76–77; reserve components and, 176, 184, 189; Taliban and, 3, 18, 211, 219–20, 278–85, 297n149, 334n68, 338; terrorism and, 338, 341–47, 352, 356; Trump and, 3, 11, 42, 56, 219–20, 270, 278–84, 296n119, 296n121, 297n135,
297n148, 299, 330n34, 343, 346–47, 352; war powers and, 299, 330n34; withdrawal from, 18, 28, 42, 204, 219–21, 222, 225, 280–86, 297n148, 299, 330n34, 338, 344, 346; Woodward on, 52
African Americans, *55*, *61*, 233–34, 236, 250, 261n71
Albright, Madeline, 25
Aldrich, John, 42
Alien and Sedition Acts, 6
Alito, Samuel, 156
Allied powers, 235
Allison, Graham, 266
all-volunteer force (AVF), 176, 179–80, 183, 196
al-Qaeda: Bush and, 6, 278, 333n62; September 11, 2001, and, 6, 33n37, 333n62; terrorism and, 6, 11, 33n37, 130, 278, 295n92, 333n62, 334n68
America First, 27, 347, 352
American Civil War, 179
American Jobs Act, 152
American National Election Study (ANES), 20, 203, 350, 352, 354
American Political Science Review, 24
American Taxpayer Relief Act, 156
Angola, 339, 340
Antifederalists, 13
Arabs, 33n37, 148, 151, *166*, *241*, 258n30
Article I (US Constitution), 2, 16
Article II (US Constitution), 13–14, 264, 316
Article III (US Constitution), 315

Ashcroft, John, 272
Asian Americans, 261n71
Assad, Bashar al-, 341
Authorization to Use Military Force (AUMF): Bush and, 14, 337n107, 342; Iraq War and, 21, 54, 73n75, 341–42, 347; language of, 14, 33n37; Office of Legal Counsel (OLC) and, 14, 317, 337n107, 342; September 11, 2001, terrorist attacks and, 14, 33n37
Awlaki, Anwar al-, 11
Axis powers, 235

Bagram Air Base, 285
Baker, Peter, 281
Balkans, 342
Bandow, Doug, 299
Bannon, Steve, 273, 292n51
Barr, William, 264
Barratt, Bethany, 109
Bay of Pigs, 153, *161*, 269
Beinart, Peter, 42
Benjamin, Medea, 42
Berinsky, Adam, 212, 235
Beschloss, Michael, 1–2
Biden, Joe: Afghanistan and, 3, 18, 28, 204, 219–21, 225, 278, 284–86, 297n148, 344, 346; approval ratings of, 7–8; bipartisanship and, 344, 357–58; bureaucratic politics and, 284–86; China and, 357; counterterrorism and, 284; executive norms and, 312–13; "Made in America" campaign and, 357; NATO and, 357; post-9/11 context and, 284–86; public opinion and, 28–30; Syria and, 42; Ukraine and, 95, 354–57; US Constitution and, 28; as vice president, 67, 278, 284; war powers and, 95, 313
bin Laden, Osama, 33n37, 152, *171*, 278, 284
bipartisanship: Afghanistan and, 79; anti-presidential, 18, 41, 77–84, 90–95, 106, 345; Biden and, 344, 357–58; checks and, 76–79; China and, 95; Cold War and, 79, 83, 94; Congressional Quarterly and, 82–92, *93*, *96–97*, 103n40, 103nn43–44; Congressional Research Service and, 103n35; counterterrorism and, 80; cross-partisanship and, 77–81, 87, 90, 94, 103n44; defining, 78; Democrats and, 76–96; domestic policy and, 76–95;

drones and, 11–13; electoral context and, 81–82; elitism and, 77, 80; foreign policy and, 76–96; frequency of, 84–87; ideologies and, 81–82; Iraq War and, 79; military and, 80–81, 95; NATO and, 95; Obama and, 83, 94–95, 344; partisan gap and, 7, 8, 50; polarization and, 76–96, 98n1, 98n4; political alignments and, 80–82; post-9/11 context and, 87, 94; pre-9/11 context and, 80, 84, 94; presidential powers and, 94; procedural votes and, 77; pro-presidential, 77, 79, 84, 90–94; Republicans and, 76–96; research methodology on, 82–84; security and, 80–82, 95, 103n35, 357–58; September 11, 2001, terrorist attacks and, 80; strong, 78, 79, 83–86, 95; Trump and, 83, 94–95, 345–46, 357–58; US Congress and, 76–96, 343–49; varieties of, 76–97; Vote Smart and, 83–92, *97*, 103n36, 103n43; voting data and, 82–84; widening fractures and, 343–49
Bipartisan Student Loan Certainty Act, 157
Bissell, Dick, 294n90
Blair, Dennis, 276
Blankshain, Jessica D., 22–23, 175–202, 251
Blinken, Antony, 284–85
blue states, 50, 60
Boland amendments, 339
Bolton, John, 297n148, 348
Borgida, Eugene, 42
Bosnia, 25, 151, *167*, 184, 316
Bowles, Chester, 276–77, 294n90
Brookings Institution, 276
Brownlow Report, 264
Budget Control Act, 152
Bundy, McGeorge, 262
bureaucratic politics: accountable expertise and, 286–88; Afghanistan and, 264, 270, 276–87, 295n98, 296n119, 297nn147–48; bargaining and, 264–75; Biden and, 284–86; George W. Bush and, 263, 271–72, 278; Capitol attack and, 301–3, 306–10, 321; casualties and, 278, 282; checks and, 24–26, 264; CIA and, 262, 270, 272, 275–79, 287; Cold War and, 265; counterterrorism and, 279, 284; deep state and, 24–25, 273, 287, 299–310, 319–21, 329n28; Eisenhower and, 269–71, 286; elitism and, 287–88; FBI and, 272; foreign policy and, 262–67, 270, 273, 275–86; gender

INDEX

and, 282; imperialism and, 277; Iraq War and, 273, 275, 277–79, 293n70; isolationism and, 361n47; Kennedy and, 263, 268–69, 274, 276, 288n4; military and, 269–70, 273–74, 277–87, 290n24; Nixon and, 269, 273; Obama and, 276–81, 284, 287, 288n8, 296n121, 362; opposition and, 263, 278; organizational processes and, 266–67, 273–75; Pentagon and, 262, 266–74, 277, 282–84, 287; post-9/11 context and, 275; presidential powers and, 264, 286; principal-agent problems and, 15, 266, 268–76; Reagan and, 267; Russia and, 263, 283; security and, 262–63, 267–73, 276–86, 288n4, 290n24, 297n148; September 11, 2001, attacks and, 264, 275, 285; Taliban and, 278–85, 298n148, 333n62, 334n68; terrorism and, 264, 275, 277–81, 284–85; Truman and, 277, 286; Trump and, 263–64, 270–73, 278, 280–87, 291n45, 292n51, 296n119, 296n121, 297n130, 297n135, 297n148; unilateral power and, 24–25, 263, 267; US Congress and, 264–68, 271, 275–77, 280, 283; US Constitution and, 263–67; US Department of State and, *169*, 267, 272–76, 279, 282, 296n119; Vietnam War and, 273, 285; war powers and, 272, 299–322; World War II and, 265, 291n45
Bureaucratic Resistance and the National Security State (Ingber), 306
Bureau of Investigative Journalism (BIJ), 11
Burundi, 4
Bush, George H. W.: background of, 147; China and, 147; CIA and, 147; domestic policy and, 147–50; failed reelection of, 147–50; first Persian Gulf War and, 147, 151, 204, 347; foreign policy and, 138, 144, 147–51, 347; midterm elections and, 144, 151
Bush, George W.: Abu Ghraib torture scandal and, 118; Afghanistan and, 2, 42–43, 51–52, 66, 211, 225, 278, 347, 356; al-Qaeda and, 6, 278, 333n62; Authorization to Use Military Force (AUMF) and, 14, 337n107, 342; bureaucratic politics and, 263, 271–72, 278; casualties and, 51, 66, 115, 225, 278; counterterrorism and, 42, 357; as divider, 6; Energy Policy Act and, 156; executive norms and, 312, 333n58;

369

FBI and, 272; foreign policy and, 139, *141*, 152–56, *166*, *169*, 350; gender and, 211–12, 215–16, 219, 225; Global War on Terror (GWOT) and, 356–57; imperialism and, 1–2, 30; Intelligence Reform and Terrorism Prevention Act and, 156; Iraq War and, 6, 16, 19–20, 51–52, 66–67, 106, 115, 118, 130, 152, 154, 156, 202, 211–12, 219, 225, 278, 313, 347, 356; isolationism and, 350; midterm elections and, 16, 19–20, 139, *141*, 152–54, 202; Office of Legal Counsel (OLC) and, 14, 271, 313, 337n107, 342; opposition and, 106, 115, 118, 130; partisanship and, 42–43, 51–52, 55, 66–67; presidential powers and, 1, 3, 6, 7, 14, 16, 19–20, 342, 347; reelection of, 19–20, 118, *141*, 156, 202; Rumsfeld and, 14–15, 275–77, 295n92, 342; second term of, 202; September 11, 2001, terrorist attacks and, 1, 6, 14; "shock and awe" campaigns of, 347; "Stellar Wind" surveillance and, 271–72; Taliban and, 333n62; US Constitution and, 14; veto power and, 16; war powers and, 14, 312

Cambodia, 340
Camp David, 148, 153, *161*, *164*, 283
Capitol, attack on: accountability and, 287; bureaucratic politics and, 301–3, 306–10, 321; checks and, 301–3, 306–10, 321; deep state and, 26, 306, 309, 324n13; FBI and, 304, 309; as insurrection, 26, 287, 301–4; National Guard and, 303–4, 308, 324–25nn12–14, 327n15; as outlier, 287; Pentagon and, 310, 313–14; Trump and, 301, 306, 308, 324–25nn12–14, 327n20; US Congress and, 302–3, 308, 324n13, 327n15
Carter, Jimmy: China and, 151; foreign policy and, *140*, 151, 156, *164*; Phase II energy plan and, 151; presidential powers and, 6–8; SALT II and, 151, *164*; US Department of Education and, 151
Carville, James, 138
casualties: Afghanistan and, 356; automatic withdrawal and, 16; bureaucratic politics and, 278, 282; Bush and, 51, 66, 115, 225, 278; communal groups and, 231–53, 258n34; consent and, 242–44; drones and, 12, 128, 232; empathy and, 205, 242–44,

casualties (*cont.*)
251; Obama and, 12, 51, 66, 278; opposition and, 21, 107–15, 121–23, 127–28; public opinion and, 22, 24, 122, 176, 203, 206, 234–36, 249, 251–53, 254n14, 258n34; reduction of, 12–13; reelection and, 107; reserve components and, 176–78, *187*, 194–96; sensitivity to, 231–53, 258n39; terrorism and, 236, 338, 352, 361n44; tolerance of, 242, 244, 252–53, 258n34; war powers and, 12, 16, 21–24, 309, 316

Cato, 13

Central Intelligence Agency (CIA): Bay of Pigs and, 153; bureaucratic politics and, 262, 270, 272, 275–79, 287; George H. W. Bush and, 147; Eisenhower and, 153; foreign policy and, 153, *160–61, 63, 168*; Hayden and, 336n82; Iran and, *160*; Panetta and, 262, 275–76, 279, 295n109; Trump and, 270

Chapp, Christopher, 363n63

checks: bipartisanship and, 76–79; bureaucratic politics and, 24–26, 264; Capitol attack and, 301–3, 306–10, 321; on commander in chief, 2–3, 15, 41, 356; communal groups and, 232; congressional, 3–5, 18–19, 42–43, 76, 79, 344; domestic, 1–8, 13–28, 264, 348; erosion of, 232; partisanship and, 41–44, 73n74; presidential powers and, 1–28; public opinion and, 19–24; reassessing, 15–26; reserve components and, 177; separation of powers and, 13, 41–44, 264–65, 304, 310, 319–22; terrorism and, 340, 343, 348–49, 353, 356; undermining efficacy of, 3–15; US Congress and, 16–19, 40–60, 63–67; war powers and, 320–21, 329n31

Cheney, Dick, 6, 271–72, 342

Cheney, Liz, 323n8, 346

Childree, Aaron, 23, 176, 186, 202–30, 232, 250

China: Biden and, 357; bipartisanship and, 95; Carter and, 151; Cold War and, 65; foreign policy and, 147, 151, 154, *160–62, 165–67*; Mao Tse-tung and, 40; Taiwan and, 95, 151, *161*, 355; Tiananmen Square and, 147; Trump and, 357

civil liberties, 1, 336n82

Civil Rights Act, 145, 155

Clark, Wesley, 212

Clark amendment, 339

Clean Power Plan, 153

Clemens, Jennifer, 205, 224

Clinton, Bill: approval ratings of, 7; Dayton Peace Accords and, 151; domestic policy and, 25, 75n88, 138, 148, 153–54, 157–58, 172n9; FBI and, 157; foreign interventions of, 67; foreign policy and, 25, 136–39, *141*, 148–54, 157–58, 172n9; gender and, 204, 212; Good Friday Peace Accords and, 157; as governor of Arkansas, 148–49; humanitarian interventions of, 4; Kosovo and, 4; Lewinsky and, 154, 157; NATO and, 154; partisanship and, 67, 75n88; presidential powers and, 4, 7–8, 20, 25; Putin and, 154; reelection of, 67, 150, 157–58, 172n9; Russia and, 151, 154, 157; START III and, 157; terrorism and, 342–43; Wye River Memorandum and, 157–58

Clinton, Hillary, 20, 296n109

coercion: communal groups and, 242, 250; diplomatic, 108; military and, 178–96, 198n22; war powers and, 334n64

Cohen's kappa, 73n71

Cohn, Gary, 270

Cohn, Lindsay P., 22–23, 175–202, 251

Cold War: bipartisanship and, 79, 83, 94; bureaucratic politics and, 265; China and, 65; end of, 342, 347, 354; foreign policy and, 154, 157; gender and, 204; partisanship and, 48, 65; presidential powers and, 4, 9, 25; reserve components and, 179; US Congress and, 31, 33, 48, 65, 79, 94, 98n2, 154, 265, 339

Comey, James, 271–72

commander in chief: checks on, 2–3, 15, 41, 356; domestic policy and, 3, 15, 206, 299; partisanship and, 40–41, 45; public opinion and, 203, 347; reserve components and, 175; Trump as, 270, 284, 299, 304; Vietnam War and lessons for, 341; war powers and, 2–3, 15–18, 40–41, 45, 175, 203, 206, 270, 284, 299, 304, 341, 347, 356

communal groups: Afghanistan and, 236; Black people and, 148, 233–36, *237, 241*, 249–53, 256n20, 256n23, 261n71; casualties and, 231–53, 258n34; checks and, 232; coercion and, 242, 250; conscription and, 231; costs of war and, 234–35; Democrats and, 232; draft and, 259n41; efficacy and,

234, 248–51, 261nn72–73; elitism and, 235, 253; empathy and, 205, 242–44, 251; ethnicity and, 231–47, 250–53, 258n30; foreign policy and, 235, 238; gender and, 237, 239, *241*, 250, 258n39; homophily and, 246–48; ideologies and, 232, 237–39, *241*, 247, 251, 258n39; Iraq War and, 236; Israel and, 233, 237–53, 257n28, 258nn29–30, 258n39, 259n41; military and, 231–53, 258n34, 258n39, 259nn40–41, 260n54; minorities, 24, 233, 253, 256n23, 261n71; NATO and, 270, 272, 283; non-Ashkenazic Jews, 233, *237*, 238, 240, *241*, 248–49, 259n41; nonwhite, 233, 236, 239–52, 260n54; opposition and, 232–35, 238, 243–45, 249; patriotism and, 239, *241*, 244, 246, 249, 260n68; polarization and, 232, 235, 252; political alienation and, 248–50; public opinion and, 234–36, 249–53, 256n26; racial, 231–51, 258n30, 259n42; regression analysis and, 240–43, 258n37; religious, 232–33, *237*, *241*, 251, 258n39; Republicans and, 253; research methodology on, 237–50; soldier motivation and, 238, *241*, 244–46, 250–51, 258n30; terrorism and, 236; United Kingdom and, 252; US Congress and, 232; Vietnam War and, 235–36, 249; World War II and, 235
communism, 148, *160*, 339–40
Confederacy, 179
Congo, 236
Congressional Quarterly: Almanac, 84–92, *93*, *97*; bipartisanship data and, 82–92, *93*, 96–97, 103n40, 103nn43–44; key votes and, 82–83
Congressional Record, 52, 72n66
Congressional Research Service, 103n35
conscription: Civil War and, 179; communal groups and, 231; degree of compulsion and, 176–78; gender and, 202; public opinion and, 177–78; reserve components and, 175–80, 197; threat of, 9; war powers and, 9, 22–23
conservatism, 3, 47, 80–81, 155
conspiracy theories, 24, 300
Cooper, John, 4
Corwin, Edward, 16
Costa, Robert, 284
costs of war: in Afghanistan, 280, 356; casualties, 12 (*see also* casualties); communal groups and, 234–35; "forever wars" and, 9; increasing submersion of, 8–13; opposition and, 108; political, 202–25; post-9/11 context and, 8–13; public opinion and, 223; reserve components and, 197; spending cuts and, 353–54, 362nn52–53; taxes and, 11
Costs of War Project, 8
counterterrorism: Biden and, 284; bipartisanship and, 80; bureaucratic politics and, 279, 284; Bush and, 42, 357; drones and, 11; Obama and, 42, 279, 284, 357
cover-ups, 155, *163*
Crimea, *171*
C-Span, 45
Cuba, 153, *161*, *168*, *171*, 266, 274
culture war, 363n63

Dallek, Robert, 145
Dayton Peace Accords, 151
D-Day, 270
Dean, Howard, 212
deep state: bureaucratic politics and, 24–25, 273, 287, 299–310, 319–21, 329n28; Capitol attacks and, 26, 306, 309, 324n13; existence of, 299; Goldsmith on, 305–6; historical use of term, 305; #Resistance and, 305–7, 321; rhetoric and, 305–7, 319; security and, 24, 305–6, 317, 324n13; Trump and, 25, 273, 287, 299–300, 305–6, 309, 313, 317, 329n28
"Deep State Thwarted Trump's Afghanistan Withdrawal, The" (Bandow), 299
Democracies and Coercive Diplomacy (Schultz), 108–9
Democrats: Benjamin on, 42; bipartisanship and, 76–96; blue states, 50, 60; communal groups and, 232; dovish, 17, 28, 42, 48–52, 57, 61–62, 66, 205–6, 345; foreign policy and, *140–41*, 142–47, 150–56; gender and, 202–9, 212–25; hawks and, 20, 28, 42, 48–52, 57, 61–63, 66, 206; opposition and, 108, 111–12, 115–20; partisanship and, 42–44, 47–66; presidential powers and, 3–8, 16–24, 27–29; reserve components and, 182–83, 186, *187*, *195*; terrorism and, 344–51, 354, *355*; war powers and, 319–20
desertion, 198n22
Dictus, Christopher, 21, 41, 135–74, 363n65

Director of National Intelligence (DNI), 156, *169*, 275–77, 294n82
Dolan, Kathleen, 205, 224
domestic policy: bipartisanship and, 76–95; George H. W. Bush and, 147–50; Clinton and, 25, 75n88, 138, 148, 153–54, 157–58, 172n9; commander in chief and, 3, 15, 206, 299; vs. foreign policy, 21; foreign policy and, 136–38, 144–59, *160–71*; Johnson and, 144–47; midterm elections and, 21, 135–38, 144, 151–54, 157–59, 363n65; Nixon and, 139, 142
Donnelly, Thomas, 277
Don't Ask, Don't Tell, 25, 152, *166*
doves: Democrats and, 17, 28, 42, 48–52, 57, 61–62, 66, 205–6, 345; ideology of, 17, 28, 42, 48–54, 57, 61–62, 66–67, 122, 205–6, 345, 348, 353; polarization and, 48; Republicans and, 17, 28, 48–52, 57, 61–62, 66, 205–6, 345
Downs, Anthony, 270
draft: Civil War and, 179; communal groups and, 259n41; conscription and, 9, 22–23, 175–80, 202, 231; degree of compulsion and, 176–78; end of, *162*; pardoning evaders of, *164*; presidential powers and, 9–10, 14; public opinion and, 176–78; reserve components and, 176–81, 184, 189, *190*, 201n55; Selective Service System, *10*, *162*, 176, 199n25; Vietnam War and, 9, 179, 189
drones: Afghanistan and, 11–13, 285; bipartisanship over, 11–13; casualties and, 11–13, 22, 128, 232, 285, 337n107, 354–57; counterterrorism and, 11; increased use of, 11–13, 22, 128, 232, 285, 337n107, 354–57; Obama and, 11–12, 337n107, 356–57; Trump and, 11–12
Dunford, Joseph, 281

Economic Opportunity Act, 145
efficacy: communal groups and, 234, 248–51, 261nn72–73; domestic checks and, 3–15; institutional changes and, 27; troop surges and, 66–67; undermining, 3–15
Eichenberg, Richard, 204, 207
Eisenhower, Dwight D.: bureaucratic politics and, 269–71, 286; CIA and, 153; Civil Rights Act and, 155; foreign policy and, *140*, 151, 153, 155, *161*; Landrum Griffin Act and, 153; National Defense Education Act and, 155; NATO and, 270; presidential powers and, 6–8, 15; reelection of, 151, 155; Sixth Fleet and, 155; Soviet Union and, 153; Taft-Hartley and, 153; West Point and, 270
electoral context: of Abu Ghraib torture scandal, 118; bipartisanship and, 81–82; ideologies and, 72n61; Iraq War and, 111–12, 114–15, 118–22; moderating role of, 58–61; opposition and, 111–12, 114–15, 118–26; partisanship and, 18, 46, 50, 58–61, 64, 72n61, 74n79; reelection and, 19 (*see also* reelection); research methodology on, 58–61
Elementary and Secondary School Act, 138, 155
elitism: bipartisanship and, 77, 80; bureaucratic politics and, 287–88; communal groups and, 235, 253; gender and, 203–15, 219, 223–25; polarization and, 3, 6, 28, 77, 80, 235; presidential powers and, 3, 6, 22–23, 28–29; public opinion and, 6, 22–23, 28–29, 176–78, 203–15, 219, 223–25, 357–58; reserve components and, 176–78, 196; terrorism and, 340, 348, 353–54, 357
empathy, 205, 242–44, 251
Energy Policy Act, 156
Energy Policy Conservation Act, 152
Environmental Protection Agency (EPA), 276
Esper, Mark, 282–83
Essence of Decision (Allison), 266
ethics, 307, 314
ethnicity: African Americans, 55, *61*, 233–34, 236, 250, 261n71; Arabs, 33n37, 148, 151, *166*, *241*, 258n30; Asian Americans, 261n71; Black people, 148, 233–36, *237*, *241*, 249–53, 256n20, 256n23, 261n71; casualty sensitivity and, 24; communal groups and, 231–47, 250–53, 258n30; constituents and, 81; empathy and, 205, 242–44, 251; foreign policy and, 142; gender and, 221, 224; homophily and, 246–48; Jews, 24 (*see also* Jews); Latinos, 55, 57, *58*, *61*, 252–53, 261n71; minority groups, 24, 233, 253, 256n23, 261n71; political alienation and, 248–50; reserve components and, 182; terrorism and, 350, 354

executive norms, 311–13, 333n58
executive orders (EOs), *171*; Clinton and, 25; First Amendment and, 309; Obama and, 152, 157; pluralism and, 267; Reagan and, 267–68; time of issuance and, 290n34

Fair Deal, 154
Farber, Daniel, 262
Feaver, Peter, 235–36
Federal Bureau of Investigation (FBI): bureaucratic politics and, 272; Bush and, 272; Capitol attack and, 304, 309; Clinton and, 157; Mueller and, 272; war powers and, 304, 309
Federal Election Commission Act, 152
Federalist essays (Madison), 40, 265, 289n16
Federalists, 179
feminists, 205
filibusters, 44
Finland, 95
First Amendment, 309
Ford, Gerald: bureaucratic politics and, 288n4; foreign policy and, *140*, 147, 152, 156, *163*; Nixon and, 288n4; presidential powers and, 7; terrorism and, 339, 341; US Constitution and, 339; Whip Inflation Now (WIN) and, 152
Fordham, Benjamin, 20–21, 40, 42, 67, 178, 259n42, 341
foreign policy: adventurism and, 9, 177, 341, 356; Afghanistan and, *168*, 338, 344, 346; Bay of Pigs and, 153, *161*, 269; bipartisanship and, 76–96; bureaucratic politics and, 262–67, 270, 273, 275–86; Bush and, 139, *141*, 152–56, *166*, *169*, 350; Carter and, *140*, 151, 156, *164*; China and, 147, 151, 154, *160*–62, *165*–67; CIA and, 153, *160*–61, *63*, *168*; Clinton and, 25, 136–39, *141*, 148–54, 157–58, 172n9; Cold War and, 154, 157; communal groups and, 235, 238; constraints in, 353–55; cover-ups and, 155, *163*; Democrats and, *140–41*, 142–47, 150–56; diversionary, 21, 135–36, 155; domestic policy and, 21, 136–38, 144–59, *160–71*; Eisenhower and, *140*, 151, 153, 155, *161*; Ford and, *140*, 147, 152, 156, *163*; gender and, 205–6, 219; Gulf War and, 151, *166*; Iraq War and, 138, 147, 151–56, *167–69*, *171*; isolationism, 27–28, 340, 344, 348–53; Israel and, 148, 151, 154, 157, *160*, *162*, *164*, *166–68*; Johnson and, 138, *140*, 142, 144–47, 155, 172n6, 174n38; Korean War and, 154, *160*, *162*, *168–69*; military and, *164–68*; NATO and, 151, 154, *160*, *166–67*; Nixon and, 136, 139–44, 147, 151, 155–56, 159, *162–63*; Obama and, *141*, 152–53, 156–59; opportunities in, 353–55; partisanship and, 40–67; polarization and, 135, 156–59; post-9/11 context and, 135, 158–59, *170*, 275–86; presidential powers and, 1–29, 135–36; public opinion and, 3, 17, 19, 23, 26, 151, 208, 252, 342, 349, 353–54, 361n45, 361n47; Reagan and, *140–41*, 147, 152–53, 157–58, 347; reelection and, 21, 135–44, 147–51, 154–59, 172n6, 172n9; Republicans and, 136, 139–45, 150–53, 156, 159; reserve components and, 181; second-term presidents and, 154–58; security and, 173n17; Soviet Union and, 138, 147–48, 151, 153, 157, *161*, *164–66*; terrorism and, 42, 80, 154, 156, *169*, 284, 339–58; Truman and, *140*, 151–55, *160*, 172n6, 174n38; Trump and, 139, *141*, 159, 347–48; US Congress and, 40–60, 63–67, 135–40, 143–59, *160–71*; US Constitution and, *160*, *168*, 172n6; US Department of State and, *169*; veto power and, 153, *160*, *162–63*, *165*, *167*, *169*; Vietnam War and, 142, 146, 151–52, 155, *162–63*, *166–67*, *169*; "wagging the dog," 136; war powers and, 299–300, 320; World War II and, 139
Fried, Daniel, 282–83
Fukuyama, Francis, 24

Gallup polls, 6, 7; gender gap and, 210, 213, 217, 229n45, 229n47; opposition and, 116, 121; Ukraine and, 356
Gartner, Scott, 109, 235–36
Gates, Robert, 278, 280, 287
Gaza Strip, 158
Gelb, Leslie, 272
Gelpi, Christopher, 235–36
gender, 23; Afghanistan and, 203–4, 207, 209–25; American National Election Study (ANES) and, 203, 350; bureaucratic politics and, 282; Bush and, 211–12, 215–16, 219, 225; Clinton and,

gender (*cont.*)
204, 212; Cold War and, 204; communal groups and, 232, *237*, 239, *241*, 250, 258n39; conscription and, 202; Democrats and, 202–9, 212–25; elitism and, 203–15, 219, 223–25; ethnicity and, 221, 224; feminism and, 205; foreign policy and, 205–6, 219; Gulf War and, 204; ideologies and, 205, 224; Iraq War and, 203–4, 207, 209–25; military and, 23, 54, 57, 176, 182, 200n50, 202–8, 216, 220–21, 224, 239, *241*, 258n39, 282, 354; Obama and, 211, 219, 224, 229n50; opposition and, 206–9, 212–13, 217, 220–24; partisanship and, 203–24, 229n48, 229n50; post-9/11 context and, 202, 221; public opinion and, 202–3, 206–11, 214, 220–21, 223–24; racial groups and, 224; regression analysis and, 213–17, *218*, 227n18; Republicans and, 205–9, 212–25; reserve components and, 176, 182, 200n50; terrorism and, 204, 211; US Congress and, 212, 216, 227; Vietnam War and, 204, 225; Violence Against Women Reauthorization Act and, 156; World War II and, 203–4
Ghani, Ashraf, 285
Gilmour, Robert, 262
Glasser, Susan, 281
Glennon, Michael, 277
Global War on Terror (GWOT): Bush and, 3, 14, 312–13, 347, 356–57; conclusion of, 339–40; institutional response to, 340–43; Israel and, 349; post-GWOT syndrome, 340–41, 349–53, 356–57; September 11, 2001, terrorist attacks and, 339, 350
Golden, Marissa, 270–71
Goldsmith, Jack, 44, 305–6, 356–57
Goldwater, Barry, 145, 155
Good Friday Peace Accords, 157
Gorbachev, Mikhail, 138, 157
Goren, Paul, 363n63
Gowa, Joanne, 47
Great Depression, 211
Great Society, 138, 145–46, 155, 265
Green Berets, 356
Greene, Marjorie Taylor, 348
Green-Riley, Naima, 235–36
Grenada, 339, 347
Guam, 268

Guantanamo, 313, 318
Gulf of Tonkin Resolution, 110, 340
Gulf War: George H. W. Bush and, 147, 151, 347; foreign policy and, 151, *166*; gender and, 204; Hussein and, 151; manpower system knowledge and, 189; reserve components and, 189; terrorism and, 339–42, 347

Haberman, Maggie, 270, 291n45, 292n49
Haiti, 4, *166*, *170*, 316
Halperin, Morton, 265, 289n22
Hamilton, Alexander, 179
Hanania, Richard, 277
Hansen, Michael, 205, 224
"Hastert Rule," 27
Hastings, Alcee, 345
Hatfield, Mark, 4
Hawaii, 153
hawks: Democrats and, 20, 28, 42, 48–52, 57, 61–63, 66, 206; ideology of, 20, 28, 42, 48–54, 57–67, 74n80, 122, 130, 206, 239, 249, 258n39, 339, 347; polarization and, 48; Republicans and, 20, 28, 48–52, 57, 61–63, 66, 206, 237
Hayden, Michael V., 336n82
Hill, Christopher, 273
Hobbs, William, 137–38
homophily, 246–48
Horowitz, Michael, 178, 183
Housing Act, 146
Howell, William, 129
Hoyer, Steny, 308
human rights, 25, 151, *164*, *169*
Hunter, Robert, 262
Huq, Aziz, 13
Hussein, Saddam: Bush and, 51, 151, 156, 211–12; capture of, 215; Gulf War and, 131, 151, 156, *169*, 211–12, 215

ideologies: bipartisanship and, 81–82; communal groups and, 232, 237–39, *241*, 247, 251, 258n39; conservatism, 3, 47, 80–81, 155; of Democrats, 4 (*see also* Democrats); dovish, 17, 28, 42, 48–52, 54, 57, 61–62, 66–67, 122, 205–6, 345, 348, 353; electoral context and, 72n61; gender and, 205, 224; hawkish, 20, 28, 42, 48–54, 57–67, 74n80, 122, 130, 206, 239, 249, 258n39, 339, 347; interventionism, 27–28,

INDEX 375

30, 344, 350–52; isolationism, 27–28, 340, 344, 348–53; liberalism, 3, 47, 80–81, 144; loyalty and, 47–49; opposition and, 111, 128–31; partisanship and, 41–67, 69n18, 71n51, 72n58, 72n61, 74n79–80, 345–49; polarization and, 3–4, 6, 18, 41, 47–48, 80–82, 98n1, 131, 232; presidential powers and, 17–18; of Republicans, 4 (*see also* Republicans); research methodology on, 57; reserve components and, 196–97; war powers and, 319

impeachment, 4, 136, *167*, 172n9, 283

imperialism: bureaucratic politics and, 277; Bush and, 1–2, 30; founding fathers and, 321; Johnson and, 338; Nixon and, 30, 338; partisanship and, 40, 44, 77; presidential powers and, 1–2, 25–26, 30, 40, 44, 77, 277, 321, 338, 344; Schlesinger on, 2; terrorism and, 344; war powers and, 321, 338

Imperial Presidency, The (Schlesinger), 2

inequality, 9, 250

Ingber, Rebecca, 25–26, 264, 267, 299–337

Insurrection Act, 287

Intelligence Reform and Terrorism Prevention Act, 156

interventionism, 27–28, 30, 344, 350–52

Iran-Contra affair, 4, *165*

Iraq War: Authorization to Use Military Force (AUMF) and, 21, 54, 73n75, 341–42, 347; beginning of, 51; bipartisanship and, 79; bureaucratic politics and, 273, 275, 277–79, 293n70; George H. W. Bush and, 147, 151, 204; George W. Bush and, 6, 16, 19–20, 51–52, 66–67, 106, 115, 118, 130, 152, 154, 156, 202, 211–12, 219, 225, 278, 313, 347, 356; communal groups and, 236; electoral context and, 111–12, 114–15, 118–22; Fallujah contractors and, 118; first Persian Gulf War and, 147, 151, 204; foreign policy and, 138, 147, 151–56, *167*–69, *171*; gender and, 203–4, 207, 209–25; Hussein and, 51, 131, 151, 156, *169*, 211–12, 215; Kuwait and, 108, 138, 147, 151, *166*; manpower system knowledge and, 189; Obama and, 20, 43, 51–54, 66–67, 152, 210–11, 219, 224, 278–79, 341; opposition and, 106–17, 127–31; partisanship and, 43, 50–67, 73nn76–77, 74n79, 363n62; Powell Doctrine and, 341–42; presidential powers and, 3, 6, 8–11, 15–23, 28; public opinion and, 6, 23, 37, 116, 130, 202–4, 207, 209–25, 229n45, 236, 254n14; research methodology on, 52–67, 73n71, 73nn76–77; reserve components and, 176, 184, 189, *190*; Shinseki and, 106–7; terrorism and, 341–43, 347–48, 352–57; Trump and, 347; war powers and, 313

Ireland, 157

ISIS, 285, 337n107

isolationism: Bush and, 350; presidential powers and, 27–28; public opinion and, 361n47; terrorism and, 27–28, 340, 344, 348–53, 361n47; Vietnam War and, 353–54

Israel, 24; communal groups and, 233, 237–53, 257n28, 258nn29–30, 258n39, 259n41; foreign policy and, 148, 151, 154, 157, *160*, *162*, *164*, *166*–68; funds for, 27, 29; Global War on Terror (GWOT) and, 349; political alienation and, 248–50; public opinion and, 224; Wye River Memorandum and, 157–58

Israel Defense Forces (IDF), 258n30

Jackson, Henry "Scoop," 48

Jacobson, Gary, 6

January 6, 2021, insurrection. *See* Capitol, attack on

Javits, Jacob, 4

Jefferson, Thomas, 179

Jentleson, Bruce, 349

Jeong, Gyung-Ho, 48

Jews: Mizrahi, 233, *237*, 238–40, 243–49, 253, 260n59; non-Ashkenazic, 233, *237*, 238, 240, *241*, 248–49, 259n41; political alienation and, 248–50; Sephardic, 233, *237*, 238–49

Johnson, Lyndon B.: Civil Rights Act and, 145; Dallek on, 145; domestic policy and, 144–47; Elementary and Secondary Education Act and, 138, 155; foreign policy and, 138, *140*, 142, 144–47, 155, 172n6, 174n38; Great Society and, 138, 145–46, 155, 265; Housing Act and, 146; imperialism and, 338; Land and Water Conservation Fund Act and, 146; memoirs of, 145–46; midterm elections and, 144–47; Office of Economic Opportunity, 145;

Johnson, Lyndon B. (*cont.*)
  opposition and, 130, 138; presidential powers and, 7, 11, 22; public opinion and, 202; reelection and, 202; reserve components and, 176, 201n54; Ruby and, 174n38; sweep of 1964 and, 144–47; taxes and, 11; Twenty-Fourth Amendment and, 145; US Constitution and, 145, 172n6; Vietnam War and, 11, 22, 130, 138, 146, 155, 176, 201n54, 338; Voting Rights Act and, 155
Johnson, Mike, 27
Joint Comprehensive Plan of Action (JCPOA), 153, 159

Kagan, Elena, 319
Kahneman, Daniel, 180–81
Kant, Immanuel, 22
Kanter, Arnold, 265
Karl, Jonathan, 282
Katyal, Neal, 286
Kaufman, Herbert, 271
Kelly, John, 271
Kennedy, John F.: Bay of Pigs and, 153, *161*, 269; bureaucratic politics and, 263, 268–69, 274, 276, 288n4; foreign policy and, 139, *140*, 142; midterm elections and, 151
Kennedy, Robert, 146–47, 151
Kenya, 157, 341
Kerry, John, 156, 212, 225, 345
Khrushchev, Nikita, 153
Kinzinger, Adam, 346
Kissinger, Henry, *163*, 262, 274, 288n4, 339
Klarevas, Louis, 206
Korean War: foreign policy and, 154, *160*, *162*, *168–69*; manpower system knowledge and, 189; opposition and, 106; partisanship and, 40, 65; presidential powers and, 4, 11, 17; public opinion and, 17, 204, 235, 249; reserve components and, 189, *190*; Truman and, 4, 16–17, 25, 40, 65, 153–54, *160*
Kosovo, 4, 236
Krebs, Ronald, 24, 179–82, 194, 196, 201n56, 231–61
Kreps, Sara E., 1–76, 79, 105, 131, 209, 320, 338–63
Krimmel, Katherine, 202–30, 232
Kriner, Douglas L., 1–76, 79, 105, 113, 131, 185, 202–32, 320, 338–63

Kucinich, Dennis, 113
Kurds, 42
Kushner, Jared, 287
Kuwait, 108, 138, 147, 151, *166*

LaFeber, Walter, 342
Land and Water Conservation Fund Act, 146
Landrum Griffin Act, 153
Laos, 340
Latinos, 55, 57, *58*, *61*, 252–53, 261n71
Lawson, Gary, 331n35
Lebanon, 130, 148, 152, 155, *161*, *163*, *165*, 238
Leber, Andrew, 235–36
Lee, Barbara, 113, 347
Lee, Frances, 4
Levendusky, Matthew, 183
Levinson, Daryl, 41, 320
Levy, Jack, 108
Lewinsky, Monica, 154, 157
liberalism, 3, 47, 80–81, 144
Libya, 67, 272, 316, 337n107, 342, 345
Lieberman, Joe, 48
Lincoln, Abraham, 1, 287
Lindsey, David, 137–38
Lockheed-Martin, 277
logit models, *187*, *195*, 220–21, 222

Mabe, William, 108
MacArthur, Douglas, 25
"Made in America," 357
Madison, James: checks and, 41, 265, 320–21; *Federalist* essays, 40, 265, 289n16; Glennon on, 277; volunteer militia and, 179; war powers and, 1
"Make America Great Again," 357
Mao Tse-tung, 40
Markey, Edward, 18–19
Marsh, Kevin, 279–80
Marshall Plan, 29
Mason, Robert, 144
Mattis, James: bureaucratic politics and 266, 270, 281, 283, 297n130; as secretary of defense, 266, 270, 281–82, 330n34, 346; Trump and, 270, 281–83, 297n130, 330n34, 346, 348
Mayhew, David, 19
McCain, John, 4, 20, 67, 345
McChrystal, Stanley, 279–80, 343

McConnell, Michael, 276
McConnell, Mitch, 308, 341, 346
McEntee, Johnny, 284
McKiernan, David, 278–79
McMaster, H. R., 281, 296n119, 348
Meacham, Jon, 147–48
Medicaid, 138, 155, *162*
Medicare, 138, 145, 152, 155, *162*, *168*
Meier, Kenneth, 269
Menendez, Bob, 18–19
Mexico, 151, *167*, *170*, 352
midterm elections: Bush and, 16, 19–20, 139, *141*, 152–54, 202; domestic policy and, 21, 135–38, 144, 151–54, 157–59, 363n65; first-term, 150–52; foreign policy and, 135–44, 150, 156, 158–59; impact of, 150; Johnson and, 144–47; Kennedy and, 151; Nixon and, 136, 139–44, 151; Obama and, 20, *141*, 153, 156–59, 202; second-term, 152–54; sweep of 1964 and, 144–47; Trump and, 139, *141*, 159; US Congress and, 16, 19–21, 135–44, 150, 156, 158–59, 202, 212, 344, 363n65
military: adventurism and, 9, 40, 106–9, 177, 341, 356; in Afghanistan, US, 79 (*see also* Afghanistan); all-volunteer force (AVF), 176, 179–80, 183, 196; bipartisanship and, 80–81, 95; bureaucratic politics and, 269–70, 273–74, 277–87, 290n24; casualties and, 16 (*see also* casualties); Civil War and, 179; coercion and, 178–96, 198n22; communal groups and, 231–53, 258n34, 258n39, 259nn40–41, 260n54; contracts with, 277; desertion and, 198n22; draft into, 9 (*see also* draft); drones and, 11–12 (*see also* draft); empathy and, 242–44; foreign policy and, *164*–68; framing and, 180–81; gender and, 23, 54, 57, 176, 182, 200n50, 202–8, 216, 220–21, 224, 239, *241*, 258n39, 282, 354; gender gap and, 23, 54, 57, 176, 200n50, 203–8, 221, 224; Iraq War and, 21 (*see also* Iraq War); Korean War and, 40 (*see also* Korean War); manpower system knowledge and, 188–90, *191*; misadventure and, 40; norms, 178–81; opposition and, 105–14, 118, *123*, 127–31, 206–9, 212–13, 217, 220–24; partisanship and, 40–51, 54–58, *61*, 65–67, 73n76; patriotism and, 180, 192, *193*; political culture and, 178–81;

presidential powers and, 2, 5, 8–30; prospect theory and, 177–81; public opinion on, 178–81, 184–88, 195–97, 200n43, 206–14, 217, 220–24; racial groups and, 234–36; research methodology on, 181–88; reserve components and, 175–97, 200n50; security and, 180, 202; "shock and awe" campaigns of, 347; soldier motivation and, 192–94, 238, *241*, 244–46, 250–51, 258n30; spending cuts and, 353–54, 362nn52–53; status quo and, 180–81; terrorism and, 338–48, 353–57, 361n44, 362nn52–53; troop surges, 43, 52, 66–67, 79, *169*, 210–11, 219, 345; Vietnam War and, 9 (*see also* Vietnam War); voluntarism and, 175, 177, 179–80, 183–94, 197; war powers and, 299–308, 312–17, 322, 324–25nn13–14, 327n15; West Point and, 270; World War I and, 179, 189; World War II and, 4 (*see also* World War II)
Miller, Christopher, 282, 284, 303, 308, 327n15, 332n48
Miller, Jason, 348
Milley, Mark, 283–84, 308
minority groups, 24, 233, 253, 256n23, 261n71
mobilization: degree of compulsion and, 176–78; National Guard and, 23, 176, 183–84, 189, 196, 201n54, 324–25nn13–14; prospect theory and, 177–81; public opinion on, 177–78; reserve components and, 22–23, 175–97, 201n54, 302, 324–25nn13–14
monarchy, 13, 40, 44
Mondale, Walter, 157
moral issues, *164*, 260n68, 276, 314, 328n27
Mueller, Robert, 272
Mullen, Mike, 273, 287
Mulvaney, Mick, 60
Murphy, Chris, 42

National Defense Education Act, 155
National Economic Council (NEC), 270
National Guard: Capitol attack and, 303–4, 308, 324–25nn12–14, 327n15; manpower system knowledge and, 188–90, *191*; mobilization of, 23, 176, 183–84, 189, 196, 201n54, 324–25nn13–14; as reserve component, 23, 176–77, 180, 183–84, 189, 196, 201n54, 202, 303–4, 308, 310, 324–25nn13–14, 327n15, 327n18;

National Guard (*cont.*)
significant role of, 177; Trump and, 303–4, 308, 324n12, 331n46, 332n48, 346
National Rifle Association (NRA), 81
National Security Council (NSC), 262, 267, 280–84, 339
NATO, 75n80; Biden and, 357; bipartisanship and, 95; communal groups and, 270, 272, 283; Eisenhower and, 270; foreign policy and, 151, 154, *160*, *166–67*; Libya and, 272, 345; Obama and, 345; Russia and, 357; Trump and, 283, 357
Neustadt, Richard, 25, 265, 286
New Deal, 100n12, 265
New START, 152, *171*
Nicaragua, 148, 153, *165*, 339
Nicholson, John W., 282
Niger, 341, 356
Nincic, Donna, 235
Nincic, Miroslav, 235
Niskanen, William, 270
Nixon, Richard M.: bureaucratic politics and, 269, 273, 288n4; domestic policy and, 139, 142; foreign policy and, 136, 139–44, 147, 151, 155–56, 159, *162–63*; imperialism and, 30, 338; Mason on, 144; midterm elections and, 136, 139–44, 151; Phase Three and Four price controls and, 156; presidential powers and, 7; reelection and, 155–56; reserve components and, 179; resignation of, 156; "Social Issue" and, 142; supersecretaries of, 273; veto power and, 340; Vietnam War and, 142, 179, 338–40; War Powers Resolution and, 340; Watergate and, 16, 40, 155–56, *162–63*, 291n37
North Korea: foreign policy and, *162*, *168*; Truman and, 25; Trump and, 27, 281–83, 287; war plans for, 287

Obama, Barack: Afghanistan and, 11, 28, 42–43, 49–56, 61–63, 66–67, 211, 224, 276–78, 281, 284, 287, 296n121, 341–45; American Jobs Act and, 152; American Taxpayer Relief Act and, 156; bipartisanship and, 83, 94–95, 344; Bipartisan Student Loan Certainty Act and, 157; Budget Control Act and, 152; bureaucratic politics and, 276–81, 284, 287, 288n8, 296n121, 362; casualties and, 12, 51, 66, 278; Clean Power Plan and, 153; counterterrorism and, 42, 279, 284, 357; Don't Ask, Don't Tell and, 152; drones and, 11–12, 337n107, 356–57; executive norms and, 312; foreign policy and, *141*, 152–53, 156–59; gender and, 211, 219, 224, 229n50; Iraq War and, 20, 43, 51–54, 66–67, 152, 210–11, 219, 224, 278–79, 341; JCPOA and, 153, 159; Libya and, 67, 337n107, 342, 345; meteoric rise of, 202; midterm elections and, 20, *141*, 153, 156–59, 202; NATO and, 345; New START and, 152; Office of Legal Counsel (OLC) and, 342; Paris Climate Accords and, 153, 159; partisanship and, 42–45, 49–56, 61–67, 72n66, 75n88, 344–45; post-9/11 context and, 278–80, 287; presidential powers and, 7, 11–12, 20, 28, 33n37, 312, 334n64, 336n85, 337n107; reelection of, *141*, 156, 267; rhetoric and, 45; Romney and, 156; Russia and, 341, 357; STOCK Act and, 152; Syria and, 157, 344; troop surges and, 43, 51, 66–67, 72n66, 211, 219, 278–81, 345; US Constitution and, 342, 344; Veteran Suicide Act and, 153; Violence Against Women Reauthorization Act and, 156; war powers and, 312, 333n55, 334n64, 336n85, 337n107, 342; Woodward on, 52; Yemen and, 11, *12*, 33n37
O'Brien, Robert, 283–84
O'Connell, Anne Joseph, 262
Office of Economic Opportunity, 145
Office of Emergency Preparedness (OEP), 268
Office of Legal Counsel (OLC): Article III and, 315; Authorization to Use Military Force (AUMF) and, 14, 317, 337n107, 342; Bush and, 14, 271, 313, 337n107, 342; executive norms and, 313; legal interpretation and, 313–17; Obama and, 342; presidential powers and, 14, 271–72, 313–17, 335n71, 335n78, 336n79, 337n107, 342; self-citations of, 289n11; September 11, 2001, terrorist attacks and, 342; surveillance and, 271; Trump and, 317; US Congress and, 14, 313, 316, 337n107, 342; War Powers Resolution and, 14, 272, 316–17; Yoo and, 14
Office of Management and Budget (OMB), 267

INDEX

Operation Desert Shield, 235, 249
Operation Desert Storm, 235, 249
opposition: Afghanistan and, 106–8, 128, 130; benefits of early, 105–31; bureaucratic politics and, 263, 278; George W. Bush and, 106, 115, 118, 130; casualties and, 21, 107–15, 121–23, 127–28; communal groups and, 232–35, 238, 243–45, 249; costs of war and, 108; Democrats and, 108, 111–12, 115–20; Eichenberg and, 204, 207; electoral context and, 111–15, 118–26; gender and, 206–9, 212–13, 217, 220–24; ideologies and, 111, 128–31; institutional constraint and, 105–6; Iraq War and, 106–17, 127–31; Johnson and, 130, 138; Korean War and, 106; military and, 105–14, 118, *123*, 127–31, 206–9, 212–13, 217, 220–24; partisanship and, 206–9, 212–13, 217, 220–24; polarization and, 115, 131; preconflict, 20, 107–10, 113, 116–18, 122–24, 130; public opinion and, 122; punishment for, 109–10; recency bias and, 127–28; reelection and, 107, 111, 118, 126, 129; regression analysis and, 116; Republicans and, 111, 114–15, 117–26; research methodology on, 110–22; rhetoric and, 131; terrorism and, 130, 344–48, 353, 355; US Congress and, 105–16, 120–22, 126–31; Vietnam War and, 106–9, 114, 128–31, 134; war powers and, 303; World War II and, 108–9, 128
organization theory, 266

Pakistan, 11, *12*, 33n37, 278, 284
Palestine, 29, 154, 157, *168*, 349
Palmer, Max, 202–30, 232
Panetta, Leon, 262, 275–76, 279, 295n109
Paris Climate Accords, 153, 159
Paris Peace Accords, 338–40
partisanship: Afghanistan and, 40–43, 49, 51–67, 73n71, 74nn77–79; anti-presidential, 18, 41, 77–84, 90–95, 106, 345; Bush and, 42–43, 51–52, 55, 66–67; checks and, 41–44, 73n74; Clinton and, 67, 75n88; Cold War and, 48, 65; commander in chief and, 40–41, 45; cross-, 77–81, 87, 90, 94, 103n44; Democrats and, 42–44, 47–66; Eichenberg and, 204, 207; electoral context and, 18, 46, 50, 58–61, 64, 72n61, 74n79; foreign policy and, 40–67; gender and, 203–24, 229n48, 229n50; hedging and, 61–65; ideologies and, 41–67, 69n18, 71n51, 72n58, 72n61, 74nn79–80, 345–49; imperialism and, 40, 44, 77; Iraq War and, 43, 50–67, 73nn76–77, 74n79, 363n62; Korean War and, 40, 65; loyalty and, 46–47; military and, 40–51, 54–58, *61*, 65–67, 73n76; Obama and, 42–45, 49–56, 61–67, 72n66, 75n88, 344–45; opposition and, 206–9, 212–13, 217, 220–24; polarization and, 41, 47–48, 50, 65; post-9/11 context and, 41, 43; presidential powers and, 44, 54; public opinion and, 45, 50, 206–11, 214, 223–24; reelection and, 50, 60, 67; regression analysis and, 55, *58*, *61*; Republicans and, 43–44, 47–67; research methodology on, 52–67, 73n71, 73–74nn76–77; rhetoric and, 18, 44–64, 72n58, 74n79, 212–13; security and, 47; separation of parties and, 41–42; teamsmanship and, 4; terrorism and, 42, 51; tribalism and, 6–8, 232; Truman and, 40, 65; Trump and, 42, 344–45; US Congress and, 40–60, 63–67; US Constitution and, 41, 44; Vietnam War and, 48, 65; War Powers Resolution and, 40
patriotism: blind, 239, *241*, 249, 260n68; communal groups and, 239, *241*, 244, 246, 249, 260n68; military and, 180, 192, *193*
Pearl Harbor, 1, 270
Pelosi, Nancy, 67, 308
Pence, Mike, 308, 331n46
Pentagon: budget of, 266; bureaucratic politics and, 262, 266–74, 277, 282–84, 287; Capitol attack and, 310, 313–14; Mullen and, 273; National Military Command Center and, 270; presidential powers and, 30; September 11, 2001, terrorist attacks and, 30; Syria and, 282; war powers and, 302–3, 310, 324–35nn13–14; Weinberger and, 267
Pevehouse, Jon, 129
Pew Research Center, 29, 183, 200nn41–42, 211, 236
Philippines, 341
Pickering, Jeffrey, 178
Pildes, Richard, 41, 320
Planned Parenthood, 81
polarization: anti-presidential, 18, 41, 77–84, 90–95, 106, 345; bipartisanship and,

polarization (cont.)
    76–96, 98n1, 98n4; communal groups and, 232, 235, 252; electoral context and, 50; elitism and, 3, 6, 28, 77, 80, 235; foreign policy and, 135, 156–59; hawks vs. doves, 48; ideological, 3–4, 6, 18, 41, 47–48, 80–82, 98n1, 131, 232; opposition and, 115, 131; partisanship and, 41, 47–48, 50, 65; presidential powers and, 3–6, 7, 17–18, 24, 28; strong, 78–80, 84, 87–89, 94; terrorism and, 344; variations of, 87–93
Polk, James, 1, 172n6
Pompeo, Mike, 283
post-9/11 context: Biden and, 284–86; bipartisanship and, 87, 94; budget deficits and, 358; bureaucratic politics and, 275; costs of war and, 8–13; foreign policy and, 135, 158–59, 170, 275–86; gender and, 202, 221; Obama and, 278–80, 287; partisanship and, 41, 43; presidential powers and, 3, 9, 11, 16, 26, 30, 340; public opinion and, 338, 349; reserve components and, 176–77; Trump and, 280–84; US Congress and, 343; war powers and, 300; withdrawal from Afghanistan, 3, 18, 28, 42, 51, 66, 204, 219–21, 222, 225, 280–86, 296n119, 297n148, 299, 330n34, 338, 344, 346
Potter, Philip B. K., 21, 41, 135–74, 363n65
poverty, 145–46, 279
Powell, Colin, 25
Powell Doctrine, 341–42
pre-9/11 context: bipartisanship and, 80, 84, 94; isolationism and, 350; presidential powers and, 1, 4, 340, 350, 358
"Presidential Administration" (Kagan), 319
Presidential Power (Neustadt), 25
presidential powers: Afghanistan and, 1, 3, 8–13, 17–18, 23, 26, 28; approval ratings and, 6–8; Article I and, 2, 16; Article II and, 13–14, 264, 316; bipartisanship and, 94; bureaucratic politics and, 264, 286; Bush and, 1, 3, 6, 14, 16, 19–20, 342, 347; Carter and, 6–8; checks and, 1–28; Clinton and, 4, 7–8, 20, 25; Cold War and, 4, 9, 25; commander in chief as, 2–3, 15–18, 40–41, 45, 175, 203, 206, 270, 284, 299, 304, 341, 347, 356; Democrats and, 3–8, 16–24, 27–29; draft and, 9–10, 14; Eisenhower and, 6–8, 15; elitism and, 3, 6, 22–23, 28–29; executive norms and, 311–13; executive office and, 13, 16, 26, 40, 43–44, 264–65, 300–302, 306, 310–22, 333n58, 342; executive orders (EOs), 25, 152, 157, *171*, 267–68, 290n34, 309; Ford and, 7; foreign policy and, 1–29, 135–36; ideologies and, 17–18; impeachment and, 4, 136, *167*, 172n9, 283; imperialism and, 1–2, 25–26, 30, 40, 44, 77, 277, 321, 338, 344; Iraq War and, 3, 6, 8–11, 15–23, 28; isolationism and, 27–28; Johnson and, 7, 11, 22; Korean War and, 4, 11, 17; military and, 2, 5, 8–30, 23–24; Nixon and, 7; Obama and, 7, 11–12, 20, 28, 33n37, 312, 334n64, 336n85, 337n107; Office of Legal Counsel (OLC) and, 14, 271–72, 313–17, 335n71, 335–36nn78–79, 337n107, 342; partisanship and, 44, 54; Pentagon and, 30; polarization and, 3–6, 7, 17–18, 24, 28; post-9/11 context and, 3, 9, 11, 16, 26, 30, 340, 343, 353, 358; pre-9/11 context and, 1, 4, 80, 84, 94, 340, 350, 358; public opinion and, 2–3, 6, 8, 17–24, 26, 28–29; Reagan and, 4, 7, 13; Republicans and, 3–8, 17–20, 27–29; separation of powers and, 13, 41–44, 264–65, 304, 310, 319–22; September 11, 2001, attacks and, 1–19, 26–30, 33n37; terrorism and, 11, 14, 340–44; Truman and, 16–17, 25, 29; Trump and, 3, 7, 11–14, 25, 27, 299–313, 317, 323nn7–8, 324n12, 327n20, 328n25, 329n28, 329n31, 330n34; unenumerated, 13–14; unilateral, 24–25, 44, 76, 301, 305, 313, 316–17, 342–45; unitary executive theory and, 13–15; US Congress and, 1–5, 11–21, 26–29; US Constitution and, 2, 13–14, 16, 24, 28, 339, 342, 344; veto, 16, 153, *160, 162–63, 165, 167, 169*, 340; Vietnam War and, 4, 9, 11, 22–23, 28; war powers, 14 (*see also* war powers); World War II and, 4, 6, 9, 16–19, 33n34, 356
primus inter pares, 15, 26
principal-agent problems: bureaucratic politics and, 266–76; information asymmetry and, 266; unitary executive theory and, 15
privacy, 1, *163*
prospect theory, 177–81
Public Agenda Forum, 236

public opinion: ABC News/Washington Post poll and, 220; Afghanistan and, 203–4, 207, 209–25; ANES and, 20, 203, 350, 352, 354; Biden and, 28–30; casualties and, 22, 24, 122, 176, 203, 206, 234–36, 249, 251–53, 254n14, 258n34; checks and, 19–24; commander in chief and, 203, 347; communal groups and, 234–36, 249–53, 256n26; conscription and, 177–78; costs of war and, 223; culture wars and, 363n63; draft and, 176; elitism and, 6, 22–23, 28–29, 176–78, 203–15, 219, 223–25, 357–58; foreign policy and, 3, 17, 19, 23, 26, 151, 208, 252, 342, 349, 353–54, 361n45, 361n47; Gallup polls and, 6, 7, 116, 121, 210, 213, 217, 229n45, 229n47, 356; gender and, 202–3, 206–11, 214, 220–21, 223–24; Iraq War and, 6, 23, 37, 116, 130, 202–4, 207, 209–25, 229n45, 236, 254n14; Israel and, 224; Johnson and, 202; Korean War and, 17, 204, 235, 249; military and, 178–81, 184–88, 195–97, 200n43, 206–14, 217, 220–24; mobilization and, 177–78; opposition and, 122, 206–9, 212–13, 217, 220–24; partisanship and, 45, 50, 206–11, 214, 223–24; Pew Research Center and, 29, 183, 200nn41–42, 211, 236; post-9/11 context and, 338, 349; presidential powers and, 2–3, 6, 8, 17–24, 26, 28–29; reserve components and, 175–78, 184–88, 195–97, 200n43; Roper Center's iPoll, 216; Truman and, 202; Vietnam War and, 11, 23, 130, 235–36, 249, 254n14, 349; Zaller's reception axiom and, 208

Putin, Vladimir, 154

Quasi-War with France, 6
Quirk, Paul J., 48

racial groups: African Americans, 55, 61, 233–34, 236, 250, 261n71; Arabs, 33n37, 148, 151, 166, 241, 258n30; Asian Americans, 261n71; Black people, 148, 233–36, 237, 241, 249–53, 256n20, 256n23, 261n71; casualty sensitivity and, 24; communal, 231–51, 258n30, 259n42; empathy and, 205, 242–44, 251; gender and, 224; homophily and, 246–48; Jews, 233 (*see also* Jews); Latinos, 55, 57, 58, 61, 252–53, 261n71; marriage and, 94; military and, 234–36; minorities, 24, 233, 253, 256n23, 261n71; nondominant, 234–36; nonwhite, 233, 236, 239–52, 260n54; political alienation and, 248–50

Ralston, Robert, 24, 180, 182, 194, 196, 201n56, 231–61
Rapport, Aaron, 180, 182, 194, 196, 201n56
Reagan, Ronald: bureaucratic politics and, 267; foreign policy and, *140–41*, 147, 152–53, 157–58, 347; Gorbachev and, 157; Iran-Contra affair and, 4, *165*; Mondale and, 157; Nicaragua and, 153, 339; presidential powers and, 4, 7, 13; reelection of, *141*, 157–58; Soviet Union and, 153, 157; terrorism and, 339, 345, 347, 354; US Constitution and, 13, 339; veto power and, 153; Vietnam syndrome and, 339; Water Quality Control Act and, 153

Real Majority, The (Scammon and Wattenberg), 142
Reconstruction, 250
red states, 50, 60–61
reelection: Bush and, 19–20, 118, *141*, 156, 202; casualties and, 107; Clinton and, 67, 150, 157–58, 172n9; Eisenhower and, 151, 155; foreign policy and, 21, 135–44, 147–51, 154–59, 172n6, 172n9; Johnson opting out of, 202; Mayhew on, 19; Nixon and, 155–56; Obama and, 156; opposition and, 107, 111, 118, 126, 129; partisanship and, 50, 60, 67; Reagan and, *141*, 157–58; second-term presidents and, 154–58; Truman opting out of, 17, 172n6, 202; War on Poverty and, 145

regression analysis: communal groups and, 240–43, 258n37; gender and, 213–17, *218*, 227n18; opposition and, 116; ordinary least squares (OLS), 116; partisanship and, 55, 58, 61; reserve components and, 186, 189, 194; terrorism and, 350, 354

Rehnquist, William, 157
Reifler, Jason, 235–36
religion: Civil Rights Act and, 145; communal groups and, 232–33, *237*, *241*, 251, 258n39
Republicans: bipartisanship and, 76–96; communal groups and, 253; doves and, 17, 28, 48–52, 57, 61–62, 66, 205–6, 345; foreign policy and, 136, 139–45, 150–53, 156, 159; gender and, 205–9, 212–25; Hastert

Republicans (*cont.*)
  Rule and, 27; hawkish, 20, 28, 48–52, 57, 61–63, 66, 206, 237; opposition and, 111, 114–15, 117–26; partisanship and, 43–44, 47–67; presidential powers and, 3–8, 17–20, 27–29; red states, 50, 60–61; reserve components and, 182–83, 186–89, *195*; terrorism and, 344–47; war powers and, 319–20
reserve components: adventurism and, 9, 177, 341, 356; Afghanistan and, 176, 184, 189; all-volunteer force (AVF), 176, 179–80, 183, 196; casualties and, 176–78, *187*, 194–96; checks and, 177; coercion and, 178–96, 198n22; Cold War and, 179; commander in chief and, 175; conscription and, 175–80, 197; costs of war and, 197; degree of compulsion and, 176–78; Democrats and, 182–83, 186, *187*, *195*; desertion and, 198n22; draft and, 176–81, 184, 189, *190*, 201n55; elitism and, 176–78, 196; ethnicity and, 182; foreign policy and, 181; framing and, 180–81; gender and, 176, 182, 200n50; Gulf War and, 189; ideologies and, 196–97; Iraq War and, 176, 184, 189, *190*; Johnson and, 176, 201n54; Korean War and, 189, *190*; manpower system knowledge and, 188–90, *191*; military and, 176, 182, 200n50; mobilization and, 22–23, 175–97, 201n54, 302, 324–25nn13–14; National Guard, 23, 176–77, 180, 183–84, 189, 196, 201n54, 202, 303–4, 308, 310, 324–27nn13–15, 327n18; Nixon and, 179; perceptions of motivations of, 192–94; political costs of, 176; post-9/11 context and, 176–77; prospect theory and, 177–81; public opinion and, 175–78, 184–88, 195–97, 200n43; regression analysis and, 186, 189, 194; Republicans and, 182–83, 186–89, *195*; research methodology on, 181–88; rhetoric and, 176, 178; security and, 180; Selective Service System and, *10*, *162*, 176, 199n25; September 11, 2001, attacks and, 177; status quo and, 180–81; US Congress and, 175, 177; Vietnam War and, 176, 179, 189–90, 196; voluntarism and, 175, 177, 179–80, 183–94, 197; World War II and, 179, 189, 200n44
#Resistance, 305–7, 321

rhetoric: deep state and, 305–7, 319; electoral context and, 50; hedging and, 61–65; importance of, 44–50; loyalty and, 46–49; as mechanism of persuasion, 44–45; nuanced, 61–65; Obama and, 45; opposition and, 131; partisanship and, 18, 44–64, 72n58, 74n79, 212–13; research methodology on, 52–64; reserve components and, 176, 178; US Congress and, 18, 44–64, 72n58, 74n79
Riedel, Bruce, 279
Roberts, John, 156
Rodman, Peter, 286–87
Romney, Mitt, 156, 352
Roosevelt, Franklin, 263–64
Roosevelt, Theodore, 1
Roper Center's iPoll, 216
Rothkopf, David, 287
Roudebush, Richard, 139
Rourke, Francis, 262–63, 273, 287–88
Ruby, Jack, 174n38
Rudalevige, Andrew, 25–26, 262–98, 300, 342–43
rule of law, 24, 142, 303
Rumsfeld, Donald, 14–15, 275–77, 295n92, 342
Russia: bureaucratic politics and, 263, 283; Clinton and, 151, 154, 157; Crimea and, *171*; NATO and, 151, 154, *167*, 283, 357; Obama and, 341, 357; online interference by, 45; Soviet Union, 29, 138, 147–48, 151–53, 157, *161*, *164*–66, 274, 287, 295n98; Trump and, 27, 283, 345, 348, 357; Ukraine and, 27, 29, 94, 348, 354–57
Rwanda, 4

SALT II, 151, *164*
Saudi Arabia, 151, *166*
Savage, Charlie, 272, 334n64
Scalia, Antonin, 157
Scammon, Richard, 142
Schake, Kori, 287
Schlesinger, Arthur, Jr., 2, 40, 294n90
Schultz, Kenneth, 108–9, 123
Schumer, Chuck, 308
Schwarz, Frederick, 13
security: bipartisanship and, 80–82, 95, 103n35, 357–58; bureaucratic politics and, 262–63, 267–73, 276–86, 288n4, 290n24, 297n148; civil liberties and, 1;

INDEX

deep state and, 24, 305–6, 317, 324n13; Department of Defense, 14, 16, 130, 263, 267–74, 279, 282, 302, 313, 318, 324–25nn13–14; Department of Homeland Security, *168*, 276, 309, 330n34; false sense of, 357–58; foreign policy and, 173n17; Internal Security Act, *160*; military and, 180, 202; Mutual Security Act, 174n38; National Security Act, *160*; National Security Council (NSC), 262, 267, 280–84, 339; partisanship and, 47; privacy and, 1; reserve components and, 180; September 11, 2001, attacks and, 1; social, 145, 152, 155–56, *160–63*, *165*; terrorism and, 339–43, 346, 349, 357; United Nations and, 113, 316–17; war powers and, 305–6, 309, 316–17, 324n13, 330n34
Segura, Gary, 109, 235–36
Seidman, Harold, 262
Selective Service System, *10*, *162*, 176, 199n25
Senate Committee on Foreign Relations, 18, 95
Separation of Parties, Not Powers (Levinson and Pildes), 320
September 11, 2001, terrorist attacks: al-Qaeda and, 6, 33n37, 333n62; Authorization to Use Military Force (AUMF) and, 14, 33n37; bipartisanship and, 80; bureaucratic politics and, 264, 275, 285; Bush and, 1, 6, 14; Costs of War Project and, 8; Global War on Terror (GWOT) and, 339, 350; lasting effects of, 42, 80, *169*, 284, 339–58; later Afghanistan withdrawal and, 3, 18, 28, 42, 51, 66, 204, 219–21, *222*, 225, 280–86, 296n119, 297n148, 299, 330n34, 338, 344, 346; Office of Legal Counsel (OLC) and, 342; Pentagon and, 30; post-9/11 context and, 3, 9, 11, 16, 26, 30; pre-9/11 context and, 1, 4, 80, 84, 94, 340, 350, 358; presidential powers and, 1–19, 26–30, 33n37; reserve components and, 177; security and, 1; World Trade Center and, 30
Serbia, 151, 154, *167*
Shaheen, Jeanne, 18–19
Shen, Francis, 113
Shinseki, Eric, 106–7
Simpson, Erin M., 178
Sixth Fleet, 155

Snyder, James, 45
social media: Capitol attack and, 309; Congressional rhetoric and, 45; #Resistance and, 305–7, 321; Twitter, 280, 299, 327n20, 328n25, 329n28
social security, 145, 152, 155–56, *160–63*, *165*
soldier motivation: communal groups and, 238, *241*, 244–46, 250–51, 258n30; logic of consent and, 244; pay, 245–46; perceptions of, 192–94
Somalia, 4, 11, *12*, 33n37, 130, *166*, *169*
Soviet Union: bureaucratic politics and, 287; Cold War and, 157 (*see also* Cold War); collapse of, 29, 138, 147–48; Cuba and, 274; Eisenhower and, 153; foreign policy and, 138, 147–48, 151, 153, 157, *161*, *164–66*; Gorbachev and, 157; Reagan and, 153, 157; Truman and, 151; U2 flights over, 151
Spratt, John, 60, 113
Stam, Allan C., 178
standard operating procedures (SOPs), 274–76, 286
START III, 157
"Stellar Wind," 271–72
Stevenson, Adlai, 155
STOCK Act, 152
suicide, 8, 153, *171*
suicide bombers, 285
Sullivan, Jake, 284
Sullivan, John, 36n67, 42, 69n17
surveillance, 6, *162*, 271–72
Sweden, 95
Syria: Beinart and, 42; Biden and, 42; foreign policy and, *171*; Obama and, 157, 344; Pentagon and, 282; Trump and, 42, 282–83, 317, 330n34, 346, 352; withdrawal from, 42, 283, 330n34, 346

Taft, Robert, 348
Taft-Hartley, 153
Taiwan, 27, 95, 151, *161*, *168*, 355
Taliban: Afghanistan and, 3, 18, 211, 219–20, 278–85, 297n149, 334n68, 338; bureaucratic politics and, 278–85, 298n148, 333n62, 334n68; Bush and, 333n62; Karzai regime and, 279; terrorism and, 3, 18, 45, 211, 219–20, 278–85, 295n92, 297n148, 333n62, 338, 346; Trump and, 3, 219, 281–84, 297n148, 346; US Congress and, 45

Tama, Jordan, 18–19, 41, 76–104, 106, 320
Tanzania, 157
Tax Reduction Act, 152
Teeter, Bob, 148
terrorism: Abbey Gate, 344; Afghanistan and, 3, 18, 28, 42, 51, 66, 204, 219–21, 222, 225, 280–86, 296n119, 297n148, 299, 330n34, 338, 341–47, 352, 356; al-Qaeda and, 6, 11, 33n37, 130, 278, 295n92, 333n62, 334n68; bin Laden and, 33n37, 152, *171*, 278, 284; bipartisanship and, 80; bureaucratic politics and, 277–81, 284–85; casualties and, 236, 338, 352, 361n44; checks and, 340, 343, 348–49, 353, 356; Clinton and, 342–43; communal groups and, 236; Democrats and, 344–51, 354, *355*; elitism and, 340, 348, 353–54, 357; ethnicity and, 350, 354; Ford and, 339, 341; foreign policy and, 42, 80, 154, 156, *169*, 284, 339–58; gender and, 204, 211; Gulf War and, 339–42, 347; GWOT and, 340 (*see also* Global War on Terror [GWOT]); imperialism and, 344; institutional response and, 340–43; Intelligence Reform and Terrorism Prevention Act and, 156; Iraq War and, 341–43, 347–48, 352–57; ISIS and, 285, 337n107; isolationism and, 27–28, 340, 344, 348–53, 361n47; military and, 338–48, 353–57, 361n44, 362nn52–53; opposition and, 130, 344–48, 353, 355; partisanship and, 42, 51; polarization and, 344; post-9/11 context and, 340 (*see also* post-9/11 context); presidential powers and, 11, 14, 340–44; Reagan and, 339, 345, 347, 354; regression analysis and, 350, 354; Republicans and, 344–47; security and, 339–43, 346, 349, 357; September 11, 2001, attacks and, 1, 6, 14 (*see also* September 11, 2001, terrorist attacks); Taliban and, 3, 18, 45, 211, 219–20, 278–85, 295n92, 297n148, 333n62, 338, 346; Trump and, 3, 219, 281–84, 297n148, 343–49, 352, 356–57, 361n47, 362n53; US Congress and, 338–49, 353–54; US Constitution and, 339, 342, 344; US Department of State and, 342; war powers and, 339, 342, 344, 350, 356–57
Thailand, 340
Tillerson, Rex, 270, 287

Ting, Michael, 45
Tora Bora, 278
tribalism, 6–8, 232
Truman, Harry S.: bureaucratic politics and, 277, 286; Fair Deal and, 154; foreign policy and, *140*, 151–55, *160*, 172n6, 174n38; Korean War and, 4, 16–17, 25, 40, 65, 153–54, *160*; partisanship and, 40, 65; presidential powers and, 16–17, 25, 29; public opinion and, 202; Soviet Union and, 151; US Constitution and, 172n6; war powers and, 16–17, 29, 40
Truman Doctrine, 151, *160*
Trump, Donald: Afghanistan and, 3, 11, 42, 56, 219–20, 270, 278–84, 296n119, 296n121, 297n135, 297n148, 299, 330n34, 343, 346–47, 352; America First and, 27, 347, 352; ANES and, 352; approval ratings of, 7–8; Beinart and, 42; bipartisanship and, 83, 94–95, 345–46, 357–58; bureaucratic politics and, 263–64, 270–73, 278, 280–87, 291n45, 292n51, 296n119, 296n121, 297n130, 297n135, 297n148; Capitol attack and, 301, 306, 308, 324–25nn12–14, 327n20; China and, 357; CIA and, 270; as commander in chief, 270, 284, 299, 304; deep state and, 25, 273, 287, 299–300, 305–6, 309, 313, 317, 329n28; defense spending and, 362n53; drones and, 11–12; executive norms and, 311–13; foreign policy and, 139, *141*, 159, 347–48; Iraq War and, 347; "Make America Great Again," 357; Mattis and, 270, 281–83, 297n130, 330n34, 346, 348; midterm elections and, 139, *141*, 159; National Guard and, 303–4, 308, 324n12, 331n46, 332n48, 346; NATO and, 283, 357; North Korea and, 27, 281–83, 287; Office of Legal Counsel (OLC) and, 317; partisanship and, 42, 344–45; Pence and, 308, 331n46; post-9/11 context and, 280–84; presidential powers and, 3, 7, 11–14, 25, 27, 299–313, 317, 323nn7–8, 324n12, 327n20, 328n25, 329n28, 329n31, 330n34; Russia and, 27, 283, 345, 348, 357; Syria and, 42, 282–83, 317, 330n34, 346, 352; Taliban and, 3, 219, 281–84, 297n148, 346; terrorism and, 3, 219, 281–84, 297n148, 343–49, 352, 356–57, 361n47, 362n53; Twitter and, 280,

299, 327n20, 328n25, 329n28; Ukraine and, 348, 357; US Constitution and, 14, 264, 308, 317; war powers and, 14, 287, 299–313, 317, 323nn7–8, 324n12, 327n20, 328n25, 329n28, 329n31, 330n34
Tunney amendment, 339
Turkey, 305
Tversky, Amos, 180–81
Twenty-Fifth Amendment, 308
Twenty-Fourth Amendment, 145
Twenty-Second Amendment, 139
Twitter, 280, 299, 327n20, 328n25, 329n28

Ukraine: Biden and, 95, 354–57; deep state and, 329n28; Obama and, 157; Russia and, 27, 29, 94, 348, 354–57; Trump and, 348, 357
unilateral power: bureaucratic politics and, 24–25, 263, 267; presidential, 24–25, 44, 76, 301, 305, 313, 316–17, 342–45; war powers and, 301, 305, 313, 316–17
unitary executive theory, 13–15
United Kingdom: communal groups and, 24, 233, *237*, 238–40, *241*, 244, 246–51, 252, 258n29; nonwhite groups in, 240, 244–49; political alienation and, 248–50
United Nations, 21, 113, *167*, 316–17
US Commerce Department, 267
US Congress: approval of, 16, 20, 42, 44, 46, 111, 313, 325n14; Article I and, 2, 16; Article II and, 13–14, 264, 316; bipartisanship and, 76–96, 343–49; bureaucratic politics and, 264–68, 271, 275–77, 280, 283; Capitol attack and, 302–3, 308, 324n13, 327n15; checks and, 3–5, 16–19, 40–60, 63–67, 76, 79, 344; Cold War and, 31, 33, 48, 65, 79, 94, 98n2, 154, 265, 339; communal groups and, 232; *Congressional Record* and, 52, 72n66; enumerated powers and, 16; foreign policy and, 40–60, 63–67, 135–40, 143–59, *160–71*; gender and, 212, 216, 227; Gulf of Tonkin Resolution and, 110, 340; impeachment and, 4, 136, *167*, 172n9, 283; loyalty and, 46–49; midterm elections and, 16, 19–21, 135–44, 150, 156, 158–59, 202, 212, 344, 363n65; Office of Legal Counsel (OLC) and, 14, 313, 316, 337n107, 342; opposition and, 105–16, 120–22, 126–31;

partisanship and, 40–60, 63–67; polarization and, 3–5 (*see also* polarization); post-9/11 context and, 343; presidential powers and, 1–5, 11–21, 26–29; reserve components and, 175, 177; rhetoric and, 18, 44–64, 72n58, 74n79; separation of powers and, 13, 41–44, 264–65, 304, 310, 319–22; Taliban and, 45; terrorism and, 338–49, 353–54; veto power and, 16; Vietnam War and, 339; voting data and, 82–84; war powers and, 14, 40, 175, 300–13, 316–22, 340, 342
US Constitution: Article I, 2, 16; Article II, 13–14, 264, 316; Article III, 315; Biden and, 28; bureaucratic politics and, 263–67; George W. Bush and, 14; Contra affair and, 339; Corwin on, 16; First Amendment, 309; Ford and, 339; foreign policy and, *160*, *168*, 172n6; Johnson and, 172n6; Obama and, 342, 344; partisanship and, 41, 44; presidential powers and, 2, 13–14, 16, 24, 28, 339, 342, 344; Reagan and, 13, 339; terrorism and, 339, 342, 344; Truman and, 172n6; Trump and, 14, 264, 308, 317; Twenty-Fifth Amendment, 308; Twenty-Fourth Amendment, 145; Twenty-Second Amendment, 139; war powers and, 2, 308–9, 316–20, 327n15, 342, 344
US Department of Defense: bureaucratic politics and, 263, 264–67, 279, 282; Gelb and, 272; opposition and, 130; Pentagon and, 272 (*see also* Pentagon); presidential powers and, 14, 16; Rourke on, 262–63; Trump and, 270, 313; war powers and, 272, 302, 313, 318, 324–25nn13–14
US Department of Education, 151
US Department of Energy, 276
US Department of Homeland Security (DHS), *168*, 276, 309, 330n34
US Department of State: bureaucratic politics and, *169*, 267, 272–76, 279, 282, 296n119; foreign policy and, *169*; terrorism and, 342; war powers and, 313, 318
US Federal Reserve, 152
US Justice Department: bureaucratic politics and, 271, 289n11; war powers and, 304, 313–14, 318, 335n71. *See also* Office of Legal Counsel (OLC)

US Marines, 155
US Supreme Court, 94, 103n46, 156, 265

Veteran Suicide Act, 153, *171*
veto power: George W. Bush and, 16; foreign policy and, 153, *160, 162–63, 165, 167, 169*; Nixon and, 340; Reagan and, 153; US Congress and, 16; War Powers Resolution and, 340
"Vietnam syndrome," 28, 339, 350
Vietnam War: bureaucratic politics and, 273, 285; communal groups and, 235–36, 249; draft and, 9, 179, 189; foreign policy and, 142, 146, 151–52, 155, *162–63, 166–69*; Gartner on, 109, 235–36; gender and, 204, 225; Gulf of Tonkin Resolution and, 110, 340; isolationism and, 353–54; Johnson and, 11, 22, 130, 138, 146, 155, 176, 201n54, 338; lessons for role of commander in chief, 341; Nixon and, 142, 179, 338–40; opposition and, 106–9, 114, 128–31, 134; partisanship and, 48, 65; political effects of, 176, 338–43, 347–53; presidential powers and, 4, 9, 11, 22–23, 28; public opinion and, 11, 23, 130, 235–36, 249, 254n14, 349; reserve components and, 176, 179, 189–90, 196; Rourke on, 273; Segura on, 109, 235–36; US Congress blamed for, 339
Violence Against Women Reauthorization Act, 156
Volcker, Paul, 152
Vote Smart, 83–92, *97*, 103n36, 103n43
Voting Rights Act, 138, 155

Walker, William, 310
War of 1812, 274
War on Poverty, 145
War on Terror, 312
war powers: Afghanistan and, 299, 330n34; Article I and, 2, 16; Biden and, 95, 313; bureaucratic politics and, 299–322; Bush and, 14, 312; casualties and, 12, 16, 21–24, 309, 316; checks and, 1–30, 320–21, 329n31; coercion and, 334n64; of commander in chief, 2–3, 15–18, 40–41, 45, 175, 203, 206, 270, 284, 299, 304, 341, 347, 356; conscription and, 9, 22–23; Democrats and, 319–20; executive norms and, 311–13, 333n58; FBI and, 304, 309; foreign policy and, 299–300, 320; Gulf of Tonkin Resolution and, 110, 340; ideologies and, 319; imperialism and, 321, 338; Iraq War and, 313; legal interpretation and, 313–17; litigation-driven decision-making and, 317–19; military and, 299–308, 312–17, 322, 324–27nn13–15; North Korea and, 287; Obama and, 312, 333n55, 334n64, 336n85, 337n107, 342; Office of Legal Counsel (OLC) and, 14, 272, 316–17, 335n78; opposition and, 303; Pentagon and, 302–3, 310, 324–25nn13–14; post-9/11 context and, 300; presidential control and, 319–21; Republicans and, 305–6, 309, 316–17, 324n13, 330n34; security and, 305–6, 309, 316–17, 324n13, 330n34; terrorism and, 339, 342, 344, 350, 356–57; Truman and, 16–17, 29, 40; Trump and, 14, 287, 299–313, 317, 323nn7–8, 324n12, 327n20, 328n25, 329n28, 329n31, 330n34; unilateral, 301, 305, 313, 316–17; US Congress and, 175, 300–13, 316–22; US Constitution and, 2, 308–9, 316–20, 327n15, 342, 344; US Department of State and, 313, 318
War Powers Resolution: bureaucratic politics and, 272; Nixon and, 340; Office of Legal Counsel (OLC) and, 14, 272, 316–17; partisanship and, 40; presidential powers and, 14, 16; US Congress and, 14, 40, 316, 340, 342; veto power and, 340
Washington, George, 179
Washington Post, 220, 276
Watergate scandal, 16, 40, 155–56, *162–63*, 291n37
Waterman, Richard, 269
Water Quality Control Act, 153
Watson Institute, 8
Wattenberg, Ben, 142
Waxman, Matthew, 357
Weber, Max, 299
Weinberger, Caspar, 267
Weinberger Doctrine, 339–42
West Bank, 157–58
Whip Inflation Now (WIN), 152
Williamson, Oliver, 269
Wilson, James Q., 271
Wilson, Woodrow, 266
Wolfowitz, Paul, 342

INDEX

Woodward, Bob, 52, 284
World Trade Center, 30
World War I, 179, 189
World War II: Allies and, 235; Axis powers and, 235; bureaucratic politics and, 265, 291n45; communal groups and, 235; D-Day and, 270; foreign policy and, 139; gender and, 203–4; opposition and, 108–9, 128; presidential powers and, 4, 6, 9, 16–19, 33n34, 356; reserve components and, 179, 189, 200n44

World War III, 348
Wye River Memorandum, 157–58

Yalu River, 106
Yeltsin, Boris, 157
Yemen, 11, 12, 33n37
Yingling, Paul, 177
Yoo, John, 14

Zaller, John, 208
Zelikow, Philip, 289n22